Sean Dorney was born in Townsville in 1951, son of a prominent North Queensland surgeon, Dr Kiernan Dorney. He joined the ABC in 1971, and first went to Papua New Guinea in 1974. He has been there (with some interruptions) ever since. He is highly regarded for his reporting of events in Papua New Guinea, and has won commendations two years running at the Thorn/EMI Australian television industry awards. (He considers his own most outstanding achievement is captaining the Papua New Guinea Rugby League team, the Kumuls, in 1976.)

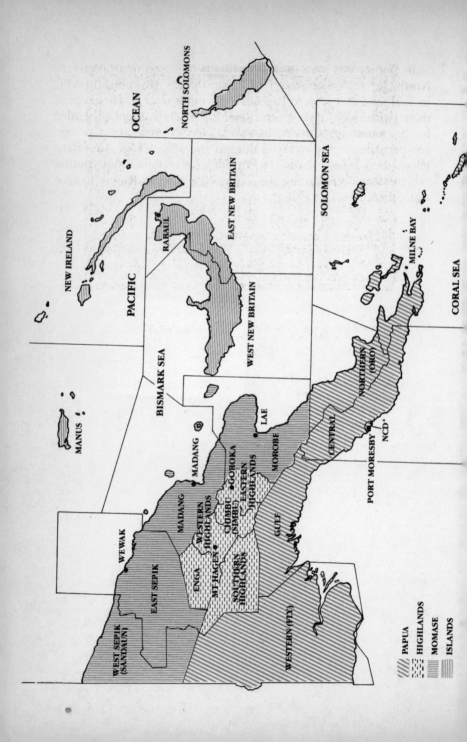

**PEOPLE POLITICS AND HISTORY
SINCE 1975**

Random House Australia Pty Ltd
20 Alfred Street, Milsons Point, NSW 2061

Sydney New York Toronto
London Auckland
and agencies throughout the world

First published 1990
Reprinted 1990, 1991, 1993
Copyright © Sean Dorney, 1990, 1993

All rights reserved. No part of this publication may be reproduced, stored in a retrieval system, or transmitted in any form or by any means, electronic, mechanical, photocopying, recording or otherwise, without prior written permission of the Publisher.

National Library of Australia
Cataloguing-in-Publication Data

Dorney, Sean, 1951-
 Papua New Guinea.

 Bibliography.
 ISBN 0 09 169461 2.

 I. Papua New Guinea – History. I. Title.
995.305

Typset by Midland Typesetters
Printed by Australian Print Group
Production by Vantage Graphics, Sydney

CONTENTS

	Author's Note	vi
	Prologue	1
1	Fleeting Glimpses	10
2	Long Taim Bifo—The Past	24
3	Parliamentary Democracy—PNG-Style	52
4	Handling the Economy	83
5	Bougainville—Land Rights or Secession?	117
6	Provincial Government—Secession's First Solution	150
7	Could a Coup Succeed?	180
8	Conflicting Interests	215
9	Irian Jaya—Border Trauma	248
10	Crime, Punishment, Justice and the Future	288
	Epilogue to Fourth Printing	319
	Appendix	331
	Index	333

AUTHOR'S NOTE

Having reported almost daily on the politics, personalities and peculiar happenings that have made news in Papua New Guinea for more than eleven of the past sixteen years, I believe I should record my debt of gratitude to a large number of people who have been astonishingly accessible, even at the worst of times.

All of Papua New Guinea's Prime Ministers during PNG's first fifteen years of Independence — Michael Somare, Julius Chan, Paias Wingti and Rabbie Namaliu — have rarely avoided requests for interviews and have seldom balked at the tough questions. Hundreds of politicians, public servants, businessmen and people in the village or the street have been far more open with me than I have had any right to expect.

Throughout this book I have attempted to source all quotes and excerpts taken from official records or published material. Generally, if no other source is given, then the quotes have come from interviews or recordings that I have taped myself.

I was approached to write this book in early 1987 and it took me the best part of three years to complete it. I found it difficult to choose a time frame and eventually decided it should take in events up until the end of the 1980s. The Epilogue brings affairs a little further up to date. Currency fluctuations over time make accurate conversions difficult. I have used as a conversion standard the exchange rate that was effective through much of the late 1980s: K1.00=$A1.50. Papua New Guinea devalued by ten percent in early 1990.

There are many Papua New Guineans who have generously shared their wisdom with me and I would like to mention two: Sir John Guise, Papua New Guinea's first Governor General, and Tony Siaguru, who in early 1990 was elected Deputy Secretary General of the Commonwealth. Amongst others whose perceptions I have valued are Professor Jim Griffin, Rowan Callick, Peter Hastings, David Hegarty, Hank Nelson, Tony Regan and Frank Senge. The person to whom I must pay most tribute is my wife, Pauline, whose practical common sense and rigid grip on reality have kept me sane though not always out of trouble.

Sean Dorney
May, 1990

PROLOGUE

ONLY two days after being thrown out of Papua New Guinea in September 1984, I was dazed and hurt. I had not wanted to leave PNG, it is true, but my pain was physical, not mental. Blood was flowing through my hair and down my face. I had just split open the crown of my head on the concrete end of a motel swimming pool. I hit the wall in a thrusting misjudged mid-butterfly stroke, while demonstrating to my two children how John Sieben had just won Olympic Gold for Australia. The Cairns doctor who sewed eight stitches into my scalp and made me wear a padded dressing under a ridiculous-looking onion-bag hairnet for the next two days chuckled that I would have been safer staying in PNG.

No doubt I would have been happier. I had wanted to stay. That I had no choice enhanced my reputation as a journalist. The notoriety associated with being an Australian correspondent expelled from Papua New Guinea following an affair involving Indonesia, PNG and the Australian Broadcasting Corporation helped lead to this book, so I have no grounds for complaint. However, my wife, Pauline, detested the publicity. She is from Manus Island and, as a wife and mother of two young children, she became the focus of much media attention because, if she was to keep the family together, she had to accept being a Papua New Guinea citizen thrown out of her own country.

Below its front-page photo of a rather glum-looking family of four under sentence of deportation, PNG's largest circulating newspaper, the *Post Courier*, began its lead story on 29 May 1984 with a direct quote:

> 'It's awful . . . but expected, in a way,' said Mrs Pauline Dorney, wife of ABC journalist Sean Dorney last night. 'We had hoped the Government would come down lightly but, realistically, the action taken was sort

of expected. The Government had to do something. They were pushed into a position where they had to do something.' Asked about how she felt about leaving PNG, even with the Government's invitation to return at any time, she said: 'Well it's home here, but I feel like an alien at the moment.' Mrs Dorney said her worst moment was finding her widowed mother in tears mid-afternoon. 'She lost Dad just last year and thought she was losing me for good, but I explained that the Government action was nothing personal against us, and that we can come and go as private individuals.'

The previous day, 28 May 1984, PNG's Foreign Minister, Rabbie Namaliu, told the national parliament that my work permit was to be revoked because the ABC's television program, 'Four Corners', had broadcast an interview with the Irian Jayan rebel leader, James Nyaro, despite earlier assurances from the ABC that it would not let the interview go to air. The work permit was valid for another three and a half years but, he announced, it would be cancelled in September. The four-month gap between the proclamation of the order in May and its execution in September resulted from the courtesy of Somare's speech writer asking me when my ABC term as correspondent was up for renewal. September 21, 1984 —the day of our enforced departure — was the fifth anniversary of my taking the job as resident ABC representative in Port Moresby.

Pauline and I had met several years before that — in 1975 in fact, Papua New Guinea's year of Independence — when I was on secondment from the ABC to the central newsroom of the National Broadcasting Commission of PNG. She was a broadcast officer with Radio Manus, visiting headquarters for a three-month training course. We married in 1976 and spent three years in Australia, where the children were born. I was appointed the ABC's PNG representative in 1979.

The offending interview made no dramatic revelations. In less than a minute of halting English, James Nyaro revealed that his men had no guns to fight the Indonesians, only bows and arrows, and that he could not understand why PNG's Prime Minister Somare did not love the West Papua rebels. But it was not what he said that so upset the authorities in PNG. It was where he said it — on Papua New Guinea soil. The ABC became an easy target for retribution because, as events unfolded, it was exposed to the accusation that it could not be trusted to keep its word. Whereas ABC management had given PNG's Secretary for Foreign Affairs a commitment that the interview would not be broadcast, the ABC Board reversed that management decision following a huge media outcry in Australia at what was seen to be the ABC's self-censorship in response to threats from a foreign government. The Australian Department of Foreign Affairs played no small part in the fiasco.

'Four Corners' reporter Alan Hogan visited PNG in April/May 1984 to do a comprehensive story on the troubled PNG/Indonesian border. Nineteen-eighty-four was a year of high tension in the relationship between Port Moresby and Jakarta. An abortive uprising in February in the Irian Jayan capital, Jayapura, by elements of the Organisasi Papua Merdeka (OPM) and a subsequent crackdown by the Indonesian military led to more than ten thousand Melanesian Irianese fleeing across the border into PNG. They did not all cross at once. The influx began at the most northern end of the border with a few hundred, mostly those involved or implicated in the Jayapura uprising. They slipped out to sea at night in canoes and landed at the PNG coastal town of Vanimo just over the horizon to the east. Gradually the cross-border sweep moved southwards down the 750-kilometre land border.

As the months passed, a series of border incidents involving the Indonesian military caused great annoyance in Port Moresby. Hogan's interview with James Nyaro came just after PNG's Foreign Minister Namaliu had returned from a torrid trip to Jakarta during which he thumped the table and accused the Indonesians of abrogating the border agreement between the two countries. Namaliu was angry that two Indonesian Air Force jets had buzzed a PNG Government station, terrifying the inhabitants. The Indonesians brushed the incursion aside and thumped the table in return, accusing PNG of breaking the border agreement itself by providing OPM rebels with sanctuary. Namaliu strenuously denied this, pointing to PNG's oft-stated policy of recognising Irian Jaya as an integral part of Indonesia and to the many hard-line anti-OPM public statements by the PNG Government. The Indonesians felt their case was proved by an incident in which a Swiss mission pilot captured by the OPM in Irian Jaya was released inside PNG. Two Indonesian officials were slaughtered when Nyaro's men ambushed the mission plane and snuck over the border into PNG with the Swiss pilot as a political hostage. The pilot was held for several weeks and then released into the hands of the Swiss honorary consul to PNG and the Catholic Bishop of Vanimo.

The PNG/Indonesian border is impossible to seal. Small bands of OPM rebels operate in the rugged mountainous region, spending a good part of their time on the PNG side. The border is a line on a map. On the ground, especially in the north, the border traverses jungle with the only markers being concrete survey posts thirty-five kilometres apart. The Indonesians have argued for years for the same 'hot pursuit' rights as they have in Borneo along their border with Malaysia. But PNG has never agreed. The border is a complex problem for Port Moresby, not the least because of the pan-Melanesian sentiments of much of the population, including a good many PNG border officials. Namaliu and the head of the PNG Department of Foreign Affairs, Paulias Matane, returned home from the tough, table-thumping exchange in Jakarta to hear that the ABC was intending to interview Nyaro. Such an interview would show the world that, contrary to PNG's undertakings, the OPM did operate from PNG soil. Matane set out to stop the interview.

Despite the terrain and their lack of sophisticated weaponry, the OPM has a crudely efficient communications network. I put Hogan in touch with a number of my contacts and left it to him to line up any interview. I did not seek to know the details. When Matane rang me at the ABC office in Port Moresby on 3 May, he told me Hogan should not do the interview because if he did he would be breaking the law, no matter where the interview took place. If it was conducted in Indonesia then Hogan would have crossed the border illegally. If it was conducted on PNG soil then his crime would be one of enticing an illegal immigrant, Nyaro, to enter PNG. Matane would not concede that Nyaro spent a good part of the year in PNG anyway. He warned me that unspecified 'action' would be taken if the interview went ahead.

Matane banned commercial charter flights to any of the border posts. He also contacted the Police Minister, John Giheno, and the Police Commissioner, David Tasion, who were in the border area at the time, telling them to stop Hogan. By the time he spoke to them on their return to the provincial capital of Vanimo that evening, the Police Minister and Police Commissioner were well aware of Hogan's presence. They had spent most of the day with him and his television crew. That morning Giheno and Tasion had met Hogan and invited the 'Four Corners' team to join them on the police helicopter for an inspection of border posts.

During our telephone conversation, I had told Matane 'Four

Corners' operated independently of me and I could not issue them with directions. All I could do was pass on a message. By the time Hogan returned my call the next morning, enabling me to pass on the Matane message that no matter where the interview took place, Matane would regard it as breaking the law, Hogan said he could cut me short as he had already spent several hours speaking with the Police Commissioner. Hogan told me he was no longer sure of getting the interview but he felt he had reached an 'arrangement' whereby if he did interview Nyaro it would not be presented in such a way as to make 'mischief' for PNG. The border was so impossible to define that he would explain that nobody could tell exactly which side they were on and this illustrated the nature of the problem confronting PNG. Hogan gave no commitment to the Police Commissioner not to interview Nyaro, a fact later confirmed in parliament by the Police Minister, Giheno.

I called Matane back to explain that I had spoken to Hogan, that he had already had a long discussion with the Police Commissioner, that he was not sure whether the interview would go ahead but that he was not out to make 'mischief' for PNG. My notes from the time indicate that Matane replied, 'I hope they keep their word!' Fearing he might believe I had halted any interview attempt, I repeated that Hogan doubted whether he would get the interview but if he did he was not out to make mischief.

Interviewing Nyaro was no scoop! Alfred Sasako, a Solomon Islands journalist working for the Niugini Nius in Port Moresby trekked into the bush twice to interview Nyaro — once when Nyaro was still holding the Swiss mission pilot captive. Photos of their encounter appeared in the PNG and Australian media. *Pacific Islands Monthly* later commissioned Sasako to write up one of these interviews for republication in its magazine and PIM ran the item over several pages boasting how much better the interview was than the one secured by 'Four Corners'! Several visiting Australian print journalists also went to the border during those early months of 1984 and talked to other OPM identities. Damien Murphy from the *Age* made the front page of both the *Age* and the *Sydney Morning Herald* for his interview with the 'President' of the OPM Senate. Bill Mellor of the *Sun Herald* won splash treatment for his assignation at a secret location in Vanimo with a 'Mr X' from the OPM. No allegations of law breaking were publicly levelled against these journalists.

The difference was that the PNG Government knew beforehand about the proposed 'Four Corners' interview, had tried to stop it and had failed. Matane was furious. After finding out that Hogan had recorded an interview, he threatened me with deportation if the interview was shown on air. I relayed the threat to the ABC management in Sydney but I was not as worried by it as they were, or as convinced (as the Australian Department of Foreign Affairs apparently was) that this threat from a senior bureaucrat would win full political backing. Matane maintained that Hogan had deliberately broken an undertaking that he would not interview Nyaro. The Foreign Secretary also alleged the law had been broken. The Australian High Commission in Port Moresby relayed his allegations to the Department of Foreign Affairs in Canberra, which in turn telexed the ABC in Sydney, saying that the department 'viewed with concern the allegations, if correct'. I was surprised that nobody from the Australian High Commission had bothered to temper their report of Matane's allegations with an account of what I might know. However, relations between the Australian High Commissioner, Robert Birch, and most of the journalists working in Port Moresby at that time were poor and the High Commission did not even ring.

On the evening of Friday, 11 May 1984, Matane called me to his home and handed me a letter officially threatening to 'review the continuing presence of the ABC representative in Papua New Guinea' subject to the 'nature of the explanation and assurances' from the ABC regarding the conduct of the 'Four Corners' crew and demanding that the interview not be broadcast. He asked me for my reaction. I told him that the story of the threat to close down the ABC office would make front page news across Australia. He replied that the ABC would then be breaking 'an undertaking of confidentiality'. I said I could promise I would not write a story on the threat because I was the channel of communications between him and the ABC. But, I said, once the letter reached Sydney, if efforts were made to stop the interview being used, it was the nature of the ABC that the story would leak. He asked to have the letter back and I went home, mistakenly believing I might have headed off the crisis.

I had not. ABC management, after consulting with 'Four Corners' about the intrinsic importance of the Nyaro segment, rang Matane and gave him a verbal undertaking that the interview would not be shown. On 15 May the Deputy Secretary for Foreign Affairs handed me the letter that Matane had retrieved from me the previous Friday. But, as I had warned Matane, the matter quickly became front-page news in Australia. The first break on the story of the ABC's being in trouble over the 'Four Corners' interview came from PNG. It was not my doing, but a story filed by the Australian Associated Press correspondent, Chris Pash. Pash was making his own trip along the border and found himself stranded in Vanimo on 14 May, after he was refused permission to board a regular commercial light aircraft flight to border stations. Chris rang Foreign Minister Namaliu, who told him 'he had written to the Australian government about an ABC Four Corners crew which had interviewed James Nyaro'.

The story quickly became a major 'freedom of the press' issue. I was in the invidious position for a journalist of knowing the story but not being able to tell it. One ABC radio current affairs program, 'The World Today', even mentioned that week that they had been unable to speak to the PNG Prime Minister, the PNG Foreign Minister, or the ABC management about the issue and added: 'our own correspondent in Port Moresby, Sean Dorney, has refused to comment!' The story picked up huge momentum in Australia and, on 25 May, the ABC Board met and reversed the ABC management decision not to show the interview.

In a statement, the Board said it believed that the ABC's independence 'would be compromised by the ABC yielding, or being seen to yield, to pressure from anyone, whether Government or otherwise, concerning the content of its programs'. It went on:

> The Board has considered the dispute with the PNG Government and recognised the rights of its senior executives to exercise editorial responsibility. The Board accepts that the decision taken by management in the first instance was made in the best long-term interests of the Corporation. However, the statement on May 24 by Prime Minister Michael Somare has elevated the original issue into a matter of principle which, in the Board's view, concerns the independence of the ABC.

On 24 May Somare had said that if the ABC broke its commitment not to show the interview, the threat to close the ABC's Port Moresby office would be carried out.

The reason the ABC Board gave — that it was Somare's statement, nothing else, that had raised the importance of the issue to one of censorship — created anger in Port Moresby. The interview went to air the next night as part of what was perhaps the best and most comprehensive report in the Australian media all year on the difficulties and problems PNG had with its land border with Indonesia. Some avid watchers were crowded into the Narimo Hotel in Vanimo where a television set linked to a satellite dish pulled down the ABC's outback service. A loud cheer went up when James Nyaro appeared on the screen. The next Monday, Namaliu told parliament I would have to go and the ABC would not be allowed back until it was prepared to 'obey the law like everybody else'.

The four months between the expulsion order and our departure were particularly trying for Pauline. She was 'a good story' — a PNG citizen who would have to leave her own country for her family's sake. Our children were a little mystified, but going to Australia held for them the singular attraction of swimming in Grandpa's pool. Initially, I was confident I would be able to find a way around the problem and that the ban would be lifted before the four months expired. I had captained PNG in Rugby League and foolishly believed the government would reconsider throwing the four of us out. Pauline was more realistic in believing that the PNG Government wanted to prove a point.

Senator Neville Bonner made a trip on behalf of the ABC Board to try to devise a formula that might resolve the issue, but all attempts failed. PNG's Foreign Ministry demanded that the ABC acknowledge that it had knowingly and deliberately flouted PNG's immigration laws. When I argued that Hogan had not enticed Nyaro across the border because Nyaro was in PNG at the time, it was explained to me that, technically, he was still guilty because he had 'caused an illegal immigrant, Nyaro, to remain in PNG for the duration of the interview'.

Lest the impression be given that PNG's motivation was purely capitulation to Indonesian pressure, it must be noted that the PNG Government took its toughest line ever against Indonesia that year. Namaliu scolded Indonesia in the United Nations and raised with ASEAN foreign ministers the difficult problems Indonesia's transmigration program and ten thousand refugees were creating for PNG. Also, I was not the only one sent from the country. Indonesia's Defence Attaché was threatened with expulsion. The Indonesians averted that indignity only by pulling him home before he was thrown out.

Our day of departure was an emotional one. I thought I was bearing up well until Pauline's mother broke down fifteen minutes before we had to board the aircraft. To my surprise, I wept.

The ban on the ABC basing an Australian correspondent in Port Moresby was lifted after one year but, by then, I had left the Corporation and Trevor Watson was appointed temporary PNG correspondent. The opportunity for me to return came another year and five months later, in February 1987, and I grabbed it. Pauline, the children and I arrived to the same sort of local media coverage that we had received on our forced departure. Ekonia Peni, the ABC's Papua New Guinean journalist who had worked on alone after I left, was there to greet us.

Papua New Guinea is a boisterously exciting country of ultimate strategic importance to Australia. It has its share of difficult, nay insoluble, problems. But it has survived its immediate post-Independence traumas in much better shape than many another developing country. The pessimists, who at Independence were predicting a rapid deterioration into tribal chaos accompanied by a massacre of the white women and children, have been proved wrong. In this book I hope to put some perspective on the continuing, intriguing story that is Papua New Guinea today.

CHAPTER ONE
FLEETING GLIMPSES

HER voice quavers: 'The natural state of our land has been exploited and all our resources have been gone forever. The people think this land will never be restored to its natural state. That's why my people are demanding ten billion Kina.' Pepetua Serero, president of the new Panguna Landowners' Association, is ill. But, sitting in the bright, mid morning sun at Guava village, high up on a mountain ridge above the world's third-largest open-cut mining pit, she is resolute. 'When the mine started most of my people were ignorant. I was a small girl when the company came and I have grown with the company. And I know what's good and what's bad!' It is early December 1988, a week after the start of a campaign of sabotage and terror against Bougainville Copper Limited.

Pepetua is to die of pneumonia and worry within six months. She'll be mourned by her husband and five children and, from the jungle, by her first cousin, Francis Ona. In most Melanesian societies first cousins are very close. They call each other Brother and Sister. Anger and frustration bound these two, Pepetua and Francis, even tighter. Together with another first cousin, Cecelia Gemel, they forged the new Landowners' Executive which ousted the older men in late 1987, and vowed to drive the Australian mining giant, CRA, off their land and out of Bougainville.

'*Mipela ol meri husat i founda* . . . We women who have been the backbone of the land . . . ' says Cecilia Gemel, standing on the shoulder of the rough gravel road where it peters out several hundred metres short of the main cluster of village houses. 'We cried out in the good times, the times of peace, endlessly to CRA to give us the compensation we wanted. But the company would not understand. Our appeals were dashed against rocks. Now it is in the hands of our men.'

In a message from his jungle hideout Francis Ona asks the Catholic priest at Koromira to send rosary beads. He says his men say the rosary three times a day. His bishop, Gregory Singkai, does not speak out against the killings. 'The land is equivalent to their life,' says Singkai. 'So precious that you can say land is really what they live on, live off. They cannot do without it. Not like in any other country where you live on cash.'

Thomas Torame Wabo stares intently out the car window at the high-rise office blocks and apartment towers along Port Moresby's Ela Beach and asks whether human beings built them. Torame is fascinated by the tall buildings. Much more so than by the jet that has just brought him down to the capital in his first trip out of the Highlands in his sixty-plus years. But his question reveals an inquiring, not a bewildered, mind. Torame wants to know because if they were built by humans then development like this could come to his area — to Mount Kare. Mount Kare! Where a late twentieth-century gold rush made his people suddenly wealthy. Torame, a traditional bigman who speaks no pidgin, let alone English, has flown to Port Moresby to visit the PNG Companies Office to register Mount Kare Investments Proprietary Limited.

In the airline bag clutched tightly under his arm is a gold nugget three times the size of his kneecap. He has kept this one as a souvenir. An estimated $100 million in gold has been recovered from the bare, three-thousand-metre-high slopes of Mount Kare in the six months since a labourer working for CRA accidentally uncovered a nugget a short distance downhill from the company's exploration drill. By law any surface gold belongs to the local landowners. Just how many local landowners there are is a perplexing question. Torame's clan is just one claiming Mount Kare as traditional land. This drear, coarse, isolated patch of PNG is too high for the planting of food gardens and so, before the rush, nobody lived here. Mt Kare was just occasional hunting ground for tribal groups living lower down to the north-west and north in the Enga province and to the south in the Southern Highlands. The confusion is greater because people claiming kinship or even friendship with any of these groups have also trekked in.

'I walked for three days from Paiala,' says Clement Nantz, a police constable from Banz in the Western Highlands who has taken special leave without pay to join the rush. 'Two nights I slept on the hills and the third I arrived.' Clement's face is daubed with a whitish clay and he stands, pan in hand, looking down into the muddy watercourse three metres below, where a mass of people are wedged shoulder to shoulder scooping handfuls of soil out of the eroding banks. Some are thigh-deep in mud. 'Their language is foreign to me,' he admits. 'It is hard to communicate. But conditions here are very, very bad. The water is very polluted. The people have nowhere to go to the toilet. They just do it anywhere and some are getting sick.' Then he smiles wryly. 'I haven't found any stones yet. Just a little bit of dust. I'll try my luck for a few weeks more.'

Malip Tindiwi, a former schoolteacher, has done better. One of a new breed of Papua New Guinean entrepreneurs, Malip has set himself up in the makeshift goldfield market as a gold buyer. He does speak the language and has K30,000 ($45,000) in cash in the bag under his squatting haunches. Malip deftly readjusts his scales after pouring his latest purchase into a large glass coffee jar already half-filled with alluvial gold and declares, 'I am thinking of investing in real estate in Port Moresby.'

Gold rushes are not new in PNG. The search for gold led to the first outside 'discovery' of the heavily populated Highlands in the 1930s. White prospectors edged up into the Highlands from the eastern end and, in 1933, Jim Taylor and the Leahy brothers, Mick and Dan, reached as far west as Mount Hagen on a patrol jointly funded by the Australian Government and the Bulolo Gold Dredging Company. Gold prospecting began at Kuta south of Mount Hagen the following year. But it was the late 1960s before Torame's people, 130 kilometres further west, were officially classified as 'under control' by the Australian administration. By then, Torame was already a middle-aged man. Unlike those earlier gold rushes, this one is a totally Papua New Guinean affair. A few white carpetbaggers have been physically run off the fields. While some of the Papua New Guinean landowners have squandered their sudden wealth on Toyota Scouts, others such as Torame have grasped the economic possibilities. It is not an easy matter to register a company when you cannot read, write or speak the language the forms are written in. But it can be done. And is.

A thousand warriors jog in rough formation down the winding dirt road to where it fords a stream in the mountainous Kuma country rising south of Minj in the Western Highlands. They clasp spears, brandishing them aloft. Held closer to the chest are axes, bows and fists full of arrows. They chant — a haunting, penetrating, valley-striding warcry.

'That's the sound they make when they go to fight,' a jeans-and-T-shirt-clad youth says knowingly as he stands on the adjacent hill which the warriors from the Nenega clan will scale next. They are fierce-looking men, their faces daubed black. 'That's my crowd!' he boasts. 'They're going to Minj for the peace ceremony.' Fifty pigs were slaughtered the previous day, their terrified squeals silenced by a ferocious club on the forehead in a ceremony performed on the eighth fairway-cum-football oval opposite the Plumes and Arrows Inn at Minj. The meat and fat of the fifty pigs will be shared by the Nenega and Konombuga people to conclude an eight-month-long tribal war. The war has brought tragedy to a dozen families on either side but fireside glory to numerous others, especially the young men.

'I fought,' he says as his 'crowd' streams across the rough wooden bridge and begins the ascent. 'Yah! I did fight!' Pointing to the forest of approaching spears, he smiles. 'Those spears and shields they're carrying — they're holed . . . damaged. They'll burn them at Minj!' There will be a bonfire lit with petrol and supervised by the police — a ritual burning of weapons to show the war is over, to seal the peace. 'They'll burn those ones. But the best ones, the good ones, they've left the good ones at home.' He grins broadly. 'Keep them for next time. For the next fight!'

'Software Laboratories is the mother company, one hundred per cent Papua New Guinean owned. All the shares are owned by me,' says Gideon Kakabin leaning forward on the desk in his converted office suite in Port Moresby's plush Pacific View apartments. He has been up since 3 a.m. finalising a computer program to meet an 8 a.m. deadline. He has just packed up his portable computer and will head off shortly to meet the client. The door to the suite bears a sign saying 'Computers and Communications'. 'Computers and Communications is a subsidiary, seventy-six per cent owned by Software Laboratories,' Gideon goes on. 'A couple of other guys own the rest. The way we have arranged things is that Software Laboratories does all the software work, all the programming — the consultancy work. Computers and Communications supplies hardware and operating systems. In the first ten months of this year we have turned over more than one million Kina ($1.5m).'

Gideon Kakabin, aged thirty-two, from Nanga Nanga village on the Gazelle Peninsula of East New Britain, is a specialist computer programmer who branched out on his own in 1983. After completing primary and secondary school on the Gazelle, Gideon went to the Darling Downs Institute of Advanced Education in Toowoomba, graduating in 1979 with a degree in business studies. He won a graduate traineeship with International Computers Limited (ICL) in Sydney. 'I don't think they were aware there was a Papua New Guinean in Australia who would be interested,' he says. 'When I applied, they thought it would be a good idea to concentrate a lot of training on me so they could send me back up here.' After eighteen months in Sydney, Gideon returned home and worked for ICL in Port Moresby for two years. But the cut in pay that he took as a Papua New Guinean citizen in PNG compared with what he would have earnt in Australia prompted him to set up his own computer software company.

'From a situation in 1984 where I was on my own downstairs, we quickly grew out of that office. We took the office next-door to that. Then we expanded up here.' The downstairs office on the ground floor of the Pacific View apartments displays the saleable hardware. Computers and Communications is the PNG agent for Compaque computers. 'At the beginning of this year there were only four of us,' Gideon says. 'Now we have eleven and we're looking for more because of the workload. We are concentrating on the private sector. Some of our clients are the larger corporate entities operating in PNG. But we also have quite a large number of smaller clients where the number of employees is between ten and twenty.'

Gideon admits that businessmen who meet him for the first time are sceptical that a Papua New Guinean would have the expertise to design a computer program to meet their company's needs. However, that problem is diminishing. 'What I found worked best for me initially was that I was able to sell my services based on work I'd previously done. So I would say, "If you really want to check up if I can write a program, then ring this fellow and ask him." I suppose we have not put much concentration on marketing.' Gideon's companies still do not have a number listed in the Yellow Pages. But the work is flowing in. 'We have drawn up a range of specific programs for companies involved in merchandising and processing work and they seem satisfied. For the future we are looking at expanding to places like Vanuatu and the Solomons where we already have a number of clients.'

One program Gideon designed for the United Nations office in Port Moresby is now being studied in Geneva for possible application in United Nations field offices throughout the developing world.

A watermelon shatters at his feet. The old Tolai women from his father's side of the family wail as they splinter sticks of sugarcane for him to walk over, and cast white, powdery lime on his legs. His father presents him with a spear, places a band around his head and bids his own, leaf-bedecked, sacred Tubuan spirit figure to dance around his son. Rabbie Namaliu, masters graduate, has come home to his people of Raluana village in East New Britain as prime minister. 'Tolai traditional society is very strong,' Namaliu confides after the ceremony is over. 'If you come from it and don't accept it as being part of your backbone you won't be accepted as a leader, as a true leader.'

His fellow Tolai parliamentarian, John Kaputin, draws heavily on the traditional symbolism in his welcoming address. 'In the context of our traditional customs and in particular with regard to the concept of a Kunubak and the secrecies that surround it, the preparation for a dance is now complete,' Kaputin says. 'The feathers, the costumes, the decorations, and all the instruments are now in place. On behalf of our elders and our people, I now invite you, Rabbie To-Namaliu, to lead your fellow dancers from the Taraiu or the Marovot [sacred places for the Tubuan society in Tolai custom] to the village — the village is Papua New Guinea — to dance. The dance is yours — you know the parts and you know how to put them together. Hopefully all participants know their parts and can sing the dance in the language that is yours!'

'The "liu" in the name "Namaliu" means above other people,' Margaret Nakikus, Nàmaliu's wife, explains. 'He was born a leader and he's always been expected to lead.' These two, Rabbie and Margaret, are a handsome first couple who would impress in any company.

Born in 1947, he was part of the first intake into the University of Papua New Guinea in 1966. After graduating in history and English in 1970, he went to Canada's Victoria University, securing a masters degree in history and political science. Turning down an offer of a job at the United Nations in 1972, Namaliu returned home to the beginnings of an academic career. He tutored, then lectured at the UPNG for a year before being recruited by Chief Minister Somare as his principal private secretary. Immediately following Independence, he spent several months as a Visiting Fellow at the University of California, returning to PNG to become provincial commissioner of East New Britain. Several years as chairman of the PNG Public Services Commission followed. Namaliu won the seat of Kokopo in the 1982 national elections and Somare appointed him Minister for Foreign Affairs.

Margaret Nakikus graduated from the UPNG in arts in the early 1970s, then spent a year doing post-graduate studies in municipal planning at London University. She began work as a nutritionist but rose rapidly through the PNG public service to become acting head of the National Planning Office. Departing the public service in the mid-1980s, she helped found Kina Securities, an investment consultant/stock broking firm in Port Moresby. When, in 1986, Rabbie and Margaret decided to move their family back to Rabaul so that their two young sons would not lose contact with their Tolai culture, Margaret became personnel manager with Kina Gillbanks & Co., a joint venture between Kina Securities and Gillbanks, the British agricultural management company. She has a teenage daughter from a previous marriage. Both their fathers, Rabbie's and Margaret's, are Methodist pastors.

Paias Wingti's mother buried his umbilical cord and the tree that now stands where it was buried is tall and straight. She was the sixth wife of the prime-minister-to-be's father and gave birth to him at Moika village near Mount Hagen in the Western Highlands province on 2 February 1951. Together the six wives produced fifteen children. Paias Wingti is a Catholic. But, while not church married, he has two sons, Karl and Nathan, whom he likes to be with if he has any free time.

Wingti did not go to school until he was over ten. But then, after six years of primary school and four years of secondary at Mount Hagen High, he enrolled at the University of Papua New Guinea in Port Moresby in 1974, studying for an economics degree. His first trip to Australia was to Monash University and an Australian Union of Students conference representing the UPNG Students' Representative Council. At university he became president of the PNG-China Friendship Society. Later, when deputy prime minister, he led a government delegation to the People's Republic.

The 1977 elections came along before he could complete his university degree and he campaigned successfully for the Mount Hagen Open seat. Joining Michael Somare's Pangu Pati, Wingti won a ministry in 1978 and served as minister for transport and civil aviation until the fall of the Somare Government in a vote of no confidence in 1980. Two years later, when Pangu did so well in the general elections of 1982, Wingti was made deputy prime minister as leader of Pangu's Highlands block. He split with Pangu in early 1985 following a succession feud and took a quarter of the party with him into Opposition. After eight months as PNG's Opposition leader, Wingti defeated Somare in a parliamentary no-confidence vote and became prime minister at the age of thirty-four.

Wingti possesses an intriguing, slightly messianic aura. One of his great gifts is patience. His performance in building the numbers between the conclusion of the counting in the 1987 elections, when it seemed certain Michael Somare would put together another coalition, and the day when the new parliament sat for the first time five weeks later and re-elected him Prime Minister astounded some of the most weathered of PNG's political observers. Despite that achievement he could not hold the numbers and fell eleven months later in a vote of no confidence. But his conduct on the day of his defeat won him new respect. A crowd of Highlanders several thousand strong massed near the front steps of parliament. The police were nervous. They had cause. Rumours were rife that Highlanders would rampage if Wingti lost. Memories were still fresh of the rioting in 1986 when Iambakey Okuk died of cancer. Paias Wingti went to the crowd, told them to sit down, and then in a measured and patrician way told them not to create trouble. He was a young man, he said, with a full political life still ahead of him. Let the system work and he would be back. The crowd listened and dispersed meekly.

Within minutes of the regional lands court magistrate upholding the appeal, a young Masandanai man lies dead outside the Wewak district court house on Hill Street. The blood running from his knife wounds soaks the dirt. Blood from three other seriously wounded people, two Masandanais and a Tambunam, smears the clothes of those supporting them. Armed police keep the

Masandanais and the Tambunams apart. But it has taken an hour to restore order. Both sides are armed with machettes, sticks, iron bars, stones, pocket knives and bows and arrows. Tension built through the morning as the two clans waited for the ruling. The magistrate, Vincent Linge, was handing down his decision on an appeal by the Masandanai against a local land court's granting to the Tambunams of rights to a long-disputed piece of land bordering their territory in the Angoram district of the East Sepik province.

The portion of land near the Sepik River is considered prime value for hunting and fishing. Tambunam village is on the main Sepik River while Masandanai is on a tributary. The disputed land lies between. Mr Linge reversed the lower court decision and awarded the land to the Masandanai. As he left the courthouse, somebody lunged at him and the fight between the two groups erupted. It has been many years since tribal trouble like this has been seen in the streets of Wewak. In the Highlands tribal clashes are still frequent. But the fact that this inter-tribal dispute has burst into violence and death here on the north coast, in an area with a relatively long history of outside contact, illustrates the passionate importance of land to all Papua New Guineans.

Ninety-seven per cent of Papua New Guinea is traditionally owned. But little of it is surveyed and registered. Disputes are endemic. Claims over the three per cent that was alienated in colonial times are never ending. The Government faces innumerable demands for compensation for the use of what is seen as tribal land, even land devoted to such public benefit purposes as schools. On Manus Island one electricity extension project had to be abandoned because the Electricity Commission could not meet the compensation demands that village people lodged for felled coconut trees along the proposed route. As a result they have forgone reticulated power. Telecommunications between the North Solomons province and the outside world were lost for several days in mid-1988 when one group claiming ownership of Mount Takaniat 'repossessed' their mountain top. They chopped up cables, shutting down the repeater station to press demands to the PNG Posts and Telecommunications Corporation for more rent. A corporation official later told the Goroka Chamber of Commerce of what he described as the 'unbelievable' compensation claims being made on all seventy-five repeater stations throughout the country. The largest, he said, was a demand for about $50 million.

The brightest child in grade five at the Ambullua Community School in the Upper Jimi valley will not get the chance to go to high school. The reason is that Philipina Kolma's older brothers have done too well in PNG's fiercely competitive battle for education. Only three out of five children in that part of the Western Highlands get to go to primary school. Of those who make it through to the final year of primary schooling, grade six, only one in three will be accepted into the nearest provincial high school. The odds are even worse for girls. Philipina's excellent results would normally mean she would overcome the obstacles and win a high school place. But the academic success of her brothers has excited too much jealousy.

The eldest brother is a journalist in Port Moresby. The next is attending the Catholic tertiary college in Madang, the Divine Word Institute. And the brother just five years Philipina's senior is in grade ten at Fatima High School. When a tribal fight broke out between Philipina's Walkai clan and the nearby Tapia clan, her parents withdrew her from school. She would have had to walk through Tapia land on her seven-kilometre trek to the Ambullua School classrooms and they feared she would be chopped to death.

Two opposing villages in the Morobe province were in dispute over the distribution of royalty payments from a foreign timber company logging in their area. The company was making payments to one group and not the other. The dispute was threatening to turn nasty, so the Morobe provincial Premier, Utula Samana, was called in to preside over a meeting between the two sides. Anger had all the disputants on edge.

'We were meeting under a mango tree,' Samana recalls, 'and a dragon lizard fell from the top of the mango tree right into the centre of the village meeting.' It startled them all. 'Everybody was scared and started running in all directions.' Samana's secretary reached down and picked up the dragon lizard. Slowly the villagers returned. 'When they came back I told them, "You realise you were all arguing over timber resources and arguing how you were going to benefit monetarily. But you forgot that the animals also own those resources as well. You forgot to invite them to this meeting. You forgot to indicate to them where they fit in, how they are being affected. They are trying to show you that they are not happy that you have not invited them here too to hear their views about how

you are disturbing the environment and destroying their habitat." '
Samana says that solved the whole problem. 'The people did not
argue any further. They understood that kind of a sign. They came
to terms and decided to make sure the distribution was equitable.'

That story is one of Utula Samana's favourites. Samana was
premier of Morobe, Papua New Guinea's most populous province,
for a record seven and a half years before being elected to the national
parliament in 1987. He mobilised the unemployed youth of Lae,
the provincial capital, into a potent political force during his tenure
as premier. A former student leader, Samana is one of the few
politicians in PNG with a well-developed political philosophy and
agenda. Some see him as dangerous. He has published a book, *Papua
New Guinea: Which Way?*, subtitled 'Essays on Identity and Development', which is extremely critical of the nature of the Australian
inherited bureaucracy, the high level of Australian aid and the
concentration of successive governments in PNG on large-scale
mining nucleus estate agricultural developments.

'I think that big-scale development is good for the State and good
for the investors,' Samana says. 'It makes quick money to run the
State and State affairs and quick profits for the investors which
they can then reinvest elsewhere. But it leaves behind sociological
and environmental destruction beyond repair when you look at it
at the village level. In terms of quality of development — by that
I mean improving village conditions — the big projects don't do
that. I think it's devil-upment. It destroys the people. I believe the
expansion of large scale developments directly contributes to the law
and order problems in this country by breaking down social order.'

The handwritten letter dated 12.11.86 referred to the approaching
election and sought 'assistance from your company to me and the
party'. The assistance being solicited was mostly in the form of
'cabbages'. Under the heading 'Party', New Ireland Premier, Robert
Seeto, asked Michael Sia, a Malaysian logging contractor, for a 'Cash
advance of 10 Cabbages, URGENTLY.' He said his provincial
Forestry Minister, Samsom Gila, also needed help. Under Gila's
name, the Premier wrote: 'Request additional 3 more Cabbages,
already collected 2 Cabbages last time.' Beneath the heading 'Self
Personal' there were two entries: a request for '50 Cabbages as a
form of Loan for 12 months'; and one for '8 Cabbages ready in
Singapore, wife will collect on her way to Taiwan next month'.

According to Mr Justice Tos Barnett who conducted the two-year-long commission of inquiry into corruption in PNG's forestry industry, a 'Cabbage' in Mr Seeto's code meant K1000 ($1500) while an 'Apple' meant K100. In the various letters tabled in the PNG national parliament in the detailed appendices included in Judge Barnett's twenty-volume report, there are many more requests for 'Cabbages' than there are for 'Apples'. In the 12.11.86 letter — following the list of cabbage requests — is a final paragraph headed 'Favourable Return'. It reads: 'I will release additional concession on East Coast Namatanai immediately, which your company will have three areas operated — West Coast Namatanai, Tabar and East Coast Namatanai.'

Mr Justice Barnett found that the New Ireland timber industry 'is out of control and has blighted the hopes of landowners and devastated a valuable timber resource for very little gain to the people or government of Papua New Guinea.' He said he found 'irrefutable evidence of full-scale transfer pricing and other fraudulent marketing practices of the foreign companies controlling the marketing of New Ireland logs.' He said that 'without exception' in New Ireland he found that all marketing companies were transfer pricing commonly at the rate of $US10 per cubic metre. This amounted to millions of dollars of profits transferred abroad.

'Knowing full well that the foreign companies were transferring secret funds into overseas accounts,' the judge reported, 'several provincial and national politicians attached themselves to those companies like leeches, making repeated demands for personal benefits and for political campaign funds.'

A line of chanting women advances towards the makeshift platform in the centre of the Kundiawa airstrip in the mountains of the Simbu province. A semi-trailer, backed up adjacent to the platform, disgorges carton after carton of South Pacific Lager beer which the women methodically hoist on to their heads. Shuffling away, their chanting uninterrupted, they file back to the section of the tarred runway that their clan line has claimed for the day and stack their cartons in a pile for later distribution. Atop the central platform, which is itself made out of more than a hundred cartons of SP and SAN MIG stubbies, the National Party leader, Iambakey Okuk, decked out in his finest traditional Highlands regalia, raises the megaphone to his lips again.

'Karimui,' Okuk barks pointing to another group amongst the thousands who have poured onto the airstrip. 'Karimui . . . Fifty cartons!' The women of Karimui strike up a chant and wend their way forward to accept this election 'wealth distribution' gift from the Deputy Prime Minister and Minister for Transport who so desperately wants to become the country's first Highlands prime minister. It is the Saturday before the three weeks of voting begins for the 1982 national elections and the ceremony goes on all day. Okuk gives away a total of 96,000 bottles of beer in nine hours.

His striking headdress of bird of paradise feathers and brilliant red plumes demands that he hold his head rigidly imperious. As the hours pass the muscles in his neck reveal the strain but this Simbu warrior is not one to flinch. The runway is closed because he, as minister for transport, is having it extended so that Air Niugini, the people's airline, can start flying into the Simbu provincial capital for the first time. As transport minister, he has also signed the national airline into buying aircraft he thinks can do the job in this mountainous valley country — short-take-off-and-landing De Havilland Dash Sevens. That was a flight, convincing Cabinet retrospectively to endorse his signing, while on a trip to Canada, of legally binding contracts to purchase them — a fight he won against the finance bureaucrats who called it 'lunacy'.

In the lounge of Chimbu Lodge, the hotel perched on the ridge alongside the Kundiawa airstrip, the former liquor licensing commissioner turns back from the window and says contemptuously, 'They'll drink his beer but they'll vote for me!' John Nilkare, Pangu candidate, is right. He scores a shock win over Okuk. But his ploy to retain the seat five years later will be just as futile. Nilkare will spend thousands of Kina of his National Development Fund grants buying school exercise books for all the primary school children of Simbu. For six months running up to the 1987 poll, each weekday afternoon the students will carry home to almost every Shimbu household those exercise books that will feature Nilkare's portrait on the back cover and the slogan 'John Nilkare Cares About Your Education'. But this is the toughest seat in the country and this tactic will be as unsuccessful for Nilkare as the beer-gift day was for Okuk.

Back on the Kundiawa airstrip, despite the thronging crowd, Iambakey Okuk is running out of clan groups to distribute the few remaining cartons to. It is late afternoon and the sun is dropping behind the mountains. Two semi-trailer loads have all but gone. Upwards of four thousand cartons have been handed out. Then in the failing light he spots me standing a short distance away from his beer platform with my tape recorder slung over my shoulder. With a twinkle in his eye and a broad grin creasing his face, he raises the megaphone again. He points in my direction and croaks, 'The expatriates . . . Twenty cartons!'

CHAPTER TWO
'LONG TAIM BIFO' — THE PAST

A quick way to cause grievous offence in Papua New Guinea is to compliment someone on how quickly their people are making the transition from the cannibalistic stone age. Papua New Guineans have a deep pride in their rich and varied cultures but equally they resent being tagged 'backward'. In parliamentary debates a most effective taunt is to describe one's opponent as a 'primitive'. There is an understandable sensitivity to the regular description of the country in the world's media as a land lost in time. The *Times of PNG* columnist, Daka, reacted pricklishly not so long ago when the *Economist* mentioned that Kuru was a disease afflicting 'cannibals in New Guinea when they eat each other's brains.' Showing marvellous tact, the Clemenger advertising group suggested a tourism promotion for PNG a few years ago along the lines: 'Travel in modern comfort and experience the thrill and excitement of a tropical land which brings you face to face with primitive stone-age people.' Stephen Ranck, a former geography lecturer at the University of Papua New Guinea, tells of a glossy brochure produced by Society Expeditions of Seattle, carrying the banner 'Expedition into the Stone Age' across a picture of an American commentator squatting next to a Highlands family sheltering from rain in a rock overhang!

The truth is, Papua New Guineans are not the world's last cave dwellers. In fact the Highlanders of PNG were amongst the earliest members of the human race to grow food intensively. Agriculture led to human settlement in permanent villages in a number of different parts of the world 8000 to 10,000 years ago. Western civilisation can perhaps trace its cradle to the Tigris/Euphrates valley in the Middle East where the Mesopotamians evolved a form of writing in about 4000 B.C. But several thousand years before this, the people living in PNG's Western Highlands were draining swamps and practising both wet and dry land agriculture in the Waghi Valley. Archaeologists working at Kuk, near Mount Hagen, have found evidence of an extraordinarily complex system of agricultural drains and culverts that date back about 10,000 years.

These early Highlands gardeners dug geometrically precise drainage channels some kilometres long. The food they grew was most likely starch crops such as taro and cooking bananas. Sugarcane was also cultivated. Indeed, sugarcane originated in PNG and what is now growing in the Queensland and northern New South Wales canefields could be descendant varieties of what these ancient agriculturalists were planting in the PNG Highlands some 8000 years before Christ. Although the type of agriculture they practised had disappeared from the Highlands by the time of first contact with Europeans in the 1930s, the methods they employed could well be similar to what is still happening today in the Baliem Valley of Irian Jaya. There the Dani people still dig extensive ditches in their swamplands to drain and irrigate raised garden plots. The men wade waist-deep in the muddy drains, scooping out the fertile debris from the floor of each drain with oar-like, fire-hardened wooden poles and dumping it on the garden plots to either side. At Kuk similar wooden oars have been found that would have been in use 400 years ago.

The Kuk excavations began after an accidental discovery when the land was being cleared for a tea plantation. Even more recent scientific work indicates there were other, large-scale agriculture works under way in the Highlands from a very early date. In the Eastern Highlands, the PNG Electricity Commission is building the massive Yonki Hydro-electric scheme and, due to some enlightened thinking, the commission has encouraged archaeological studies of areas that might be affected. These studies have excited the researchers involved, who feel they have proved the existence of elaborate ancient agricultural terraces on the mountainsides. Fortunately most won't be inundated by the hydro scheme's dam and some diggings will continue. Dr Marjorie Sullivan, associate professor of physical geography at the University of Papua New Guinea, says it is the first time evidence has been found that terrace gardening was practised in PNG. The terrace formations had previously been dismissed as benching caused by prehistoric flooding.

'The work at Yonki is, in a sense, related to the work at Kuk in the Western Highlands,' Dr Sullivan says. 'The difference is the environment in which the agriculture in the Western Highlands and the agriculture at Yonki in the Eastern Highlands would have been carried out. In the Western Highlands, there is an excess of water most of the year and one of the problems for anyone gardening there would have been to drain the swamp. At Yonki, on the far eastern side of the Highlands, there is a pronounced dry season in most years. The problem there would have been to find water or to ensure water got to the roots throughout the year. The people's solution at Yonki seems to have been to construct enormous, very complex and far reaching terrace systems. We've found steep back walls and flat terrace platforms extending for hundreds of metres along gentle hill slopes, terraces undoubtedly built for the purpose of growing food.'

Dr Sullivan says the terraces in the Arona Valley at Yonki extend for more than twenty square kilometres. Since finding the Yonki terraces, Dr Sullivan and her fellow geographers have gone back and looked in the area near Kainantu, south-west of Yonki, where they have found similar terraces extending over the same sort of area. They have also found other sites near Goroka in the Bena Bena Valley. Altogether she believes they could have found more than 100 square kilometres of terraced hillslopes.

The obvious question is: If agriculture had such early beginnings in the PNG Highlands, why didn't this lead on, as it did elsewhere — in the Middle East, India and China for instance — to a post-agricultural society? It's a question without a proper answer yet. But one of the crucial differences between the agriculture-based life in the PNG Highlands six thousand to ten thousand years ago and the agriculture-based life in the Middle East of the same period was the type of crops cultivated. In PNG, they were root crops such as yams, taro and bananas, crops that grew at most times of the year but which could not be stored easily because they rotted. In the Middle East they were grain crops, seasonal and long lasting, which could be stored in vast quantities. In Asia it was rice. These crops could be traded and thus commercially exploited. In PNG any excess production had to be disposed of quickly.

Rather than lead to the creation of towns, the huge agricultural infrastructure established in the Highlands over thousands of years was itself abandoned several hundred years ago with the introduction of the sweet potato, *kaukau*. It arrived in the Highlands from South America via a circuitous route. The Spanish took it first to Europe. Later they and the Portuguese introduced it to their colonies in the Far East. From there Malay traders introduced the sweet potato to the coastal areas of Irian Jaya and it gradually found its way via trade routes up into the Highlands. Marjorie Sullivan says sweet potato wrought a rapid change in lifestyle and habits, a change that has been labelled the Ipimeian Revolution.

'With the coming of the sweet potato the previously cultivated crops assumed a secondary role. Sweet potato grows pretty well anywhere on any sort of soil. It feeds a large number of people. It tastes good and it's very much easier to grow than the other crops,' she says. 'Faced with the choice of intensive land manipulation for the production of taro or relatively simple gardening for the growing of sweet potato on the same areas, the people apparently decided, "Why bother with taro?" Producing a large quantity of food became relatively easy and the complex drainage systems at Kup and the terrace systems at Yonki were no longer necessary.'

One effect of the expanded food production was the domestication of more pigs. The great pig exchange ceremonies in the Highlands, like the Moka, are believed to date back to this agricultural change of direction about four hundred years ago. Pigs were important before that. In excavations in the central Highlands evidence has been found of pig exchange dating back 2500 years. But the Highlanders found it easier to rear pigs with a food crop that grew readily. They could also grow sweet potato higher up the mountains because it had far greater tolerance than the foods it replaced. One theory is that the Ipimeian Revolution even led to a greater incidence of tribal fighting because the population expanded, creating greater pressure on the land, and people had more time for such activities, being freed from the extra labour the earlier crops had required.

Piecing together PNG's pre-history jigsaw is a challenging task being tackled by scientists from a surprising range of disciplines. Some intriguing work is being done by geneticists at the PNG Institute of Medical Research in Goroka. A group led by Doctor Kuldeep Bhatia has been attempting to track down the origin of people in the South-East Asian region. Part of their research involved collecting the placentas of 145 women from throughout PNG just after childbirth. The team is studying the genetic material, Mitochondrial DNA. This is not the DNA that determines the size of your nose or the colour of your eyes. It is a form of DNA that comes from outside the nucleus, in a compartment of the cell called the mitochondrion, which produces the energy to keep the cell alive.

Mitochondrial DNA is inherited only from the mother and so allows the tracing of matrilineal lines thousands of years. Some of Doctor Bhatia's collected placentas were sent off to Berkeley (UCLA) in the United States where a study team was engaged in a much broader investigation into Mitochondrial DNA from the placentas of women from around the world. This team has since expounded a theory that the whole of present-day humankind may have evolved from the one woman who lived about two hundred thousand years ago. What slight variations there are in Mitochondrial DNA have resulted from accidental mutations over generations and this genetic stamping allows some comparisons of the relationships between people of different races.

Dr Bhatia says one of the revelations of his research is the exceptional homogeneity of the Mitochondrial DNA collected from the placentas of women from the Highlands. It has long been established that the peoples of the Highlands and many of those now populating the coastal areas of PNG came from different stock. So Doctor Bhatia was not surprised to discover that the Mitochondrial DNA collected from the placentas of coastal women was closer to that of Asian women than to their fellow countrywomen in the Highlands. But he was surprised at the almost rigid uniformity amongst the samples from different parts of the Highlands. This has led him to believe that the Highlanders have been a separate people for a very long time, and that they all may have evolved from relatively few people who entered the Highlands about 15,000 years ago. Doctor Bhatia has now turned his team's attention to studying the isolated Hagahai people on the periphery of the Highlands to see which of PNG's present day people they are related to — the Highlanders or the coastals, or indeed if they may predate both.

Papua New Guinea and Australia were linked by land up until six thousand years ago. As the last Ice Age ended and ocean levels rose, the waters from the Pacific and Indian Oceans poured through the Torres Strait, cutting off the Australian continent from the world's second-largest island. Archaeological work in both Australia and PNG indicates that both places could have been populated about fifty thousand years ago. Those first immigrants were hunters, gatherers and fishermen. It is speculated that there must have been movement along what would have been the connecting Cape York isthmus up until the land link was broken. The present Torres Strait Islanders are similar to some of the coastal Melanesians of PNG, but the Melanesian penetration of Australia never went much further.

The diversity of the people and cultures of PNG is the nation's most distinctive trait. Archaeological work in the coastal areas presents its own challenges. Because the sea level has risen some thirty metres since the end of the last Ice Age, coastal village remains from before that time are now well under the ocean in most parts of the world. But the main Papua New Guinea island mass is tilting, with the northern side rising and the southern side sinking. This is naturally a slow process but, along with the changing levels of the sea over the past fifty thousand years, it makes for fascinating discoveries as to where coastal settlements really were in the past. The lift of the Huon Peninsula coastline on the north coast between Lae and Madang, for instance, has been faster than the rising sea, with spectacular flights of coral reef terraces rising up the northern side. Their staggered, stair-like formation came from the joint action of the upward tilting of the coast and the falling sea levels during cold glacial periods. Prehistory students from PNG University have found waisted axes from what would have been a coastal settlement on Reef 3 on Fortification Point. These have been carbon dated at about thirty-six thousand years old. The change in the sea levels has meant, for instance, that the rich Murik Lakes culture on the Sepik coast cannot have been in that location more than three thousand years because the lakes would not have been there before then. The sea coast would have been further inland.

There's more to Papua New Guinea than the mainland. Six hundred other islands together make up fifteen per cent of the country's total landmass. Some of the largest of these islands form the Bismarck Archipelago. The archipelago curves from Manus, which is just below the Equator, east to New Hanover, and southeast down the long thin finger of New Ireland before cutting back abruptly south-west through the major island of New Britain. Further off to the east are Buka and Bougainville, the northernmost islands of the Solomons chain.

It was once thought settlement on these islands came much, much later than settlement on the mainland. However, excavations on the coral islands north of New Hanover have indicated that people were there as early as thirty thousand years ago and that they had the capacity to make dangerous sea voyages. There is increasing evidence, too, that the first human movement out into the rest of the Pacific islands began from the Bismarcks. Tools made from the volcanic glass, obsidian, mined from Manus and from Talasea in West New Britain have been found as far west as Fiji. Obsidian from Manus was also traded westwards to Indonesia.

One beguiling prehistory mystery in the New Guinea islands is the origin of Lapita pottery. This elaborately etched pottery has been found across the Pacific, in Fiji, New Caledonia and in the Polynesian islands of Tonga and Samoa. 'This Lapita pottery,' says Pamela Swadling from the PNG Museum, 'dates from about 3500 years ago to just about the time of Christ and then it dies out or it stops being recognisable as Lapita. In parts of the eastern Pacific it's associated with the people who first settled there. Of course it's not associated with the first people who got to PNG because we're expecting dates of about fifty thousand years ago. And we have an established date of thirty-eight thousand years so far. Curiously, when you look at the material being found in eastern Indonesia in their old sites it's a lot older. But they have found no pottery which, to an archaeologist's eye, would be the ancestor of the Lapita. So we are puzzling as to where Lapita Pottery became Lapita. It might be that small groups of potters arrived from the west, found the New Guinea people they joined had already domesticated certain agricultural plants, and not having to spend so much time finding food, they may have specialised more and celebrated by producing very elaborate pots,' Swadling says.

Just why Lapita died out is not known. But the increasing body of information being collated is gradually helping Papua New Guineans find out more about their history and how they came to be such a diverse people. 'The information that is now coming from such a wide variety of sources is gradually giving us a slow understanding of how regional sequences have led to the current development of the extraordinary cultural complexity in PNG,' Pamela Swadling says. 'You just can't describe the prehistory of the whole of PNG by concentrating on one little place because every little place has its own story. There are certain general patterns which we are slowly getting some understanding of but there's a long way to go and probably work for many generations of archaeologists.'

The differences in physical appearance amongst Papua New Guineans can be quite marked. It does not take a foreign resident long to distinguish a Sepik from a Trobriand Islander, a Highlander from a Tolai, or a Bougainvillian from a Mekeo. Skin colour ranges from the midnight black of the Buka people through all shades of brown to the pale brown of some of the people of the Central province. While the vast majority of Papua New Guineans are classified as Melanesians, the tiny populations of the western islands of the Manus province are of Micronesian descent and those of the furthest flung eastern islands in the North Solomons province are Polynesian. Societies may be patrilineal, matrilineal, or an amalgam of both. But what shows up the remarkable patchwork of PNG's multiple societies best is the languages they speak.

An oft-repeated statistic about Papua New Guinea is that its people speak over seven hundred different languages. But that is just part of the story, because these languages evolved from many different roots and are of widely varying antiquity. Studies have shown that even languages in the one province can come from a number of radically different language groups. A language spoken by the people of one area may be similar in grammatical structure to the one spoken by the people five kilometres away or it may bear no relationship to it at all. Nearly all these 700-plus languages evolved within Papua New Guinea but they are generally classified into two broad groups: Austronesian and non-Austronesian. The most recent languages to arrive in PNG are from the Austronesian family, a grouping that also embraces the languages of Indonesia, the Philippines and the rest of the Pacific island countries. The Motu people from the Port Moresby coastal area speak an Austronesian language, as do the people around Lae and in Manus, most of New Ireland and New Britain. But up in the Highlands, in pockets of New Britain, New Ireland and Bougainville and along two thirds of the southern mainland coast and half the northern coastline there exist hundreds of other, presumably older, non-Austronesian languages that defy simple classification.

The complexity of PNG's language map is well illustrated by the linguistic puzzle on the spectacular volcanic island of Karkar off the Madang coast. Twenty-five thousand people live on Karkar, which is some twenty kilometres in diameter. The Karkar Islanders speak two entirely different languages. Those living in the villages on the south-eastern side of the island speak Takia, an Austronesian language believed to be about fifteen hundred years old. On the other side, north-west of Karkar, the people speak Waskia, a trans-New Guinea phylum language of much more ancient heritage. Culturally the Karkar Islanders appear to be just about identical, yet their two languages could hardly be more different. The language distribution in PNG is the most complex in the world. In practice it means Papua New Guineans have an extraordinary facility to learn languages. While the average third-generation Australian struggles with just the one language, the average Papua New Guinean speaks three or four. And those who've been to school and been taught English have learnt it, not as their second language but perhaps their fifth. In the national parliament three languages are spoken — English, Pidgin and Hiri Motu. Pidgin and Hiri Motu are both languages of convenience which evolved separately in New Guinea and Papua out of the need for some common means of communication. Pidgin had its origins amongst the blackbirded Melanesians labouring on the Queensland sugarcane plantations last century. Hiri Motu was a trading language used along the Papuan coast before European contact.

The manifestation of cultural diversity is not limited to the 700-odd languages. Not many societies in traditional PNG could even have agreed on the result of two plus two. This is not meant disparagingly; rather, the simple fact is that there were probably more than fifty separate ways of counting. Whereas the decimal system in modern use has a base of ten, in PNG the bases ranged down as low as two. That is, after two, there was no three, you went back to one. In some communities there is no word in the indigenous language for numbers beyond the first few digits. Anything beyond two or three is 'some', and more than 'some' is 'many'. But it can also operate the other way. There is one group in the Eastern Highlands with a counting base of no fewer than 47. Their 47 digits are represented by 23 points on the right hand side of the body — fingers, toes, joints — and 23 on the left. The 47th digit is the nose. Then it starts all over again.

This probably makes as much sense as the imperial system's base of twelve and may go some way to explaining why some Papua New Guineans have difficulty grasping Western mathematical concepts. One ingenious solution has been devised in PNG to help small store owners with relatively limited education overcome these difficulties. The Department of Small Business was looking for a way to combat the problem of too many tradestores going broke because their owners had great trouble keeping track of what mark-up they should put on their goods. Even giving change can be a major difficulty. Some lateral thinking led the small business development officers to supply tradestore owners with pocket calculators and short courses showing them which sequence of buttons produced the right answer. Just a few easy steps to work out a percentage mark-up . . . The theory was the same as learning to drive a car: One does not need to know how the car works to make it go.

A major factor contributing to the rich diversity of peoples and cultures in PNG is the nature of the geography. Geologically it is a young, violent land. Located between the old, stable continental mass of Australia and the Pacific Ocean's deep basin, the segment of the earth's crust on which most of PNG sits is highly mobile. The friction caused by its constant movement has created the folded and faulted mountain ranges which continue to shake and occasionally explode to this day. There are fourteen active volcanoes in Papua New Guinea and twenty-two dormant but potentially dangerous ones. When Mount Lamington (near Popendetta) erupted in 1951, 3466 people died. Before it blew, Lamington had not been considered dangerous. Most parts of the country regularly shudder from the force of tectonic earthquakes under the Solomons Sea.

The beautiful town of Rabaul is the only urban centre in the world actually built inside the crater of a giant volcano. Volcanologists say it is inevitable that the town will be destroyed again, probably before the end of this century. Rabaul last exploded in 1937 and an eruption almost happened in 1984 when intense pre-eruptive activity led the authorities to declare a 'State Two Eruption Alert'. All the shakings, movement and eruptions over the past half-million years have resulted in a jagged and disparate topography. The main island's most dominant feature is the central cordillera. Running 2400 kilometres from the Voglekop in Irian Jaya through the Highlands to the Owen Stanley Ranges, it drops below the sea off the south-eastern tip of the PNG mainland to reappear in the D'Entrecasteaux Islands and the Louisiade Archipelago of the Milne Bay province.

The highest point in the cordillera is in Irian Jaya. In PNG, the tallest mountain is Mt Wilhelm, which reaches 4508 metres, more than twice the height of Mt Kosciusko. Upwards of a million Papua New Guineans live at a height above sea level at least equivalent to Kosciusko's peak. Some of the biggest mountains occasionally have snow on their peaks. The central cordillera takes up about half of the mainland. It is a haphazard system of ranges separated in many places by broad upland valleys. At its broadest the cordillera, with its encased Highlands valleys, is up to two hundred kilometres wide. At its edges the drop to the coastal plains is steep with falls of two thousand metres and more in the space of ten or twenty kilometres, producing spectacular waterfalls.

To the south the drop is to the swampy Papuan lowlands and to the north it is into the Sepik, Ramu and Markham river valleys. The Papuan plains are widest in the west directly above the Torres Strait. These vast lowlands are traversed by the Fly and Strickland rivers. Low ridges and plateaux break the major flood plains but the region is renowned for its sago swamps. Both the Fly River in the south and the Sepik in the north are navigable for up to eight hundred kilometres. The Fly River has become the highest earning waterway in the country, with barges plying from the river port of Kiunga to the river's mouth. They carry copper and gold concentrate from the Ok Tedi mine to the mine's floating sea port, an anchored ore carrier in the Gulf of Papua.

The three major northern rivers, the Sepik, the Ramu and the Markham, are hemmed in by a second chain of mountains fringing the north coast and running parallel to the central cordillera. These northern ranges are generally lower and much narrower than the central spine, except on the Huon Peninsula north of Lae where the highest peak tops four thousand metres. The islands that complete the nation of PNG have their own contrasts. They generally consist of mountain ranges rising directly from the sea or from narrow coastal plains. Volcanic landforms dominate the northern part of New Britain and Bougainville and some of the smaller islands are entirely volcanic. Goldmining geologists have discovered potentially huge riches in these volcanic islands rimming the so-called Pacific Ring of Fire. Other islands are beautiful coral cays.

Weather patterns in PNG vary to a surprising degree. Cool nights are the norm in the Highlands and frosts are common, sometimes being so severe as to wipe out food gardens and cause considerable deprivation. For eight months of the year Port Moresby is brown, hot, extremely dry and dusty, whereas Lae and Rabaul are green, hot, humid and wet all year round. The dense jungles covering many lowland areas are like those of Malaysia, while the savanna country around the capital and in the broad Western province resemble parts of northern Australia.

PNG's steep, jagged slopes, rushing rivers, broad swamps and thick forests present considerable engineering difficulties. The engineers designing the infrastructure for the Ok Tedi mine in the Star Mountains were staggered by how much they underestimated the challenge. Ok Tedi suffered a cost overrun of some fifty per cent — $500 million. Not only was the terrain difficult, it kept moving. Roads were cut in mountainsides only to disappear under landslides or fall out of sight down the slopes themselves as the earth below gave way. The engineers found the land in the Star Mountains to be so young that it had not settled. The attempt to build the main tailings dam was abandoned in total frustration. The tailings dam was a central requirement of the original environmental impact study. But it was destroyed before it could be finished. The dam wall was being built across a valley that had quite gently sloping walls. But one of these gently sloping walls gave way soon after the job began, and smothered the construction site. The main tailings dam has never been finished.

The land presents such a barrier that the capital, Port Moresby, is not connected by road to any of the country's other major cities or towns. The Japanese Government is funding a study aimed at providing a road link from Port Moresby to Lae, the second city and the nation's major port and industrial centre. If it goes ahead it will be one of the world's major construction projects of the 1990s.

The difficult terrain enforced the isolation in which so many groups once lived. Traditional life in Papua New Guinea was dominated by fear of one's enemies and, more importantly, fear of the spirits. The ancestors and spirits of dead relatives were active players in everyday life and great effort and attention went into placating them so as to ward off ill-fortune and death. It is tempting to generalise about PNG traditional society but the reality is that each group lived out its existence, developing its own solutions to explain the world in which it lived. Anthropologists have swarmed across the country, and for good reason, for PNG is an extraordinarily rich field. However, their hosts have not always appreciated the attention. Some provincial governments have moved to restrict anthropologists' access to their people, arguing that visiting anthropologists contribute nothing to the people and are just making careers for themselves. There are some Papua New Guineans who believe the academic brawl that erupted over Derek Freeman's questioning of Margaret Meade's seminal work on Samoa would be nothing compared with what they would like to say about Meade's more extensive writings on PNG. Papua New Guinea's first ambassador to the United States, Sir Paulius Matane, used to argue with Margaret Meade face to face in New York in the mid-1970s. When she died, he stalked out of her funeral service, enraged at what was being said in the funeral oration about her 'good work' amongst the New Guineans.

The impact of contact with outside forces has resulted in many of the old practices being discarded. Papua New Guineans are an adaptive people. Massive reassessments continue to take place as formal education and experience of outside cultures teach people to question and doubt the explanations their grandparents had for why things happen as they do. Nevertheless, Papua New Guineans retain much closer links to a spiritual world than do people of a Western background. Few urban Papua New Guineans have totally dismissed the power of magic and sorcery. Senior public servants have been known to seek the help of 'sanguma' men, people Australians might refer to as witchdoctors. A few years ago, the then chief executive of PNG's compulsory private enterprise superannuation scheme hired a wizened old man with a big reputation as a sorcerer to sit in his organisation's office to determine, through magic, who the chief executive's in-house enemies were. He was paid consultancy rates.

In the more remote areas life can still be dominated by fear. American anthropologist Bruce Knauft has detailed how the Gebusi people near Nomad on the Strickland plain of the Western province were attempting to interpret life and survive in the early 1980s. Knauft did his fieldwork between 1980 and 1982 amongst the Gabusi, who live in one of PNG's least contacted areas. Reviewing Knauft's published work, John Burton from the University of Papua New Guinea's Anthropology Department said the Gebusi believe they are terrorised by angry sorcerers and their traditional solution has been to find and violently deal with the offenders.

> Sickness is attributed by the Gebusi to a variety of sorcery methods: 'ogwili', 'bogay', 'bap' and an epidemic bringing sorcery are the main

types. An 'agwili' is a real man or group of men from a hostile group who have turned magically into an invisible death-dealing warrior; the 'ogwili' stalks its victims when they are alone in the bush. 'Bogay' sorcery is the kind of sorcery where the sorcerer is believed to obtain personal leavings of the victim. The sorcerer 'knots' this into a parcel, causing sickness. If the parcel is then burnt, the victim dies. In bap sorcery, the attacker sends a snake to replace the victim's spirit with stone; it is allegedly most often directed at children by jealous old women. In the past, sorcery suspects could be killed outright and this was the basis of an extraordinarily high homicide rate. Knauft calculates this at over 500 per 100,000 per year. If his figures are accurate, the Gebusi have rated as one of the world's most violent societies and something like one third of adults could expect to meet a violent death. While we certainly have similar figures for other PNG societies who were traditionally engaged in constant warfare (the Whagi valley may have been as violent as this before 1933), it is particularly startling that among the Gebusi the majority of these killings were carried out by members of the community itself, not by enemy warriors or outsiders.

Belief in spirits or ghosts was universal. Merlyn Wagner, in her 1970 article, 'The Enga Concept of Fear' (for the book, *Studies in Missionary Anthropology*), relates the story of a man coming into the mission station with four mangled fingers. He had unsuccessfully tried to hack them off with an axe to placate the ghost who was attacking his son. In Enga even birds are to be feared. 'Much of creation is arrayed in battle against the Enga, and ghost inhabited birds form part of the army. Not only are certain birds ghost-inhabited, but their cry can have specific meaning and invoke specific behaviour. The cry of the "tinalupi" bird (a small bird with a white tail) is a summons to sacrifice pigs or opossums, and failure to heed the signal will cause sickness or death. Likewise the cry of a "kau" (a small brown bird), "tidi" (a flying fox), "wangamatai" (a medium-size brown bird with a long tail) and to a lesser extent the "pisetulio" signify ghost presence, a call to sacrifice and punishment if this does not occur. The degree of fear varies from valley to valley, but the cry of a bird can strike terror in the ears of some.'

Daniel Kumbon, an Engan journalist, tells the story of how a ghost told him he would not only get to high school but also take out first prize in his final year of primary school. It was Christmas, 1971. 'The ghost, it was claimed, was an only son of a middle-aged couple from Laiagam living in Kandep at the time. The ghost or "*timongo*" of the dead son spoke to us through the mother,' Daniel says. He and a cousin were staying with relatives after their grade six exams. He says they were sitting around at night sharing pork when the woman from Laiagam asked the girl nearest her if she had taken her portion by mistake. The girl said no and offered to light a candle. That is when the ghost spoke, according to Daniel.

' "No don't light a candle for it is I who got it mother," somebody said in a low pitched whistle. "Mother, my mother, I am putting your pork back, you can eat it," the ghost said. Through the night many of the people asked questions about lost property and wanted to know a host of other things too. My cousin asked if I would be accepted into high school. The ghost replied: "Your cousin will go. Your cousin will go. He will go to Pausa High School and win a torch for coming first in the class," the ghost replied.' Daniel says these two predictions came true. Then he makes the comment: 'Up until now I had forgotten about this experience until a copy of the book *Studies in Missionary Anthropology* came into my possession. Everyone may agree with me that in modern society, due mainly to Christian influence, not many Engans believe in ghosts any more and they may no longer be offering pig sacrifice to *timongos*. But it was a fact of life of all Engans before the white man came.'

The first white people to see the mainland of PNG may have been the Portuguese expeditionary parties led by Antonio d'Abreau and Francisco Serrao in 1511-12. Within a century, Christianity had made its first assault — a brief but undoubtedly traumatic one for those involved. It was in 1606 and the Spaniards Luis Vaez de Torres and Diego de Prado raided a village, capturing fourteen girls and boys to carry them off to Manila for instruction in the Catholic faith. It was a long time before any serious white colonisation was attempted. Whereas Captain Cook's 1770 reports on his trip up the eastern coast of Australia led Britain within just eighteen years to send out Captain Phillip with boatloads of convicts to annex Australia as a penal colony, it was well over three centuries after the report of the first European sighting that efforts were made to colonise Papua New Guinea. And even then it was done most reluctantly, by the British at least.

After repudiating successive claims on behalf of the Crown to the eastern part of the main island of New Guinea — in 1845 by Charles Yule, in 1873 by Captain John Moresby and in 1883 by

Henry Chester on orders from the Queensland Premier, Thomas McIlwraith — Britain finally moved in 1884, much to the relief of the Australian colonies, who were worried about Germany's plans. The Dutch had claimed the western half of the main island (now the Indonesian province of Irian Jaya) in 1848. The Germans took the north-eastern quarter, calling it Kaiser-Wilhelmsland and raising the German flag on 3 November 1884. Three days later the British flag was raised over British New Guinea in Port Moresby. The border between the two was settled the next year. Sitting in a room in Europe, pouring over a map of this distant land, the British and German negotiators pulled out a ruler and inked in a line splitting the eastern half of New Guinea in two. The name of British New Guinea was changed to Papua after Australia assumed responsibility for its administration in 1906.

While Holland, Britain and Germany became the colonisers, the names 'Papua' and 'New Guinea' were coined by men from two other European countries, Portugal and Spain. Jorge de Meneses, the Portuguese Governor-General of the Moluccas, first used the name 'Papua' in 1526, taking it from the Malay word for frizzy hair. The Spaniard, Inigo Ortiz de Retez, wrote 'New Guinea' on his map in 1545 because he believed the people resembled the people of Guinea in Africa. When Carteret named New Ireland several hundred years later, he was prompted by different logic.

The administrations of the two colonies could not have been more different. The Germans chartered a private business firm, the Neu Guinea Kompagnie, to run its colony and it pursued an aggressive policy of economic exploitation. This was resented mightily by the local inhabitants, especially the Tolais of the Gazelle Peninsula, who resisted, at times fiercely, the taking of their land for copra plantations. In Papua, first the British, then the Australians followed what was then believed to be an enlightened policy of protecting the native people from exploitation and their land from expropriation. Ironically, today many people in Papua believe the Germans did a better job.

Whereas British policy may have been influenced by the missionaries who were the first foreigners to reside in Papua prior to 1884, the Germans were impressed by the foreign planters who had moved into the fertile New Guinea islands. Emma Forsayth, known as Queen Emma, was the first of these. She arrived in the Duke of York Islands in the late 1870s and over the next thirty years established a coconut plantation empire with its base near Kokopo in East New Britain. The Germans encouraged other planter settlers. As a consequence of their ruthless money-making policies some of the New Guinea island provinces are now the most prosperous in the country, while the Papuan provinces are generally poor and undeveloped. By 1914, when Australia sent a military contingent to take control of New Guinea at the outbreak of World War I, the Germans had alienated more than 280,000 hectares of land on New Britain. And by then more than 100,000 islanders had been pressed into service as plantation labourers, one quarter having died on the job.

A common difficulty facing both administrations was the absence of any powerful local rulers. Unlike the colonisation process in other parts of the world where the colonial power subdued and then dominated the indigenous political leaders, in PNG there was no unified system of pre-colonial administration. There were no large tribes or regional despots. The people were scattered in mostly small and often hostile groups. Hank Nelson in the ABC radio series, 'Taim Bilong Masta', elaborated on this point when talking about the role of the Australian patrol officer, the Kiap, in the administration of law several decades later: 'A problem in Papua New Guinea was that the traditional political units were so small. There was no centralised system that the colonial authority could take over and modify. It was a case of imposing Western law over an infinite variety of subtly changing local customs and values. The process had to be repeated over and over again. The Australian field and legal officers did not oversee the work of sultans or chiefs; they themselves determined innocence or guilt, and decided on the appropriate punishment.' It was the type of colonial rule that required close, constant control if it was to be effective.

After World War I, the League of Nations granted Australia a mandate to administer the former German colony. The vigorous and talented Lieutenant Governor of Papua, Sir Hubert Murray, argued that he be given responsibility for New Guinea too. But the Australian Government decided the land alienated from the local people by the Germans would provide an ideal soldier settlement scheme. The plantations were expropriated, the Germans turned out of their homes and Australian returned servicemen encouraged to take up a new life. Many failed. A separate administration was set up in the old German colonial capital of Rabaul under orders to make the mandated territory pay for itself if possible. A gold rush at Bulolo in the late 1920s helped towards this aim, as did the New Guinea administration's parsimonious approach to spending on the welfare of the indigenous people.

Australia's annual report to the League of Nations' Permanent Mandates Commission in 1921 revealed that Australia spent twelve pounds ($24) on native education that year. Fifteen years later, in 1936, the commission questioned whether the priority put on native education by the Australian administration was high enough. It represented one per cent of the territory's budget. Australia had even suggested to the Commission in 1934 that it should abandon native education altogether and hand it over completely to the missions. The suggestion was rejected. But the result must have been about the same because, although it defies belief, Australia spent less on education for the Melanesians in New Guinea in the 1930s than it did in the 1920s!

Sir Hubert Murray in Papua was constantly starved of cash and he was regularly under attack from resident Europeans for allegedly being 'absurdly paternal', for inhibiting their attempts to expand their commercial activities. Murray was a first-class honours graduate from Oxford. While studying in England, he had won the British Amateur Heavyweight boxing title and was more than capable of looking after himself. His concern for looking after the Papuan people extended to reviewing all the court cases involving Papuans in every district station. He personally signed the release papers of anyone he felt had been jailed unfairly. In the words of Ivan Champion, who worked in the Papuan service, Murray constituted a 'court of appeal' for the local people. 'He didn't worry about Europeans; they could appeal somewhere else.'

Murray was a remarkable character and according to *Pacific Islands Monthly* in 1933, after twenty-five years as Lieutenant Governor, Murray's 'ability, vision, scrupulous integrity and rigid adherence to a high code and a splendid ideal has given him a world wide reputation.' He served as head of the Australian administration in Papua from 1908 until he died in office in 1940. After the outbreak of World War II, Murray, at the age of seventy-eight, received instructions that in the event of an attack on Port Moresby he was to retire inland and direct guerilla activities. His son, Terrance, who had become a professional soldier, had already been retired by then on the grounds of age.

The coming of World War II to the Pacific forced Australia to abandon the separate administrations in New Guinea and Papua. The Japanese invaded and took control of all coastal New Guinea and the Oro and Milne Bay districts of Papua. Their attempts to take Port Moresby from the sea were frustrated by the Battle of the Coral Sea. Over land they were beaten back by Australian diggers on the Kokoda Trail. The war had a huge impact on those areas affected by it. The myth of the all-powerful white man was destroyed. Those local people who worked with the Americans were astonished to see negro soldiers apparently on a par with their white comrades. The Australian soldiers were friendly and not at all like the prewar 'mastas'. As the war swung around, Manus became the largest naval base in the South-west Pacific, with one million Americans passing through as they prepared to attack the Philippines. At the end of the war 150,000 Japanese soldiers lay dead in the PNG soil.

In July 1945 the Australian Government acknowledged that Australia owed a 'debt of gratitude' to the PNG people and it promised a new postwar order. A single administration was set up to govern both the Australian Territory of Papua and the United Nations Trust Territory of New Guinea. Australia made a reasonably good start although there was a scandal over war disposals. In the five years to 1950 the budget given to the unified administration of Papua and New Guinea by the Labor Government totalled sixteen million pounds — forty times what had been spent on both prewar administrations in the five years leading up to the war. The first postwar administrator, Colonel J K ('Kanaka Jack') Murray, is fondly remembered by the older PNG leaders who knew him.

Fondly remembered and honoured too is a giant of Australia's postwar colonial period in PNG, Dr John Gunther. Gunther was appointed director of a practically non-existent public health service at the close of the war. 'We had five doctors, about four Australian-trained nurses and twenty-three European paramedical workers, so it was a fairly desperate situation,' Gunther told the ABC's 'Taim Bilong Masta' radio series in 1980. Gunther's imaginative and novel approach to solving the severe health problems confronting the people of PNG transformed the health delivery system. He arranged with Dr H C 'Nugget' Coombs, the head of postwar reconstruction, to tap funds from the Commonwealth training scheme for returned servicemen. 'It was really stretching the provisions of the scheme to the ultimate to apply it to Papua New Guineans,' Gunther admitted. 'But we grabbed this and started what I called the "Native Medical Assistant Training Scheme", which afterwards became known as the "Aid Post Orderly Scheme". I say it quite proudly that we were just twenty years in front of the Chinese barefoot doctor. We trained people, complete illiterates, we taught them to recognise major killing diseases, to use the specific drugs, and we sent them back to their villages.' Some people died as a result of their ministrations but many thousands were saved.

To overcome the severe shortage of qualified doctors, Gunther visited postwar migration camps in Australia and recruited forty European migrant doctors, many of them refugees. Most spoke only a little English and they were debarred from practising in Australia. 'I was abused by the Australian Director General of Health,' Gunther recalled. 'The words he used were that I was "letting Australia down".' A few impostors had to be weeded out but the plan worked. A man of dynamism and foresight, Gunther became deputy administrator in the 1960s and the first vice chancellor of the University of Papua New Guinea.

The Australian politician who came to dominate the formulation of policy for Papua and New Guinea in the first twenty years after the war was Sir Paul Hasluck, Minister for Territories in the Menzies Government from 1951 to 1963. Hasluck says in his book, *A Time For Building*, that he returned from his first trip to PNG in 1951 'revolted at the imitation of British colonial modes and manners by some of the Australians who were there to serve the Australian Government . . . and never before in my life had I come across so many Australians who had lost so quickly any capacity to clean their own shoes or pour themselves another drink without the attention of a "boy".' The Acting Public Service Commissioner in the territory, Mr E A Head, told him 'a disheartening story' about the state of the service and the incompetence of some of the key men. Head summed it up for Hasluck by suggesting that if the Commonwealth public service was taken as a yardstick to be 100 per cent efficient, it would be 'an optimistic view' to think of the PNG service as being twenty-five per cent efficient. Hasluck set about his task as Minister with a determination to raise standards and instil in the people of PNG a respect for the institutions of government.

In his first year, 1951, Hasluck stated publicly that it was hoped PNG would eventually develop to some form of self-government but 'that is a long way ahead. It may be . . . more than a century ahead.' Unfortunately, Australia did not have those 100 years that would have been needed to see Sir Paul's vision through. From the time he took responsibility for the two territories, it had a bare twenty-four years to prepare PNG for Independence. But nobody suspected that at the time.

Hasluck was a demanding man never happy with the standard of performance of the territory administration and constantly badgering his department and the administrator to produce better results. This bred much resentment and probably lessened his effectiveness. In an address delivered at the end of his term as minister he said his objective had been to create the conditions that would allow sustainable self-government for the people of PNG. He was dismissive of newly independent African States in which the façade of democracy had quickly collapsed.

> For success a self-governing country needs not only a parliament but also a competent public service; an independent judiciary and magistracy; a sufficient number of educated and competent men and women to become candidates for public office; and a sufficient number of knowledgeable and well-informed persons to give popular leadership in the electorates. For success a self-governing country also needs sources from which it can draw its public revenues to support its services and utilities, funds to maintain and extend its capital equipment, and sources of investment for the development of its resources. . . . It also needs economic activity to support the standard of living of its people and give them gainful occupation. . . . Building a public service, helping a country to become economically viable and laying a broad base for political activity are all much more difficult than creating representative institutions or drafting constitutions.

He was critical, too, of his fellow Cabinet ministers in the Menzies Government for not appreciating Australia's obligations. 'One disillusionment is that in my twelve years as Minister for Territories,' he wrote in 1975, 'Cabinet never had a thorough and well-informed discussion of our policy and objectives in Papua New Guinea, although I was always trying to get one. . . . For example Cabinet approved that target dates should be announced but neither originally nor later faced the associated question of how to give effect to the announcement.' He said that in debates in Cabinet on the annual budget the territory was treated the same as other departments, with no debate on policy or what the goal was. 'The most devastating objection to an increase concerned the capacity of the Administration to use the money granted and the weakness of its financial control, but Cabinet never concerned itself with the attendant problem of Australian responsibility to make the Administration efficient. At times it almost seemed as though the view held was that, since Australia had met imperfectly its responsibility to govern the Territory efficiently and provide adequate staff, it had lessened its obligation to provide funds.'

Hasluck's book makes no claims of success. He says that whereas he looks with pride upon what he achieved in the other responsibilities of his portfolio — the Northern Territory and the smaller island territories, Papua New Guinea 'was a task for Sisyphus. I think I did just as well as Sisyphus did and certainly got just as tired.' The *Encyclopedia of Papua and New Guinea* in 1972 summed up Sir Paul's ministry: 'The extended period during which he was the minister responsible for PNG saw vast changes in the Territory, the virtual completion of its exploration and great expansion in government services and economic development. While the merits of some of Sir Paul's policies were warmly debated, there is no question that he brought to the administration of his Territory portfolio the force of a trained mind and a seriousness of purpose that were something quite new.'

Under his successor, Charles Edward Barnes, Australian policy in PNG seemed to lose direction. The same encyclopedia is eloquent in its silence about Mr Barnes's achievements. For all its three volumes and 1231 pages just six lines are devoted to this man who held Australian ministerial responsibility for PNG for a crucial eight years. Those six lines simply record that he was the Country Party member for McPherson in Queensland, that he became minister in 1963 and that his portfolio's name was changed to External Territories in 1968. Hasluck had proposed that Gunther be made secretary of the Department of Territories in Canberra for two years and that he then be sent back to PNG in 1966 as administrator. Barnes decided otherwise and appointed an economist, George Warwick-Smith, from the Trade Department as his departmental head.

In the late 1960s Barnes was saying Independence would not come to PNG before the end of the twentieth century. Certainly his policies reflected that attitude. In 1970 — just five years before PNG became Independent, there were just 122 Papua New Guinean students doing their sixth year of secondary schooling. Even in fourth year — the final year at most high schools in PNG — there were only 1731 students. The country's population at the time was 2.5 million.

The Barnes years were studded with bumbling insensitivity. Although it certainly was not the goal, this tended to promote greater political awareness amongst Papua New Guineans. An issue that ignited some indigenous political activity came in 1964 when the administration decided that Papua New Guineans employed in the public service should be paid less than their Australian equivalents. The PNG pay was set at forty per cent of that of an Australian doing the same job. The economic argument, a valid one, was that an independent PNG would not be able to afford Australian rates of pay. But Independence seemed so far away on the Barnes political agenda that none of the PNG public servants of 1964 would be around to enjoy it when it eventually came. The announcement was appallingly handled. At the time, fewer than 200 Papua New Guineans had been promoted into the second and third levels of the public service, to the sorts of positions where they competed with Australians. But more were on the rise. There was a protest march and many were galvanised into political action for the first time. Amongst these were some who would lead PNG to Independence. Bob Hawke travelled to Port Moresby in 1966 to represent the public servants as their industrial advocate. One witness he called was Michael Somare.

The year 1964 also saw most adult Papua New Guineans casting their first vote. A Legislative Council had been set up in 1951 but only three of its twenty-nine members were Papua New Guineans, all three selected by the administration. Of the twenty-six whites, sixteen were public servants appointed by the administrator. By 1961 the number of indigenous members in an enlarged Council had grown to a bare seven. The United Nations visiting mission in 1962 led by Britain's Sir Hugh Foot was very critical. Sir Hugh recommended a 100-seat Assembly with no special electorates for European members. This horrified some in the Australian resident community. Foot's proposals did, however, help dissipate opposition to the establishment of a House of Assembly of 64 members — 10 of them officially appointed, 10 elected in 'special' non-indigenous electorates and the remaining 44 from open electorates where anybody could stand. Not surprisingly, few of the PNG members elected were educated beyond primary schooling.

Only one of those forty-four members is still in parliament today: Sir Pita Lus. He has stood in every election since and he has never been beaten. In the 1987 national poll, Sir Pita won a commanding 53.33 per cent of the vote in his electorate of Maprik in the East Sepik. His was the fifth-highest vote recorded in the elections, in which only seven of the 109 members polled over 50 per cent. Sir Pita has been a tough and demanding Minister in his time but his reputation is built on his outstanding and witty pidgin oratory. Rarely does a parliamentary sitting day pass without Sir Pita having the public gallery and half the parliament in uproar, mostly with laughter.

Those first House of Assembly elections in 1964 introduced the word *democracy* to many Papua New Guineans. Within nine years, Australia was giving PNG self-government, to be followed shortly thereafter by Independence, all in the hope that somehow, after such a short time, democracy would have taken root. The second House of Assembly elections in 1968 saw the first real political party in PNG campaigning on the hustings — the Pangu Pati. Pangu had been formed the year before out of the informal 'Bully Beef Club' at the Administrative College. Michael Somare, a former broadcast officer and journalist with the administration Radio Service won the seat of East Sepik and became Opposition Leader. That Assembly consisted of ninety-four members, ten still appointed by the administration. The special electorates for the non-indigenous had been replaced by fifteen regional electorates but candidates standing for these had to have acquired a certain minimum education level. There were sixty-nine open electorates.

Although Mr Barnes was resisting any quick move towards independence, troubles were growing for the administration. There were disturbances on the Gazelle Peninsula, where the Tolais were objecting to a multi-racial council, disquiet on Bougainville over land matters related to CRA's opening of the Bougainville Copper Mine, and a rising agitation amongst the better educated Papua New Guineans. Then came Gough Whitlam. In 1969 he visited and proclaimed that self-government should be given within three years, by 1972, and Independence by 1976. In two highly publicised subsequent trips in 1970 and 1971, Whitlam, as federal Opposition Leader, visited the Gazelle Peninsula and gave John Kaputin's dissident Mataungan Association warm support. Whitlam had gone close to toppling the Liberal Government of Prime Minister John

Gorton in 1969 and he pledged that, when Labour won the 1972 Australian elections, he would ensure there was early self-government followed by quick Independence.

Affairs began to speed up. The Liberal Government adjusted its policies, Barnes was removed from the portfolio of External Affairs, and the youthful Andrew Peacock took up the job. The emerging Papua New Guinean political leaders struck an immediate rapport with Peacock. Here was a man their age, someone they could speak to. Although Peacock had the job barely a year, he made a profound impact. When Michael Somare patched together a coalition after PNG's 1972 elections, his new government established excellent relations with the new minister in Canberra. Ironic as it may seem, amongst today's Papua New Guineans who were at the political forefront in those years, Andrew Peacock is regarded more highly than the man who succeeded him when Whitlam did win the Australian elections in late 1972. It was Bill Morrison who saw Papua New Guinea through to self-government and Independence, but Peacock was in the job when it all became possible.

In the end, Independence came with a rush. It was handed over before any mass struggle arose. Despite the political skirmishes on the Gazelle Peninsula and Bougainville, a majority of Papua New Guineans were not demanding their freedom. In fact if there had been a referendum in the early 1970s, Independence would have been rejected by a majority. The Whitlam Government was keen on a timetable. One was set that would give PNG self-government in December 1973 and Independence a year later. Somare made numerous trips throughout the country in 1973 and 1974 trying to sell the idea of freedom from colonial control and to persuade the people that this would not bring disaster. As Independence approached, a peculiar reversal of roles came about, whereby Somare and the so-called 'radicals' of the late 1960s were urging a slow-down while the Government in Canberra was pushing for a quick end to Australia's colonial rule.

Australia could not have delayed giving PNG its Independence for many more years without there having been far more strife and consequently far greater post-Independence problems. The debate is not 'Did PNG get Independence too early?' but 'Did the preparations start too late?' Writing in 1964, eleven years before Independence, Paul Hasluck said that he was 'quite certain' in his own mind 'that a form of self-government will come to Papua and

New Guinea before the country is economically viable and before it is fully equipped either to finance or to staff the various departments and agencies of government. Someone other than the people of Papua and New Guinea will have to underwrite self-government.' He went on to describe what needed to be done — a strengthening of the public service, an expansion of education, the building of the economy — but he predicted that the work would not be completed in time. 'Self-government will be an improvisation when it comes but the more we can manage to do now the better the improvisation will be.' Australia should not be ashamed of its tutelage of PNG. Much was done in a relatively short time from an extraordinarily narrow base. But more could have been done and opportunities were squandered.

Highlanders especially were wary of early Independence. Their first contact with the outside world had come fewer than forty years earlier. Then came the war. It was not until the 1950s and even the 60s that large parts of the Highlands were pacified. Even as late as 1970 an area of some 170,000 hectares was still classified as not being under administrative control. The opening up of the Highlands is a modern epic. The enthusiasm with which the Highlanders wanted to 'catch up' is reflected in the fact that by 1970 almost half of the workforce employed in lowland areas was made up of Highlanders, most of them working as contract plantation labourers. Coffee became a Highlands crop. The people saw the opportunities it offered and, from 1954 on, village cash-crop coffee production exceeded what was being produced on the settlers' plantations. Many Highlanders believed they needed more time to narrow the gap; that if Independence came too quickly, they would be dominated by the better educated coastals. It was a fear that European planters in the Highlands played on and the political party that stood on that platform in the 1972 elections, the United Party, won most of the Highlands seats. Those elections were very close.

The officially appointed administration members were no more. There were 102 seats of which the conservative, anti-early Independence United Party won 42. Somare's Pangu Pati won 24. The rest were won by a range of mostly regional groups and independents. The United Party was sure it had won, but the Pangu Pati expertly cobbled together a coalition. In an exciting few weeks leading up to the first sitting, Pangu was able to persuade enough of the smaller parties and independents that their only chance to play a role in shaping an independent PNG was to join together behind Somare. The first Somare coalition government grouped Somare's Pangu Pati; Julius Chan's People's Progress Party; the Mataungans from the Gazelle; the Bougainvillians; a collection of Papuan Independents led by the wily John Guise, the former Speaker, who became deputy chief minister; and a selection of Highlanders under the banner of the National Party.

The vigorous Iambakey Okuk played a key role in securing this necessary Highlands representation. Okuk, a crash-through-or-crash politician, who much later became Opposition leader and then deputy prime minister in the 1980–82 Chan Government, died of cancer in 1986. By then he had become a Highlands symbol and his death brought widespread grief, mourning and riots. But in 1972, when he first won a seat in the parliament, he was a young man in the small Highlands-based National Party at odds with most of the other Highlands politicians. Somare and Okuk had been students together at the Sogeri National High School in the mountains behind Port Moresby and Somare relied on Iambakey and his National Party Leader, Thomas Kavali, to drag the necessary Highlanders into the coalition.

Here is Iambakey Okuk's own version of how it was done, taken from an address to a lively university student audience during the run up to the 1982 PNG national elections:

'We went and greased up one bloke called Kaibelt Diria.' (In Pidgin 'grisim' or 'to grease' means to trick somebody into doing something by flattery or lies.) 'Kaibelt Diria was a deputy leader for the United Party. And, you know, we told him: "Papa, the Australian Government has already announced that Somare is to become the first Prime Minister." And he says: "WHAT!"' The students burst into laughter.

Okuk went on, 'Kaibelt Diria said, "WHAT!" And we said: "Yeah. They announced it on the radio that we have already got the number and we're forming a government. But we don't have enough Highlanders and we want to give some ministries to some people."' By this time the students had really warmed to the story and there was more laughing.

'So we said: "But, Papa, there is only a few of us and we are still young and we are looking for some elders to take the important positions."' By this time Okuk himself was chortling along with his audience.

'And he said: "Yeah? Wait, wait . . . OK! We go now!" And we said: "Look, hang on, hang on, it's OK. The position won't run away. You'll get it. But you must also bring another five or something like that." "Oh, that's no problem," he said, "I'll bring seven!" ' With this the students roared.

'So he brought back seven people so we made the number. This is how Somare claims he got self-government,' Okuk said. 'But we did the dirty job which you don't know. I had to tell lies to my old father who had more pigs and more wives than Somare, you know. Many, many wives. Many, many pigs. Big coffee plantation — more things than Somare, myself or Chan put together. Anyway, the poor guy, we greased him so he had to come and become a minister.'

Okuk's punch line had his University student audience in convulsions of laughter: 'We made him the Minister for . . . Telephones!'

Politics, but in a new, distinctly PNG style.

CHAPTER THREE
PARLIAMENTARY DEMOCRACY — PNG-STYLE

PAPUA New Guinea's Culture Minister, Aruru Matiabe, was desperate to retrieve a seemingly impossible situation. Working at night with Prime Minister Namaliu's staff, he facsimiled a news release to all the PNG media urging journalists not to read 'undue meaning' into statements he had made at noon that day at a news conference called by the Opposition Leader's office. He was worried that the media might interpret what he had said as indicating that his loyalty to Mr Namaliu's government was less than total. What Mr Matiabe had said was: 'I am happy to announce to the public that I have resigned as a minister'; and 'With Paias Wingti as prime minister and myself as the deputy we can once again get PNG moving on the right path'; and even 'Rabbie Namaliu has not provided the strong, firm and decisive leadership this country needs so I have decided to withdraw my support'. Mr Matiabe's excuse for making these statements into which he was urging the media not to read 'undue meaning' was that he had been 'under duress'.

The noon news conference that day, 7 November 1989, was supposed to have been the Opposition's coup de grace against Namaliu on the eve of a parliamentary vote of no confidence. Mr Matiabe's defection was to have swung the finely balanced numbers Wingti's way. The lobbying for numbers in the 109-seat parliament had been frantic for a week. Few members, ministerial staff or Opposition office workers had slept more than four hours a night. The preceding evening, Opposition supporters smashed the back window and deflated the tyres of a car in which the Police Minister,

Mathias Ijape, and the Minister for Trade and Industry, John Giheno, were sitting at the Port Moresby airport waiting for the government whip to arrive from the Highlands. The whip was a possible defector. When the aircraft did arrive, the Opposition delegation swarmed onto the tarmac ahead of the two ministers. But in vain — the government whip was not on board.

Some time between noon and dusk on the seventh, Mr Matiabe changed his mind. Prime Minister Namaliu held enough members and the next morning, the Opposition withdrew its motion minutes before the no-confidence vote was to be taken. Mr Matiabe's double crossing of the floor saved his ministry. Another minister was not so lucky. The Administrative Services Minister, Theodore Tuya, followed more conventional channels and notified Prime Minister Namaliu of his resignation in writing before going to the media. It was accepted and the Prime Minister used the ministry to attract an Opposition member, William Ank, to defect to him. At Mr Ank's swearing-in at Government House, a weary Mr Namaliu rued PNG's no-confidence motion roundabout. 'It can be very destabilising because it takes your mind off everything else, including governing, and concentrates your mind entirely on the vote,' he said.

Despite its inherited Westminster-style parliament and democratic institutions, PNG's political system has rapidly evolved its own mores and distinctive practices. The scramble for numbers each time there is a motion of no confidence is the most obvious manifestation. Governments change not at the ballot box but during parliamentary sittings. In the three elections since Independence, two have resulted in the retention of the prime minister who went to the polls. But both fell later in mid-term votes of no confidence. To understand the peculiarities of PNG's post-Independence politics it is important to know how the politicians see their role. Parliamentarians in PNG regard themselves more as leaders of their people than as their representatives.

The difficulty members have rationalising their own expectations with those of their electors is evident in one debate after another. But nothing focuses the mind on what a job entails better than a discussion over pay. The following are extracts from parliamentary debates in 1983 on members' retirement benefits and a private members' Bill to change the Constitution to remove the independence of the Parliamentary Salaries Tribunal. The Member for Enga, Paul Torato, wanted the tribunal membership altered so that the Prime

Minister, the Opposition Leader and the Speaker would decide members' pay and conditions. The disarming frankness of speech is characteristic of political debate in PNG:

'I face transport problems so I always travel by PMV [Public Motor Vehicle — bus] like ordinary people,' the member for Lagaip Porgera, Mark Ipuia, told the House. 'No one knows whether I am an elected member of parliament or not. The dust usually covers my face and even the people travelling in the same PMV cannot recognise me. I have nothing which will show other people I am a member.' Mr Ipuia, a former minister, continued: 'I know some ministers and members fall into the trap of accepting bribes because they are not satisfied with what they receive.' He suggested the government should not only provide all members with cars but that a house should be built for him in his electorate. Public servants, he complained, 'get higher salaries than us, they have good houses and they have cars, but not me. . . . I am looked upon as a bigman because I am the elected member for Lagaip Porgera. Many people come to me and say, "Member, can you help me with K100 [$150] because I want to send my son to school?" Sometimes I have to tell my own people to get lost.'

Paias Wingti, then deputy prime minister, was also unhappy about the disparity with public-service pay. 'My executive officer who is on Level One earns more than me! I see no justification for this! Everybody wants to see Paias Wingti because he is the deputy prime minister. I have to paint a good picture in public,' Mr Wingti said. 'I represent 60,000 people from the Hagen electorate. They come to my house every time I go to Hagen. They expect something all the time. What about the secretaries of departments, do they have the same problems as you and me? They do not! And yet they are paid highly!'

The member who moved the constitutional amendment, Mr Torato, claimed PNG politicians were amongst the worst paid in the world. Comparisons of this nature are never easy but a PNG backbencher's pay is roughly equivalent to five times the PNG urban minimum wage. In 1990 an ordinary member earnt K15,400 [$23,100] a year. 'If people see us travelling in taxis or PMVs,' Mr Torato told parliament, 'they are going to wonder what has gone wrong with the system. "He is supposed to be travelling in a VIP car because he is a bigman." I am ashamed because of this. When the people elect me to parliament,' he went on, 'they think I own the Bank of PNG. People demand you buy them motor vehicles or give them money because they have been your campaign managers or cast their votes in your favour. They demand you produce K10,000 and buy them a car.... People have this kind of mentality that when we become MPs, we inherit wealth. I call this cargo cult.'

'In our tradition,' the member for the Papuan electorate of Abau, Jack Genia, said, 'leaders are leaders because they are wealthy men. By wealth, I mean pigs, material goods and sometimes many wives. Sometimes they are leaders because they have magical powers and can use these powers to catch fish, win negotiations, make rain and many other things.' Mr Genia, who was a former Lands Department secretary, complained that the leadership code in the Constitution created a dilemma for members by preventing them from going into business, thus prohibiting them from accumulating the wealth leaders were expected to have and share. 'Our people blame us all the time,' he lamented. 'When I was a public servant as head of a department my salary was two or three times more than what I am getting now.'

The Justice Minister and member for Wewak, Tony Bais, who had been a district commissioner, echoed this sentiment: 'When I told [my electors], they were very surprised members of parliament are paid less than public servants.' The Member for Manus, Michael Pondros, said his wife was the one to suffer: 'I just don't want to spend my time in this parliament to talk and talk, and when I go back to my house and see no food, I might hit my wife for no good reason.' Mr Pondros suggested entertainment funds could be the answer. 'If I go to Manus my people want me to make a party for them because they voted for me. Mr Minister, if I were you I would allocate K5000 for the ordinary members, the ministers K10,000, the Prime Minister K40,000 — to entertain the people.'

According to the member for Wabag, Albert Kipalan, the members who were complaining loudest about how much their electors demanded were the most to blame for raising their people's expectations. 'I am sorry because you members are the most miserable people I have ever seen,' he said. 'I have no doubt in my mind, Mr Speaker, that when they campaigned, they said, "I am going to fight for you." I am wondering if anyone of you here would be honest enough to say, "I will fight for my salary, allowance and accommodation!" ... Our people have been spoilt because people handed out money hoping they would be elected.'

But no matter who is to blame, the high expectations are a reality in the electorate. The member for Tambul Nebilyer, Thomas Negints, saw the issue quite starkly: 'You must have money to stand for election in the Highlands. I was elected to parliament [in 1982] because I am a young man and I have no businesses. But I must have K100,000 [$150,000] to face the 1987 elections or I will lose my seat. The same goes for every member. We must be realistic and face the facts. We should not oppose this Bill just because we think the people will not agree with us. We should not pretend nothing is wrong. As elected leaders, we have the duty to upgrade our status and living standards in the community.' Mr Negints did win again in 1987.

The Provincial Affairs Minister, John Nilkare, added that members in the Highlands were expected to lead by example. 'Members are expected to kill five pigs if the people kill only one. He must contribute the most. This has been carried on from traditional society. It used to be pigs in the past but nowadays it is money. . . . Our electors blackmail us,' he said. 'I would be happy if the members went on strike. We ministers will support you and there will be no one to make decisions.' One other minister did support industrial action to convince the Salaries Tribunal that members needed more money. 'We have never gone on strike and so they do not know whether we are happy with what we are getting,' said Lukas Waka, Forests Minister. 'It seems they are not concerned. They feel we are the leaders and cannot go on strike so they are not doing anything for us.'

The late Sir Iambakey Okuk, then Opposition leader, came straight to the point. 'At the moment, with the meagre salaries, we have the problem of members trying to become Ministers so they can earn more. We are opening the door to bribery and corruption so I feel an increase is very much justified. Naturally we can expect some criticism but we have to take the initiative.' The corruption argument was also used by the mover of the amendment, Mr Torato. 'If we are going to be looked up to as the supreme legislators then we must be the ones to decide our own salaries, conditions and privileges,' he maintained. 'We will not be in parliament all the rest of our lives. Some of us will be replaced at the next election and I would like to pose the question that when we leave the parliament, what have we got to go back to?' Mr Torato, who lost in 1987, admitted to parliament: 'To satisfy our people, some of us have turned to bribery and corruption and I think this is disastrous for this country.'

In 1988 the parliament did vote to change the Constitution to put the Speaker in charge of the commission setting members' pay and conditions. The pay did not rise but the benefits and facilities immediately improved. Amongst the new provisions were an office in each member's electorate, a car, staff, a subsidy for office-running costs and higher allowances for travel within the electorate. In response to adverse media publicity about the new deal for members, the Speaker, Dennis Young, revealed in November 1989 that the 'total cost of all services to a member of parliament, excluding airfares, and his staff, vehicles and office is K54,000 [$81,000] per year.'

Although members may bemoan their lot, there is no shortage of people wanting to grab their seats. A record 1515 candidates contested the 109 electorates in the 1987 national elections — an average of 14 per seat. The total was up 35 per cent on the 1982 elections and more than 70 per cent on 1977. The seat that attracted the highest number of candidates was Kerowagi in the mountainous Simbu province in the Highlands with 45. PNG has a first-past-the-post voting system, so whoever scores the most on the first count wins. In Kerowagi the winner received only 7.9 per cent of the popular vote. He went into parliament even though more than 90 per cent of the voters of Kerowagi chose otherwise.

Election Time

The ballot paper at the village polling station near the Kerowagi High School is so large that a child could hide behind it. It is as big as a glossy wall poster. It needs to be, and probably has cost as much to produce. PNG's electoral commissioner has ruled that in each electorate in the 1987 elections a passport-like photograph of each candidate must appear on the ballot paper next to the candidate's name. Alongside that, if the candidate has party endorsement, a second photograph of the candidate's party leader has to be shown.

At Kerowagi, in the Simbu province, this has meant a super-sized ballot paper, printed on both sides, with forty-five photographs of candidates and five more of party leaders. Twenty of these, and a ballot box is stuffed full. As the voters edge forward in single file to have their names recorded and their fingers daubed with indelible ink, they are handed the giant ballot papers while hundreds of others line the roped-off, mobile ballot station, watching. The policeman in charge of protecting the polling team nods in the direction of one man with a cap standing under a tree and says: 'He's a candidate. Last time, when he lost, he fired a shotgun off at the school.'

The sitting member for Kerowagi, David Tul, from Paias Wingti's People's Democratic Movement (PDM), is to lose. He polls 1753 votes — 7.4 per cent of the total cast. He runs second to Jim Yer Waim, an independent who later joins Michael Somare's Pangu Pati and gets the Environment ministry in the 1988 change of government. Mr Yer Waim scrapes in ahead of Mr Tul by 124 votes. He gets 1887 — support from a mere 7.9 per cent of people credited with valid votes. This means 92.1 per cent of the voters of Kerowagi backed men who lost.

Supporters of one losing candidate threaten to burn down the Kerowagi High School. The anger is explainable. Back at that ballot station near the school, students are in the queue lining up to vote. They are wearing their Junior High School uniforms. Some look no more than sixteen. But under PNG's electoral laws, people whose names are not recorded on the electoral roll are still allowed to cast what is called a 'sectional vote'. In practice, all they have to do is give the presiding electoral officer their name, swear that they have lived in the electorate for more than six months and that they are over eighteen. The harassed electoral official at Kerowagi goes through the formalities. But when the third, clean chinned student in succession claims he is 'eighteen and a half', the official lets out a strangled, exasperated cry of, 'Jesus!'

Of the members elected in 1987, forty-one got into parliament with the endorsement of fewer than one out of every five of their constituents. In the Highlands, only one of the thirty-nine winners polled more than forty per cent of the popular vote. That was Prime Minister Wingti in the Western Highlands regional seat with 40.1 per cent. With so many losers supported by so many people, some trouble was inevitable. In the Southern Highlands the Pangia High School was wrecked by followers of the defeated member for Ialibu/Pangia, Pundia Kange. Mr Kange, a Pangu/Somare man, from the Wiru clan on the Pangia side of the electorate, was beaten by Roy Yaki, a Paias Wingti man, from the Kewa clan on the Iabibu side. As the result became clear several days after the election, fifty men from three Wiru villages attacked the Pangia High School with axes. Their reasoning was that Pundia Kange had 'built' the high school when he was a Pangu minister and therefore his people could rip it down. Roy Yaki and Paias Wingti could build it up again. The Wiru people were also angry with two of their clan members, one a teacher at the school and the other the chairman of the school board, who stood for the election, splitting the Wiru vote and allowing the Kewa clansman, Roy Yaki, to take the seat from the Wiru people.

The nomination of 'friendly' candidates to split a powerful opponent's clan vote is a common tactic. Under the 'first past the post' system the more candidates there are in an electorate covering a multitude of often mutually envious villages, the greater the chance each candidate has of winning. In most of PNG there is no genuine party vote and the general belief is that anybody can win. Prospective candidates are attracted by the rich rewards they have seen members acquire in terms of status, power, privileges and money. While candidate numbers are proliferating so are parties. In the 1987 election, fifteen political parties nominated candidates, although for some it was more a case of the candidates selecting the parties than the parties selecting the candidates.

On the floor of the parliament between elections, parties are constantly being formed or dissolved, securing new or losing old members. It is almost impossible to give an accurate count of party numbers in the parliament at any specific time. A list compiled one day can be misleading a week later. Back in 1981, when there were seven parties in the parliament, only one could give an honest count on its exact strength. That was Panal, the Papuan National Alliance, which had only one member, its founder, Waliyato Clowes. Panal disappeared when Ms Clowes lost in 1982. The first time any of the journalists in PNG could get a correct fix on party numbers in the outgoing parliament in 1987 was when the electoral commissioner, Luke Lucas, published lists of candidates who had received party endorsement. Even he could not put complete faith in the lists that party executives had given him! Advertising the endorsed candidates' names after nominations closed, Mr Lucas called on anybody named who did not agree that they were standing for the parties claiming them to contact his office. The electoral commissioner wanted to start printing the ballot papers but knew he must double check.

Parties in PNG are organisationally feeble, with most having no paid-up members outside parliament. The best organised, Pangu, has a strong business arm and a national executive. But, despite attempts to build up a nationwide structure and fight provincial elections, even Pangu has limited grassroots membership. Whereas Pangu took seats in sixteen of the nineteen provinces in 1982, it lost support in the Highlands and Papua in the 1987 elections and became predominantly a party of the New Guinea mainland coast with some hold on the New Guinea islands. A number of other parties have a purely regional or even provincial focus. Parties that form in parliament tend to be groupings around a dominant personality and the party grows or shrivels depending upon the strengths or fortunes of the leader. Leaders are always keen to recruit because the ability to deliver numbers is the basis of bargaining power. A leader's overthrow mostly results in the party splitting in two or shattering completely.

There is rarely any ideological cement binding a party together. For example, no working class culture has had time to develop in PNG and although some trade unions launched a Leiba (Labour) Party to contest the 1987 elections it never won a seat. The increasing number of university-educated members has contributed to a rise in the amount of left-wing rhetoric heard in parliament but the few socialists are well outnumbered by the pro-business lawyers. The most persuasive of the anti-capitalists is Utula Samana, leader of the Melanesian United Front who has published a book advocating village community-based self-reliance. Generally, though, party platforms advance bland policies promising such things as agricultural development, easier access to bank loans, free primary schooling, better roads, and lower air fares, while honesty and accountability are popular catchwords.

Roughly half the MPs lose their seats at any election. In the 1987 poll, forty-eight members who recontested were tossed out, while fifty-six were returned. The tenuous nature of a member's hold on his seat contributes much to the way the parliament operates. Sir Julius Chan, PNG Prime Minister from 1980 to 1982, says PNG politics become logical if this lack of security is taken into account. 'Our politics [are] still regionalistic, and tribally based,' Sir Julius

PARLIAMENTARY DEMOCRACY 61

says. 'Each member has a strong commitment to directly benefit his immediate electorate — much more so than in, say, Australia, where only a minority of seats are considered "marginal". In PNG, over fifty per cent of members lose their seats at the polls. There are very few "safe" seats. Appreciate this and you go a long way to understand the logic of PNG politics,' Chan says. 'I have often read foreign commentators refer to our politics as "crazy and without ideology". Ideology is a luxury marginal members cannot afford. It becomes a case of delivering the goods — a pragmatic approach. Just as it is in marginal seats in Australia before election day, with both sides offering election bonuses. The Australian parties play Santa at every Federal and State election. For us it is a full-time job!'

Sir Julius argues this is 'in a way a good thing', in that it puts pressure on members to service the people who voted for them. 'But our politics [are] not illogical, crazy, unstable or even unpredictable,' he claims. One clue to what distant observers might see as the puzzle of PNG politics is that the Constitution makes the parliament more powerful than the government. Theoretically that may be the case in Australia. But between elections in Australia, the government can get on with running the country without worrying about parliamentary revolts. It was only during the constitutional crisis in 1975 when the Senate blocked Gough Whitlam's supply Bills that the Australian parliament (in modern times) exercised the power that is an everyday fact of life for prime ministers in Papua New Guinea. The PNG Constitution gives the parliament the power to decide who should be prime minister. But unlike the Australian Constitution, it gives no power to the prime minister to decide when elections should be held. No PNG prime minister can go to the Governor-General and seek a dissolution of parliament.

Parliamentary terms are set at five years and only parliament itself can decide whether there should be an early poll. The members' knowledge that there is no guarantee of being returned, that half of them are destined to lose, effectively rules out the possibility that a majority would ever vote for a dissolution. Once, when a motion to dissolve parliament was introduced, an amendment was immediately moved that would have had the opposite effect. It was in 1979, and the Commerce Minister, Pita Lus, moved that instead of calling a snap election the motion be reworded to delay any poll until 1984. That would have given members an extra two years without facing the people, extending the parliament's life to seven years!

With parliament's term rigidly fixed, a prime minister has to be alert to regular challenge on the floor of the House. The only periods of grace he gets are the first six months after he is elected and the final twelve months of the parliament's five-year term. In between, the prime minister is subject to overthrow through votes of no confidence. To ensure continuity, the Constitution says any no-confidence motion must nominate an alternative prime minister. Party discipline is paltry because loss of endorsement or expulsion is no penalty. All of this elevates the power of the ordinary member. As one Somare staff member put it in early 1985, 'PNG suffers from the dictatorship of the backbench.' Keeping members on side is an endlessly absorbing task and the best lure, a ministry, is effective only for half the number the prime minister needs. The Constitution limits the number of ministers to one quarter of the members plus the prime minister. With 109 members, this sets a maximum of twenty-eight ministers. It takes fifty-five votes to stay on top.

In the first two years of Independence none of this was a problem. From 1975 until 1977, Michael Somare as Prime Minister enjoyed the generous support of the Opposition Leader, Tei Abal, when it came to crucial questions of stability. Sir Tei deserves an honoured place in PNG's history for not exercising the considerable powers of destabilisation at his disposal in the years when he led the Opposition, from 1973 until 1977. A traditional bigman from the Highlands' Enga province, Sir Tei led the United Party (UP) which then held by far the largest number of seats in parliament. The UP had campaigned vigorously against Independence in the 1972 House of Assembly elections, receiving sturdy financial support from Australian planters and businessmen. But once Somare was confirmed in power and the process of self-government and Independence began, Sir Tei swung his UP in behind Somare on some of the most difficult issues, thus enhancing the smooth transition to nationhood.

The Somare/Chan Government did well at the 1977 elections. Both Somare's Pangu Pati and Sir Julius's People's Progress Party (PPP) emerged with their party numbers enlarged. Somare formed another coalition from Pangu, the PPP and regional groups. The UP lost numbers and the new Opposition leader, Iambakey Okuk, was the head of the other Highlands-based party, the National Party (NP). Aggressive and ambitious, Mr (later Sir) Iambakey Okuk had broken with Somare in 1974 after having helped form the 1972 coalition. He knew no other way than to attack. In 1978 and 1979 he tried three votes of no confidence against Somare. Somare easily survived them.

The successful Somare/Chan combination came apart in late 1978 when Somare, urged on by some of the newer, younger members of his Pangu Pati such as Nahau Rooney and Paias Wingti, decided to make PNG's strict leadership code even tougher. The proposals would have severely limited the business interests of politicians. Chan's family is heavily involved in shipping and accommodation in the New Guinea islands and his party is essentially a businessman's party. While this dispute over tightening up the leadership code simmered, Somare reshuffled his ministry, removing Chan's PPP ministers from economic portfolios. Chan withdrew from the Government, saying Somare had forsaken consultation. In a manoeuvre often repeated in PNG politics since, Somare coaxed a party over from the Opposition to survive. His new coalition partner was Pangu's old foe, the much-reduced United Party.

Somare's new coalition had a poor 1979. Confidence in the Government was rocked by a series of events, the most serious and damaging being the 'Rooney Affair', which resulted in a constitutional crisis, more than half the judges resigning from the Supreme Court and a thousand prisoners breaking out of jail. It had its origins in the decision by the Deputy Leader of the United Party and Primary Industry Minister, Roy Evara, to hire a Guyanian academic, Ralph Premdas, as a personal adviser to help him 'assume control over the policy-making of his department'. Dr Premdas was head of the Politics Department at the University of Papua New Guinea. Evara had been his student. But Premdas was also a part-time adviser to Opposition Leader Okuk. A Pangu ministerial committee became convinced Premdas had some mystical power over Evara because Evara repeatedly ignored Somare's demands that he sack the foreign academic. The committee ordered Premdas deported. Premdas won a temporary injunction. In a fury, the Justice Minister, Ms Rooney, publicly attacked the totally expatriate Bench. She also wrote a stinging letter to the Chief Justice, Sir William Prentice.

Minister Rooney was charged with contempt of court. The full bench of the Supreme Court heard the case, found the Justice Minister guilty and jailed her for eight months. Somare made himself Acting Justice minister and set Ms Rooney free the next day, pending an appeal to the mercy committee. Five judges including the chief justice

and deputy chief justice resigned. Upon learning of Nahau Rooney's
release prisoners throughout the country followed the Justice
Minister out of jail — but over the fences, not through the front
gates. Papua New Guinea's Chief Ombudsman, Ignatius Kilage,
investigated the whole extraordinary affair and reported to parliament that, 'had Evara been candid with Premdas' instead of
making false assurances to him that Somare sanctioned his role as
Evara's adviser, Premdas would undoubtedly have resigned and 'the
harsh consequences that were to follow would have been avoided.'

Evara played a role in Somare's defeat a few months later, in
March 1980. This first successful vote of no confidence is worth
examining in detail because it set the pattern for those that followed
and reveals the limited capacity any PNG prime minister has to
exercise discipline over errant ministers or argumentative coalition
partners. Whereas Somare had not been troubled by the three earlier
no-confidence motions, he set the scene himself for a much more
difficult test by a thorough ministerial reshuffle in January. Like
the reshuffle in 1978 that had led to Chan's withdrawal, the New
Year reshuffle in 1980 upset Somare's coalition team members. This
time it was fatal. He disaffected one and a half of the parties in
his three party coalition. One change was to sack Evara. But, while
this seemed inevitable following the Rooney fiasco, Evara, as deputy
leader of the United Party, took half of the UP members with him
and crossed the floor. The irony of having a United Party split
down the middle was made more exquisite when the two factions —
the United Party (Government) and the United Party (Opposition) —
fought over the party's bus, which was plastered with the slogan
'United We Stand — Divided We Fall'.

Somare may have survived his shedding of the troublesome Mr
Evara if, at the same time, he had not decided to discipline the
third grouping in his coalition. This group, which soon took the
name Melanesian Alliance (MA), was led by Father John Momis,
Minister for Decentralisation. Momis had played a major part in
framing the PNG Constitution but, as Independence approached
and his differences with Somare intensified, he resigned his seat
and became a leader of the 1975 Bougainville secession movement.
Succession was averted with the introduction of provincial government and Momis stood for parliament again in 1977. He led a team
campaigning for decentralisation and swept all four Bougainville
seats. Somare made Momis Decentralisation minister, giving him

carriage over the introduction of provincial government to the other eighteen provinces. Momis's best ally on the Constitutional Planning Committee, John Kaputin, who had been a leader of the anti-colonial Mataungan movement in East New Britain, also won his seat again in 1977 and was made Central Planning minister.

In the January 1980 reshuffle Somare switched Momis to the Minerals and Energy portfolio and Kaputin to Higher Education. Both were provocative steps. Momis was not only stripped of the portfolio he had fought so hard for but, as Minerals and Energy minister, he would be put in what he saw as an untenable position. The renegotiation of the Bougainville Copper Agreement was due in 1981 and Momis would have had to combat the provincial government he had helped create. Kaputin plummeted from number five in the ministry to twenty-six. He was annoyed for another reason as well. A few months before, when the 'Rooney Affair' was still dominating the news, the national court had jailed Kaputin for ten weeks for failing to comply with a court order relating to company returns for the Mataungan Association's business arm. Upon his release, Kaputin bitterly attacked Pangu ministers for leaving him in jail by failing to grant a conditional pardon.

Momis and Kaputin were outraged they had not been consulted about the reshuffle. They announced their intention to resign, but when after one week they had not, Somare sacked them. Kaputin, Momis and the three other Bougainvillians joined the vote of no confidence in Somare that nominated Sir Julius Chan as the alternative prime minister. In a last-minute flurry, Somare appointed three new ministers — two of them from amongst Evara's disaffected UP backbenchers. But the list of those who had real or imagined grievances against Somare had grown too large and Chan defeated Somare 56 to 52. Four of the five political parties in the new coalition government had been allies of Somare in one or another of his three earlier governments. Somare took the defeat with good grace and, leading by example, made sure there was a smooth, violence-free transition.

Okuk had accepted that to get into power he would have to rally support behind Chan and he became Chan's deputy prime minister. Evara, Momis and Kaputin all became ministers again. The five-party Chan/Okuk Government was bedevilled by in-fighting, much of it instigated by Okuk. Okuk has been accurately described an 'Oppositionalist' figure, whether in government or opposition. The five parties covered the complete spectrum. At one end there was the Melanesian Alliance, which saw itself as defending the rights and interests of the exploited village people; and at the other end was Okuk's National Party, representing aggressive, indigenous Highlands business interests. In between were Chan's centrist pro-investment PPP, the 'new government' half of the split United Party and the Papuan separatist group, Papua Besena.

The most radical policy differences in PNG politics throughout this period were not between the Government and the Opposition but within the Government itself. In one memorable exchange Father Momis accused Deputy Prime Minister Okuk of 'being addicted to the principle of the acquisitive private businessman', while Okuk accused Momis of being 'a communist'. On a trip to Australia, Momis won headlines with the claim that the Government he served in was 'unstable and corrupt'! John Kaputin, as Finance minister, regularly castigated other ministers, especially Okuk, for extravagance and he publicly attacked specific Cabinet decisions as 'economic lunacy'. Chan confessed to a forum of university students in 1981 that he was regularly subjected to 'political blackmail'. However, he kept the government intact and built up his numbers to more than seventy as various members quit their former allegiances and crossed the floor. A close Chan adviser described these switches as 'disgustingly transparent' and said the sole attraction was the perceived benefit of going into the 1982 elections with access to the Government's purse strings.

Those 1982 elections were a personal triumph for Somare. There were 1126 candidates and nine political parties competing for the 109 seats but Somare's Pangu Pati achieved a phenomenal thirty-four per cent of the national vote. Pangu, which had thirty-five members in the outgoing parliament, won fifty seats — almost half. Iambakey Okuk, who had spent a fortune to persuade Highlanders that this was their one and only chance to elect a Highlands prime minister, lost his seat. His NP, which went to the polls with twenty-three seats, came away with only twelve and without either Okuk or his deputy, Thomas Kavali. The wife of a leading NP official in the Southern Highlands sliced off one of her ears in grief over Okuk's loss. Chan's PPP also suffered a rebuff, dropping from twenty members to fourteen. All but one of the five governing coalition parties lost members. The exception was Father Momis's MA which gained two seats — up from six to eight. Of twenty-six ministers who stood, twelve were rejected.

A feature of the immediate post-election phase in PNG is the scramble by parties to grab the support of the new members. This is not limited to the clutch of newly elected independents. Every member is fair game and in the month or so between the declaration of the polls and the first sitting of parliament, no rules apply. The MA soon lost its two new members to other parties. Pangu offered free tickets to Goroka to any members who would accept them. The newly elected member for Koroba Lake Kopiago, Aruru Matiabe, was one who did. 'We were locked up in hotel rooms, refused the free use of telephones and told that we had to swear our allegiance to supporting the formation of a Pangu government under Somare,' Mr Matiabe claimed. He said he was chased through the streets of Goroka when he escaped from the hotel. Mr Matiabe threw his support behind the former Defence Force commander, Ted Diro, who had gone to the elections leading a group known as the Ted Diro Independents, eight of whom, all Papuans, were elected.

Within a week, Diro was leading not only his Diro Independents but also Okuk's suddenly leaderless National Party. Okuk and Diro made this decision with few members of either group being consulted. Pangu countered Matiabe's claim that he had been locked up in Goroka with accusations that Diro's men 'hijacked the Pangu member for Sohe, Mackenzie Jovopa, and drove him twenty-five kilometres out of Port Moresby and threatened him with explosure [sic] in his electorate' unless he left Pangu's ranks.

The membership of the disunited United Party fell to nine. Its post-election leader was Roy Evara. Somare, needing a cushion to get his numbers comfortably above sixty, disregarded his earlier troubles with Evara and invited him into coalition along with a number of pro-Somare Independents. What was left of Chan's old coalition was in disarray and Sir Julius stepped down from the prime ministership. A few days before the new parliament met, a new, short-lived party — the National Alliance — made up of the MA, the NP and Mr Diro's Independents was formed, with Father Momis put forward as leader to contest the vote for prime minister against Somare. Somare won comfortably, 66 to 40. The National Alliance disintegrated. Diro became Opposition leader.

The new-found unity in the United Party lasted eight days. Somare had given the UP three ministries for its nine MPs. Two of the nine promptly deserted the UP to join Pangu. And at a caucus meeting the four remaining UP backbenchers outvoted the three UP ministers to elect a new leader, Paul Torato, dumping Evara. Mr Torato announced that he would leave it to Prime Minister Somare to ponder the 'protocol implications' of having the leader of the coalition's junior partner on the backbench. Torato remained on the backbench. He won a ministry only when he led his part of the UP into Paias Wingti's government more than three years later following a second successful vote of no confidence in Mr Somare.

Pangu's exceptionally strong showing in the 1982 elections led a number of analysts to speculate that the party system was taking root in PNG. The backing of 34 per cent of the disparate PNG electorate for a single party was a remarkable achievement. But Pangu could not withstand the strains of a battle within its ranks over succession. By the 1987 elections, Pangu had split three ways and it secured only 15 per cent of the national vote. Its offshoots, Paias Wingti's Peoples Democratic Movement(PDM), and Tony Siaguru's League for National Advancement (LNA) won 11 per cent and 5 per cent of the national vote respectively — a combined total for the three (31 per cent) that fell short of Pangu's 1982 effort.

Early in the 1982-87 parliament, Somare was considering retiring from politics at the end of the term. He even spoke on ABC radio in February 1983 about his plans for his remaining four and a half years in office. But two months later he changed his mind and in late April issued a statement saying he would lead Pangu into the 1987 elections. The turnaround came because serious divisions were appearing in the Pangu caucus just ten months into the new government's term. The divisions were over who would take Somare's place. One of Pangu's worries was that Somare was the only Pangu politician whose appeal cut across regional boundaries.

Paias Wingti had become deputy leader but that was more in recognition of Pangu's strong performance in the Highlands than any consensus that he should be Somare's successor. The Public Service Minister, Tony Siaguru, a Sepik like Somare, was extremely well qualified. He had headed PNG's Foreign Affairs Department for five years and had studied at Harvard. But Mr Siaguru was in his first term and lacked wide support. Others in contention were the Foreign Minister, Rabbie Namaliu, from East New Britain; the Finance Minister and former Police Commissioner, Phillip Bouraga, a Papuan; and the provincial Affairs Minister, John Nilkare, another

Highlander. All were bright men in their thirties, with solid education or experience, but not one could command the support of half the party. Mr Wingti was the most active, busily organising Pangu backbenchers, many of them Highlanders, into a block of 'Wingti men'.

Iambakey Okuk returned to parliament in July 1983, winning a by-election after convincing one of his National Party members to resign. During the campaign, Okuk, irrepressibly aggressive, claimed Sir Julius Chan had 'stabbed him in the back' during the 1982 elections. Sir Julius retorted that working with Okuk was like 'living with a time bomb'. It was not long before Okuk replaced Diro as opposition leader and parliament lurched towards more motions of no confidence. In November 1983 Okuk suffered a humiliating 70-to-0 defeat after the government converted a threatened motion of no confidence into a thumping vote of confidence. Okuk, who stormed out of the chamber before the vote, claimed that he had been doublecrossed by the United Party, whose leader, Paul Torato, he claimed, had approached him, saying the UP was deserting Somare. Amongst those who voted with Somare was ex-Opposition leader Diro.

Towards the end of 1984 the strains in the Pangu caucus had become such that Paias Wingti was accusing Tony Siaguru of being a 'dangerous element' in the government and Siaguru was accusing Wingti, without naming him directly, of being 'one of those members of government plotting against and back-stabbing the Prime Minister.' The final parliamentary sitting for 1984 was dominated by talk of a motion of no confidence. Paias Wingti first submitted and then withdrew his resignation as deputy prime minister. At Christmas, Somare conducted a Ministerial reshuffle, disciplining Wingti by moving him from the National Planning portfolio to Education. Three months later Wingti resigned as deputy prime minister only minutes before the first sitting for 1985 began. Sir Julius Chan tabled a motion of no confidence in Somare, nominating Wingti as the alternative prime minister. Motions of no confidence sit before the parliament for a week before a vote is taken. Wingti claimed Pangu had lost touch with its roots.

Wingti took fifteen members across the floor. To survive, Somare pulled together another unlikely coalition. He turned first to the Nationals. Okuk was temporarily out of parliament, having been stripped of his by-election win on a technicality. He was back in the Highlands, busily campaigning to win the seat a second time. Somare sent the government aircraft to collect Okuk and fly him down to Port Moresby to persuade the NP to join the Government. As the crucial day for the no-confidence vote approached, Somare was still in danger even with the Nationals locked on side.

The night before the vote, the Opposition leader, John Momis, stunned observers by agreeing to join Somare. Father Momis, who had taken the Opposition leadership from the disqualified Mr Okuk, had been relentlessly attacking Somare's leadership and demanding a Royal Commission into government corruption. Somare had responded publicly, telling Momis that politics were no place for Catholic priests. But political necessity conquered logic. Somare, with the Nationals and the MA behind him, defeated Wingti, 68 to 19. Wingti had stalked from the House with eighteen other members before the vote was taken when the government gagged, 62 to 40, Sir Julius Chan's no-confidence-motion speech. It was the seventh parliamentary session in less than six years that had been dominated by manoeuvring around motions of no confidence. More were on the way.

Father Momis became deputy prime minister. Prior to the March sitting, he had been advocating a vote of no confidence in Somare but he explained away his switch to the Government side by saying there was more than one way to achieve change. 'A lot of people are misled to think that if you have more than half a dozen complaints then the only way to correct the Government is to move a vote of no confidence and change it,' Father Momis told reporters. He said the Melanesian Alliance was also concerned about stability: 'I think no one in his right mind would take a step to further destabilise our country.' Stephen Tago, temporary leader of Okuk's Nationals, put no gloss on his members' motives. 'We decided which way the political wind was going to blow,' he said.

The handsome size of Somare's victory was ephemeral. Somare had the impossible task of carving up the Ministry in a way that would satisfy both his loyal supporters and his new-found partners. The NP demanded five ministries and the MA two. Somare had only two portfolios spare because Wingti took no Ministers with him, just a huge swag of the dissatisfied Pangu backbench. Somare tried sacking three loyal Pangu Ministers, offering the Melanesian Alliance two portfolios and the Nationals three. But with further splits in Pangu threatening, Somare pulled back. Instead of sacking anyone, he accepted the resignations of Tony Siaguru and Barry Holloway, two of Pangu's most competent men. They went to the backbench. Somare split up the spare Ministries two each. While that ensured that the Melanesian Alliance was happy, the National Party was not. Wingti became Opposition Leader and formed his Peoples Democratic Movement (PDM).

Five months later, when the parliament met in August 1985, there was another motion of no confidence tabled by Sir Julius Chan, again naming Wingti as alternative prime minister. Chan claimed the country was being hopelessly mismanaged and Somare had lost control of his ministers. Somare adjourned the session one week early to avoid a vote. By this time, Iambakey Okuk was back in parliament having re-won the seat of Unggai Bena. Immediately upon his return, he had demanded that Somare repay him with a ministry for his work in March. When Somare would not, Okuk deserted the Government, leading most of his NP members back into the Opposition. The two Nationals who had been made Ministers declined to follow.

In November, Somare fell to Paias Wingti in the third motion of no confidence for 1985. Wingti won, 57 to 51. 'There will be a different style of leadership,' he promised. 'There will be discipline. We will control expenditure.' Amongst those to vote against Somare were the two National Party Ministers whom he had sacked at the last minute, and John Kaputin of the Melanesian Alliance who had never been pleased with Father Momis's earlier decision to join Somare. The new six-party coalition consisted of Wingti's PDM; Chan's PPP; Okuk's Nationals; the UP under Torato; Ted Diro's group, which adopted the name the People's Action Party (PAP); and the Papua Party (PP) led by Galeva Kwarara. Once again, despite the intensity of the power plays, PNG's mid-term change of government was peaceful.

Paias Wingti did not have to worry about motions of no confidence for the remainder of the 1982-87 parliament because the timing of the change of government meant there was just over eighteen months to go to the elections. He had six months before he could be challenged and any defeat in the last twelve months would have brought the elections on early. Few members wanted that. But Wingti had other concerns. He had almost as much trouble controlling Okuk as Chan did in 1980-82. By mid 1986, Okuk, now Sir Iambakey, Agriculture Minister, was threatening to sponsor a vote of no confidence against Sir Julius as the Finance and Planning minister. They were in bitter dispute over which of them should control the Agriculture Bank. However, Sir Iambakey was terminally ill and died of cancer in late 1986. Okuk's death changed the nature of the 1987 campaign. Wingti was left as the most easily identifiable Highlander. But gone as well was the image of chaotic turmoil that Okuk's explosively disruptive style created.

The 1987 campaign was different for Michael Somare too. In June 1986 Tony Siaguru and four other Pangu members announced they were leaving the party and forming the League for National Advancement (LNA). They claimed PNG had outgrown Somare's 'leadership style', which they criticised as 'based on charisma, patronage and compromise.' The loss of Siaguru together with one of the founding members of Pangu, Sir Barry Holloway, was evident in Pangu's approach to the 1987 election, which lacked the polish and drive of the extremely effective 1982 campaign. But Siaguru and Holloway suffered from the split as well. Despite a slick campaign, the LNA performed poorly. Siaguru, Holloway and John Nilkare, who had won Okuk's seat for Pangu in 1982, all lost their seats.

The innovation by the Electoral Commissioner in 1987 to have the faces of party leaders on the ballot papers next to the faces of their endorsed candidates was aimed at strengthening the party system. But, as the votes were counted and the post-election scramble for numbers began, this quick identification tag served only to emphasise the party system's fragility. No fewer than twenty-two members were elected with a blank spot next to their photograph — so twenty-two out of the 109 were immediately classified on the electoral commission computer printouts as Independents. In previous elections, parties had endorsed two or three candidates in the one seat but this new 'leader photo rule' meant that these supplementary candidates did not show up on the official lists of party-endorsed winners. As well, the switching between parties that occurred became all the more obvious. Many new members whose faces had appeared on every ballot paper in their electorates adjacent to one party leader showed no embarrassment embracing a different one, or several different ones, in the weeks that followed.

Immediately after the declaration of the poll, Somare seemed best placed to win back government. Although Pangu fared poorly, dropping a net nine seats to twenty-six, its worst result for fifteen years, it remained the largest party. Somare struck quick deals with a number of other leaders to stitch together a coalition. He signed up the new National Party leader, a lawyer turned rich Highlands coffee businessman, Michael Mel, who announced the NP would pull out of the Wingti coalition. Mel, a new member, had been the NP's national president during the turbulent Okuk years. The Nationals had gained two seats to hold a dozen. Father Momis's MA, which had entered a pact with Pangu prior to the elections, also gained, finishing with seven seats. A new force, the former Premier of the Morobe province, Utula Samana, committed his four, first-time members to Somare. And the LNA, reduced to three, threw in its lot with Pangu. With several independents declaring themselves supporters, Somare seemed unassailable.

They all flew to Rabaul for a post-election lock-up. At Rabaul, sixty-two parliamentarians swore their allegiance to Somare, and the party leaders set about apportioning ministries. Parliament was three weeks away and some of the sixty-two began to doubt that they would make the select twenty-eight-member ministerial team. The slide began. With eight days to go to parliament's first meeting, the number was down to fifty-four, the absolute minimum needed to win. Only 106 members would vote because deaths of candidates had forced a delay in polling in three seats. A day before parliament met, a crucial defection ruined Somare's chances. Dennis Young, the veteran Pangu member for Milne Bay, switched. 'We spent our time in Rabaul talking about who would be the deputy prime minister and where the ministries would go,' Mr Young said. 'This is one of the things I admire about Prime Minister Wingti's camp. There's been no talk of ministries at all. The understanding is that the first priority is to elect the prime minister and once that's done the leaders will sit down and discuss ministries. Somare should have kept his options open.' Mr Young became Wingti's Public Service minister and, later, Speaker.

Stories of deals and counter-deals abounded. The new member for Usino Bundi, Theodore Tuya, a former journalist with the ABC, revealed that he was offered K10,000 in cash to switch from supporting Wingti to supporting the Opposition. He declined. Scuffles occurred in Parliament House on the day of the vote, as waverers were manhandled by members delegated to make sure they remained true. Wingti defeated Somare, 54 to 51. The new Wingti coalition was made up of his PDM, Chan's PPP, Diro's PAP, Galeva

Kwarara's PP and various independents. Mr Diro emerged leading the most powerful Papuan group the parliament had seen. Called the Papuan Block it consisted of his PAP, Mr Kwarara's three-member Papua Party and a string of independents, including two naturalised citizen MPs; smallgoods manufacturer, Hugo Berghuser; and the Pink Pussycat nightclub proprietor, Robert Suckling, who won two of the Port Moresby seats.

The Papuan Block demanded the deputy prime ministership for Diro. But the day after the vote for prime minister, Diro was implicated before a Judicial Inquiry into the PNG forestry industry and Sir Julius Chan retained the deputy prime minister's post. This infuriated the eighteen-strong Papuan Block. They kept up the pressure on Diro's behalf well into 1988, and this helped precipitate the first vote of no confidence crisis for Prime Minister Wingti. But before 1987 was out, Wingti had built up his parliamentary majority from three to more than twenty. One of his major gains was to attract Utula Samana and his three followers across on the very last sitting day of the October parliamentary session.

The six months' grace period, during which Mr Wingti as a newly elected Prime Minister could not be challenged, ended in February 1988. The first session of the parliament for the year was scheduled for April. The weeks leading up to the sitting were dominated by speculation about a vote of no confidence. Although Mr Wingti appeared to have sufficient numbers to survive, the Papuan Block became more and more aggressive over its demands that Diro be reinstated to the ministry and made number two in the Government. The growing power and influence of Utula Samana had at the same time led to the formation of distinct left and right factions within the Government's ranks — factions that tended to blur across party lines. Samana led the left, and within the right the naturalised businessmen politicians saw Diro as their best hope of providing a counterbalance.

On the weekend before the session began, Wingti's PDM caucus became so worried about the possibility of the Papuan Block defecting en masse and catapulting the PDM into Opposition that it outvoted Wingti on the Diro issue. Mr Wingti had said he would not reinstate Diro until after the forestry inquiry matters had been cleared up. But the Prime Minister accepted his caucus decision and agreed to Diro's reinstatement. The April session began with the Deputy Opposition Leader, Father Momis, giving notice of a motion of no confidence in Wingti and nominating Somare as the alternative prime minister. To avoid a vote, Wingti aborted the session after less than three hours, adjourning the parliament until late June.

Eight weeks of political confusion and turmoil followed, including two doomed attempts to form a grand coalition of national unity. In the wake of the collapse of the first of these, and with what remained of his Pangu Pati threatening to disintegrate, Somare stepped down from the party leadership in late May. Pangu was just three weeks short of its twenty-first birthday. Rabbie Namaliu took over as the new Pangu leader. The second grand coalition attempt failed when none of Wingti's ministers would resign voluntarily to make way for others in the proposed National Unity Cabinet. With the June/July session of parliament approaching, Wingti attracted half of the National Party across from the Opposition and he dumped Ted Diro, while keeping all the other Papuan ministers.

The Grand Coalition Dance

Many of the diplomats, departmental heads and journalists summoned to the PNG parliament are deep in eyebrow-raised conversation as they wait for the Prime Minister and Opposition Leader. The magnificent National Parliament building incorporates three traditional architectural styles and the invitation to be in attendance specified the majestic Reception Room in the Highlands Roundhouse amenities block. Surely there can be no second attempt at a grand coalition of national unity so soon after the first was stillborn? That first grand coalition was announced to almost the same audience in this very room just last month when Prime Minister Wingti and the father of PNG's Independence, Michael Somare, shook hands behind the superbly carved, tropical hardwood conference table. There was surprise then. Now it is wonder. The first attempt collapsed because of the impossible conditions set by both sides. Each tried to dictate who in the opposite block should be excluded from the grand coalition Cabinet. Somare resigned as Pangu Pati leader five days ago and Rabbie Namaliu now leads Pangu.

In they come, Wingti and Namaliu, beaming. They go behind

the table and sign an 'irrevocable' commitment that their two parties, PDM and Pangu, the largest in parliament, will join forces in government until the 1992 elections. Wingti, enthusiastic, says into the microphone that this will end the 'political power games that have relegated good government to second place'. He says they will invite other parties to join them 'so that the problems we have been facing over the past fifteen years can be overcome. Constitutional changes can be made with the numbers we have.'

Mr Namaliu takes the microphone: 'The Pangu Pati believes no Prime Minister must be pushed into a corner where he is not able to perform to the best of his ability.' The agreement, he says, will end the instability that followed the 1987 elections. 'We have made ourselves available to assist in restoring credibility and confidence in the system of government that we opted for at Independence.' Prime Minister Wingti says a new Cabinet will be named tomorrow.

Six days later, no new Cabinet has been named. The country's administration has been in paralysis for a week. Mr Wingti claims that he needs time to convince his governing coalition partners to remain with the Government. To make way for Pangu, he will have to sack seven ministers. How can he do it and still retain loyalty? Pangu's impatience grows. The only specific ministry announced is Michael Somare as Foreign Minister. But Somare's wife, Veronica, convinces him that he needs a break. When Wingti is informed that Somare will not be taking a Ministry, he seizes upon the news, and claims Somare's presence in Cabinet is an essential, if unwritten, understanding behind the grand coalition concept.

Instead of proceeding with the 'irrevocable commitment', Mr Wingti announces a new coalition government leaving Pangu out and drawing in instead another opposition party, the National Party.

Diro had quick revenge. When parliament met on 27 June 1988 it was only the second day's sitting for the year. The motion of no confidence that had been moved on the first day back in April, nominating Somare as alternative prime minister, was withdrawn and replaced with another, nominating Namaliu. Somare officially stood down as Opposition leader. Wingti tabled an interim report by the judge investigating corruption in the PNG forestry industry, heavily implicating Diro. Four ministers from the Papuan Block, including the Finance Minister, Galeva Kwarara, resigned, and although Wingti claimed he was well rid of 'the destabilising influence of Mr Diro's supporters' he fell in the vote on 4 July 1988 to Rabbie Namaliu, 58 to 50. Namaliu had been a short-term Opposition leader — seven days after officially taking over the job from Somare he was prime minister. Wingti's bid to shore up his numbers by recruiting the National Party failed. The Highlands-based Nationals split in two.

One National Party member soon let everybody know that he regretted his vote when he was overlooked in the new ministerial allocations. Mr Namaliu worked for four days to sort out what he hoped would be a carefully balanced ministry. But just as he was telling the media he could not please everybody, the Highlands member for Baiyer Mul, Joel Paua, showed how true that was. Mr Paua, from the Western Highlands like Wingti, interrupted the news conference to loudly object to the ministerial allocations. Mr Paua shouted that Highlanders had lost a prime minister and he claimed that since it was the Highlands-based National Party that had helped make Mr Namaliu prime minister earlier that week, the Nationals would break him too.

Prime Minister Namaliu's six months' grace from challenge ended on 4 January 1989. Several defections from the backbench fuelled speculation that a no-confidence motion would be introduced when parliament began its first session for the 1989 year on 21 February. It did not happen that day. But on the seventh day of the session Utula Samana gave the necessary notice that the Opposition would be supporting Paias Wingti in a challenge to Mr Namaliu. The vote was due on 9 March, seven days later. But a sudden adjournment won Namaliu a four-month reprieve.

A few nights before the next session began in July, PNG's Communications Minister, Malipu Balakau, was shot dead outside his home in Mount Hagen. People from Balakau's home province of Enga rioted. The Opposition withdrew its no-confidence motion out of respect for the slain minister, whose body was brought into the Chamber so that members could pay their respects. The rest of that session was subdued but the lobbying for numbers intensified again as the year went on. In November 1989 Utula Samana moved another no-confidence motion, again nominating Paias Wingti as the alternative prime minister. After an exhausting week in which the Opposition was convinced that it had the numbers till the night before the vote, Utula Samana withdrew the motion just as vote was due. Mr Samana was angry with members who 'broke their word'.

Smooth, steady government is practically impossible under the present system where no prime minister can ever be certain of the loyalty of any government backbencher or even, as has been shown repeatedly, any member of his Cabinet. Although it has been argued by some in PNG that the no-confidence-vote mechanism is an important release valve allowing regular changes of government and thereby preventing a dangerous build-up of frustration, many others believe that the system must be changed for the long-term good of the country. Attempts at reform have been made. But the difficulty is that while constitutional change in PNG requires the overwhelming support of the parliament, most of the changes seen as vital are aimed at limiting the freedom and power of the very people who would have to vote those changes through — the backbenchers.

This has stymied earlier efforts to overhaul the system. Back in 1982 the Pangu Pati election campaign platform included a series of constitutional and electoral law amendments aimed at stabilising parliamentary politics. Tony Siaguru, Pangu's chief strategist in that campaign, presented an eloquent case for reform in a forty-five minute radio documentary which the ABC ran on the eve of the 1982 poll. The first constitutional change proposed was to strengthen the Prime Minister's position by giving him the option of calling elections if he lost the confidence of parliament. A second amendment would have forced any member who switched parties to face an immediate by-election so that his constituents could endorse or reject the move. And the third proposal was to change the electoral Act to discard the first-past-the-post polling system and revert to the optional preferential system that the Australians introduced to PNG in the 1960s.

'The peculiar situation existing in PNG is that when people go to vote, especially in the rural areas where the majority live,' Siaguru said, 'they consider themselves bound by social and family obligations to cast their first vote for their relative or a person from their own clan, house line or language group. It might not be that that person is the best candidate in the judgment of the voter! But he or she is obliged because of social traditions to vote for him. I know of elections in the past, when the optional preferential system was in use, where candidates went around the electorate saying

"Don't vote for me as your first choice. I know you will have to give your first vote to your line candidate. But give me second." And they did get in on second preferences or third preferences. They did it with far greater representative support than, say, the member who has got in with less than ten per cent of the vote. That is ridiculous!'

In advocating compulsory by-elections for parliamentarians who deserted the party that backed them in a national election, Siaguru argued that parliamentary stability would come only from a strengthened party system. 'This country's problem has been the chopping and changing by members of parliament. They change for the sake of what I would call the paraphernalia associated with political elective office — a house, a nice car — that's a great temptation. When such offers are made — not necessarily directly — members are very much tempted to move from one party to another. If you had the situation where a person thinking about changing allegiance was faced with the possibility of a by-election, that would naturally discourage him and he would stay on. I am convinced this would lead to more stability.'

Within three months of Somare's solid win in the 1982 elections, Cabinet approved the drafting of all three changes. They were put on the parliamentary notice paper but they withered for lack of caucus support. Constitutional and Electoral Act amendments such as these require a two-thirds majority of parliament at two separate sittings not less than two months apart. That means the support of seventy-three members, not once but twice, with a gap between the votes. There was an outside chance that Somare could have pushed these amendments through in the first twelve months of the 1982–87 parliament. No PNG government has ever been in a stronger position that Somare's was then. But he would still have had to rely on some Opposition support. He had won the prime ministerial vote, 66 to 40 — a good majority for normal legislation but seven short of the seventy-three needed for this Constitutional change. Somare never pushed the issue.

There was little enthusiasm from his own backbench and none whatsoever amongst the members of his fractious coalition partner, the United Party. After the first twelve months it was all a lost cause as government numbers drifted and Pangu's own internal problems intensified. Siaguru's frustration with the inability of the system to deliver what he had seen as essential change was underscored with his defection from Pangu in 1986 to create an entirely new political party, the LNA. By then, the Wingti Government was in power and Siaguru's proposed constitutional change, the one that would have forced him to face a by-election for leaving Pangu, was then brought on for debate and speakers made ironic references to Siaguru's position. Wingti's PDM members were in a similar situation. Debate was adjourned and the proposed changes were destined to be wiped off the notice paper as unfinished business at the close of the parliament's five-year term.

Tony Siaguru lost his seat of Moresby North East in the 1987 elections to what he sees as another failure in the operations of the Electoral Act, sectional votes. Voters whose names are not on the roll can claim the right to vote by swearing that they did attempt to enrol, that they have lived in the electorate for six months and that they are eligible to vote. Thousands turned up to polling booths around Port Moresby demanding sectional ballots. Siaguru claims that his scrutineers found he outscored the man who eventually defeated him by more than two to one amongst registered voters in his electorate. But 7753 votes — fifty-five per cent of the total counted — were sectional votes, cast by people whose names did not appear on the roll. There were widespread allegations in all four Port Moresby seats that voters had been trucked into the city to vote.

Proposals to limit the ability of members to switch political parties were also recommended by the general constitutional commission established in the early 1980s to review the entire Constitution. Its final report tabled in 1983 recommended that any member who deserted one party and joined another in the first twelve months of being elected should lose his seat. The commission did not want to abolish the practice altogether, so there was a supplementary recommendation that would have allowed members three switches in the last four years of each parliamentary term!

The personal staff of all four prime ministers since Independence have wistfully commented during the regular parliamentary challenges to each of their bosses that one solution would be to make half the members of parliament ministers. This is not possible under the Constitution, which limits the total ministry to 28, 27 short of an absolute majority of 55. Casting about for alternatives, the Leader of Government Business under Mr Wingti, Gabriel Ramoi, proposed that 27 government backbenchers be made chairmen of the boards of 27 statutory authorities. In a confidential memo to the Prime Minister in February 1988, Ramoi listed the 27 statutory authorities and the members who should head their Boards. These jobs for the backbench boys included the chairmanships of the Central Bank, the PNG Banking Corporation, the National Airline Commission (Air Niugini), the Posts and Telecommunications Corporation, the Harbours Board and the Housing Commission. The professed aim was to make the authorities 'more answerable to the people'.

Somare, Chan, Wingti and Namaliu all advocated change to the present system when in power. One proposal discussed at length in the late 1980s was a constitutional amendment to extend from six months to two and a half years the period in which motions of no confidence are banned following the election of a new prime minister. Mr Namaliu suggested that this change, if approved, take effect after the 1992 elections, the reasoning being that members in the 1987-92 parliament may feel less threatened by prospective legislation.

As the 1990s began, the parliament had before it a comprehensive report on ways in which the electoral system could be overhauled to lessen the strains that make PNG parliamentary politics so volatile. Prepared by two academics with a long association with PNG, Tony Regan and Ted Woolfers, and fully backed by the electoral commissioner, Luke Lucas, the report canvassed a wide range of amendments to the Constitution and the electoral law. The report grew out of a suggestion by the Acting Director of the Institute of Applied Social and Economic Research, Michael Walter, that the institute sponsor a review of the 1987 elections. In his introduction to the report, Dr Walter said that the political system in 'PNG no longer functioned as it was intended to by the Constitution'.

Referring to a rampant lack of discipline in the political arena, Dr Walter proposed, as a starting point for reform, a constitutional change to give the Prime Minister power to dissolve parliament at any time and call elections. Dr Walter argued that the existing system was like a game in which the rules had become so warped that all the players had lost sight of the desired end result. He said the system encouraged politicians to respond to the opportunities and demands of the game at the expense of the needs of the nation. This was courting social and political upheaval. He warned the politicians that if they did not recognise the 'mismatch of needs and deeds' and the necessity to change the Constitution, then eventually more dramatic change might be forced upon them by others. He suggested that this could be the armed forces via a coup. But it may take more than dark talk about a possible coup to shock Papua New Guinea's parliamentarians into altering a system from which so many of them benefit.

CHAPTER FOUR

HANDLING THE ECONOMY

On the morning of 19 April 1975, the day Papua New Guinea's currency was launched, the wife of the country's first Finance Minister, Julius Chan, gave birth to a baby son in Rabaul. News of the birth reached Sir Julius in Port Moresby during the currency launching ceremony. Word spread amongst the official guests outside the central bank in Douglas Street and Sir Julius responded to urgings to honour the occasion with a PNG custom reserved for events of great significance. He named his new son 'Toea' after the smallest unit in the new currency. Lady Stella Chan learnt the name of her newborn child when Michael Somare announced it to the crowd at the currency launch in an address broadcast nationally. The names 'Kina' and 'toea' come from traditional currency units. A *Kina* is a valuable pearl shell traded in the Highlands and Sepik while a *toea* is an arm shell prized in Papua for bride price payments. Toea Chan, now in his teens, plays soccer for his father's Alma Mater, Marist Brothers, Ashgrove. The PNG currency had to mature early.

Back in 1975, when the Kina was introduced five months before Independence, some people were not convinced that the new currency had healthy prospects. A number of Australians working in PNG demanded that their contracts be written in Australian dollars. They were fearful that PNG's economic management would falter and the Kina would rapidly depreciate. They were wrong and soon lost money. Within six months of the new currency being released from dependency on the Australian dollar on 1 January 1976, PNG revalued by five per cent. The trend continued. At the close of the 1980s K1 was worth $1.50. In early 1990 PNG devalued because of the Bougainville copper mine closure but even after that the Kina was worth $1.36 — still an exchange rate to horrify tourists. PNG's Finance Department very early adopted what was called the 'hard Kina' strategy.

Outlining the 'hard Kina' strategy the day the Kina was launched and Toea born, Finance Minister Chan said it meant taking deliberate action on two fronts to ensure that the external value of the currency did not weaken. These were: 'The accumulation and maintenance of adequate international reserves to assure the credibility of the policy and appropriate internal policies of economic management. The "Hard" strategy means facing up to the difficult choices before, rather than after, we get ourselves into big trouble.' It was a tough time for PNG to move to monetary independence. The worldwide commodity boom of 1973-74, during which inflation in PNG hit thirty per cent, was followed by a bust. 'The boom and the pattern of colonial administration before 1973 had left PNG with a legacy of real government expenditure far in excess of what could be sustained,' Dr Ross Garnaut, a government economic strategist wrote later. 'It had also left a legacy of real urban wages far in excess of levels that were consistent with low levels of urban unemployment. A weak trading of the balance of payments, capital outflow generated by political uncertainty associated with independence, and anxiety about the new currency itself caused a sharp rundown in bank deposits and potential foreign exchange reserves.'

The 'hard Kina' strategy worked. An independent review of the economy in 1985 commissioned by both PNG and Australia described as 'remarkable' the achievements in the first ten years of Independence. While recommending a change of emphasis in economic policy to ensure that the gains were not wasted, the review by Goodman, Lepani and Morawetz commended PNG, saying that political and economic stability had been achieved and maintained against the odds; the direction of the economy had been placed firmly in indigenous hands; the institutions of economic policy-making — non-existent under the Australian colonial administration until 1972 — had been created and had operated efficiently; a new currency had been introduced and its value maintained; inflation had been kept low at a time of worldwide inflation; effective commodity and mineral stabilisation schemes had been established; the benefits of development had been spread quite widely, if unevenly, amongst villagers and townspeople; and policy makers had shown flexibility in responding to changing international and internal circumstances.

The good record over that first ten years was a result of careful, tough-minded management against some determined opposition. Finance ministers had to fight to overcome more powerful ministers wanting to spend big. At one point in the early 1980s, the Finance Minister, John Kaputin, called a news conference to ridicule proposals by the Deputy Prime Minister, Iambakey Okuk, for a mini-budget to borrow as much as possible before the 1982 elections. Mr Okuk had found on his overseas trips that PNG had an excellent credit rating and he demanded that this be used to full advantage. He compiled a list of expensive capital works projects he wanted under way by election time and he abused the Finance Department for being overly cautious. When doubts were raised about the economic wisdom of borrowing to the hilt, Okuk accused the country's most senior economic advisers of 'disloyalty and subversion'. They were, he claimed, 'scandal mongering'. Finance Minister Kaputin denounced the Deputy Prime Minister and blocked Okuk's expedient generosity, perhaps averting economic disaster.

The 'hard Kina' strategy was softened in the early 1980s because, while it had achieved its prime objectives, its unintended effect had been to hinder export growth and discourage industries competing with imports. The high Kina reduced returns to exporters and made imports cheaper. In early 1983 the Australian dollar depreciated substantially and the Bank of Papua New Guinea, which sets the exchange rate each morning, decided to let the Kina drop with it. The central bank then adopted a policy of fixing the value of the Kina against a basket of currencies according to a formula reflecting the relative importance of those currencies in PNG's mix of imports. Over the next five years the Kina gradually declined against most major currencies. This happened mainly because the Australian dollar was falling and Australia dominates PNG's import trade. In the late 1980s, the basket of currencies mix was changed to reflect both imports and exports and the Kina appreciated once more against the Australian dollar. In early 1990, to combat the slump in export revenue caused by the shutdown of the Bougainville copper mine, the bank devalued the Kina by ten per cent against the basket.

There are two economies in PNG — the market economy and the subsistence or non-market economy. The market economy is narrowly based. Bougainville Copper provided about ten per cent of market Gross Domestic Product (GDP) in 1988. The mine's output that year provided well over one third of total exports. The market economy is also extremely vulnerable to fluctuations in world trade and the troubles at Bougainville coincided with poor world commodity prices. In 1988 exports made up forty-three per cent of GDP while imports of goods and services were equivalent to forty-eight per cent of GDP.

Village Shareholders

A thermostatically controlled, high-pressure mist blower is keeping sixty thousand hens in considerably more stable climatic comfort on the outskirts of Port Moresby than many of their 2500 owners in the villages of the Goroka, Unggai and Asaro census divisions in the Eastern Highlands. But the hardy Highlanders, whose village huts don't have running water or electricity, know a profitable venture when it is outlined to them and they do not begrudge the hens a thing. For their jointly owned business, the Gouna Development Corporation, has seized opportunities galore since being set up in April 1975, five months before Independence. It is now one of PNG's most successful, diversified companies.

The people contributed K120,000 in share purchases during the first two years of Gouna's existence. Now they own the Erinvale and Lahamenegu coffee plantations in the Eastern Highlands, a plantation management agency servicing smallholder clients who have more than 130 hectares under coffee, a new K350,000 coffee processing factory on Lahamenegu plantation, a renovated coffee factory in the Chimbu province and another in the Western Highlands, three service stations, the BP depot and agency for the Goroka area, a fuel tanker, Gouna Motors — the Mitsubishi agent in the Eastern Highlands, a commercial printing business, an egg-carton manufacturing plant, commercial and industrial land and two poultry farms, including the new thermostatically controlled one outside Port Moresby, which is the country's largest and most modern.

Japan and West Germany have been PNG's two largest markets. In 1988 Japan bought 40 per cent of Papua New Guinea's exports — K496 million ($744m) — mostly in the form of copper and gold concentrate. West Germany took 21 per cent — K266 million

HANDLING THE ECONOMY

($399m) — in mineral concentrate and agricultural products. Australia was fourth on PNG's export market table behind South Korea. Although Papua New Guinea has duty-free access to Australia for most goods, PNG sold Australia just K67 million ($101m) worth of produce in 1988, 7 per cent of its total exports. The trade balance between the two was more than seven to one in Australia's favour. PNG imported K513 million ($770m) worth of goods from Australia, half its total imports bill, mostly food and manufactured goods. Foreign reserves at the close of 1989 stood at K388 million ($582m), 3.6 months' import cover. The 1990 devaluation was aimed at cutting imports and boosting exports to ease the effects of the sharp drop in mineral revenue.

Gold was Papua New Guinea's most valuable single export throughout the 1980s, although in 1988 a recovery in the world price of copper and increased production at the Ok Tedi copper mine edged copper back into first place. Copper, gold and silver made up 69 per cent of PNG's total exports in 1988, with copper earning K447 million ($670m) and gold K405m ($607m). Agricultural commodities accounted for 20 per cent of exports. The largest agricultural crop is coffee. Coffee exports in 1988 were worth K114 million ($171m) — more than twice as much as cocoa, at K46 million ($69m). Next came copra and copra oil — K37 million ($56m); palm oil — K30 million ($45m); tea — K6 million ($9m); and rubber — K4 million ($6m). The only other significant export was tropical forest logs, which earnt K91 million ($136m), about 8 per cent of total exports. Papua New Guinea has vast fisheries resources but there is only a small local industry which, in 1988, exported barramundi, lobsters and prawns worth K8 million ($12m), not even one per cent of total exports.

Papua New Guinea's external debt is close to 100 per cent of GDP but the majority is private debt. Government borrowing, which began to balloon in the early 1980s was brought back under control towards the end of the decade. In 1989 outstanding public debt stood at K1.15 billion ($1.7b), 36 per cent of GDP down from 42 per cent just a few years before. In the 1990 Budget, the Government committed itself to no more overseas commercial borrowing and a reduction in total new borrowing to K144 million ($216m), most of it coming from concessional sources such as the World Bank and the Asian Development Bank. Debt service payments in 1990 were budgeted at K254 million ($381m), 16 per cent of expected exports. A survey of the PNG economy by the Australian International Development Assistance Bureau (AIDAB) in February 1989 said that PNG's ratio of public debt service to exports compared favourably with those of Indonesia and the Philippines, which had 1987 ratios of 28 and 23 per cent respectively.

Despite the generally sound job that successive Finance ministers have done at the macroeconomic level, growth of the PNG economy was sluggish in the 1980s and, as a result of the Bougainville crisis, the economy was expected to contract in 1990. GDP in 1989 was K3.2 billion ($4.8b). With a population of 3.8 million, that translates into an average income per head of K842 ($1263). Per capita, GDP rose in the first five years after Independence. But in the early and mid-1980s economic growth was so low that it barely kept pace with population growth, which was estimated at 2.3 per cent per year. An upswing in performance in 1987 and 1988 ended abruptly in 1989 with the shutdown of the Bougainville copper mine. The importance of the mine to the PNG economy was such that its closure for seven and a half months cut the nation's economic growth to zero. The expected shutdown throughout 1990 was estimated to mean negative growth; GDP was expected to shrink by four per cent in real terms.

In 1988 Bougainville's exports of gold, copper and silver earnt K493 million ($740m). PNG's Finance Department had predicted that in 1989 the mine would contribute nine per cent of total market-sector GDP and thirty-five per cent of total export earnings. That was before the trouble. The Bougainville story and its lessons for all — landowners, mining companies, national and provincial governments — will be covered in detail in the next chapter. The shock to the PNG economy in 1989 and 1990 of the Bougainville shutdown would have been more traumatic had it not been for substantial investment in other mining projects and big spending by oil exploration companies. Real GDP in 1989 would have shrunk but for construction beginning on the big Porgera goldmine early in the year, the Misima goldmine going into production in June and fifteen exploration wells being sunk in the Southern Highlands.

Oil and gold hold significant promise for the future growth of the PNG economy. But while there are tricky problems to be overcome in satisfying landowners in the prospectively rich areas — who are demanding to be involved — a more fundamental economic problem must be faced in Papua New Guinea, namely employment.

HANDLING THE ECONOMY

Even if the hoped-for mining and oil boom occurs, the most optimistic predictions of new jobs to be created by the mining and oil industries is 20,000. The concern facing any government in PNG is how to provide work for a rapidly expanding population. The figures are frightening. 'Approximately 1.85 million Papua New Guineans are potentially employable,' the Namaliu Government's 1990 'Development Policies' document said, 'while only 225,000 are actually employed in formal wage labour.' That means there are paid jobs for just twelve per cent of people of working age. The situation is getting worse. More than fifty thousand per year are joining the 'potentially employable' group, while growth of total formal jobs is around only six thousand per year.

The twelve per cent of the potential workforce in paid employment does not mean an unemployment rate of eighty-eight per cent, although chronic unemployment is a big and growing problem in the cities and towns. More than eighty per cent of Papua New Guineans live in villages and the basis of the PNG economy is village agriculture. The continued active participation of villagers in the non-wage economy is the country's major hope for the future. About 1.5 million Papua New Guinean villagers of working age are involved to varying degrees in three types of agricultural activity: subsistence food production, growing food for sale at markets, and cash cropping. The statisticians put a notional figure on the value of the first of these, non-marketed subsistence production. It is estimated to be worth about fifteen per cent of GDP. In 1990 it was set at K450 million a year. 'Subsistence production', or work that is not paid for in cash, covers more than just food grown in village gardens, pigs killed and wildlife or fish caught for the family to eat. It covers all the non-paid work done in the village, such as the production of food for domesticated animals, the collection of firewood, the building of houses out of traditional materials and the construction of items such as canoes.

During his term as prime minister in 1985–88, Paias Wingti constantly stressed the promotion of agriculture as the economic saviour of PNG. His government's 1988 economic strategy proclaimed that, since the majority of the population lived in rural areas, 'it is here that income earning opportunities are most needed: to solve both the fundamental village problems of malnutrition and the lack of basic goods and services and to prevent migration and the associated problems of lawlessness and urban deprivation.' Mr

Wingti, who studied economics at the University of Papua New Guinea before entering politics, also committed his government to the full-scale pursuit of economic growth. Under a heading 'The Imperative for Economic Growth', the Wingti government's strategic plan claimed that the Government would 'move from being a passive actor in the economy to become a major stimulant of investment and growth'. Mr Wingti swung money away from the law-and-order and social-welfare sectors of government activity towards those promoting and directing economic development. The 1988 strategy paper claimed that the Wingti government would 'not repeat the mistakes of previous governments by compromising its growth objectives to the achievement of subsidiary social goals'.

It was perhaps the first time in PNG that a clear political division emerged on basic economic philosophy. This division had little to do with party politics. Both sides in PNG, the Government and the Opposition, take in so many groups that all shades of philosophy are covered on both sides. The difference came with the individual. Paias Wingti committed himself and his government to economic growth at all cost. Under Mr Wingti's 1988 Budget, spending on law and order (police, army, prisons, courts and justice) fell below ten per cent of government outlays for the first time since Independence. Planned spending on 'social welfare' — health, education, youth and women — dropped to a bare 10.6 per cent of total expenditure. In contrast, allocations to economic portfolios were boosted, with more money going to agriculture in particular. The Wingti strategy said that growth demanded that present consumption be postponed and resources go to investment instead. By diverting its own resources into investment and encouraging the private sector to do likewise, the Wingti Government planned to raise the proportion of GDP allocated to investment from 20 per cent to 30 per cent within five years.

While the strategy may have been commendable economic policy — and it certainly had World Bank endorsement — implementation was another matter. The Government's economic agencies, such as the Department of Agriculture and Livestock, were not ready or able to spend the extra money. Mr Namaliu, who took power in July 1988, accused Mr Wingti of jeopardising any growth by ignoring law and order. Mr Namaliu's government switched the emphasis back to social welfare to meet its obligations under what was described as the Government's 'social contract' with the people.

The Namaliu Government's 1990 Budget strategy said the need was to create favourable conditions for development. It listed the priorities as 'law and order; proper, and relevant education and manpower development; economic growth and job creation; and administrative reform.'

Administrative reform is essential. Mr Namaliu's government, like Mr Wingti's, found its plans lapsing because of failures in implementation. While the emphasis may have been different on where recurrent spending was directed, both governments committed themselves to boosting investment spending. And both governments found the administrative machinery unable to deliver. The Namaliu government's 1989 Budget had proposed capital spending under the Public Investment Program (PIP) of K232 million ($348m), almost one quarter of the Government's total spending on goods and services. The revised 1989 Budget approved late in the year revealed that actual spending on investment projects was only K161 million ($242m) — a shortfall of K71 million ($107m) or 30 per cent below target. Recurrent spending blew out more than K50 million ($75m). In a frank admission of failure, the Government said it 'recognised [that] the lack of capacity to implement many capital works, maintenance and other investment projects has reduced the government's influence on economic activity and development'. In addition, the poor implementation rate reduced and postponed the use of soft concessional loans from overseas donors, with an adverse impact on the balance of payments.

This Job Is A Killer

'This job is a killer and I don't want it!' PNG's Finance Secretary blurted out angrily. The chairman of the parliamentary Public Accounts Committee and his fellow members were taken aback. It was 2 March 1988. The head of the Finance Department was being questioned by the Public Accounts Committee in Conference Room B3 on the third floor of the members' wing at Parliament House. The committee was conducting public hearings into the Auditor-General's report on PNG's 1986 public accounts.

The secretary, John Vulpindi, was on extended leave but he appeared for interrogation by the Public Accounts Committee after the committee chairman was quoted by the PNG media as saying

Mr Vulpindi should be sacked. Mr Vulpindi's appearance before the committee was an extraordinary performance, even by PNG's often extravagant standards. He stunned committee members with an angry and bitter tale of his own personal frustrations over five years as the country's chief finance officer. Responding to critical questions, he said he had 'no confidence PNG's public accounts were either accurate or in order.' Mr Vulpindi told the Public Accounts Committee members that they were wasting their time on 'nuts and bolts when the whole system is defunct'.

The committee was asking why there had been no bank reconciliation done on the Finance Department's Salary Drawing Account since June 1985. The Auditor-General pointed out that about K130 million ($195m) passed through the account in 1986, but that at the time of audit in May 1987 the Finance Department had failed to submit bank reconciliations for almost two years.

Mr Vulpindi told the committee it 'shouldn't concern itself with peanuts' when, he said, the fundamental problem was that the whole government accounting system was inadequate, the control points were 'weak or non-existent' and there were '140 cashier officers around the country operating without supervision'. The Finance Secretary had not been a popular departmental head, often in dispute with other key bureaucrats and at odds with senior officers within his own department. He won little sympathy from the committee when he claimed his lone efforts at reform were constantly sabotaged by expatriates.

Asked to name the alleged expatriate saboteurs, he refused, calling them 'non-entities'. When he repeated that he, as Finance Secretary, had 'no confidence in the government's public accounts' and that the committee was 'just wasting its time', the committee chairman told him to stop behaving like a child. Mr Vulpindi was relieved of his job shortly afterwards.

In the fourteen years from Independence until 1989, Bougainville Copper provided twenty per cent of the Government's total revenue. The mine closed in May 1989, but the Government was partially insulated from what should have been a devastating loss of revenue by some prudent planning stretching back to the 1970s. The insulation came from a 'buffer fund' known as the Mineral Resources Stabilisation Fund (MRSF). The MRSF was set up after the 1974 renegotiation of the Bougainville Agreement with CRA, which established a minerals tax regime giving PNG the bulk of any super profits from large mining ventures. The fund was designed to give PNG insurance against wildly fluctuating mining revenues. The MRSF took in tax and dividends (the PNG government owns nineteen per cent of Bougainville Copper Limited) as they gushed or dribbled in each year depending on the world price of gold or copper. But the fund was able to provide a steady flow of predictable revenue for annual budgets. In drawing up its 1990 Budget, the Government was able to draw down K80 million ($120m) from the MRSF even though Bougainville Copper Limited (BCL) would contribute nothing to the fund in 1990. Even after that withdrawal, the fund balance was still expected to be more than K60 million ($90m).

Nevertheless, many of the Government's Budget predictions for 1990 had to be revised when the decision was taken to put the mine under 'care and maintenance' in early 1990. More than a thousand Bougainvillians were employed by BCL when the troubles began in late 1988. But the Bougainvillians were much better placed to endure any loss of employment than the remainder of the mine workforce, the 500 expatriates or the 2000 other Papua New Guineans. With 'mothballing', only a few employees were kept on. The expatriates and the other Papua New Guineans had to leave the island but the Bougainvillians could always move back to the village and turn to village agriculture and cash cropping to wait for a resolution.

Rural Papua New Guineans enjoy a great advantage over their counterparts in most other developing countries in having efficient subsistence agriculture to fall back on. They are not single-crop-market peasants working land that is no longer theirs. Villagers move into and out of the cash economy as they see fit, often without any dramatic change in their standard of living. They can engage in cash cropping, but if the prices fall below what they think is worthwhile they can opt out. Parents will turn to cash crops to fund their children's school fees and once the immediate demand for cash is over they may well turn their energies to other things. The subsistence economy has proved remarkably resilient because village root crops — especially sweet potato, but also yams and taro — are very efficient in terms of food energy produced per unit of labour input. (One field study in Fiji found that the energy efficiency of root crops is three to four times that of rice.)

Barry Shaw, an Australian rural economist who did a major study into agriculture in PNG in 1985 for the privately funded Institute of National Affairs, points out that a Papua New Guinean rural family can produce sufficient food in twenty hours or less labour per adult per week to cater not only for the family's needs but also for ceremonial food exchanges and feed for pigs, while still probably having a surplus for insurance or sale. He says this compares favourably with the returns from any other work available to unskilled labour. In analysing why certain agricultural projects had failed dismally while others, mostly with little or no government encouragement, had just as dramatically succeeded, Shaw debunked some pessimistic theories about rural PNG. Drawing on the work of other researchers and his own field studies, Shaw pointed out that subsistence food production had kept pace with the expanding population; that people would not abandon their food gardens for any chance to get into the cash economy; that nutritional levels were not declining but appeared to be improving; and that village people were not slow to grasp agricultural opportunities provided the returns were worth their while.

A United Nations Food and Agriculture Organisation study in 1983 concluded that the view of PNG 'being a country suffering from malnutrition, where food systems are under stress and . . . things are getting worse, is by no means universally held. . . . Certainly most pressure for something to be done about food and nutrition has arisen from within government bureaucracy. There appears to be little political pressure coming from rural areas for resources to be devoted to food production. Indeed the demands most voiced by the rural people are for better roads, improved communications and higher incomes from cash crops.' In some parts of the country, however, food shortages are a cause for concern. One area under great stress is the Wosera area of the East Sepik, where the population density is 200 per square kilometre. The reason is that traditionally the Sepik region around Worsea was an area of fluid land ownership. In the 1930s, the Australian administration brought fighting to a halt and those unlucky enough to be short of land at the time lost, while those with more land seem to have gained permanently.

Estimates vary on the value of produce sold through PNG's countless local markets but the industry is believed to be bigger than coffee, PNG's major agricultural industry. In coffee's best year, 1986, it earnt more than K200 million ($300m). After analysing the local market economy, Barry Shaw concluded that it was dynamic and innovative. He said that although politicians complained of poor infrastructure, the continued viability of the markets implied returns were good and the industry had a bright future. Bureaucratic efforts to stimulate the sale of village food production have failed. The Food Marketing Corporation was set up in the 1970s amid much publicity. Its aim was to put village produce on to the dining tables of Port Moresby. The capital city is isolated from the areas the Government tried to stimulate and, in 1981, the corporation collapsed having accumulated losses of K3.1 million ($4.7m) and frittered away K4.3 million ($6.5m) in capital. 'Yet,' Shaw comments, 'Papua New Guinean people have, without government intervention or direct assistance, developed a food production and marketing system which is serving the country extremely well in spite of the continued comments of politicians and policy-makers to the contrary.'

Port Moresby's markets are bustling these days. One of the sights of the city now is the patchwork of food gardens, which blanket many of the hills through the capital. Squatter settlements are not the only sight now on the slopes around Port Moresby. Urban migrants, Highlanders many of them, are hard at work most days, tending their hillside food gardens. They rent this ground from the traditional Papuan landowners and the produce is bought and sold in the city's markets. One project pushed relentlessly, but with ultimate futility, by the Australian administration in the 1950s and 60s and by successive PNG governments in the 1970s and 80s has been rice growing on the Mekeo plains in the Central province adjacent to Port Moresby. It has never been a success. The Mekeo landowners today are doubtlessly making far more from selling betel nut to Port Moresby's betel-nut-mad Papua New Guinean residents than they ever would have made from rice. Betel nut is such an essential part of average householder spending that fluctuations in its price affect the CPI.

Another notable government-backed failure was smallholder cattle projects. International Development Association credits of K6.7 million ($10m) and PNG government funds of K7 million ($10.5m) were provided. Up until 1978 the PNG Development Bank provided 2850 loans totalling K7 million for small herds. There is little to show for any of it now, except 'unpaid loans, disillusioned project owners and large numbers of feral cattle'. A fifteen-breeder cattle project was estimated to give net returns of K600 for a labour input of 100 person days. While this return of K6 per day may have seemed attractive compared with the then rural minimum wage of K2 per day, the farmer saw very little of the money. A loan of about K5000 was required, repayable over five or six years at eight per cent. Repayments plus interest meant the annual net cash flow was a negative K500–600 a year for five to six years before the cattle turned a net surplus. The poor village farmer had to find other cash work just to meet his repayments!

The great success story of smallholder involvement — coffee — happened with minimal government assistance and almost no bank loans. Coffee was introduced to PNG late last century by the Germans, but its growth as an industry came after World War II with the extension of administration control over the Highlands. Expatriate planters were granted land and they began to plant estates. From 1951 to 1965 the area planted by estates rose from 150 to 4950 hectares, with 7.9 million trees. But by 1964 the number of trees planted by smallholders had reached 12.2 million. Today seventy per cent of coffee produced in PNG is grown by smallholders on village plots averaging half a hectare. Some of the smallholders have expanded to take over estates and ninety-five per cent of production is owned by Papua New Guineans. Statistics from the 1980 Census showed that 260,000 families depended on coffee-growing as a source of income. In the main producing provinces, the Eastern and Western Highlands, virtually all households that can grow coffee do.

Barry Shaw argues that Papua New Guineans make extremely rational economic decisions when it comes to choosing what to devote their labour to. 'The events of the past 15 years have proved the farmers right and many agricultural planners wrong: and at considerable cost,' he says. Shaw also claims that too many farmers in PNG have been encouraged to borrow money that they do not need. 'There is a widespread belief in PNG that credit is the greatest constraint to agricultural development. Over the years the PNG government has put considerable pressure on the commercial banks and the Agriculture Bank to increase agricultural lending to the point that the amount of money lent to agriculture was seen as the prime indicator of agricultural development.' But, he says, unnecessary credit can lower incomes, create mistrust and disillusionment and increase the cost of failure. 'The great cattle push of the 1970s will have left a legacy of producers who have repaid loans from other income or who still owe money, or have lost by diverting labour and land from other uses, and of taxpayers who will be repaying foreign loans for the projects for years.'

The great need in agriculture in PNG is not snap loans to small village farmers, but more well-trained agricultural extension officers, more research and a better infrastructure, such as roads in rural areas. The Planters Association of Papua New Guinea, which represents thousands of copra and cocoa growers (both large and smallholder) in PNG's coastal areas, has pleaded with the Government for more money for extension and research. But, it says, the funds should go to private bodies that can do the job and the Government's own departments should not be involved. It says that services provided by the Department of Agriculture and Livestock are 'beyond redemption' because of 'institutional rigidities and lack of both discipline and incentives for those who do good work. The Planters Association says the unfortunate pattern, though, has been for the government to hand over the work but not the money. 'We see an alarming trend for government to divest itself of functions with no corresponding reduction in expenditure or staff.'

Papua New Guinea's main agricultural export industries are all plagued by the volatility of world commodity prices. In the mid-1980s agricultural exports earnt the country between K300 million ($450m) and K400 million ($600m) a year. In the best year, 1984, they accounted for almost half the nation's export earnings. Price collapses in the late 1980s drained industry stabilisation funds and cut agricultural export earnings by one third. In 1989 world coffee prices collapsed to half of what they were in 1986. Although coffee is grown in about fifteen provinces throughout PNG, about 90 per cent is produced in the five Highlands provinces. In 1986-87 the Western Highlands accounted for 47 per cent of national production and the Eastern Highlands 31 per cent. The mild type of Arabica coffee grown in the Highlands is of a high quality and is in high demand. Coffee production for 1989 was forecast at 1.2 million bags, and production could double by the end of the century. The coffee industry is served by about eighty coffee-processing factories located mainly in the Eastern and Western Highlands provinces.

Copra and cocoa are grown in the coastal areas of Papua New Guinea and the 1980 census found that, of the 316,000 households in the fourteen cocoa and coconut growing provinces, 70,000 families were involved in cocoa production and 107,000 in copra, with many producing both. World prices in 1989 were poor. A tonne of copra, which had been worth K525 ($790) in 1984 earnt just K250 ($375) in 1989. Cocoa slumped from K2021 ($3032) in 1985 to K900 ($1350). There has been extensive replanting of cocoa on plantations in recent years. Cocoa production grew by more than 40 per cent in the six years to 1988 to more than 37,000 tonnes. Copra production tends to vary with the available price, with annual production moving between about 77,000 and 103,000 tonnes.

Palm oil is produced on nucleus estates owned half by the Government and half by foreign investors. The major foreign investor is the British Development Corporation and the estates service surrounding smallholders. New estates are being planted and production in the 1990s is expected to pass 200,000 tonnes a year. Production in 1988 was 103,000 tonnes. The price, which reached K561 ($842) per tonne in 1984, was averaging K355 ($533) a tonne in 1988.

While cash croppers play a major part in PNG agriculture, there are still about 650 plantations or estates in PNG of fifty or more hectares. The church missions derive a significant proportion of their operating revenue from plantations. Between them, the major churches own about thirty per cent of all plantations in PNG. The copra, cocoa and rubber plantations and the coffee, tea and palm oil estates employ about 43,000 people, mostly unskilled labourers, or about one fifth of the total formal workforce. Wages on the plantations are low although not as meagre as the wages paid in rural areas of PNG's main trading competitors in tropical commodities, such as the Philippines. Productivity was improved by a relaxation of wage rules in the early 1980s to allow the payment of piece work rates. PNG's rural minimum wage in 1989 was K20.50 per week (about $30). But it is in the urban centres that economists are most critical of PNG's wages structure. The urban minimum wage is well over double, almost treble, its rural counterpart. In 1989 an unskilled labourer in any of the major towns in PNG was earning K53.90 per week (about $81).

Although that is not much money in a high-cost city such as Port Moresby, the economists say it is too much if PNG is to compete and so encourage job growth. A 1982 report commissioned by the PNG Government on exchange-rate and macro-economic policy recommended drastic action to reduce urban wages to bring 'balance' back to the economy. The study, by Ross Garnaut and Paul Baxter, heavily criticised the wage structure left by the Australian administration. Pay rates were not the only legacy. PNG is one of only four countries in the world with institutionalised long-service leave. The others are Australia, New Zealand and South Africa! Wages constitute only sixty per cent of labour costs. The other forty per cent comes from Australian-style loadings, penalties, and fringe benefits. Both Garnaut and Baxter had worked in PNG. At the time of Independence, Garnaut was first assistant secretary for Finance, responsible for financial and economic policy, while Baxter was the national accounts statistician. They said wages in PNG's towns were too high for the level of unemployment. They recommended wage cuts of twenty-five to thirty per cent for adult workers in Port Moresby, and that there be 'a substantially larger reduction' in wages in other urban centres and for youth everywhere.

The explosion in wages in Australia that occurred during the Whitlam years flowed through to PNG. While parity between wage rates for Papua New Guineans and Australians doing the same work was severed in 1964, the rates of pay still followed similar methods of adjustment in the early 1970s. Between 1972 and 1976 the urban minimum wage in Port Moresby leapt from K8 a week to K27.18 — more than 300 per cent in four years. Discounting inflation, the real cost of labour more than doubled. From 1976 through to when Garnaut and Baxter did their study in 1982, wage adjustments were indexed to cost-of-living rises. Following the Garnaut/Baxter report the Government successfully argued for a change in the way the Minimum Wages Board set the rates. Under the system in place from 1983 to 1989, once-a-year adjustments were applied, based on a modified cost of living index with a maximum possible increase of five per cent. PNG's inflation rate in the 1980s was low, so the effect of the policy was a slow cut in real urban wages amounting to about five per cent by 1989 — well short of the twenty-five to thirty per cent deemed necessary by Garnaut and Baxter.

One difficulty facing any PNG government wanting to cut wages is the stark fact that the expatriate workforce numbering some fifteen thousand is so well paid. To attract skilled expatriates to Port Moresby, for example, private companies have to offer enticing packages. The costs of putting an expatriate family into secure accommodation is huge, with rents for apartments in the Port

Moresby town area ranging from K350 ($525) a week to K670 ($1000) a week. The Government, too, faces an enormous annual expense in housing its 1700 expatriate contract officers. The big costs of accommodation in urban PNG are not helped by the banks' demand for repayment of home loans over five years. The government is attempting to encourage banks and other financial institutions to introduce long-term home loans for Papua New Guineans but the scheme is moving slowly.

The official policy of cutting real wages remains. The Government mounted a major case before the 1989 Minimum Wages Board for a tough set of rules to keep wage increases well below inflation. When the Board ruled that the formula to apply from 1989–91 would provide for six-monthly indexation — up to three per cent in the first six months and a six per cent maximum for a full year, provided inflation did not exceed ten per cent — the Government accepted the decision but announced it would apply only to those on the minimum wage. Practice had been that minimum-wage adjustments flowed through to other wage earners. But the Government said it was up to employers and the unions to negotiate. For its part, the Government would enter negotiations with the Public Employees Association on pay increases for employees earning more than the minimum wage. Going into the negotiations, the Government said it intended 'to achieve a reduction in real wages in the range of 3 per cent to 4 per cent'.

In its 1990 economic policy statement the Government said it was requesting the 'same level of restraint' from other workers and trade unions. 'Real wage reduction,' it said, 'will help the economy overcome the setback of the short-term impact of the Bougainville mine closure and begin to implement the necessary structural adjustment required for the creation of additional productive employment opportunities in the non-mining private sector.' The trade unions argued before the Minimum Wages Board for hefty real wage increases to make up for the spending power lost since the early 1980s. As the 1980s ended some unions were taking industrial action in support of claims for a ten per cent pay rise.

The official policy of job creation does not include making more jobs in the public service. PNG's national government employs about thirty thousand people while the nineteen provincial governments employ another twenty thousand. Despite a major exercise to trim the public service in 1983, governments still employ one in every five people with paid jobs. It is a very large public service for a developing country of 3.8 million people. 'The cost to the country is very large,' a government statement in 1988 admitted. 'Terms and conditions of employment in the public service are significantly more generous for junior public servants than in most non-government organisations and certainly higher than in most other developing countries.' The statement commented critically that 'services have not improved to the extent that would be expected from the growth in the number of government employees. Indeed in some areas services have deteriorated since Independence. Further, the growth in the public service has largely been in administrative areas which have not had any significant impact on improving investment or in improving services.' The major retrenchment exercise in 1983 turned into a farce, with public servants who accepted lump sum retrenchment packages moving back into the service later in other departments.

While direct government employment stands at about fifty thousand, another twenty thousand wage earners are working for government statutory authorities or public enterprises in which the Government or its financial corporations have a forty-nine per cent or greater controlling interest. There was great enthusiasm at the time of self-government and Independence for government involvement in business. The enthusiasm carried through to the nineteen provincial governments as they became established. A survey in the early 1980s found that more than half of the provincial Development Corporations were making losses, many heavy. The same study found most national government ventures into the private sector performed poorly, too. The Government was then involved in commercial enterprises covering air transport, telecommunications, power supply, banking, insurance, broadcasting, shipping, forestry, sugar and rubber. Some of the more exotic ventures included experimental power alcohol production and performing dolphins.

The performing dolphins company, Sea Park Pty Ltd, was a disaster. Sea Park was an oceanarium and underwater observatory built at Ela Beach in Port Moresby as a tourist attraction. The original estimated cost was about K250,000 ($375,000) but by the time the dolphin pool, a public seating area, a kiosk and an observatory were built in the late 1970s, K1.5 million ($2.25m) had been spent. So the proposed bird aviary, library, auditorium and research facility were abandoned. The tiny tourist trade all but ignored the Sea Park and the general Port Moresby public showed little interest. The Sea Park eventually closed hopelessly in debt in 1986. Professor Michael Trebilcock, a Canadian economist who studied PNG's public enterprises, said that in terms of creating employment, the Sea Park venture was by far the least successful. Each job cost the taxpayer K175,000 ($263,000) and none of the jobs lasted.

The Wingti Government in 1987 adopted a policy of privatisation to gradually extricate the State from a whole range of industries. The Cabinet agreed to a phased approach to sell off many of the forty or so government enterprises. First to go was the PNG Shipping Corporation. The shipping corporation began operations in 1977 as a joint venture between the Government and the New Guinea Australia Line, a wholly owned subsidiary of Hong Kong's John Swires group. Five years later it went into receivership having lost K3.7 million ($5.6m). The receivers set up a creditors' scheme of management to trade out of difficulties but got into more; and after another five years accumulated losses had risen to K8.5 million ($12.8m). In July 1987 the Government sold the PNG Shipping Corporation to the Steamships Trading Company, a diversified company with its own shipping division which has operated in PNG for more than sixty years.

In 1989 the Namaliu Government declared it, too, believed in privatisation 'unless national security is an overriding consideration'. The delay in getting rid of most of the government-owned concerns was said to be due to problems in valuation, the terms on which state equity should be offered and finding suitable buyers. 'The State's investment portfolio comprises 29 firms,' a statement said. 'The government's shareholding in 14 of these is valued at less than K1 million [$1.5m]. The shareholding ranges from 3 per cent to 100 per cent. Only two are currently paying dividends.' Of the fifteen in which the government's stake was more than K1 million, only four were paying dividends while six were in the process of liquidation and three — PNG Forest Products, Niugini Insurance and New Guinea Marine Products — 'were in the first phase of privatisation'. Amongst measures to help the Government divest itself of these unwanted businesses is the proposed establishment in the 1990s of a PNG stock exchange on which the companies could be floated publicly.

Some of the more successful areas of government activity in PNG are those under the control of what are called the commercial statutory authorities. These are the Electricity Commission (Elcom), Air Niugini, the Posts and Telecommunications Corporation (PTC), the Harbours Board and the Water Board. Most ran into problems in the early years after Independence, but their efficient operation was so critical to the economy that the Government abandoned public service practice in 1983 and ordered their managements to adopt 'strictly commercial methods of operation'. Elcom, PTC and Air Niguini are amongst the best run PNG operations. PTC has performed best and is the only one that will meet the government's guidelines of a return on investment of between sixteen and twenty-two per cent in 1990. Half the profits have to be paid over to consolidated revenue. The success of these commercial statutory authorities has prompted the Government to try to convert a number of government departments into corporations. One will be a National Housing Corporation.

The National Housing Commission, which will be part of the new Corporation, is well into its own vigorous privatisation scheme — selling its houses to their occupants. Hundreds of houses are part of the controversial scheme. The *Government Gazette* in mid-May 1988 published the names of 6 government ministers, 15 former ministers, 1 backbench member of parliament and 199 public servants who had successfully met the criteria for purchasing their government-supplied homes. Also gazetted were the reserve prices the lucky residents would have to pay. The PNG *Post Courier* carried a front-page story quoting real estate firms as saying that some of the government houses in the Port Moresby town area that had reserve prices of K50,000 could fetch K250,000 on the open market.

Papua New Guinea's manufacturing sector has been crippled by the relatively high cost of labour, the low productivity of workers, the competition of cheap imports because of the 'hard Kina' strategy and the limited size of the market in PNG for manufactured goods. The fact that the capital (and largest) city, Port Moresby, has no road link with any other major centre has tended to retard industrial development or force the duplication of small, inefficient factories on either side of the mainland. Coastal shipping costs mean that it is often cheaper to import items into Lae and the Highlands from overseas than to buy them from Port Moresby. Other restraining factors that the Government itself has identified are 'excessively bureaucratic procedures for regulating foreign investment' and shortages of land 'aggravated by complex allocation procedures'.

A number of secondary industries have become established. Beer, cigarettes and soft drinks have all been produced locally since before Independence. There have been various attempts to replace imports. PNG created its own sugar industry in the early 1980s — at some cost in increased price to the local consumers — and sugar imports are banned. Meat canning now takes place in both Madang and Port Moresby and the country is self-sufficient in chicken. There are a few clothing and metal fabrication factories and PNG is exporting nails to northern Queensland. There is a well-developed financial services sector, the transport industry is healthy and building and construction, especially in the capital, was booming at the end of the 1980s.

Nevertheless, the Government admits that 'growth of investment and production in the non-mining private sector has proceeded at very disappointing levels'. Total non-mining-sector investment has been generally declining or stagnating as a proportion of GDP. It fell from 9 per cent in 1982 to 7.9 per cent in 1986. In an attempt to stimulate investment, the Government in 1987 promised 'a considerable easing of administrative red tape and delays for those foreign activities which are declared as "open" under proposed new procedures' to be adopted by the foreign investment regulatory body, the National Investment and Development Authority (NIDA). It also promised 'improved administrative procedures to speed up land transactions' and a 'considerable relaxation' of the regulations governing the issuing of work permits and entry visas for 'approved enterprises and occupations'.

A string of other measures — such as 'streamlining' the administration of foreign exchange control, 'de-emphasising' price control in selected activities, 'speeding up' decision-making, 'deregulating' business-licensing requirements and 'further improving the Government's own accounting system' to quicken the processing and payment of government accounts — were all announced. But the private sector had heard it all before and had seen little happen. In mid-1987 Sir Julius Chan, as acting prime minister, ordered an inquiry into complaints against bureaucratic delays in the issuing of work permits and entry visas. A letter from the Rabual Chamber of Commerce sparked the inquiry but Sir Julius, as Trade and Industry minister, had been deluged by similar letters of complaint. The report of the 'Committee of Inquiry into the Work Permits Division of the Labour Department and the Immigration Division of the Foreign

Affairs Department' was presented in September 1987 and was never adopted.

But the committee's findings are worth reviewing because they show how bureaucratic obfuscation has been well learnt in PNG. The Department of Foreign Affairs did not like this inquiry and so drafted, and had its minister sign, a letter to the Prime Minister which reads like a script from 'Yes Minister'. After outlining a series of objections to the way the committee had been formed, the letter requested that the terms of reference be expanded to cover philosophical matters such as the relationship between the various laws governing the entry and activities of foreigners in PNG and government policies regarding 'manpower planning, training, capacity building and localisation'. As well, it suggested that the committee should investigate the 'impact of commercial practices of foreign businesses operating in PNG on the licensing/permit issuing authorities in PNG'. In the absence of a reply from the PM, the department refused to co-operate with the inquiry.

The committee's report praised the assistance given by the work permit section of the Labour Department but said its investigation 'was hampered by an unhelpful and obstructionist Department of Foreign Affairs'. It found that while the work permit section (Labour Department) operated relatively efficiently, the migration division (Foreign Affairs Department) was plagued by 'poor organisation, much rumoured corruption, low morale and confusion'. The committee said that files were piled on desks, passports were frequently lost and even simple procedures were subjected to 'incredible' delays. It could not detail specific instances of corruption warranting prosecution but said that the number of allegations led the Committee to believe 'petty corruption was prevalent'. The report found that the immigration division was overruling the Labour Department and rejecting entry visas for people the immigration officers felt should not have been issued with work permits. 'This is not their job. If Labour and Employment issue a work permit for someone then Immigration has absolutely no authority to withhold a visa because they feel, on whim, it should not have been issued. Yet this is exactly what has been happening', said the 1987 report.

Three years later many of the same problems remained. The Government's 1990 development strategy said that work permits and visas remained the biggest concerns of business. The solution? 'Cabinet directed the Departments of Foreign Affairs, Labour and

Employment and Trade and Industry form a committee to ensure that adjustments are made in visa and work permit systems to reduce delays and difficulties for businesses in particular.' The document said NIDA was being reviewed and that 'consideration is being given to splitting' its foreign investment control and investment promotion functions because these had often been in conflict. The Finance and Planning Department, which produces government strategy papers, seems well aware of the major problems and the need for reform. 'With 19 provincial governments, 26 government departments, plus a number of statutory bodies, agencies and other institutions, it is important to ensure the effective integration and coordination of planning and implementation to achieve the government's overall development objectives,' it says. Only a handful of the departments are working in any efficient way. Finance and Planning, and Minerals and Energy are two of the best.

Despite the Government's concern that 'broadly based' economic growth will be 'severely constrained if there cannot be a significant growth in non-mining private sector investment', PNG's immediate prospects for rapid economic growth seem to depend entirely on the country's enormous mineral, oil and gas resources. While developments on Bougainville raise concerns about the smooth development of these non-renewable resources, the Government's official statements on the future of the sector are all strongly optimistic. 'Mineral and petroleum exports are expected to grow at an average annual rate of over 25 per cent in nominal terms with the major increase coming in 1993,' the Government says. 'By 1994 mineral and petroleum exports will account for 81 per cent of exports, with 22 per cent coming from oil. Imports are projected to increase up until 1991, due to the importation of capital goods corresponding to mineral sector construction activity. From 1992 construction activity declines and imports tail off. As a consequence a trade surplus is expected in 1992 growing to a level of over K1 billion [$1.5b] in 1993.' That was the prediction as the 1980s ended.

Papua New Guinea had one major open-cut mine go into production in the 1970s, Bougainville Copper, and one in the 1980s, Ok Tedi Mining. They are at opposite ends of the country — in the extreme eastern province, North Solomons, and in the Western province, close to the Irian Jayan border, respectively. Both were enormous engineering achievements in difficult terrain. Bougainville Copper began producing copper, gold and silver concentrate in 1972 while Ok Tedi mined gold from a gold cap at the top of Mount Fubilan for two years from 1984 before moving into the production of gold, copper and silver. Bougainville Copper Limited is listed on Australian stock exchanges and its major shareholders are CRA (53 per cent) and the PNG government (19 per cent). Ok Tedi Mining Limited is owned 30 per cent each by BHP and Amoco Minerals (PNG), a fully owned subsidiary of Standard Oil of Indiana; and 20 per cent each by the PNG Government and a West German consortium led by Metallgesellschaft AG.

One small goldmine — the Mount Victor mine near Kainantu in the Eastern Highlands, fully owned by PNG-based Niugini Mining—began producing in 1987. The following year there was a remarkable alluvial gold rush at Mount Kare on the border between two of the other Highlands provinces, Enga and Southern Highlands. Thousands of Papua New Guinean prospectors flocked to Mount Kare, digging up nuggets and sluicing grains of gold worth an estimated K70 million ($105m). CRA has a prospecting authority over Mount Kare and in late 1989 it was attempting to set up a 50/50 joint venture company with landowners to conduct an alluvial mining operation to recover what the diggers might have missed. The Misima goldmine, owned by Placer Pacific on Misima Island in the Milne Bay province, began producing in 1989. It cost K175 million ($263m) to open up and in its first full year was expected to produce twelve tonnes of gold and eighty tonnes of silver.

The major mine under construction as the 1990s began was Porgera, the K700 million ($1050m) goldmine in the Enga province at the remote western end of the PNG Highlands. Porgera is a joint venture between Australia's Mount Isa Mines (MIM), Placer Dome of North America and Rennison Goldfields Australia. The PNG Government has taken a ten-per-cent interest on behalf of the landowners and the Enga provincial government. Placer's interests were handed to the Australian-based Placer Pacific Limited when that company was floated in 1986. MIM's interests are now with Highlands Gold, which MIM floated as a Papua New Guinea based mining house in late 1989. The ownership of Porgera is now Highlands Gold (30 per cent), Placer (PNG) (30 per cent), RGC PNG (30 per cent), with 10 per cent held by Mineral Resources Development (Porgera) Pty Ltd as the holding company for the State's equity.

Porgera has an identified mineral resource of 490 tonnes of gold and an ore reserve of another 391 tonnes. Gold production is expected to begin in late 1990 and to average twenty-five tonnes per year for the first six years. There will be both underground mining of a high-grade zone and an open-cut mine to extract gold from lower grade ore. The underground mine will be PNG's first on a large scale. The Porgera Project Manager, Vic Botts, says the challenges have been great: 'It's very difficult because of the terrain and the location of Porgera some 700 kilometres from Lae. We have an enormous amount of material to move here up that Highlands Highway. Next, there are many landslides,' he says. 'The third point is that it's a very high technology mine and we're doing some elaborate and difficult things in a difficult country,' says Botts, who has become expert in negotiating with Engan tribesmen.

Other mines expected to open in the 1990s include Lihir in New Ireland, Hidden Valley in the Eastern Highlands, Laloki in the Central province, Wild Dog in East New Britain and Tabar in New Ireland. The most exciting prospect is Lihir. Lihir is a beautiful, tropical, volcanic island off the north-eastern coast of the long, thin island of New Ireland, about eight hundred kilometres to the north east of the PNG mainland. Discoveries made by geologists there in recent years reveal that it is exceptionally rich. 'In March 1988 Lihir's mineable reserves were upgraded to 18.4 million ounces of gold [575 tonnes],' Niugini Mining Limited's Chairman, Geoff Loudon, told shareholders at the company's annual general meeting in Port Moresby in late May 1988. 'This massive upgrading in reserves makes Lihir one of the truly remarkable gold ore bodies and probably the largest discovered outside South Africa this century.'

Mr Loudon is confident further testing will substantially raise recoverable gold reserves and Lihir could have a fifty-year life. Loudon's PNG based Niugini Mining Limited holds a minority interest in the prospect. The major owner is the British-based RTZ Corporation, following a series of big takeovers involving RTZ, British Petroleum and Kennecott. RTZ owns forty-nine per cent of CRA, which in turn is the majority owner of Bougainville Copper Limited. Following the manoeuvres, PNG's Prime Minister Namaliu stated his government's concern that it did not want one multi-national dominating PNG's mining industry. Suggestions that the Government might prevent the transfer of the exploration permit over Lihir going to RTZ prompted a quick visit to Port Moresby in January 1989 by RTZ's Deputy Chief Executive, Lord Clitheroe.

After meeting with Lord Clitheroe, Mr Namaliu said he had been assured that RTZ had no intention of selling the Lihir interest to CRA but would hold it and put considerable effort into the project. 'The involvement of the world's biggest mining company in PNG and their commitment to the project is a clear vote of confidence in the country and its economic future,' Mr Namaliu claimed.

Geoff Loudon finds it hard to contain his enthusiasm for gold prospecting in PNG. 'Probably the next-best prospect we have is the Tabar Islands. There is a large drilling program going on there at the moment and recently we have had some exceptionally good results. We expect a productive mine there as well. Another very good prospect that we are involved in is up in the Highlands, halfway between Porgera and Ok Tedi. We have interests in a company called Equatorial Gold which is drilling at a site known as Bulago. We have had very rich surface samples going up to 88 grammes per tonne.' Loudon has so much confidence in the future of PNG that his company intends to set itself up as a Papua New Guinea-based regional Mining House. 'We have a strong belief in PNG and the institutions here,' he says. 'We think government here is stable, even though the coalitions may keep changing. We like the mining law and we like the whole social fabric that allows us to get on with exploration. We obviously do have problems sometimes with landowners but we think that is part and parcel of an emerging nation and the ethic of the people.'

PNG is far from being a third-world dictatorship where multinational mining companies in league with a corrupt government ignore the interests of the indigenous people. The people are highly politically motivated and they don't hesitate to take action. Dr Roman Grynberg, an economist who worked for Prime Minister Namaliu for twelve months after several years' lecturing at the University of Papua New Guinea, says the very democratic nature of the way things operate in PNG means people with a vested interest are going to have their say. 'Conflicts will arise that have to be resolved. It must be particularly difficult for any mining company that is used to dealing with a very powerful centralised government that can impose its will on everyone. That is certainly not the case in PNG,' Dr Grynberg says. 'I am sure Kennecott would find it much easier to negotiate with Augusta Pinochet than with the government of Papua New Guinea!'

Agreements or Guidelines?

The relocation houses built by the mining company for the Ipili-speaking Porgera people are stark, white, almost windowless, aluminium-clad boxes. They have none of the charm of traditional Highlands bush-material housing, nor do they nestle into the mountainside in the same seemingly compatible way. But, be in no doubt, they are what the people demanded. The Porgera Joint Venture's first sketch proposals for wooden houses incorporating local design features and verandas were rejected out of hand. It took eight months of negotiation before the landowners settled on the current design — the most important feature of which is that they cannot be burnt or chopped down in a tribal fight.

Chairman of the Porgera Landowners' Association, Jolson Kutato, has been a tough negotiator and some of those houses are built before his association agrees to give its approval for the K700 million ($1050m) goldmine to start. The Namaliu Government's development forum process requires all parties — the company, national and provincial governments, and the landowners — to reach agreement on where the benefits will flow before mining can proceed. The joint venture partners, Mount Isa Mines, Rennison Goldfields and Placer Dome, have had frustrations. They had hoped for approval to mine last November. It is now May and all are gathered in the great hall at parliament in anticipation.

'The agreement we have is a general guideline,' says Jolson Kutato's interpreter, translating from a burst of guttural Ipili. 'But there are four important issues I want to raise before we put our signature on the paper. Firstly, all the business spin-offs, whether big or small, must go to the landowners regardless of whether they have finance, whether they have expertise, whether they have a reputation, or whether they have experience in business.' Mr Kutato argues that the clauses in the agreement are too loose, that the people who have little education will miss out and the mine service contracts will go to others who do have finance, expertise and a business reputation. 'I want to register that sentiment here and I want the news reporters to make sure all these words are recorded and we will refer to this day, at this time, and this wording in regards to contracts coming out of the Porgera project.'

Secondly, Jolson Kutato is concerned that non-landowners should not 'play around' with the landowners' five per cent equity in the mine. Thirdly, he wants a guarantee that by year seven most workers will live with their families on site, not work on a fly-in/fly-out basis. His final point is special education for Porgerans, so the landowners can have their own man in an 'executive position' in the mine to keep the people informed.

'As I said earlier,' he concludes, 'the agreement that we are going to sign today is just a guideline. ... The company and the Government must make sure the landowners are the major beneficiaries because the landowners are the people who are going to be more affected than anybody else. Even though we are not fully satisfied, we want to make [a] commitment today to allow the company to go ahead. But, as I said, if we don't address these important points properly, in the next twenty-five years there will be problems.'

By law 1.25 per cent of a mine's gross export sales is paid in royalties. Prior to 1989, 95 per cent of those royalties went to the provincial government and the other 5 per cent to the landowners. But the Namaliu Government adopted a new policy in 1989, granting the landowners a four-fold increase to 20 per cent. On Bougainville, for instance, this would have meant that the landowners would receive about K1.5 million ($2.3m) from a full year's production. The provincial governments have been compensated for their loss of royalties by an additional grant from national revenue. Landowners are also paid compensation according to a set schedule for land worked on, trees knocked down, gardens lost and fish and wildlife resources that might be driven away. The new policy provides them with equity in mining companies and preferential treatment for their companies to take advantage of spin-off businesses.

The people keep a keen eye on what goes on. At a dinner hosted by the North American Placer Dome Board for senior PNG ministers and officials in Port Moresby in early 1988, Correctional Services Minister Tom Amaiu warned the visitors that they should get the Porgera mine going quickly. Mr Amaiu, from the Enga province, said the people were getting impatient and suspicious about how many core samples were being sent south for assay. 'The people are worried you are tricking them and smuggling out their gold!'

The Canadians laughed but Mr Amaiu was not joking.

One landowners' dispute forced the indefinite postponement of an alluvial-gold dredging operation on the Lakekamu River in the Gulf province north-west of Port Moresby. City Resources of Australia spent K7 million ($10.5m) and more than three years exploring the Lakekamu basin. In a joint venture with Sydney-based Lydgate Holdings, City Resources was about to spend K30 million ($45m) on a dredging operation when the Moveave people at the mouth of the river refused to allow a barge carrying K100,000 ($150,000) worth of drilling equipment to pass their village. The Moveave claimed they owned the riverbed sixty kilometres further inland where the dredging was planned. City Resources had sealed a landowners' deal with the Kamea/Kovio people who live in the upper reaches, a deal recognised by the Gulf Provincial government and the national Lands Department. One Kamea/Kovio leader claimed the Moveave at the river's mouth were never interested in the upstream river bed until the dredging operation seemed likely. But the Moveave in turn claimed the Kamea/Kovio were mountain people who had migrated down to the riverbank only after World War II. The Moveave threatened violence if barges used the river before the dispute was resolved and so the project was postponed indefinitely.

The Porgera negotiations introduced the concept of the development forum, which is aimed at achieving harmony before mining operations begin. Through the development forum the national Government, the provincial Government and the landowners conduct tripartite negotiations leading to three separate but linked agreements. Porgera also introduced important initiatives in equity participation by landowners and provincial governments. Under existing law, the PNG Government has the option to purchase, at cost, up to 30 per cent of the equity in major mining projects and 22.5 per cent in oil and gas projects. The new policy gives the landowners and the provincial government each an option on 5 per cent of total equity in any mining project, the equity to come from the national Government's holding. Of the total shares, 4.9 per cent may be purchased at cost but may be 'carried' equity and be paid for out of future dividends. The remaining 5.1 per cent must be bought for cash at market price. The equity option confers substantial benefits. On Bougainville, for example, the capital value of 5 per cent of BCL's shares (on 1988 prices) was K35 million ($53m), while the dividend (on 1988 performance) would have been K5 million ($7.5m), or an average of about K5000 ($7500) per registered titleholder.

Papua New Guinea could become an oil exporter by 1993. In mid-1988, the country's oil and condensate reserves were estimated at 587 million barrels and its gas reserves at eight to nine trillion cubic feet. Exploration wells are being drilled at the rate of more than fifteen a year in what *Oil and Gas Australia* (the Australian oil industry publication) has described as 'a rash of interest' since the Iagifu field was discovered in 1986. Iagifu is in sparsely inhabited forest south of Lake Kutubu in the Southern Highlands province. The field is thirteen kilometres long and five kilometres across. 'Those that have invested and are operating in the country are predictably optimistic, touched with the edge of mania characteristic of those who work in high-risk areas,' the Australian oil industry publication wrote. The 'edge of mania' was heightened by the baffling and complex nature of the Iagifu-Hedinia field.

The 1986 drilling at the Iagifu 2 well site, in what is now PNG's Petroleum Prospecting Lease area PPL100, produced the country's first substantial oil discovery. But subsequent drilling was disappointing. Detailing the history of the field, IMPS Research, Port Moresby, says none of the Iagifu wells 4, 5, 6, or 6ST flowed oil, although Iagifu 6 flowed gas. 'Meanwhile, in 1988, gas was discovered on the adjacent Hedinia anticline in the same Toro reservoir. Drilling downflank (Hedinia 1ST1) resulted in the discovery of oil, part of the common Iagifu-Hedinia pool.' With no seismic data available, the appraisal of the field has been done by drilling. 'Including Iagifu 2, there have now been 21 wells drilled on the Iagifu-Hedinia field, including sidetracks. Of these, 11 flowed oil with gas, four flowed gas without oil and five were dry,' IMPS reported. The participants in PPL100 are Chevron Niugini and BP Petroleum Development, with a 25 per cent interest each, the Ampolex Group with 21.233 per cent, BHP Petroleum (PNG) with 12.5 per cent, Oil Search Limited with 10.017 per cent and Merlin Petroleum with 6.25 per cent.

Oil Search said the proven recoverable reserves in the Iagifu-Hedinia field was approaching one hundred million barrels at the end of 1989. By then the question was when, not if, the field would be developed. All exploration work has been done by helicopter and the plan is to build a fifty-kilometre road to the Government station of Poroma, which is connected by road to the Highlands Highway. A pipeline will run south from the field 274 kilometres to a sea terminal in the Gulf of Papua. IMPS Research says the marine terminal, 40 kilometres off Cape Blackwood, will be a permanently moored tanker. 'The pipeline will not involve pump stations, at least initially, gravity flow will be sufficient for field production of up to about 150,000 barrels per day.' Construction of the pipeline will take a workforce of about three thousand. Chevron, the operator, has quoted a planned field production rate of 80,000 barrels per day and a capital cost estimate of K613 million ($920m).

At the close of the 1980s the PPL100 joint venturers had spent about K220 million ($330m) on the evaluation of the field. They expected total revenue would amount to K2300 million (K3.5b). Another prospective field, Agogo, is about five kilometres from the Iagifu-Hedinia field and it may be developed in tandem. Several major oil companies are now farming into other Petroleum Prospecting Licences in PNG, and Minerals and Energy Department officials anticipate that the trend of discoveries will continue. The department commissioned a study by Coopers and Lybrand (PNG) in conjunction with Blumer Associates on the possibilities of domestic processing of PNG's oil and gas finds. One proposal is for the development of a K5 million ($7.5m) mini-refinery in the Highlands producing 2000 to 3000 barrels of petroleum products per day. These could be price-competitive with imported products, which have to be trucked up the Highlands Highway from Lae. The consultants suggested that the crude oil discovered in the Iagifu field could be converted at a mini-refinery near the well head to meet all the Highlands' needs for petrol, Avtur aviation fuel and kerosene.

The first hydrocarbon field into production in PNG will not be the Iagifu-Hedinia oil field but the Hides gas field to its northwest. A contract has already been signed between the Porgera goldmine and BP for the Hides field to provide power for the mine. The Hides gas deposits of some two trillion cubic feet will be converted to electricity at a four-turbine gas-fuelled powerhouse on the field. Seventy kilometres of high-tension powerlines will connect the powerhouse at Hides to the Porgera mine in the adjacent Enga province. The Minerals and Energy Department is studying a possible extension to feed into the mostly hydro-powered Highlands grid.

Oil and Gas Australia has complemented PNG on how well run its infrastructure is for such a young country. But it advised potential explorers that sensitive account had to be taken of the complexity of the national community. 'Disruptions are easily and inadvertently caused, slowing down operations considerably — a case in point being BP's loss of water at their Tari camp due to a hen being run over.' Chevron is confronted by demands from the Southern Highland Premier for the building of a large-scale refinery in his province. Mr Yaungtine Koromba threatened in late 1989 to get his people to block any oil pipeline construction if his demands for a major refinery were not met.

The PNG government estimates that by 1994 Papua New Guinea's total exports will be worth K3.035 billion ($4.553b), an increase of more than 250 per cent in five years. According to the estimates, gold will be earning more than K1.1 billion ($1.6b), copper K715 million ($1b) and oil K551 million ($827m). Those predictions are based on the expectation that Bougainville will be back in production. Dr Roman Grynberg says that if the predicted boom eventuates, PNG could contract what economists have referred to as the 'Dutch Disease': 'What happened in Holland when they discovered large amounts of natural gas was that the gas boom led to high wages in the gas industry which then spread to other sectors of the economy. Bougainville and Ok Tedi are geographically isolated, so the spread effects on wages has not been that large. But when you start getting six or seven or a dozen mines, where miners are paid relatively high wages, I suspect that will spread,' he says.

Dr Grynberg says that the worst hit could be the plantation sector, which relies on low wages for its existence. 'For both copra and cocoa production wage rates are already relatively high in comparison with PNG's nearest neighbours, Indonesia and the Philippines. Any increases in wages in the agricultural sector would have the same effect as they had in Nigeria. In Nigeria the oil boom devastated the production of palm oil and I suspect we are going to see a similar effect in the plantation sector in the PNG economy in the mid-1990s,' Grynberg warns.

PNG's tax laws on mining and oil have won international acclaim. But Dr Grynberg fears the possible boom may bring a crisis in the country's economic management: 'Given the current taxation laws, which are very generous to PNG, the State could get about fifty toea out of every Kina in export earnings from oil. That will be a massive injection of revenue,' Dr Grynberg says. 'I do not believe that the Government has the capacity to spend that money effectively. My fear, though, is that it will be spent. And unless the minerals and petroleum boom that's getting into swing at the moment is controlled then I fear that you will have an economic disaster here of Nigerian proportions!'

Papua New Guinea's macro-economic management over its first fifteen years of Independence gives some grounds for confidence that such a disaster can be averted. However, the Department of Finance and Planning itself admits that macro-economic control is not enough. 'Despite the good record of macro-economic management, particularly in respect of fiscal policy, balance of payments, external debt and inflation, the economy is still constrained by long-standing structural weaknesses. These include traditional land ownership patterns, a high cost structure, a lack of manpower skills and poor infrastructure. Significant segments of the population still do not have access to basic transport, electricity, running water, education and health services. Moreover, it has proven difficult to maintain the quality of these services in the areas where the infrastructure exists.' The 1990 economic strategy document says it is the Government's intention to use revenue flows from mineral and petroleum projects to complete the 'unfinished agenda of providing and maintaining Papua New Guinea's basic infrastructure.'

Given the big problems the country already has in implementing projects, the money might be more wisely used to achieve three much more limited objectives: firstly, to cut PNG's external public debt; secondly, to provide the funds necessary for the extension and research work that is essential if the country is to meet its massive employment challenges through agriculture — the industry Papua New Guineans know most about; and, thirdly, by building up the capacity of its own institutions, some of which have failed the country so badly on Bougainville.

CHAPTER FIVE

BOUGAINVILLE — LAND RIGHTS OR SECESSION?

THE novel that won Papua New Guinea's National Literature Competition in 1988 was entitled *The Call of the Land*. Runner-up was *In the Name of Land*. The literature competition attracted more than a thousand entries in all sections and it is instructive that the best and most passionate writing by Melanesians that year was on one theme — land. Deep grievance over what had happened to their land at Panguna on Bougainville Island during the previous twenty years led Pepetua Serero and Francis Ona into launching a passionate and violent confrontation with the PNG national Government in the latter months of 1988. The conflict worsened in 1989, took many lives and shook the fragile unity of Papua New Guinea.

Serero and her first cousin, Ona, grew up at Guava village in the Crown Prince range on Bougainville in the 1950s and 1960s. They were attending Catholic mission schools run by the Marist Order when CRA Exploration began drilling in the Panguna area near Guava in 1964. Their people vigorously opposed the mine. In 1967 one villager said losing land was like taking 'the bones out of a man's legs, the man would not be able to walk'. PNG history professor Jim Griffin says the Australian administration's negotiations to acquire the land were 'astonishingly crass'. Due regard was not paid to the people's feelings for their land, 'which not only represents patrimony, livelihood and future security but is also invested with mystical awe'. The people were told that although their land contained fabulous riches, they did not own the minerals, the administration did. Fr Bob Wiley, the American Catholic priest at Panguna, tells of Australia's External Territories Minister, Charles Barnes, flying into the area in the late 1960s: 'He got off and he said, "You get nothing." And he hopped back on the helicopter and was gone. The people just shook their heads. Right from the beginning frustration built.'

When construction of the giant copper mine began in 1969, Pepetua Serero was a broadcast officer with the administration radio station on Bougainville. Francis Ona joined Bougainville Copper Limited several years later as a surveyor. Like their parents and most other Bougainvillians they were highly suspicious of the motives of outsiders. J P Reynolds wrote in 1970 that the continued opposition to the copper project indicated 'the fear and distrust' many Bougainvillians had of attempts by the administration and expatriate companies 'to promote economic development which they feel is just another ruse by which the European will exploit the local people and their resources for his own ends.'

The Bougainvillians also resented the mainland Papua New Guineans who were brought in to build the mine. Geographically, Bougainville is separate from the rest of Papua New Guinea. It is at the northern end of the Solomon Islands chain (hence the name, North Solomons). Its division from the rest of the Solomons and its incorporation into PNG is a result of the same nineteenth-century colonial map dividing that has rendered Irian Jaya Indonesian. The Bougainvillians' most distinctive trait is their skin colour. Bougainville is home to the purest black people on earth. They refer to people from elsewhere in PNG as 'redskins'.

The anger in Serero and Ona grew as the open-cut pit deepened and more of their land became waste down the Jaba River. In August 1987 they called a meeting of landowners at Panguna, which installed a new executive. Pepetua Serero became chairlady (*sic*) of the new Panguna Landowners' Association and Francis Ona General Secretary. The new executive demanded K10 billion ($15b) compensation from CRA, half the profits made by BCL since the mine began production, and tighter controls on environmental damage. In November 1988 Francis Ona walked out of a meeting with the company and the national Government, furious at the findings of an independent study by a New Zealand firm of environmental consultants which said that the Jaba River water was not poisoned.

He claimed that the landowners knew fish were dying and he alleged 'a white mafia' was fooling the people. Ona resigned his job and went into the jungle. Within days, guerillas from what was to become the Bougainville Revolutionary Army (BRA) held up the mine's magazine and stole explosives. Sabotage and arson followed. They raided buildings and installations around the mine and blasted a power pylon off its legs, severing transmission lines between the Loloho power station on the east coast and the mine in the mountains. Soon after repair teams restored power, the guerillas blew down another two pylons.

The expertise with which these sabotage operations were executed astonished the national Government and BCL. Earlier in 1988 the new landowners' executive had organised protests. But those had been relatively peaceful and amateurish attempts to halt production by blocking roads with drums. The felling of the power pylons was professionally done. Charges were attached to each of the four legs and detonated in turn so that the transmission towers collapsed down mountainsides or across the mine access road. The man supervising the sabotage was a former PNG defence force soldier, Samuels Kauona, a Bougainvillian, who had returned home in late 1988 after extensive demolitions training with the Australian Army in Victoria. Ex-lieutenant Kauona deserted the PNG defence force on his return to become Francis Ona's right-hand man and military strategist.

Sam Kauona was not a landowner from any of the BCL lease areas. His village was in the nearby Kongara area at the head of the Bovo Valley, which runs up towards the mine from the rear of the town of Arawa, a coastal town of 10,000 residents that BCL built on what had been a coconut plantation. Kauona's talents went beyond running the guerilla campaign. He became adept at using the media and issued statements as Ona's spokesman. His guerilla forces, which initially numbered fewer than a hundred, operated in small bands and conducted hit-and-run raids against mine property, commercial facilities closely associated with the mine and government installations such as telecommunications towers. The security forces sent to Bougainville by the national Government found Kauona a formidable foe. The guerillas succeeded in shutting down the mine in a permanent way on 15 May 1989, through terrorist attacks on mine employees.

Insurgency Begins

Guerilla war came to PNG in the late afternoon of Tuesday 22 November 1988. Few could believe it. Young men armed with knives and axes held up members of a Bougainville copper mine detonation team when they returned unused explosives to the mine magazine. The bunkered magazine was in a cleft running back into the mountains off one of the highest benches rimming the open-cut mine. The guerillas stole more than a hundred kilograms of high explosives and disappeared into the jungle that surrounds the mine pit.

In a co-ordinated operation three nights later, they set fire to six installations around the mine. The Chairman of BCL, Don Carruthers, flew from Melbourne to Port Moresby to speak to Prime Minister Namaliu about what he termed the 'terrorist attacks', a description Mr Namaliu at first rejected. Speaking after the meeting, Mr Carruthers said CRA had a general concern that throughout PNG 'people's expectations of what they are likely to get from mining operations are being raised too much and when these expectations are not satisfied, they turn to violence and crime to draw attention to their problems.'

The following day, Prime Minister Namaliu told parliament that the police had the situation under control. 'Five arrests have been made,' he said. 'The ringleader has also been identified. He is still at large but they are tracking him down with a view to apprehending him.' The ringleader, Francis Ona, was still at large thirteen months later as the 1980s ended. By then, more than fifty people were dead, including three policemen and nine soldiers — and Francis Ona had become a PNG legend.

Back in November 1988, during that parliamentary debate after the first sabotage attacks, the Justice Minister, Bernard Narokobi, foretold what a difficult problem it was going to be for Papua New Guineans to solve. He said their natural sympathy lay with the saboteurs, not the company, despite the huge benefits the nation had received from the mine. Rejecting Opposition criticism of the Government's caution, Mr Narokobi told members not to be hypocritical. 'If we were out there as one of the Panguna men then I am sure we would have done the same thing! Let us not be dishonest!'

To the Justice Minister it was a clash of traditional and modern values. 'The question relates to the interplay between modern law and traditional law. It is one of perception, understanding the modern economy as it relates to the subsistence economy that most of our people subscribe to. I think we are being dishonest and we trick our people by blaming one another. The fact is that the people are dissatisfied with the kind of economy and kind of services they are getting from the mine. It's up to us all to recognise the real role of the landowners and develop laws and policies that satisfy all parties'.

By any third-world criteria, Bougainville Copper Limited was an exemplary corporate citizen of PNG from the day the Bougainville Copper agreement was renegotiated in 1974, the year before Independence, till the mine was knocked out of action by sabotage attack fifteen years later. It had paid a total of more than half a billion Kina (K0.55b — $0.83b) in company tax and K141 million ($211m) in dividends to the national Government. It had paid the landowners K19 million ($28.5m) in compensation for losses and disruption — at higher rates than the restitution stipulated by legislation — and K3 million ($4.5m) in royalties. BCL had paid another K55 million ($83m) in royalties to the provincial Government on Bougainville. It had built two towns, a port and a power station. It provided jobs for 3500 people and had supplied PNG with 45 per cent of its export earnings. More than 17,000 technical certificates had been issued to graduates from the mine's own training college or, under sponsorship by BCL, from technical institutions in other parts of PNG or overseas.

None of these statistics impressed the new Panguna Landowners' Association. The new executive claimed that the landowners had received little benefit. Their level of mistrust of the company was such that the only figure that was real to them was that BCL had removed 1.215 billion tonnes of their land in ore and overburden and turned 99.4 per cent of that into waste. They blamed the company for the extinction of the flying fox and refused to believe a study that showed it had been the victim of an epidemic introduced from East New Britain. They alleged other detrimental side effects of the mining, including retarded crop growth, poisoning of mango, pawpaw and banana trees, disappearance of wild pigs and possums, and ulcerous fish. They rejected expert opinion that said otherwise. BCL, to their minds, was a scourge on the island: 'Our children are born with so many birth defects: deformed hands, legs, nose and whole body. We don't remember this happening so often before. So many people become old so quickly and so many die now. Before, the girls would have developed breasts before they began to menstruate, today the girls are very young when they menstruate.'

There was little basis for communication between the company and the new landowners' executive. BCL had formed a good working relationship with the old executive, all older men. By 1988 the younger people mistrusted and hated these members of the old executive almost as much as they despised the company. The old executive, all land titleholders and village elders, had never been formally elected. The elders had formed the Landowners' Association in 1980 in an attempt to present a united front to the mine management. Its executive, which had changed little since 1980, was virtually self-appointed. Serero, Ona and other members of the new executive were not land titleholders, although they were from the landowning villages. They were classified as beneficiaries. The difference between the two — the 850 title holders and the 5000 or more beneficiaries — caused much resentment.

A major reason for this was the way payments to the landowners were structured. Put simply, there were three sorts of payments each year: royalties; compensation for the loss of land, crops and fish; and social inconvenience payments. The royalties and the various compensation-for-loss payments went directly to the 850 land titleholders. The titleholders then distributed the money, or should have, according to custom to other members of their family group who, although not holders of land title, were classed as beneficiaries. The royalties were set by law at 5 per cent of total royalties (calculated at 1.25 per cent of the mine's sales) and, in 1988, were worth K308,000 ($463,000) while the compensation payments came to K1.14 million ($1.7m). The social inconvenience payments, which amounted to K364,000 ($546,000) in 1988, were paid into a trust, the Roads Mine Tailings Lease (RMTL) Trust Fund. The trust was originally set up to provide for the future well-being of all the landowners by investing in long-term, income-producing assets. But the trust was controlled by the titleholders on the old executive who made up its Board.

Under customary law amongst the Nasioi people in the Kieta

district of Bougainville the land ownership system is matrilineal — that is, the land passes in trust from the mother of the landowning group to the eldest daughter. But when the Australian patrol officers were working out the titleholders in the 1960s, many of those who were actually registered and recognised as titleholders were not the elder sisters who, traditionally and culturally, were supposed to be the caretakers of the land. For instance, Matthew Kove, an uncle of Ona and Serero, was on the old executive as a registered titleholder from Guava village. He signed on behalf of his sister who was the real titleholder but who could not write. Matthew Kove, who had built the finest house in Guava, was abducted by the BRA in early 1989 and killed. One of those patrol officers from the 1960s, Mike Bell, was shot and critically wounded at Panguna in 1989 when he returned briefly as a consultant to BCL.

The new landowners' executive claimed that not only were some of the registered titleholders not the right people but they had become rich by not distributing the money fairly amongst all the landowners. The new executive demanded that the registration system be changed so that all the people in the landowning groups would be classified as landowners. They also alleged that members of the old executive had been bought off by the company and so were not prepared to fight for a better deal. The old executive rejected the allegations and refused to accept as legitimate the public meeting in August 1987. They claimed the new executive could not be representative as four of its eight members were from one village, Guava. The old executive said it represented the legal titleholders. BCL kept dealing with the old executive for many months, partly because they could not find the names of Pepetua Serero, Francis Ona and the others on their lists of registered land titleholders. The older men still controlled the association's money, the RMTL Trust, because under law they were the trust's Board.

The new executive demanded that the company recognise them as the legitimate unit representing the landowners. They received solid support from the provincial Premier, Joseph Kabui. Mr Kabui, from a relocated village near the mine tailings dump, was a landowner himself but he, too, was a beneficiary not a registered titleholder. He committed the provincial Government to backing a court case launched by the new executive. Support also came from Father John Momis, the Catholic priest who was the member for Bougainville in the national parliament and who, in July 1988, had returned to the Decentralisation Ministry when Prime Minister Namaliu named his Cabinet. The powerful Catholic Church on Bougainville also supported the Serero/Ona executive. The company was in a quandary. It took the legalistic view that it could not deal with the new landowners' executive because the old executive still claimed legal legitimacy.

BCL eventually went to the national court, seeking direction as to who should be paid the 1988 inconvenience payments — the RMTL trust controlled by the old executive or some new body. The matter was settled in the Kieta sittings of the national court in mid-1989 without the judge needing to make a direction. By then, the landowners in the lower tailings area did not want anything more to do with the Panguna mine landowners and they sought to set up their own trust fund. All agreed that the lower tailings people who lived down in the Jaba River valley and on the shores of Empress Augusta Bay had the right to break away. The old Panguna landowners' executive accepted the new arrangement and a representative of the new executive, one who was not a guerilla in the jungle, entered no objection. However, by that stage, the dispute had moved well beyond one year's inconvenience payments under the old distribution formula.

Just when the landowners' uprising against the company turned into a war of independence for Bougainville is not clear. Secession had been part of the political agenda in Bougainville since before PNG's Independence. In fact Bougainville had declared its unilateral independence fifteen days before Australia granted Papua New Guinea Independence on 16 September 1975. The first written evidence that secession was part of Francis Ona's plans is a letter dated 10 February 1989, about eleven weeks after he had stormed out of the meeting with the New Zealand environmental consultants and gone into the jungle. Datelined 'BRA Central Command, Camp Hide Out' and written in pidgin, the letter was sent to David Sisito, a prominent Bougainvillian, warning him to watch out for lies of the *'wait mapia'* (white mafia) that had filled the minds of those in the national parliament. Ona claimed that the whiteman's tricks, which he said were part of a 'worldwide set-up', had ruined the PNG national Government. The only way to save Bougainville was to break away — *'bruk lusim Papua New Guinea'*. Ona said he was passionately committed to this cause *'na mi redi long dai long savim ol pipol bilong mi'* (and I am ready to die to save my people).

He signed the letter: 'Mi, Father of Nation, Francis Ona'.

In another letter sent out from his jungle camp in April, Ona said secession was the 'only option' and he 'would only surrender in a coffin'. The book that most influenced Ona and other members of the new Panguna Landowners' Association was a 1972 publication, *River of Tears*, by Richard West, an English environmental journalist. West's book was a critical analysis of the worldwide interests of CRA's British parent, Rio Tinto Zinc (RTZ). It examined RTZ's operations in southern Africa, Britain and Australia and one chapter was devoted to Bougainville, which West visited in 1970 when the copper mine was under construction and again in 1972 when it had just begun production. The theme of the book was that RTZ was a ruthless, exploitative, white supremacist, multinational company determined to get its own way wherever it operated. The chapter on Bougainville slated the Australian administration for allowing Australian businesses to dominate the economic life of PNG and it claimed that the official Australian policy was to encourage 'speculative capitalists' to invest in the colony. Referring to possible self-government (which was granted the following year, 1973), West alleged that Australia was 'unlikely to subsidize Papua and New Guinea without maintaining control of industry, business and agriculture'.

Richard West's book was seen by Ona and Serero as prophetic. West had written in 1972 that the mine 'could bring great profit over the next 20 years to the shareholders of RTZ — at the cost of damage to the physical, social and spiritual well-being of Bougainville'. And he warned of the 'danger that arguments over the ownership of the mine could cause political strife, even civil war'. Members of the BRA wore T-shirts emblazoned with the words *Valley of Tears*. West's book and their own limited observations had convinced the new Landowners' Association executive that RTZ and CRA were out to dominate the world and that PNG was not run by the national Government in Port Moresby but by CRA's local agent, Bougainville Copper Limited. This allegation was made often and Ona repeated it in the April letter. 'This leads us to the root cause,' Ona wrote. 'And it is, of course, that this country is run and administered by BCL.'

To back up this claim, Ona pointed to what he saw as officially sanctioned apartheid. 'There are in this company people in top management who have South African identities and ideologies. This is why on the principles of apartheid, there are two nations in one. White and Black. Facts: Two hospitals, two schools, two drinking clubs, worst of all, two living standards. The Government of PNG is not run to safeguard our lives,' Ona argued, 'but rather to safeguard the few rich leaders and white men. This is why there will never be any peace in PNG. Our leaders are like clouds that fly over the mountains, not knowing where they will turn into rain and eventually disappear.'

The following month, Ona wrote to Prime Minister Namaliu accusing him of taking 'white mafia's advice' and turning guns on the people who were 'fighting for our much needed rights'. He called on Namaliu to withdraw the security forces from Bougainville and give the people of the North Solomons a referendum on independence. He gave the PNG Prime Minister two weeks to meet his demands. 'If you don't want to solve the crisis our way,' Ona threatened, more innocent people would die and 'you will be signing an economic death for your country'. Six days later, on 15 May 1989, the mine shut down when the workers walked off the job following a terrorist raid on a team of labourers cutting grass. All efforts to reopen the mine in 1989 were thwarted by terror attacks on mine employees and sabotage of the essential powerline. Pepetua Serero's health, fragile before the crisis, deteriorated and she died in June after a severe asthma attack.

Serero, like Ona, had been convinced that the people were being lied to constantly by white men. Speaking in her village in November 1988 she regularly returned to the theme, saying: 'We do not trust any white men.' As the more radical landowners saw a gigantic hole deepening daily where their land had once been, their sense of grievance became bitterness and then outrage when all around they could see people they considered intruders living a luxurious life. The houses the company built for its expatriate workers and senior PNG staff were hardly palaces. They were comfortable, wooden, tropical homes similar to those in suburban Townsville or Cairns. But compared with a village hut or a corrugated iron shack, they might have seemed palatial. The people from the relocated villages were angry that the company did not build them fine homes in the same style. 'They are worse than squatter camps,' Serero had complained in an interview when referring to the relocated villages. 'This resettlement scheme has made my people nomadic. Where before the coming of the company my people were used to staying in permanent, ancestorial villages, now the company has made my people nomads.'

Ona's allegation that there were two hospitals, two schools and two drinking clubs needs explanation. There were two hospitals: the Arawa base hospital run by PNG's Health Department and a private hospital, the Arawa Medical Clinic, run by the North Solomons Medical Foundation and owned by the Bougainville Copper Foundation, a philanthropic trust set up by BCL. The Medical Clinic catered for those who could pay for private medical care which, of course, tended to be the expatriates and the better paid Papua New Guineans. Similarly, the two schools did not actively promote discrimination. Throughout PNG there is a network of what are called International Schools charging high student fees and teaching a New South Wales curriculum. The system dates from before Independence, when the Australian Government funded what were then called 'A Schools' to cater for the children of expatriates working in PNG. Post-Independence, the PNG Government withdrew direct funding. But the schools have continued to flourish because the Government and companies such as BCL subsidise, as a condition of employment, the fees of the children of expatriates on contract so that their children can receive an Australian-standard education.

While some companies also pay International School fees for the children of their senior Papua New Guinean workers, many PNG parents pay the high fees themselves to give their children what they see as the advantage of a higher standard education than that available in the PNG education system. Despite the expense, more than half of the students attending international schools in PNG are Papua New Guineans. But the option is just not available for PNG families who are not part of the elite. And that included many of the Panguna landowners, especially those who were beneficiaries, not titleholders.

The white/black division on Bougainville was perhaps more noticeable than almost anywhere else in PNG because of the nature of the Bougainville mine. BCL totally dominated the economy of the island. It ran an enclave mining operation that had minimal links with the rest of the economy and was well away from the mainland. Ships delivered supplies and took away concentrate without calling in at any other ports in PNG. In this insulated setting BCL was the largest single employer of expatriate labour in PNG, excepting the national Government itself. In 1988, the expatriate workforce was 610 out of 3560 — seventeen per cent. Most of the expatriate employees, who were predominantly Australian, had their families with them. The Australian High Commission in early 1989 estimated that the Australian population of the North Solomons province was five thousand.

There were in fact two drinking clubs in Arawa, but there was no 'whites only' rule. The Arawa Country Club, which had golf links and tennis courts, tended to be where the expatriates socialised while the Nafig Club attracted more Papua New Guineans. Up at the mine itself in Panguna, the drinking club — known as the Cricket Club — was noticeably multi-racial, with a working-man's-club atmosphere. But down on the coast, at Arawa, there was a distinct genteel atmosphere about the Country Club, marking it out as the socialising centre for the expatriate population. When the Nafig Club was taken over during the State of Emergency to become the joint security forces headquarters while the Country Club remained in the hands of its mostly expatriate members, there were rumblings of discontent amongst the PNG community.

The Deputy Controller of the State of Emergency, Colonel Lima Dotaona, did attempt to turn the Country Club into a care centre for displaced village people. The white membership was outraged. The homes of the displaced Bougainvillian villagers had been burnt down by the security forces and they had nowhere to live. But the 'two lifestyles' syndrome was well summed up by one club member who protested at the threatened closure: 'We've put up with trouble for eight months. Why should we miss out on our only source of recreation?' In agreeing that the closure of the Arawa Country Club could mark the end of the old, comfortable, expatriate lifestyle, he speculated on what the club might become: 'It appears that if it's not going to be a concentration camp it will definitely be a camp for the people who have been moved out of the villages. We understand the police have burnt the villages down anyway. So now the expatriates have to suffer!'

The attitudes amongst some expatriates on Bougainville were reminiscent of what used to be heard in the Boroko RSL club in Port Moresby in 1974 prior to Independence. Because BCL was so big, because it employed so many expatriates and despite its excellent training program for Papua New Guineans, it had never taken on a Papua New Guinean identity. The upper management was still

Australian, still expatriate. That is still true of a number of companies in Port Moresby and Lae but none of these companies employs so many expatriate people and none of them absolutely dominates the economy of its area in the way that BCL dominated Bougainville. To be onside with BCL in Bougainville meant business would be prosperous. A large number of expatriates worked for companies that depended on the mine. The landowners were angry, too, that they had no companies to take advantage of these contracts. The activities of the philanthropic Bougainville Copper Foundation, which owned the supermarkets in Arawa and Panguna, stores in other centres and a substantial piggery and chicken farm at Mananau in the Jaba River Valley, also engendered resentment.

BCL admits that it could have handled its relationships with the landowners better. The company at the upper levels lost touch with the village people. Don Vernon, BCL's top executive in the late 1970s, devoted much effort to maintaining links with village elders. He occasionally loaded a carton of beer into his four-wheel-drive vehicle and headed off into the villages for a chat. His deputy and successor, Paul Quodling, had a thorough understanding of local issues, but Quodling's retirement left a vacuum. The managing director who took over in 1987, Bob Cornelius, was a mining engineer and a straight-dealing, hard-working man who ran a super-efficient mine. But Mr Cornelius and some of his senior Australian executives, all technically expert men, had a limited experience of Papua New Guinea. They relied on their senior Bougainvillian staff to keep them informed on village matters. In late 1988 the top men at BCL were questioning where Francis Ona was born, suggesting that his home village was well to the south of the mine when in fact it was on a ridge above the open-cut pit.

While the theory of relying on senior Bougainvillian staff in matters relating to village liaison would seem to make perfect sense, the problem was more complex. Any Bougainvillian who had done really well with the company and had risen to a senior management job was referred to, by the landowning village people, as a coconut — dark on the outside but white inside. Nobody in top management was a landowner. The only Bougainvillian or Papua New Guinean amongst the seven general managers was Joe Auna, GM Personnel. But Mr Auna is from Buin in the south of Bougainville. This lack of a landowner in senior management was not policy. One reason no landowner rose to that level was that there was so much disregard for the mine amongst the younger landowners that a top company job was no desired objective. Anybody who reached the upper levels would become ostracised by his own people. Some of those close to Mr Cornelius argue that the Don Vernon approach of the late 1970s was no longer appropriate in the late 1980s because the village elders had lost their influence and the new executive consisted entirely of angry, younger people.

The company may have had its faults but it could never be accused of flouting the law or breaching any of the conditions of its agreement with the national Government. The Bougainville Copper agreement of 1974, which set a new standard for developing countries in their dealings with multinationals, provided for reviews every seven years. When the first review came due in 1981 the company was prepared for negotiations all year. But the national Government led by Sir Julius Chan could not agree on a uniform approach. There were deep divisions within the Chan Government on economic issues and the Decentralisation Minister, Father Momis, and the Deputy Prime Minister, Iambakey Okuk, were in constant feud. Father Momis was also at odds with the provincial Government led by Leo Hannett. So the opportunity to alter the agreement in 1981 passed. The second seven-year review should have been in 1988. Again, BCL was ready to negotiate but, again, the national Government seemed preoccupied. It was not until after the sabotage attacks of late November to early December that Prime Minister Namaliu announced his negotiating team to start preparing the national Government's case. The 1974 agreement was still in place when the mine shut down in May 1989.

Once the magnitude of the troubles on Bougainville was brought to its attention, the national Government admitted that it and its predecessors were responsible for 'long-term neglect'. When Mr Namaliu's government took power in mid-1988, it announced plans to involve landowners more in mineral development projects. But the legacy of fourteen years of neglect meant that its word was not trusted by the Panguna landowners. Any government in PNG faces enormous demands for development from the country's 3.8 million people. There are so many calls for roads, bridges, schools and hospitals that the Government has tended to abdicate its responsibility for government services in areas that have major 'development' projects under way. BCL spent big and the areas around the mine were considered prosperous. Although the national

Government was earning large sums of money from the mine, large-scale government capital works projects went to other 'less developed' provinces. A similar attitude prevailed at the provincial level. The North Solomons Government tended to concentrate its efforts on providing services to the more remote parts of Bougainville because Panguna was relatively well serviced. However, the landowners did not see any justice in this.

The company's relationships with the North Solomons provincial Government withered in the late 1980s. Part of the reason was the emergence of Mr Kabui as premier. Premier Kabui, a landowner, was very critical of the company. But another factor was the departure from the island for post-graduate studies in Hawaii of one of the sharpest Bougainvillians in the provincial government, Melchior Togolo. Mr Togolo had been provincial secretary and had established excellent relations with people on all sides. Married to a European, Togolo provided an invaluable network of informal linkages on a social as well as a work level between the provincial Government and BCL. When he accepted an offer to do higher-degree studies at the East West Centre in Hawaii and was away for a crucial eighteen months, these links were broken. The events of late 1988 may not have run so far out of control if it had not been for a range of almost incidental factors such as this that contributed to a breakdown of confidence and trust between the company and provincial authorities.

Jungle War

The machine-gun hammers away. It shatters the morning quiet. Bullets tear through the foliage 150 metres away on the other shoulder of the saddle-shaped ridge. One soldier claims he can see the entrance to a rebel tunnel. Two others crouch and fire their grenade launchers. The first shot is off-target but the second lobs into the suspected cave entrance and explodes with a thump. The patrol has been in the Bougainville jungle for seven days. They have no prisoners.

The soldiers file up on to Guava Ridge, where there is a network of shallow trenches. These overlook the mine pit and were used by the BRA a few weeks earlier in one of the few confrontations of the campaign that was anything like a pitched battle. Soldiers from 'A' company had taken the ridge after six hours.

The patrol waits on the 'captured' ridge for a helicopter to lift them back to the temporary camp at the Panguna International Primary School, which has been converted into an army base. Major Gerry Singarok, operations officer at Panguna, is pleased with the progress his men have made over the previous few weeks. He believes that they have seized the initiative from the rebels for the first time since the whole start/stop operation began months before: 'We have really pushed into the strongholds. We have neutralised three already. We have them running. We are on the offensive.' It is late July 1989.

Two weeks later the soldiers are pulled back from the jungle and told to guard the mine and other installations. The government in Port Moresby has decided that the rebels have been hit hard and it is time for a new peace initiative.

The Minister for Decentralisation in the Namaliu government, Father John Momis, had been a critic of BCL since the late 1960s. Momis was amongst the most articulate Bougainvillians to have opposed the mine from the start. In 1971 he had written that 'it is the tragedy of the Nasioi that the economic benefits (of the mine) are not distributed in the same manner as the social costs'. During the 1987 PNG national elections, Father Momis launched what he called 'The Bougainville Initiative', which proposed a three per cent levy on the mine's total sales to go directly to the North Solomons province. He claimed that BCL had behaved like a 'wild pig'. In an election statement titled 'The Wild Pig Cannot Now Hide from the People', Father Momis said BCL had to respond to the demands by his political party, the Melanesian Alliance. 'The wild pig has rooted up the crops in the villagers' gardens', the statement read. 'It cannot now hide from the people. . . . BCL must tell us exactly how many of its senior staff above foreman level are nationals. It must tell us what it will do to restore the dignity of the people who have been reduced to passive dependence.'

Father Momis was a leader of the first Bougainville secession attempt in 1975. He entered politics in the 1972 elections, campaigning against the way the Australian administration had disregarded local sensitivities in allowing CRA to open the mine. He won overwhelmingly against the pro-administration sitting member for Bougainville, Joseph Lue. Chief Minister Somare gave Father

Momis the task of heading the committee drawing up the national Constitution. One of the major recommendations of Momis's constitutional planning committee was provincial government for each of PNG's nineteen provinces. Bougainville was the first to be granted interim provincial government on 27 November 1973, just a few days before PNG's self-government. This concession was in recognition of the Bougainville people's own belief in their special identity and followed a concerted campaign by Bougainvillians for guarantees of a large measure of local control if they were to be citizens of an independent Papua New Guinea.

In early 1974 BCL announced a huge profit for 1973 — its first full year of production — of more than $156 million. But it paid no tax! Under the mining agreement signed in 1967 the Australian Government granted CRA a generous profit-sharing arrangement under which BCL kept the bulk of early earnings via a three-year tax holiday. The size of the untaxed 1973 profit caused outrage in PNG and on Bougainville. Somare put high priority on a renegotiation of the Bougainville Copper agreement. When those talks were about to enter their fourth round later in the year BCL announced its profit for the first six months of 1974 — $118 miilion, again untaxed. Somare warned CRA that unless it started taking the renegotiation talks seriously, his government would legislate to get what it wanted. In October Mr Somare and the General Manager of BCL, Frank Espie, signed a new Bougainville Copper agreement which was widely hailed as a model for third-world countries. It removed BCL's tax concessions and introduced an innovative resources rent tax as well as tightening environmental protection measures. It gave the PNG Government an extra $55 million in 1974 alone.

On Bougainville news of the big jump in earnings for the central Government brought demands that more money be directed to the interim provincial Government. In particular, the province's leaders wanted the royalties (or rather the ninety-five per cent of royalties that did not go to the landowners). The fledgling Somare Government's problems on Bougainville were not confined to battling with a multinational and with a secessionist-minded population. There was a third restless element — the workforce at the Panguna mine. The workforce was predominantly non-Bougainvillian Papua New Guineans — 'redskins'. And in the wake of the huge profits, the miners, too, wanted a greater share. On 13 May 1975, a thousand striking workers at Panguna rioted. The Government sent three police riot squads to Bougainville to try to contain the rioters. Twelve busloads of wives and children were evacuated.

The miners eventually returned to work but the talks between the central Government and the interim provincial Government over its demands for a greater share of the money for Bougainville deadlocked. The central Government refused to budge on the question of royalties, arguing that the whole country should benefit from mining ventures, not one area. The Bougainvillians argued that they were the ones suffering the ill-effects, so they should get special attention. On 30 May 1975, the provincial assembly voted to secede. The assembly, then an appointed not an elected body, was chaired by the District Commissioner, Alexis Sarei. Somare had appointed Dr Sarei to the district commissioner's job from his own staff. But Sarei, a Bougainvillian, felt his loyalties were with Bougainville and he became a leader of the secession movement. The initial reaction from Port Moresby was that the 'secession' motion was just a tactic. But the Bougainville provincial planner, Leo Hannett, told PNG's National Broadcasting Commission: 'There is no alternative. The issue is now non-negotiable.' Momis, Sarei and Hannett — a Catholic priest, a former Catholic priest and a former trainee Catholic priest respectively — formed the core of the secessionist leadership.

Peace talks arranged for Port Moresby on 12 June 1975 lasted fifty-five minutes. The secessionists walked out. In late July, further talks between the secessionists and the Somare Government broke down. Somare's reaction was to get the House of Assembly, then meeting as the Constituent Assembly and debating the proposed PNG Constitution, to chop provincial government out of the Constitution altogether. The Bougainville secessionists proclaimed Independence on 1 September. Before a crowd of five thousand, a Bougainvillian village woman 'symbolising motherhood and birth' raised the flag of the Republic of North Solomons at the Arawa town market. Dr Sarei, who became the Republic's interim president, said the Panguna mine would be closed as an 'ultimate tactic' if necessary. Seventy-five per cent of Bougainvillians are Catholics and the Bishop of Bougainville, Bishop Gregory Singkai, who led a religious service at the flag raising, stated that his church was fully committed to the secession movement. From New York where he had gone to seek support in the United Nations for an independent

Bougainville, Father Momis sent a telegram to the Speaker of the PNG House of Assembly, resigning his seat. His UN mission was a bitter disappointment. Momis had hoped for sympathy from the African countries, especially Tanzania and Zambia, but he found them the least sympathetic.

PNG gained Independence on 16 September 1975. At first the new Independent State of Papua New Guinea took no action against the Bougainville secessionists. The national Government continued to pay public servants and to keep basic services running. But a month later, in mid-October, the Acting Prime Minister, Sir Maori Kiki, suspended the interim provincial Government and appointed a trust to determine spending priorities on Bougainville. Three thousand Bougainvillians marched in protest, but despite an ugly and explosive situation on the island an uneasy truce followed for some months. Various attempts to arrange talks failed. In January 1976 secessionists rampaged. They severed all communications for a day or two, damaged government installations in four centres and blocked two airfields.

Somare ordered police riot squads to Bougainville. But although pressure mounted on him to send in the troops, Somare refused. Instead, he issued orders to the police to avoid major confrontations if possible. And he telegrammed an appeal to the secessionist leaders: 'Do not fail Bougainville, do not fail Papua New Guinea.' Word came from Buin in the south of Bougainville that secessionists had stolen 2500 sticks of dynamite. Somare rang the secessionist leadership and, to the surprise of many, arranged a fragile truce as a prelude to talks. He flew to Bougainville in February. Negotiations began. In April, they were on the verge of collapsing when Momis and Sarei heard Somare say on national radio that Bougainville would have provincial government but it would remain within PNG. In July law and order broke down in the Buin area and all central government services to the southern part of the island were suspended. Government officers, including seventeen high school teachers, withdrew and the Buin High School shut down.

Eventually, on the weekend of 7-8 August 1976, after eleven months and a week, Bougainville's first secession attempt was over. Somare and the secessionist leaders signed a pact that kept Bougainville within the new nation. The price was the writing back into the Constitution of provincial government. Prime Minister Somare justifiably took great pride in this settlement. In parliament he said:

'Mr Speaker, members will recall that the last time I spoke on the Bougainville question I said: "While the rest of the twentieth century is impatient, violent and insensitive, we are building a nation prepared to be patient and determined to peacefully resolve our differences." . . . In Papua New Guinea our ability to seek compromise, and our patience to seek peaceful solutions is something we can show the rest of the world with pride. . . . I believe we have shown this twentieth-century world what nationhood really means, within the first year of our Independence.'

The comradeship between those early secessionist leaders did not last. Father Momis stood for the 1977 national elections and was returned comfortably. His supporters took the other three Bougainville seats, one of them from Sir Paul Lapun, a senior Pangu Pati minister. In the 1960s Lapun had been the first elected politician to champion the rights of the Panguna landowners. Despite opposition from the Australian administration-appointed members of the 1964-68 House of Assembly, Sir Paul successfully moved a Bill giving the landowners five per cent of BCL's royalty payments. The administration had argued that landowners did not have any rights to minerals. But, although he had been in favour of secession himself in the early 1970s, Lapun had remained loyal to Somare as a Pangu minister during the 1975 crisis. That killed his political career. Sarei and Hannett were soon opponents and Hannett defeated Sarei for the premiership in the late 1970s. Hannett and Momis had a big falling out. In the mid-1980s Sarei stood for Premier again and he defeated Hannett. In 1987 Sarei stood down from the premiership to contest the national elections against Momis. Father Momis polled a huge seventy-one per cent of the vote to Sarei's eighteen per cent. The new Premier was Joseph Kabui, a member of Father Momis's Melanesian Alliance party.

The role of Premier Kabui in the events of 1988-89 illustrates the complexity of the Bougainville problem. As noted, Kabui was a landowner. Thirty-five years old, about the same age as Francis Ona, he grew up with many of the same concerns and resentments. He told the *Times of PNG* in March 1989 that as a youth he witnessed the discrimination of the 'colonial mastas'. 'I saw how my people were mistreated by the whites. I saw the discrimination and arrogant attitudes of these foreigners, the damage done to my people by the war and I saw the hatred and discrimination that took place during the final term of the colonial reign in this province. I saw the suffering of my people, including my parents who had to struggle to protect our lands and our communities, and I also saw the numerous takeovers of land by foreigners.' Mr Kabui, like so many other political leaders from Bougainville, trained to be a Catholic priest. After more than eight years of religious training, he decided in mid-1978 that the priesthood was not for him. He still goes to Catholic mass every morning.

As premier, Mr Kabui was also chairman of the provincial Peace and Good Order committee. The provinces in PNG do not have their own police forces. Under the Constitution there is just the one national police force (and one prisons service) and the purpose of having nineteen provincial Peace and Good Order committees is to maintain liaison between the executive arm of the provincial government and the national Government's law and order agencies. Serving on the committee is the province's senior policeman, the provincial police commander. Peace and Good Order committees have certain powers, such as the authority to declare fighting zones if there is an outbreak of trouble in a particular area. However, in the North Solomons in the days following the first sabotage raids on the Bougainville mine, Premier Kabui was openly sympathetic to the cause of the saboteurs. He was quoted on the National Broadcasting Commission on 30 November as saying that in Bougainville 'there was silent support for the Panguna Landowners' Association's action to destroy property at the mine site'.

In December 1988 Father Momis and Mr Kabui arranged talks between Francis Ona and a national government delegation sent to Bougainville by Prime Minister Namaliu and headed by the Deputy Prime Minister, Akoka Doi. The national government delegation spent three days waiting for the meeting to occur and when it did, near Guava village, Francis Ona smashed the camera of a senior public servant who tried to photograph him standing with Mr Doi. That night Premier Kabui hosted a function at the Arovo Island resort near Kieta for Mr Doi and some of the landowner representatives and he described Francis Ona in an official speech as 'a contemporary hero' of Bougainville. This infuriated the police, whose numbers had been boosted by riot squads flown in under Prime Minister Namaliu's instructions to 'restore law and order'. Fourteen landowner representatives were arrested by the police on their way home from Premier Kabui's function in the early hours of the next morning and thrown into the police lockup.

Premier Kabui held a number of secret meetings with Francis Ona in the jungle over the following few months. In an interview the day after one of these meetings in March 1989, Mr Kabui said Ona was not a criminal. 'Francis is very happy with the way things have gone,' he said. 'I have kept Francis informed of the correspondence I've had with the national Government.' Explaining away the damage done to the mine, Premier Kabui said that was just a tactic to attract the attention of the world. Asked if he found himself in a peculiar position as chairman of the Peace and Good Order committee meeting with Ona in the bush when the police wanted to capture Ona for breaking the law, Premier Kabui replied: 'I think I am in a difficult position. But again, I see my role as a person who knows the underlying motives and the reasons and how deep the whole problem has gone.' Shortly before this clandestine meeting, Prime Minister Namaliu had announced that the landowners would get a four-fold increase in their royalty payments. Mr Kabui said Ona was pleased with that. 'When I met up with him on Saturday, he was very happy and he admitted that we have come a long way now. "What I wanted to achieve by doing what I have, you know, I'm achieving it." And we are getting there,' Mr Kabui concluded.

These secret meetings between the Premier and would-be 'Father of the (Bougainville) Nation' ceased shortly afterwards. Mr Kabui himself became a target for rebel harassment after speaking out against secession. He claimed that his life was threatened. No one could doubt the seriousness of the threat when his Minister for Commerce and Liquor Licensing, John Bika, was assassinated by the BRA in September 1989. But the police never trusted Mr Kabui. And in July 1989 he was assaulted by riot squad police who tried to force him to lick the spilt blood of a policeman who had been seriously injured by a shotgun blast in a BRA ambush. After taking their wounded colleague to hospital, the policemen set out looking for the Premier. They found him outside a canteen at the Arawa Technical College. It was a Sunday morning and Mrs Kabui and two of their children were with the Premier in his official vehicle. The police smashed the windscreen and deflated the tyres. They then took the Premier to the police vehicle that had been shot up in the rebel ambush and demanded that Mr Kabui lick the bloodstains for what 'his people' had done. When he refused they kicked and punched him. His provincial Primary Industry Minister, Michael

Laimo, was also attacked and he lost the sight of one of his eyes when a policeman poked them with a rifle barrel.

Father Momis also had a confrontation with the riot police, at his Port Moresby home. The police on Bougainville considered they were being thwarted in their efforts at capturing the BRA by the influence of Father Momis's party, the Melanesian Alliance, both at the provincial level and in the national Cabinet. The Police Commissioner, Paul Tohian, went public with the police complaints in early March 1989, saying that he was 'fed up with political interference and indecisiveness' and that negotiations with Ona were not going to work. Father Momis called for Mr Tohian's sacking. The next morning there was a knock on his door. 'I was confronted by a group of policemen,' Father Momis says. 'They demanded an apology from me and also stated that the Government should, or I should, think twice about sacking the Commissioner. At the entrance to my house there was a police truck, I think, and about ninety to a hundred policemen.' The policemen were from the riot squad and were led to Father Momis's house by the head of the Police Special Services Unit, Chief Superintendent Gabi Baki. The Chief Superintendent was temporarily suspended.

The confusion over just what the national Government expected the police to do when faced with a landowner uprising was obvious from the start. When Prime Minister Namaliu sent his Deputy Prime Minister, Akoka Doi, to Bougainville in early December 1988, heading what Mr Namaliu described as his team of 'ministerial trouble shooters', the Police Commissioner was barred from attending the crucial meeting at Guava village with Francis Ona. Commissioner Tohian was accompanying the national government team but the politicians felt Ona might not meet them if a policeman was present. So Mr Tohian spent the day on the coast while the politicians and other public servants visited Guava. At that meeting Mr Doi gave the rebel landowners an assurance that police would be confined to protecting the towns and the mine. However, the police were not a party to this undertaking. The following Sunday morning at dawn, acting on what they said were directions from the Prime Minister to restore law and order, police squads raided four landowners' villages including Guava 'in an attempt to recover stolen explosives and arrest saboteurs'. No explosives were found but police confiscated electrical goods worth several thousand Kina which they 'suspected' had been stolen.

The situation of Bougainville deteriorated in March 1989, with a series of ethnic killings. A Bougainvillian nurse and mother was murdered with a long-bladed knife when she was working in her village food garden near Aropa plantation adjacent to the island's main airport. In payback killings, Bougainvillians from the self-proclaimed 'tornado force' of the BRA shot dead three labourers from the PNG mainland in their living quarters on the plantation. The terminal at Aropa airport was burnt down at night and an aircraft wrecked by fire. The killing of the plantation labourers led to retaliation by Highlanders, who smashed up the Arawa supermarket, one of the largest in the whole of PNG. As the situation worsened, Prime Minister Namaliu sent in the troops. The troops had orders to penetrate the jungle and capture Ona and his men. Within a fortnight, two soldiers had been killed in a BRA ambush.

Killings continued. The soldiers felt hampered by legal limitations on their powers because no state of emergency had been declared. That did not happen until 26 June, and then only after further BRA activity had shut the mine and kept it closed for more than a month. In the meantime, Prime Minister Namaliu had declared a fifteen-day truce, during which he appealed to the Catholic Bishop of Bougainville, Bishop Gregory Singkai, to act as an 'independent' intermediary. Bishop Singkai met with Ona but Ona stuck to his original demands for K10 billion ($15b) compensation and a referendum on secession. Mr Namaliu declared a series of unilateral truces during 1989 in an effort to get Ona to negotiate. In the opinion of the military and the police the truces were one-sided and simply gave the BRA time to regroup.

As early as April 1989 Prime Minister Namaliu's government proposed a package of peace proposals that Mr Namaliu hoped would solve the crisis. The package provided for a substantial improvement in the money and benefits flowing to the landowners and the provincial government alike. For the landowners, the package broke down into five components. First, royalty payments would increase four-fold — up to K1.2million ($1.8m) a year based on BCL's 1988 results. Second, there would be higher rates of compensation for land, tree and crop damage and also for disruption. Third, the landowners would be given five per cent equity in BCL to come from the national Government's twenty per cent. Fourth, the Government would undertake a series of public works programs to improve life in their villages. And fifth, the Bougainville Copper agreement would be amended to ensure that the landowners were given preference in business spin-off contracts from the mine. The provincial Government would lose some royalties to the landowners but these would be more than compensated by a special yearly grant from consolidated revenue equivalent to one per cent of the mine's gross sales. It, too, would get five per cent of BCL's shares and a K200 million ($300m) development program over five years for the building of roads, schools and health facilities.

Premier Kabui was delighted with this package and took it back to Bougainville in late April 1989, following talks in Port Moresby, confident it would win support from a majority of landowners. The reaction from some of the landowners was that, while they were happy to hear what the national Government was prepared to do, they demanded a like offer from BCL. Francis Ona's response was to reject the package as a trick and demand the withdrawal of the security forces, the continued closure of the mine and a referendum on secession.

By September 1989, not only had the national government improved its package but BCL had announced its own proposals worth K40 million ($60m) to improve conditions for the landowners. Announcing the details on 8 September, PNG's Finance Minister, Paul Pora, said the national Government would spend K5 million ($7.5m) within three months on welfare projects in the landowning villages and give the provincial government an additional grant of K4 million ($6m). He said the national Government would have to accept tax losses of about K20 million ($30m) as a result of BCL's planned spending of K40 million on additional benefits for landowners. He estimated that the BCL shares that the landowners and the provincial government would receive free were worth K40 million ($60m). He said that on average each of the 850 titleholders would get equity in the mine worth K47,000 ($70,500). 'The price of peace,' Mr Pora said, 'does not come cheaply in the North Solomons province.'

But Francis Ona and Sam Kauona were not interested in peace. The condition the national Government set on its 'peace package' was that the mine resume production without interference. Ona wanted the mine to stay shut. A date was set for the signing of Mr Namaliu's 'peace package' in Port Moresby. A number of landowners indicated their willingness to sign, as did the provincial Government. A day before the Bougainville delegation was to have flown to the national capital, one of the proposed signatories, the North Solomons provincial Minister for Commerce and Liquor Licensing, John Bika, was assassinated by the BRA. The ceremony was postponed indefinitely.

Bika Assassinated

The Bougainville Revolutionary Army assassination squad burst through the front and back doors of John Bika's home in the dark hours of the morning of 11 September 1989. They shot him dead in front of his wife and young children. Then, running from the house past hibiscus bushes, they crossed the bitumen Kieta-Aropa airport road and escaped along the beach.

Bika, the North Solomons Commerce and Liquor Licensing Minister, had headed a provincial committee that rejected secession. Instead, it proposed statehood for Bougainville, with strengthened autonomous powers. The BRA's military commander, ex-Lieutenant Kauona, claimed that the BRA did not kill 'innocent' people, only those he called 'betrayers'.

Students from the assassinated minister's old school, Marist Brothers' High, Rigu, lined the path to the Catholic cathedral as Bika's body was carried to the service on the back of a Bougainville Copper Limited truck. Above hovered one of the Australian-donated PNG Defence Force Iroquois helicopters.

Inside the cathedral, mourners blanketed the coffin with flowers. Bika's wife had to be helped back to her pew, sobbing uncontrollably. The Catholic Bishop of Bougainville, Bishop Gregory Singkai, said in his short sermon that Bika had been to Sunday mass only hours before his death. But the bishop did not single out the BRA for blame. He simply said: 'Those who hated him, killed him.'

For the national Government the Bougainville crisis lurched from one disappointment to the next. Prime Minister Namaliu tried hard to find a solution but his foe would not negotiate. Mr Namaliu did not visit Bougainville until more than nine months after the troubles began. And then it was for a peace ceremony that Francis Ona boycotted. Namaliu's Cabinet was far from united on the best way to deal with the crisis. Father Momis and his fellow Melanesian

Alliance ministers, the Minerals and Energy Minister, Patterson Lowa, and the Justice Minister, Bernard Narokobi, were appalled at some Cabinet decisions, such as putting a price of K200,000 ($300,000) on Francis Ona's head. That 'reward' was fully supported by the Minister for State, and former Defence Force Commander, Ted Diro, who strongly advocated a military solution to the problem.

In a message to the Deputy Controller of the state of emergency, Colonel Lima Dotaona, in late September 1989, after the assassination of John Bika, Mr Diro said Cabinet had decided to give the Colonel 'freedom of military action' to bring about an end to BRA activities. 'The Government now wishes the security forces to take tougher measures,' Mr Diro said, and it appreciated that 'a state of insurgency exists in the North Solomons'. He said the ministerial committee on the Bougainville crisis, consisting of the ministers for Police, Defence, Correctional Services and himself as minister for State and chairman, recommended 'greater dispersion in troop deployment' and 'greater security of pylons, e.g. electrification, booby traps, landmines, patrolling, etc.' Mr Diro ended the message: 'Good Luck. Happy soldiering!' Shortly afterwards, two soldiers died in booby-trap explosions.

Mr Namaliu appointed a number of committees to work on the problem. The first, headed by Deputy Prime Minister, Akoka Doi, failed to achieve anything even though it was the only group actually to speak to Francis Ona. Another committee, set up following the outburst of ethnic violence in March and headed by the member for Rabaul, John Kaputin, took months to present its report. In the meantime, Mr Kaputin became one of the harshest critics of the Prime Minister's approach. Yet another committee wanting to be involved was the parliamentary committee on states of emergency headed by Sir Hugo Berghuser, a naturalised citizen of German extraction. Berghuser, whose committee had the job of ensuring the emergency powers were not abused, believed the major need on Bougainville was for an internment law allowing the authorities to jail anyone without trial for an indefinite period.

The Prime Minister had also appointed, as his personal adviser on Bougainville, Leo Hannett, the former North Solomons premier, by then an implacable opponent of Father Momis. There was no shortage of advice. But most of it conflicted. The situation slid further and further beyond any rational settlement. And relations with the village people on Bougainville were not helped by the occasional propaganda fiasco. In April 1989 the Defence Minister, Arnold Marsipal, appeared in a large photo on the front of both of PNG's national daily newspapers brandishing an automatic weapon and saying 'his' soldiers on Bougainville had orders to 'shoot to kill'.

A major embarrassment for the PNG Government was lack of discipline in the disciplined forces. Allegations of human rights abuses streamed out of Bougainville. One early accusation of brutality concerned the death of a youth, aged eighteen, from Pakia village on the port mine access road. Clement Kavuna was arrested by riot police in March, 1989, for allegedly throwing stones at passing police vehicles. He was later admitted to hospital with severe head injuries and died. The people of Pakia village claimed Clement had been kicked by policemen standing over him in the tray of a police vehicle travelling at high speed and that he had fallen to the road as a result of the kicking. The police countered saying Clement had leapt from the vehicle when trying to escape.

The Bougainville division of the Catholic commission for justice and peace detailed a large number of allegations of human rights abuses against both the military and the riot police. The following was typical: 'Dominic Itta, Steven Miringtore, Steven Noidau and Ephraim Tampari who were on their way to work on the 10th of April, 1989, were stopped by about fifty police and army personnel at gunpoint. They were removed from their car and beaten with gun butts and sticks. When they arrived at the Arawa police station they were beaten to the floor with punches, kicks and gun butts. During the beatings they were called "black bastards", "bigheads" and "pigs". They were bleeding from the head, nose and mouth. Dominic was also beaten with a wooden mallet. The police said they were lucky that they were taken by the soldiers as the police would have shot them and left them to stink in the bush. . . . Eventually they were allowed to go free as there were no charges.'

The national Government made various attempts through 1989 to investigate these allegations of human rights abuses. The Police Minister, Mathias Ijape, announced in late April, for instance, that more than twenty policemen involved in the North Solomons operation had been transferred out of the province and dealt with under the disciplinary provisions of the Police Force Act. Mr Ijape said some of the disciplined police had lost one month's pay and some had been charged with serious disciplinary offences and they would be either demoted or dismissed from the force. 'I would like to make it clear,' Mr Ijape said, 'that in any major operation anywhere in the world where there has been a large number of servicemen involved, there have been similar problems.' Prime Minister Namaliu also ordered the Public Solicitors office to set up a bureau in Bougainville to follow up complaints of police and soldier brutality.

In June the Prime Minister ordered both the Police Commissioner and the Acting Defence Force Commander to Bougainville to assume direct control of the security forces. He was 'deeply concerned at reports of serious incidents involving a minority of the security force members', he said. Mr Namaliu said that rebel activity over the previous weekend when both police and soldiers were wounded 'undoubtedly created tensions in the disciplined forces. However, that is not a justification for any member of the disciplined forces to behave in an undisciplined way outside the law.' Mr Namaliu said he was greatly concerned that public confidence in the security forces might have already been seriously undermined 'by the disgraceful actions of a minority'.

The police and the soldiers were regularly being shot at in BRA ambushes and they suffered large casualties and enormous frustrations. They found the Bougainvillian population unco-operative. One senior policeman, drunk, shot a hole through the roof of his police vehicle. Another shot a hole in his hotel-room wall when cleaning a gun. One soldier was shot dead and another critically wounded at a military roadblock. The official version of the incident said the two soldiers were both off duty and were travelling in a civilian vehicle with a non-soldier. 'When approaching a roadblock manned by "A" company 2RPIR and Mobile Squad 11 the vehicle carrying the two off-duty soldiers and the civilian failed to stop.' Warning shots were fired. 'When the vehicle drove off at high speed, the security forces became suspicious and fired at it, wounding the two soldiers. One of them died on the way to hospital. . . . Cartons of beer were found in the vehicle.' The roadblock was outside the Kobuan camp where earlier that evening four prison guards had been shot and wounded by the BRA.

The police believed that they were not getting sufficient support from the politicians or the Police Department bureaucrats in Port Moresby and this sapped morale. In September, when thirty-eight police promotions were announced, Superintendent Tony Wagambie, who was head of the police operation on Bougainville, went public with the frustrations of his men. He told the PNG *Post Courier* that all the officers working on Bougainville had been given the 'cold shoulder' by the Promotions Board and they were angry. 'This operation is the biggest ever in this country, most probably the biggest in the South Pacific. We are risking our lives and working in an extremely dangerous area. One of us might just get a bullet in the head and just fall down and die.' Superintendent Wagambie claimed the morale of policemen on Bougainville was at a low ebb.

The police and the soldiers were under a lot of pressure and they never had an easy job. They believed the politicians had pulled them back and sued for peace each time they were having success against the BRA, which, they maintained, put them in even further danger. But the poor level of discipline kept the downward spiral going. There were ludicrous examples of discipline lapses. In one incident, soldiers walked into a BCL mess with their guns cocked and demanded to know the identity of the catering company official who had pinned up a notice in the mess hall appealing to the soldiers to stop 'thieving' spoons. The mess manager had noticed that scores of spoons were disappearing each meal time. The reason was that there were no decent spoons in the ration packs issued to the soldiers when on patrol. But a group of soldiers marched into the next meal threatening to shoot catering staff if they did not reveal who was the author of the 'offensive' notice calling soldiers 'thieves'.

On Bougainville the administrative machinery simply was not designed to cope with a problem of this complexity. Under the provincial government system most administrative functions had been devolved to the provincial level. The crisis could be divided in two from an administrative point of view. The first was up until the start of the state of emergency in late June. Before then, the man in charge of co-ordinating the operations was the North Solomons administrative secretary, Peter Tsiamalili. Mr Tsiamalili, a Bougainvillian, was the most senior public servant in the province and, although appointed by Port Moresby, he headed the provincial administration. Mr Tsiamalili was under constant pressure and subjected to regular death threats from the BRA. He established a joint planning committee of senior national and provincial officials. But after the first few meetings it was effectively boycotted by the police because they believed any information disclosed at committee meetings leaked out and found its way rapidly to the BRA. One senior police officer claimed that the army had lost a number of men in the jungle because army officers had revealed to the joint committee where their patrols would be operating in the following few days.

The second phase of the administrative handling of the crisis began with the state of emergency. Police Commissioner Tohian was appointed emergency controller. But he was based in Port Moresby. On-the-spot command was in the hands of the deputy controller. For the first few months this was Colonel Lima Dotaona, but he was recalled in October and replaced by Colonel Leo Nuia. Colonel Dotaona is a delightfully pleasant man and he set about his work attempting to establish good relationships with the provincial Government, the company and community leaders. He had some early success. But amongst his problems was inheriting the plans that the joint planning committee had already adopted and which were to take effect when the emergency began. One of these was a relocation program for thousands of village people. They were to be moved out of their villages and into what were called 'care centres' while the military pursued the rebels.

At his daily news briefings in the opening days of the state of emergency, Colonel Dotaona did not seem keen on this enforced relocation program. But it became necessary because some of the villages no longer existed. Riot police burnt down village homes in retaliation for their men having been ambushed. Some politicians denied this was happening. A survey in late 1989 revealed that at least 1600 village homes had been destroyed. The riot police were responsible for the early burnings but the torching of village homes became a regular practice for army patrols if they found anything suspicious in a village as they passed through.

Colonel Dotaona had a further problem. The Defence Force hierarchy at Murray Barracks headquarters in Port Moresby had not wanted him in charge of the Bougainville state of emergency operation. Logistical difficulties arose. A situation developed where the Chief of Army Operations, Colonel Leo Nuia, was communicating directly with the contingent commander on Bougainville, the officer who was supposed to be answerable to Colonel Dotaona. Relations between Colonel Dotaona and his number two deteriorated to the extent that the contingent commander repossessed the military vehicle he had earlier provided for the colonel. The deputy controller was left depending upon civilians for transport. The infighting in the army was aggravated by the fact that the post of commander of the Defence Force was vacant following the suspension of Brigadier General Rochus Lokinap after an army pay riot in Port Moresby in February. Colonel Dotaona was being considered for the commander's job and there were some at Defence Force HQ determined not to let this happen. Finally, Cabinet decided to reappoint Brigadier General Lokinap, and one of his first moves upon reinstatement was to demand the replacement of Dotaona by Nuia. The Government acceded.

Colonel Dotaona made no reference to the internal factionalism within the Defence Force when his recall was announced in mid-October. Instead he was critical of the Government for lacking 'political decisiveness'. Colonel Dotaona told Wally Hiambohn, a senior journalist with the PNG *Post Courier*, that the operation would be easier if national leaders were consistent with their decisions affecting security force operations on Bougainville. Hiambohn quoted Dotaona as saying there had been many decisions that he and the men had found difficult to follow and he hoped Colonel Nuia would not be made to feel the same way. 'It's a risky business and our leaders have to make firm decisions. The morale of the troops is good, but our leaders have to make the right decisions and understand the fact [that] people can get killed. I want our leaders to be realistic. They should appreciate difficulties. Miracles will not happen . . . if you tell the troops to do something then let them do it without going and telling them how to.' Hiambohn said Dotaona also urged the national Government not to set timetables for the military to capture the militants. Colonel Nuia suffered the same frustrations as Dotaona. Almost as soon as he took over, a new truce was declared to allow for another doomed peace initiative.

The solutions drawn up in Port Moresby by Prime Minister Namaliu provided a new, better deal for the landowners. Both the provincial Government and some landowners' representatives — those not in the jungle — accepted this. But the confusion that riddled the implementation of government policy at the local level on Bougainville played into the hands of the secessionists. And every time another abuse of human rights was committed by any member of the security forces, the secessionists gained further community support. Bougainville revealed in stark terms PNG's administrative decay. While the solutions in Port Moresby were genuinely conceived, on Bougainville the lack of discipline and the frustrations flowing from what appeared, to the security forces, to be chronic political indecision sabotaged (inadvertently maybe, but sabotaged nevertheless) the national Government's efforts.

The Catholic Church is a major power on Bougainville. Before the advent of CRA, the Catholic Church had been virtually the Government by default. It had provided the majority of the education and health services to the people because of the relative weakness of the Australian administration. When CRA came, pouring in huge amounts of money and introducing large numbers of outsiders, the Church took the side of the Bougainvillians, perhaps out of apprehension that its own influence might be whittled away by the attractions of raw capitalism. From the start, in the 1960s, the Church supported the village people against both the company and the Australian administration.

The Catholic Bishop of Bougainville, Bishop Gregory Singkai, has told Father Momis he has to continue in politics 'until the Bougainville problems are solved'. This direction to a priest to remain as a politician is against the expressed wishes of the Pope. But Bishop Singkai believes Father Momis is doing more for his people in parliament than he could do in a parish. The Catholic Commission for Justice and Peace on Bougainville has strongly condemned the actions of police and soldiers, justifiably so in many cases. But the violence did begin from the BRA side. Father Momis has been one of the few in the Church publicly to condemn the ambush killings and shootings carried out by the guerillas. However, in the words of one Catholic priest on Bougainville, the landowners equate mining with violence to their land. When asked why the BRA was shooting people in company buses going to work, the priest said: 'They are not shooting at people, they are shooting at BCL.'

CHAPTER SIX

PROVINCIAL GOVERNMENT — SECESSION'S FIRST SOLUTION

FEBRUARY 24, 1984, was an illuminating but disheartening day for the auditors from the PNG Auditor-General's office faced with the mammoth task of attempting to piece together the Sandaun (West Sepik) provincial Government's financial affairs. They knew things were in a mess. But on that day in the midst of the monsoon season in the provincial capital of Vanimo, they opened a safe in the provincial headquarters to find a series of documents and papers that illustrated the almost hopeless state of the province's financial administration.

They knew from the list of financial statements forwarded to Port Moresby that the big figures were awry. For instance, three different figures showed up for the province's cash balance at the end of 1982, ranging from a credit of K2.1 million ($3m) to an overdraft of K50,000 ($75,000). But what they found in that safe told them that even the smallest matters were totally out of order. One set of documents showed financial transactions for which no proper records had been kept, including illegal loans to ten members of the Provincial Assembly. They found a deposit bag with a note inside listing provincial government collections totalling more than K1000 ($1500), but all that was left in the bag was thirty-one toea. Also in the safe were twenty-one pay packets containing unclaimed members' sitting allowances. A check of these revealed that nine had been opened and money removed. Finally, the auditors came across a bank passbook marked 'Sandaun Assembly Lounge Account'.

Asked to explain this 'Lounge Account' passbook, which disclosed a series of minor but unreported transactions in the province's financial statements, the Provincial Secretary, Paul Langro, replied: 'the Premier saw his members were getting out of hand in public so he asked for a snooker table to be bought and placed under the Premier's residence so that members [could] play games to pass the time.' Proceeds from the coin-operated table were deposited in the account, but the purpose of the withdrawals was not explained. An audit inspector visited the Premier's residence to find the snooker table had been exposed to the elements and was damaged beyond repair.

In his comprehensive report on the Sandaun provincial Government's accounts tabled in the national parliament in 1987, the Auditor-General revealed far more serious breaches of financial discipline than these — so serious that the provincial Government was suspended, legal action initiated against a number of people and an administrator appointed to restore financial order. Some of these affairs, including a damages award of more than $A1.5 million to an Australian company for breach of contract, will be detailed later. But the contents of that safe tell a graphic story of how the solution to PNG's secession problems — namely provincial government in nineteen provinces — has not worked in many parts of the country the way the visionary proponents of the system hoped it would.

The record of suspended provincial governments is a sorry one: Enga — suspended February 1984 for 'gross financial mismanagement', Premier Tindiwi jailed for misappropriation; Manus — suspended September 1984 for 'financial mismanagement', Premier Maiah jailed for misappropriation; Simbu — suspended December 1984 for 'mismanagement and misappropriation', Premier Siune jailed for misappropriation; Fly — suspended September 1985 for 'financial mismanagement', investigations into alleged malpractice continuing; Western Highlands — suspended March 1987 for 'gross financial mismanagement', former Premier Mara jailed for misappropriation; Central — suspended May 1987 for 'glaring faults in financial management', investigators turned up thirty-six separate cases of fraud; Sandaun — suspended May 1987 for 'gross financial mismanagement — the worst so far', investigations continuing; and

Morobe — suspended September 1989 following a breakdown in law and order and mass looting of stores in the city of Lae.

Only three of PNG's nineteen provinces have natural boundaries — the island provinces of Manus, New Ireland and North Solomons. The remaining sixteen all have at least one land boundary and those boundaries have little or no tribal, traditional or social relevance. All were drawn during the colonial period as district boundaries which were marked out for Australian administrative convenience. These lines of colonial convenience even divided clan groups. When the Mount Kare gold rush began in early 1988, politicians from two adjoining provinces claimed Mount Kare as their people's traditional land. The last detailed border gazettals were made two years before Independence. John Burton, from the University of Papua New Guinea, says a good example of the confusion is that nobody knows whether forty square kilometres of the Kubor Range lies in the Simbu province or the Western Highlands province.

During the ninety-one years of colonial rule, the number of administrative districts changed often. At the end of World War II, when Australia combined the administrations of New Guinea and Papua, there were thirteen districts. The whole of the Highlands was classified at that time as one district called the Central Highlands. One third of the total population lived in the Highlands but the area was only lightly contacted. Indeed, outsiders had learnt only a decade earlier, in the 1930s, that Highlanders existed. In 1951 the Central Highlands was split into three — the Eastern, Western and Southern Highlands. The number of districts rose to eighteen in 1966 when three of the larger ones were split in two. The present number, nineteen, was reached just before self-government. The only post-Independence changes have been to names, not boundaries, except in the case of a few small islands switching back and forth between the Manus and East Sepik provinces.

Populations of the nineteen provinces vary considerably. Morobe, the largest, is home to more than one third of a million people while Manus, the smallest, has a population of barely 30,000 — fewer than one tenth as many. The level of development also varies widely. Although the Australian Government instituted a system of district level administration, it did not lay any basis for the eventual creation of nineteen provincial administrations. Australia was preparing PNG for only two levels of government — national and local. Local government councils were set up throughout the country in the 1950s and 60s and by 1970 more than two million people were covered by 146 local government councils. But the Australian Government's policy adopted in the mid-1960s that councils be multi-racial — open to non-indigenous people as well as 'natives' — generated suspicion. This was strongest on the Gazelle Peninsula of East New Britain. There, by the late 1960s, the Mataungan Association had mobilised the Tolai people in virtual revolt. Elsewhere, councils tended to be dominated by their Australian council clerk and few survived in any dynamic form much beyond Independence.

The concept of provincial-level government was home grown. It was proposed by the Constitutional Planning Committee (CPC) in response to two powerful influences. One was the disparate nature of the country itself and the other was a reaction to the nature of Australian colonial rule, which was highly centralised. Government by telex, it was called. Commenting on the structure of government administration in Papua and New Guinea in 1962, the visiting United Nations mission criticised what it saw as the 'over-centralised and over-complicated' government service and recorded its 'anxiety lest a public service be created with a superstructure too cumbersome for the country to afford'. Those sentiments were echoed twelve years later by two academics hired by the CPC, Professors Tordoff from Manchester University and Watts from Ontario University. 'In our experience of political systems in Asia, Africa and the Caribbean,' they told the Committee, 'we have not come across an administrative system so highly centralised and dominated by its bureaucracy.'

Amongst those in Australia in the 1960s who could see some need to recognise the other factor — the highly fractured make-up of PNG society — was the man destined to become Australia's most controversial Governor-General, Sir John Kerr. In 1965, as Mr Justice Kerr, Director of the Council on New Guinea Affairs, he addressed a seminar on 'The Role of Law in a Developing Country'. 'The tendency towards regional pressure blocks and even towards regional separatism,' Justice Kerr said, 'makes it natural to contemplate some kind of federal structure for Papua and New Guinea, to give expression to regional aspirations whilst avoiding attempts at secession.'

The Constitutional Planning Committee was a committee of members of the House of Assembly appointed in 1972. Chief Minister Somare was the nominal Chairman but effective leadership passed to the Deputy Chairman, Father John Momis, the member for Bougainville. Somare had just put together a raw coalition which had to contend with the gradual assumption of power from a colonial administration startled by the possibility of internal self-government in less than eighteen months. The second man who came to dominate the work of the sixteen-member CPC was John Kaputin, one of the Mataungan leaders from East New Britain. Kaputin had been the first Papua New Guinean to play top-grade Rugby League in Port Moresby and he had represented PNG at the 1962 Commonwealth Games in Perth. But his political credentials came from having helped lead the Tolai people in their confrontation with the Australian administration. During the troubles, the Australian District Commissioner, Jack Emmanuel, was murdered on Kabona plantation, and his murderers were gaoled for a lengthy period. Kaputin had been elected to the House of Assembly in 1972, joining Chief Minister Somare's first government as justice minister.

With Momis and Kaputin in charge and with the support of a dedicated group of mostly foreign academic and legal consultants to flesh out the detail, the final CPC report was radically anti-centralist. Released in June 1974, after two years' preparation, the report advocated provincial government for all nineteen administrative districts. 'Colonial rule', it said, 'ignored, or opposed, or sought to alter our traditional forms of social organisation without proper consultation with our people. It deprived us of self-government, and even of self-respect. The proud independence of our local communities was replaced by dependence. . . . Our people feel powerless and frustrated. Decisions that can and should be made locally are made in Konedobu.' Konedobu was the Port Moresby harbourside suburb where the Australian administration was based. 'The structure of government bequeathed to us by our colonial rulers,' the CPC Report chided, 'has placed power in the hands of public servants, rather than the people whom the bureaucracy should serve'. The answer to this, the CPC Report confidently predicted, was to devolve power to the nineteen districts, henceforth to be called provinces.

'Public servants who work in accordance with the wishes of local leaders,' the CPC said, 'will become more effective because they will also be able to work in the name of these leaders. Their activities are therefore more likely to enjoy the full support and co-operation of the local people.' This happy confluence of objectives was to be achieved following the election of nineteen provincial assemblies of at least fifteen members each. The list of functions over which the provinces would have control included local government, local courts, health centres, aid posts and primary school education. There were two other lists — one of activities to be the absolute responsibility of the national Government, such as police, foreign affairs and defence; and the other of activities where responsibilities would cross and be shared.

Even before the CPC report was tabled, there was some support in the Somare Government for decentralisation. In late 1973 Somare had granted interim provincial government status to Bougainville and he told the House of Assembly that two other pilot provincial governments would be established, one in the Highlands and one in Papua. But things did not flow smoothly. Self-government came on schedule on 1 December 1973, but the Whitlam Government's timetable for Independence to follow in 1974 became impossible to achieve. In early 1974 Whitlam promised Somare that Australia would provide at least $500 million aid during PNG's first three years of independence. Reading the Whitlam letter to the House of Assembly, Somare said he intended to give 'the widest publicity possible' to the Australian assurance, which he said would substantially allay fears of Independence. It was a promise that Whitlam's government did not keep and one which compounded Somare's secessionist problems.

Another significant development in those early months of 1974 that was to have far-reaching repercussions was the announcement by Bougainville Copper Limited of its astoundingly large untaxed profit for 1973 of more than $156 million. This widely publicised windfall profit added impetus to both the secession movements that were to plague Papua New Guinea in the following two years — one on Bougainville itself, where the local leaders saw the copper mine as funding Bougainville's independent future, and the other in Papua, where secessionist leaders were glumly aware that Papua had nothing of the like and resented Bougainville's success.

The late Sir Percy Chatterton, missionary, politician and author of a delightful book on his life in Papua, *Day that I Have Loved*, was a fulsome critic of the type of Australian government thinking that led to deals such as the 1967 Bougainville agreement between the administration and CRA. Sir Percy, who served two terms in the House of Assembly, encouraged Josephine Abaijah to stand for his seat when he retired in 1972. Abaijah came to lead the Papuan secession movement, Papua Besena. Chatterton wrote in 1974 that Papua Besena means 'the Papuan Tribe'. 'Ethnologically this is complete nonsense. Papua, like New Guinea, is a jumble of many tribes. Yet there are ways in which it makes sense. It is one of the ironies of history that the Government of Australia, which since 1945 has striven so energetically to promote "unity" of Papua and New Guinea, might be fairly described as the first, though not the only, begetter of Papuan separatism.'

Sir Percy said that in his eight years in politics he repeatedly put the argument that development plans should take account of social and political factors as well as economic ones, but his case 'cut no ice at all with the administration-dominated government of those days which was firmly wedded to the World Bank's recipe of maximised development of the most economically promising areas without regard to social and political reactions in the neglected ones'. He said that, if he was asked to name the founding fathers of Papuan nationalism, he would include 'Robert S McNamara, President of the World Bank. For it was the policies of the World Bank during the 1960s which led to the neglect of Papuan development by the colonial government'. And Chatterton claimed that 'most of the areas of low economic potential condemned by World Bank policies to neglect were in Papua'.

The stridency of Ms Abaijah's campaign for a separate destiny for Papua began to annoy Mr Somare as 1974 drew on. She claimed that unity would not result in equality for Papuans but that they would become dominated and subservient to New Guineans who outnumbered them four to one. Abaijah's Papua Besena tactics included mass rallies and noisy demonstrations. In one, women beat their way into Chief Minister Somare's conference room, ripping down curtains, overturning chairs and smashing a glass door. By mid-1974 Somare was sufficiently concerned about Abaijah's impact that, when he moved a motion in the House of Assembly that 1 December 1974 be nominated as Independence Day, he devoted almost his entire speech to attacking Papuan separatism. The Opposition seemed more concerned about the possibility of PNG becoming independent without the protection of a constitution and Somare's resolution was amended so that Independence Day would be proclaimed 'as soon as practicable' after approval of the Constitution.

Papua v. New Guinea

The members of the Royal PNG Constabulary band playing and marching with such flourish in the middle of the Boroko Rugby League field are all drilled in riot control technique. It is half time in the 1974 Papua-versus-New Guinea 'grudge match'. Last year's game (1973) led to three days of rioting in Port Moresby. The fighting erupted in the crowd during the second half when a Papuan woman disparagingly referred to New Guineans as *'kaukau* eaters'. *Kaukau* is sweet potato. The fight between Papuans and New Guineans spilled out of the grounds and carried on in the streets of the capital the next day and the day after that.

The playing field is surrounded by a tall mesh wire fence topped with barbed wire to prevent the crowd invading the field to attack the players, or more likely, the referee. Ground capacity is more than ten thousand, but scores more spectators are perched in the branches of trees outside. Extra riot police are on stand-by. But the 1974 Papua versus New Guinea game ends peacefully.

That year (1974) was my first in PNG and although I played first grade for Paga Panthers in the Port Moresby competition, I watched the Papua-versus-New Guinea game from the stands. I made representative selection the next year. But, by then, the potentially volatile Papua-against-New Guinea clash had been abandoned in the interest of 'national unity and stability'. Our Papuan representative team was renamed Southern Zone while New Guinea had been split into 'Highlands', 'Islands' and 'Northern Zones'.

The three hundred-page final report of the Constitutional Planning Committee was tabled in that June 1974 session. It was a complex and highly controversial document proposing a sort of Melanesian Socialist democracy with extensive counterbalancing mechanisms, a strict leadership code of conduct and tough citizenship laws. In tabling the report, Somare, the committee's non-participating chairman, said he disagreed with some of the recommendations and would table a minority report proposing a much simpler constitution. Momis and Kaputin were furious. They accused Somare of sabotaging the CPC's work, of being manipulated by foreign white advisers and of betraying the trust the people put in his leadership.

Over the next four months, Kaputin, who was still Justice Minister, and Momis conducted what could be described as a media guerilla war against Somare. In the parliament they established the Nationalists Pressure Group to fight against any changes to their constitutional proposals. Fighting back, Somare demanded that Kaputin resign. He refused. Because of a quirk in the self-government arrangements, Somare had no power to sack him. After one weekend in October when Kaputin attended a public rally on the Saturday to call on workers to strike to cripple the towns, and another rally on the Sunday to give his 'moral support' to the Papuan separatists' cause, Somare went to the House of Assembly and by a vote of 52 to 12 had Kaputin sacked from the Ministry for 'inciting trouble'.

Josephine Abaijah presented a document to the Australian Government claiming that 'race hatred and racism are rife between Papuans and New Guineans' and she formed what she called an interim Papuan republican government. Soon afterwards, a meeting at Hanuabada, Port Moresby's village on the water, set Sunday, 16 March 1975 as the date for Papua's unilateral declaration of Independence. 'Papuan Independence Day' came. There were speeches and a flag-raising but no incidents, and Abaijah admitted that it was symbolic. Throughout, Somare showed remarkable tolerance. It was a tolerance that would serve him well because, despite the bravado of the Papuan separatists, the real problems of Independence Year, 1975, came with Bougainville.

The interim provincial Government on Bougainville decided to secede in late May. Peace talks broke down. Somare was getting frustrated. He still didn't have a firm date for the country's Independence and already two parts of the nation claimed they were splitting free. 'On Wednesday 18 June I decided at my breakfast table at 7.30 a.m. to test my strength,' Somare recalls. 'So I told the Cabinet that I was going to propose the date that day. The threat of Bougainville secession gave me the ideal opportunity to make a quick move. I could now test the House's feelings about national unity.' Somare caught the Opposition off guard. He rescinded the earlier motion stipulating that the Constitution had to be in place before any date was set for Independence, and he nominated 16 September as Independence Day. That was less than three months away. The motion was carried to loud applause. Debate on the Constitution still had quite a way to go. But, 'Independence has been put off too long,' Somare told the members. 'Independence will bring strength, stability and unity.'

When talks with the Bougainville secessionists broke down again in July, Somare successfully moved that provincial government be cut from the Constitution. It took just twenty minutes. A few weeks later, just a month and a day before Independence, the Constitution was passed. At about the same time Somare received a shock from Mr Whitlam when visiting Canberra. Australia, just one month before launching PNG on its voyage of nationhood, reneged on its $500-million three-year aid promise! Somare arrived back in Port Moresby saying Whitlam had not only told him there would be no long-term aid agreement but that PNG would get $36 million less than it was expecting in the following week's Australian Budget. 'I feel as though Australia has broken my back,' Somare said. 'The Australian Government has made a mess of administering the Australian economy and as a result, PNG will suffer.' He blamed the failure of his mission on 'an arrogant and ignorant bunch of Treasury advisers who know nothing about PNG's problems'.

The Australian Treasurer of the day was Bill Hayden. Years later, according to journalist Brian Toohey's the *Eye* magazine, as Foreign Minister, Hayden was to write in a memo to his Department that he considered PNG's leaders suffered from 'limited maturity'. Hayden was never much of an admirer of PNG. In 1986, with Hayden responsible for the foreign aid budget, the Hawke Government unilaterally revoked a five-year aid commitment to PNG — a document that Bob Hawke had signed only the year before. Senator Gareth Evans, not Foreign Minister Hayden, flew to Port Moresby to tell the PNG Government the bad news. As in 1975, PNG felt aggrieved.

As Independence Day approached, Somare's government carried out its first deportation. Dr Eric Wright, Josephine Abaijah's chief adviser, was expelled. Born in Australia, Dr Wright was a former Deputy Director of Health in PNG, and had spent thirty years there. A Somare government official described him as an 'expatriate promoting disunity'. Abaijah claimed that the deportation was 'another step towards dictatorship'. When Wright died in Australia a few years later, Abaijah flew to Sydney to collect his ashes, which she brought back to Port Moresby and scattered on the waters of Papua. That sad and defiant act would seem to be a fitting epitaph for Papua Besena — symbolic gestures rather than achievement. For although the movement won seven seats in the first post-Independence elections in 1977, it gradually disintegrated, with most of those parliamentarians drifting off to join other parties. In 1982 Josephine Abaijah lost her seat and she failed again in an attempted comeback in 1987. The belief amongst Papuans that they have been disadvantaged by history, however, remains and Ted Diro was able to harness that in forming his eighteen-strong Papuan Group in parliament after the 1987 elections.

It took Somare eleven months to get the Bougainville leaders to accept integration with the rest of PNG and that was only after he agreed to write provincial government back into the Constitution. But while provincial government took root in the North Solomons and became a relatively effective form of administration, that was not the case everywhere. In half a dozen of the other provinces it worked reasonably well but in the rest the first attempts at provincial government were chaotic failures. Mr Somare told parliament at the conclusion of the first Bougainville secession crisis in 1976 that the agreement he had made with the Bougainville leaders envisaged a law requiring that provinces 'exercise responsible management over their finances'. PNG's Auditor-General has found that in many cases financial management has been appalling.

Part of the reason for failure was that, while Bougainville was ready and eager for provincial government, many other provinces were not. There was a dearth of sufficiently skilled human resources. The training of Papua New Guineans to take responsible jobs in the Australian administration started very late, in most cases not until the late 1960s or early 1970s. The first indigenous heads of PNG's Public Service Departments were young men barely in their thirties when self-government and Independence came. And they were trained for a centralised public service, not one where power and authority were devolved into nineteen separate, provincial administrations. The Papua New Guineans moving into these provincial jobs did not take over an existing bureaucratic system. They had to create and run a radically different system and one based on the theory that central control was a bad thing. Rapid localisation — the replacement of Australian public servants by their junior PNG understudies — compounded the problem.

According to Tony Regan, who has seen the decentralisation process from both sides, most provinces were in no way ready. He says that in 1976 the spread of provincial government was expected to be a slow process. 'Bougainville, East New Britain, East Sepik, Eastern Highlands and Morobe — the areas with a longer exposure to the outside world — were the ones people thought might move into it more quickly but that the rest would come in over many years. The more exposed provinces,' Regan explains, 'had better educated people, people with more capacity to deliver, to set up systems. And it is largely those areas that managed better in the early years.' Regan, who worked in the Decentralisation Ministry in Port Moresby and, later, with the Islands' Premiers Secretariat in Rabaul, points out that the organic law on provincial government, which accompanied the constitutional adoption of the system, provided for a gradual acceptance of responsibilities.

The organic law proposed that powers be transferred only when provinces showed the capacity to deal with them. 'Various procedures had to be followed before provincial government was established,' Regan says. 'There had to be a constituent assembly. The province had to adopt a Constitution.' But steady devolution was not what happened. 'Amongst the politicians there was certainly some feeling that this gradual introduction of provincial government might be unrealistic,' says Regan. 'They felt once you had given something to one area, it was inevitable others would demand it. But I think that was assumed, before it really happened.' In 1977 the government engaged the international consultants, McKinsey, to advise on implementation. McKinsey recommended that all powers should be devolved at the same time to every province! The report was accepted and implemented immediately. Regan says this dismayed many bureaucrats, even those who were strong advocates of provincial autonomy. 'They felt it was totally unrealistic to introduce provincial government to areas that, first of all, didn't especially want it and, secondly, didn't have the capacity to run it.'

The country's public service was not ready for the upheaval. Heading the public service was Rabbie Namaliu, who became PNG's fourth prime minister twelve years later in 1988. As Public Services Commissioner in late 1976, Namaliu said that some idea of the 'mammoth task' facing his Public Services Commission could be obtained from the size of government payroll lists. 'We have 30,000 officers employed under the Public Service Act. There are 10,000 employed by the teaching services commission. And statutory authorities employ another 30,000 people. That makes a total of

70,000, many of whom will go across to the service of provincial government while continuing to be employed by the national Government.' Lines of authority became very confused. Under the Australian administration only the largest departments had had any district-level administration. Some of the smaller ones were hardly represented outside Port Moresby. Some had their people concentrated in a few districts and others were organised on a regional, not district basis. But few had agreed on what constituted a region. For instance, the Forests Department recognised three regions while the Public Works Department recognised five.

Even the largest department, Education, which was organised down to a District level, saw immense difficulties with provincial government. The Education Department was horrified that provincial governments were to become responsible for community schools. In late 1976 the Education Minister wrote to the Minister for Provincial Affairs suggesting there may have been a huge mistake. 'It is possible,' he wrote, 'that the national Government team engaged in negotiations with the North Solomons team was not aware that "community schools" is the new term for "primary schools". It is possible they thought they were conceding power over schools similar to village self-help schools and were not aware that they were conceding powers over about 80 per cent of PNG teachers and about one half of the Education Budget.' The Port Moresby Education headquarters foresaw nineteen separate education systems with nineteen curricula. That was avoided. But it took almost seven years of sometimes acrimonious negotiations involving church, provincial and national interests before an acceptable National Education Act was adopted that took provincial government powers into account. That Act became effective in July 1983. It kept curriculum as a national government responsibility but transferred other powers to the provinces.

The 'father' of provincial government, John Momis, returned to national politics at the 1977 elections. Somare, declaring decentralisation a 'top priority', put Momis in charge of the process. Father Momis, fresh from the exhilaration of having achieved his aim of enshrining provincial government in the Constitution, would not accept that all the people were not ready to control their local affairs. On 19 September 1977 he told those attending the official opening of the Fly Provincial Government in Daru that despite any misgivings they might have, they should have no doubts that they were ready.

'Unfortunately, too many of our leaders have been led to believe that our people are not ready for provincial government precisely because we do not have enough technicians, lawyers, capital-intensive projects and so on,' Momis said. 'Whilst important, they are not part of my list of urgent priorities. I consider the first priority to be the creation and encouragement of a genuine leadership, which will perceive the real needs and aspirations of your people, can distinguish between the options relevant to your situation and can pursue the means most suitable to achieving your development goals.'

What some of the 'leaders' were concerned about quickly became obvious. On 23 February 1978 the PNG *Post Courier* reported that the new provincial governments had been quick to set their pay scales, with Central province (which surrounds Port Moresby) members being highest paid. The next day the paper reported that the Central Provincial Assembly, rather than being embarrassed by this revelation in the previous morning's paper, had, in fact, thrown out the proposed Salaries Bill because members were dissatisfied with their proposed pay scales and wanted more!

The proliferation of governments in provinces where there had been no previous structure for governmental decision making inevitably led to problems. Some became obvious early. Bill Standish, a long-time observer of PNG affairs, told the Waigani Seminar at the University of Papua New Guinea in 1978 that one consequence was that bureaucratic morale in some provinces had become 'desperately low'. Standish, whose specialty was the Simbu province, said that the way provincial government was being implemented meant that the most senior public servant in each province, the administrative secretary, did not report to the premier and his provincial executive directly. He had to do it via a provincial policy secretariat. In Simbu this policy secretariat 'was appointed as the result of bitter factional struggles'. Standish said that in several provinces secretariat staff lacked any administrative experience or government expertise. 'Having been appointed on the recommendation of the provincial politicians, the administrative secretary's position, like that of the secretariat as a whole, remains the subject of intense political struggle between educated elite members from different parts of the province. There are signs appearing that the previously meritocratic public service could become subject to fragmentation and nepotism with a consequent decline in both its political neutrality and professionalism, and ultimately in its capacity and performance.'

That prediction of a drop in performance came true. All but two of the provinces abolished their secretariats over the following ten years. Provincial secretariats remain only in the North Solomons and Eastern Highlands provinces. Elsewhere the tensions and rivalries caused too many problems for the retention of a dual structure. In the Western Highlands the feud between the head of the secretariat and the administrative secretary got so bitter that the door between their offices was nailed up and it remained impassable for two years. There was also friction between Port Moresby and the provinces over the appointment of who should be the province's senior bureaucrat. In 1984 the matter went to the Supreme Court. The Somare Government, attempting to exercise its authority over the Morobe province, appointed a new Morobe Provincial Secretary, John Gaius. The Morobe Premier, Utula Samana, objected strenuously and the Morobe provincial government boycotted the appointment.

A series of legal moves and countermoves followed. The national Government took out a court injunction to restrain the provincial Government from interfering with Mr Gaius. Two weeks after moving to Lae to take up the secretary's job, Gaius was still being refused accommodation and was denied access to both the Secretary's office and vehicle. The injunction was aimed at enabling him to work. But the province challenged the whole constitutional basis under which the national Government had transferred public servants to serve provincial governments. Morobe won and the provincial Government retained the services of the man it wanted.

Conference of Confrontation

The annual premiers conference in Papua New Guinea is a venue for frank exchange — sometimes physical as well as verbal. There are nineteen provincial governments and once a year the nineteen premiers confront the prime minister. The 1983 confrontation was in Madang. Twenty-eight items were on the agenda for the week-long conference but discussion stalled for two and a half days on item one — the future of the provincial government system. Even after that time, no motion acceptable to all could be drafted and the item was put to the end of the notice paper. Twice there was the distinct prospect of a walkout — first by the premiers, then by the prime minister.

The premiers almost stormed out after Somare's opening address in which he lectured them about the 'collapse of confidence in relations between the national and provincial governments'. Somare warned the premiers that by 'treating the national members of parliament with contempt' the provincial governments could be courting their own demise. 'It seems to me,' Somare thundered, 'that many of you do not recognise the national parliament for what it is. It is the supreme legislative body in Papua New Guinea. If it is determined to abolish the provincial government system, it will do it. I am only one member of that house. There are 108 other members and about a hundred of them want to get rid of provincial governments altogether.' Somare accused the provincial governments of 'appalling financial irresponsibility'.

In reply, the Premier of Gulf, Sepoe Karava, told Somare that the national Government was not so pure itself. 'There's corruption also in the national Government,' he said. 'But we are not saying that we should throw out the national Government and bring back the colonial Australian Government. By the same token we ask the national Government to understand that because there's corruption in our system of government, it doesn't mean that you should suspend us and bring in the Kiap system!' The Kiaps were the all-powerful patrol officers who governed in the bush during the Australian colonial days.

But the altercations were not just between the politicians. The Premier of Simbu, Matthew Siune, punched the secretary of the premier's conference, Mark Kwapena, in the face at one of the first social events. Siune claimed Kwapena had not recognised him and this was a grave personal insult. On Kwapena's part there was both injury and insult. Prime Minister Somare asked Kwapena at the next session to apologise to the Premier.

Another premier went to the conference not to get into a fight but to get out of one. Western Highlands Premier, Nambuga Mara, turned up at the conference on the third day and pleaded with journalists not to write or broadcast that he was there. Mara's clan was engaged in a tribal fight which had arisen out of an assassination attempt on him two weeks before. He had retreated to his village but arrived at Madang after his government had sent in a helicopter to pluck him out of the fighting. Mara did not stay in Madang long. He was off again when told that the police had detained some other Western Highlanders who had gone to the Madang Hotel asking for him.

Chaos reigned in the administration of the Western Highlands in late 1987 and early 1988 when a similar situation developed, with the governments in Port Moresby and Mount Hagen selecting two different men to head the Department of Western Highlands. The Western Highlands provincial Government had been suspended early in 1987 by Prime Minister Wingti. Prior to the lifting of the suspension, Mr Wingti appointed Gabriel Waipek to the job. Then the reinstated premier, Philip Kapal, reappointed his former provincial secretary, Peter Wama. Both Wama and Waipek claimed legitimacy and each man issued orders suspending the other from duty. This farcical situation dragged on for months, with the public service in the Western Highlands cleaving down the middle, half supporting and taking directions from one man and half from the other. The crisis was resolved but not before police had to guard government property with police dogs.

The most crucial and regular confrontation, though, between the national and provincial governments is over money. The basic national government grant to the provinces was designed to ensure they could maintain the same level of services as were provided by the national Government in 1976-77. This arrangement, advocated by McKinsey, institutionalised the inequalities that existed prior to the introduction of provincial government. The additional grant that was supposed to redress this problem gradually dropped away, with the effect that the less well-off provinces were unable to do very much to overcome their problems. The better-off provinces not only stayed ahead but, being more developed, had the ability to raise a greater percentage of their revenue themselves. Best off was North Solomons, which received mining royalties — up to K4 million ($A6 million) per year. That was more than some of the smaller provinces' total budgets. In 1989, more than a dozen years after the system came into being, the Namaliu Government revised the means for calculating the basic grant, varying the base year from 1976-77. It also announced that from 1990 a 'more equitable' method would apply for calculating annual adjustments.

Provincial governments do have the power to impose a range of provincial taxes, the most common being retail sales tax, land tax and head tax. The retail sales tax on beer is significant. In some provinces beer drinkers pay up to 15 toea (22c) per litre, or 5t (7c) a stubbie to the provincial Government. Hotel accommodation is also widely taxed. The provinces have found taxes levied on companies much easier to collect than taxes levied on individuals. Provinces can charge a head tax that everyone should pay but collections have not always reached expectations. In one year, the Central provincial Government estimated it would raise K100,000 ($A150,000) in head tax. But by year's end not a single toea had been collected.

The dependence on national government grants is extreme. Up until the late 1980s, the North Solomons Government was the only one that did not rely on Port Moresby for more than seventy per cent of its revenue. In 1989 the system of apportioning mining royalties between the landowners and provincial governments was changed to give landowners a greater share, but the provinces were more than compensated by a new grant that was equivalent to one per cent of mining exports from any mine in the province.

Many provinces have not fully explored the range of powers they have to raise money. Others have occasionally overstepped the mark — and not only in money-raising matters. In July 1979 the then East New Britain premier was jailed for attempting to set up his own provincial police force. Tony Regan says there is enormous ignorance of where provincial powers begin and end. 'One reason for the apparent complexity of the organic law is that the system was designed to be extremely flexible and fluid for the shifting of functions and powers between the different levels of government. That has not been well enough understood. There has certainly not been much attempt to educate public servants and politicians about the basic philosophy underpinning the system or about the way it works in practice. The other serious problem, though,' Regan contends, 'is that virtually every power that provincial governments are exercising, every function they're carrying out, they are doing under a national government Cabinet decision made in 1977.

'The intention of the organic law was that the national government would gradually move out of a lot of legislative fields in which the provincial governments had responsibilities, leaving the provinces free to pass their own laws. These laws would then set out the powers and functions of the provincial ministers and public servants. Those laws cannot be passed at the provincial level at the moment because national legislation still covers many areas,' Regan says. 'So there is tremendous ignorance and confusion. One of the eternal complaints from provincial public servants is that the politicians are constantly treading into the implementation areas of the public service. And until that whole mess is sorted out, until there is a real attempt by the national government to do what it promised to do in the organic law, there will be a lot of confusion about legal roles and responsibilities.' In mid-1988, more than eleven years after the system was adopted, the Minister for Provincial Affairs announced that his department was in 'the final stages' of preparing a guide for provincial politicians and bureaucrats explaining the limits and extent of their respective powers.

Jealousies and tensions grew very quickly between the politicians at the national level and those in the provinces. Provincial politicians began to take credit for development at the local level and their rivals in the national parliament came to realise and envy this. Some of the provincial politicians had failed in national elections. They were often personal rivals of those who had beaten them and become ministers in the national Government. One reason official 'slush funds' for national politicians in PNG have grown is that the national government — first under Somare, then under Chan, Somare again, Wingti and then Namaliu — tried to redress the political problems back home for backbenchers. At the 1983 premiers' conference, Mr Somare harshly rebuked the premiers, telling them it was their own fault that the national parliament was moving to curtail their powers. 'As premiers you have failed to properly account for your actions and spending,' Somare declared. 'You have treated the members of the national parliament with contempt.'

Not long after this, the national Government legislated to give itself the power to suspend provincial governments. The first to go was Enga. Significantly, Enga was the last administrative district created by the colonial administration. At the far end of the Highlands Highway, Enga is the least developed of all the provinces. Like the six others that were to be suspended over the following four years, the Enga Government was accused of 'gross financial mismanagement'. The first seven suspensions all followed reports by PNG's Auditor-General. In every case, even for those provincial governments suspended as late as 1987, the audits were for the years

1982 or 1983. What the Auditor-General found each time was widespread incompetence, appalling record-keeping and dishonesty. The Auditor-General has been sharply critical of no fewer than eleven of the nineteen provincial governments for not keeping proper financial accounts.

Mr Somare's announcement of the Enga suspension listed the weaknesses: 'Proper books of account not maintained, no assets register maintained, several votes overcommitted due to poor exercise of control, payments authorised without financial delegation, lack of supporting documentation for payments, expenditure authorised regardless of limits, government order forms issued without authentication, payments made to non-existent groups, and contracts awarded without calling tenders.' Enga's suspension lasted more than two years and the return of elected government in 1986 was less than auspicious. When the results of the Enga elections were announced, supporters of losing candidates set fire to the Enga administrative headquarters in the provincial capital, Wabag. Eight motor vehicles were also destroyed and the damage bill was K500,000 ($750,000). The Acting Administrator said the incoming provincial government would 'not have reliable resources to work with'.

The second to be suspended was Manus. Prime Minister Somare said the Auditor-General found that the Manus Government had spent well over K80,000 ($120,000) on entertainment — more than five times the budget allocation. Manus has fewer than thirty thousand residents. Friday night had become party night at the provincial headquarters in Lorengau. The Manus Premier, Joel Maiah, spent more than K80,000 overseas on flags, crests and diaries without going through the proper tender procedures. The Manus Government was reinstituted in August 1985, after its previous leaders were prosecuted and jailed on charges of misappropriating public money. A new Government headed by a former university academic, Mr Stephen Pokawin, made significant progress in the late 1980s, converting Manus into a model provincial administration.

Between December 1984 and May 1987 five provinces were suspended: Simbu, Fly, Western Highlands, Sandaun and Central. The annual budgets brought down by these suspended provincial governments bore little resemblance to what actually happened. The Western Highlands budget for 1983 provided for anticipated receipts and expenditure of K4.79 million ($A7m). Actual revenue totalled K5.71 million (a jump of about $1.5 million or twenty per cent over what was expected). Retail tax on liquor provided K309,797 (more than double predictions). Motor vehicle registrations were expected to bring in K228,600. But not a single toea was collected! Much of the increased revenue came from unanticipated national government grants for high schools, maintenance and transport (more than K500,000). The total expenditure of K5.4 million exceeded the budget forecast by thirteen per cent, or almost a million dollars. But all this over-expenditure was unauthorised.

The Western Highlands provincial Government engaged a firm of accountants to prepare its financial statements. But the accountant added the following qualification to his report: 'I have prepared the financial statements — bearing in mind that much source documentation was unobtainable — from the books and records. . . . I express no opinion on whether they present a true and fair view of the position . . . and no warranty of accuracy or reliability is given.' The Auditor-General found that government cars were sold to the provincial ministers who were using them even though they should not have had vehicles.

The Somare, Wingti and Namaliu governments all suspended provincial governments. Mr Wingti abolished three in three months in 1987, including Sandaun, which he claimed had achieved a distinction all its own. 'The Auditor-General's report on the Sandaun provincial Government,' he said, 'observed the most unsatisfactory practices, believed to be the worst of all, worse even than any previously suspended provincial government.' The Auditor-General found the records so hopeless that, in concluding his report on Sandaun for 1982, he said he would not be able to do the province's books for any of the years from 1983 to 1986 because the books of accounts for those years were in such a mess.

Sandaun was one of the provinces where few facilities and minimal administrative structure were established during the colonial period. The Auditor-General's report reveals the size of the problems that resulted from trying to set up from scratch an administration with few qualified people and no existing system to refer to. 'This office was unable to make a true comparison of actual revenue and expenditure with budgeted revenue and expenditure, as proper expenditure ledgers showing expenditures against appropriation items were not available,' the Auditor-General said. 'The accounting records were not correctly maintained and the financial statements presented for audit did not agree with the underlying ledger account'.

No record was maintained on rent for government property and no checks were made that rents were collected or that collected rents were banked. 'At the time of audit the preparation of provincial government bank reconciliation statements was approximately four and a half years in arrears.'

The Auditor-General requested explanations on various matters from the chief bureaucrat in the province, the provincial secretary. His explanations illustrate the problem. The Auditor-General sought clarification on why money had been advanced to members of the Sandaun Provincial Assembly and office staff when no provision had been made for private loans in the budget and not a single one was authorised. 'Funds . . . were not properly receipted nor banked because we had workload procedures [sic],' the provincial secretary said. 'Where these cash became available, staff or members came asking for loan which I must admit that I gave the money knowing that they would refund immediately. . . . I have kept these records trusting that these people refund the money. Others have paid while others didn't pay back and when refund came in, some came back asking for loan again.'

In response to questions about money he received himself, the provincial secretary said that 'since the audit I have tried my best to reconcile my memory and briefs and have resolved that I got the money to pay for legal fees to bail my relatives. That time I got another problem . . . a debt of K1050 personal telephone bill came and I was trying to settle all at once. But a good friend helped me to settle the bill and thus I owe two people now. That is K610.00 provincial government and a friend K1050. Honestly this will be settled.' The Auditor-General also asked why certain collections totalling K26,391.67 were not banked. The secretary advised that 'the key was lost during my absence in Australia. . . . When I returned and I was told about the lost key, I tried to locate the spare but with despair, hence I left the box unopened.'

Despite all this the Sandaun provincial budget was underspent by almost K500,000 ($750,000). Tony Regan explains that underspending on capital works is all too common: 'There's a tremendous lack of trained manpower in the whole country. And very little has been done since provincial governments were established to ensure quality people are working in the provinces,' he says. 'There is also a tremendously fast turnover. A senior Finance Department official who used to work closely with provincial governments told me that in 1980 and 1981 when he went to one particular, poorly developed province there had been a 100-per-cent turnover in the heads of the working divisions. That's a common experience. There are no incentives for quality people to go to these provinces and no incentives for them to stay there. So systems for the development or the implementation of projects are not being nurtured in any way at all. This has led to massive underspending of capital works funds in a large number of provinces,' Regan says.

'In many ways that underspending of capital works is more scandalous than the odd K10,000 here and there that might be misspent on travel or entertainment. And the capital works underspending receives no attention. The incapacity of some provincial governments to deliver is far more serious than misspending. Probably the blame rests more with the entire national public service and the national government than with the provinces because no effort is being made to lift capacity. Unless there is some system developed for getting better public servants into the provinces, for establishing better understanding of legal procedures, of understanding the proper division of responsibilities between public servants and politicians then things are going to continue the way they have gone.' In 1989 Mr Namaliu's government recognised the need to improve the capacity of provinces to design and implement projects. The national government's Indicative Investment Program for 1990–94 included a line item titled 'Provincial Investment Planning and Project Preparation'. However, no money was included in the projected funding of the program for any of the five years up to 1994.

When the Provincial Affairs Minister, John Nilkare, introduced the constitutional changes in 1983 that would give the national Government power to suspend provincial governments, he claimed funds sent to the provinces were not going to development but to prop up government business arms, most of which had gone bankrupt. The history of provincial government business arms is chequered. The Bougainville Development Corporation (BDC) set a lead but its record of profitability and good management was rarely duplicated. Even the BDC ran into trouble but that was political, not financial, with the provincial Government claiming the company had been hijacked by its directors. Millions of Kina have been sunk into other provincial development corporations and many have lost everything.

The West Sepik Development Corporation, Westdeco, was one of the worst. Incorporated on 4 October 1978, it commenced trading in February 1979. It was launched by the Sandaun provincial Government as a timber milling, logging and road construction concern with the aims of promoting business activity in the province and returning profits to the annual budget. It achieved neither. In less than three years, Westdeco accumulated losses of more than K1 million ($1.5m) and liquidation proceedings began. The development corporation was overly ambitious. It signed an expensive seven-year hire purchase agreement for logging equipment but was incapable of meeting its commitments. A provincial development study into why Westdeco failed reported that the company's operations were chaotic.

'The company's management appears to have been completely unqualified to run a business of the size and complexity of the Westdeco operation,' it said. 'The company's sales and production performance was low and inconsistent. The Blackwood Hodge hire purchase agreement was based on sales production of 50,000 cubic metres [of timber] per annum with gross revenue from sales estimated at about K2.5 million [$3.3m]. Actual sales volume during 1980 was 21,615 cubic metres valued at about K1.1 million [$2.1m]. Forest planning, log extraction, loading operations and wood processing all seem to have demonstrated a lack of experience and expertise among supervisory personnel. No effective marketing strategy was ever developed. Financial control procedures were not existent. The Board of Directors appear to have had little interest or knowledge about company operation,' the investigating team concluded.

Sandaun Inc

The Sandaun provincial Government lost everything it invested in its provincial development corporation, Westdeco, and more. After the company was wound up, the province was sued as a guarantor and had to pay the Australian company Blackwood Hodge more than $1 million. But, according to PNG's State solicitor, the Sandaun province might have avoided the default pay-out if only its case had been presented to the court!

In 1979 and 1980 Westdeco signed logging equipment lease agreements with Blackwood Hodge that the then premier purported to guarantee. Westdeco collapsed. Blackwood Hodge sued. In July 1984 the PNG national court found in the Australian company's favour on the grounds that no defence had been filed. But a defence had been prepared because a copy was served on Blackwood Hodge's lawyer!

Commenting on the litigation, PNG's State solicitor said: 'For reasons known only to the previous lawyer acting for the provincial Government, this fact was never brought to the attention of any of the judges who dealt with the matter . . . the Sandaun provincial Government always had a defence to Blackwood Hodge's claim on the grounds that the then premier had no authority to enter into the guarantee agreements'. The State solicitor said there was uncontested affidavit evidence that Blackwood Hodge knew this.

In August 1984 the court dismissed the provincial government's application to set aside the default judgment. 'For some inexplicable reason,' the State solicitor said, 'the lawyer for the provincial Government did not appeal.' In March 1985 the court ordered the Sandaun government to pay the Australian company K1.35 million ($2m) plus costs. The State solicitor observed that 'the Sandaun provincial Government was very badly served by its former lawyers'. The State solicitor took over the case and a month later negotiated a settlement reducing the provincial government's pay-out from K1.35 million to K0.85 million — a saving of $750,000 on the court award.

PNG's Auditor-General reported that the former lawyers submitted a claim for K80,989.46 ($120,000) for professional services and costs. Referring to the legal firm retained by Sandaun from January 1982 to April 1985, the Auditor-General observed that one of the lawyers was the former provincial legal officer. 'In his letter of resignation he stated that his services as a barrister and solicitor would still be available to the provincial government "at no greater cost than the cost of employing me",' the Auditor-General said. 'His salary as legal officer had been K8870 ($13,300) per year. For the three-year period he was retained as legal consultant, legal fees and costs claimed by him totalled K127,532.57 ($191,000).'

There are numerous stories of foreign businessmen taking advantage of provincial government business arms. One of the more outlandish involved the business arm to the Western Highlands provincial

Government, Melpa. In November 1980 an overseas company presented the Melpa group with a Bank of America cheque for $US90,918.46 and entered an agreement with them that this would pay for a timber feasibility study. Melpa deposited the cheque with the PNG Banking Corporation in Mount Hagen. The money was later withdrawn and spent on the timber feasibility study as instructed by the Philippines firm that provided the cheque. Ten months later, the PNG Banking Corporation advised that the Bank of America had declared the cheque had been fraudulently altered from $US18.46 to $US90,918.46 and that Melpa would be required to refund the $US90,900 difference!

Not all provincial business arms have failed. As expertise and understanding have grown, some have been turned around. Gulf Papua Fisheries, 100 per cent owned by the Gulf provincial Government, is one. In 1983 Gulf Papua Fisheries bought out its Japanese partner, Gulf Sohbu, and set out on a development program that has seen it move, according to former Chairman, Mekere Morauta, from 'a non-profit-making and asset-poor position to an extremely profitable and asset-rich position'. The man who helped engineer the turnaround is himself Japanese, Hiro Muromoto, the company's chief technical adviser. Gulf Papua Fisheries bought its first vessel, Gulf Star 1, in 1983 for K800,000 ($1.2m) in cash. The next year it bought Gulf Star 2, borrowing half the money from the PNG Banking Corporation, a loan it was able to repay in ten months. Gulf Star 3 and Gulf Star 5 were designed specifically for the company and a Western Australian firm was commissioned to build them for $A1.3 million each.

Mr Morauta says the company obtained highly concessional funding from the Australian Export Finance and Insurance Corporation to buy the two prawning trawlers — a first for PNG. All the profits since 1983 have been ploughed back into the company which has even opened an office in Tokyo. The office is run by a fully owned subsidiary of Gulf Papua Fisheries, Isapea Japan Pty Ltd, which sells the prawn catch directly to wholesalers. Mr Morauta, a former head of the national Finance Department, claims that Gulf Papua Fisheries represents a model that other PNG companies could follow.

Each province is supposed to draw up its own constitution. This has led to some peculiar innovations. In the Southern Highlands the architects of the Constitution wanted to avoid the problem that so plagues the national parliament — incessant votes of no confidence. In an attempt to bring more stability they decided the Southern Highlands premier could not be removed unless he lost the support of two thirds of the members of the assembly. But this did not have the desired stabilising effect, at least for much of 1983. The Premier, Mr Ebeial, lost most of his ministers in a provincial assembly revolt and could not command a majority. However, he retained the support of just over one third of the members. Consequently he refused to resign and effective government broke down for three months. The Southern Highlands province was led by a premier who was constantly outvoted but who could not be removed. Eventually, some former supporters rejoined him.

Suggestions have often been made that PNG should scrap provincial government completely. The most serious of these came in late 1984 when the Somare Government proposed a referendum on the issue. It is probably a reflection of Somare's desire not to have to go through the same trauma as at Independence that he wanted the people to decide, not the national parliamentarians. 'In view of the constant debate in parliament and outside on the future of provincial government,' Somare argued, 'a referendum would provide a better means of gauging national opinion on the issue, which would become too complex to decide at political party level. After ten years of Independence, it is good that we should look at the system of provincial government to see if it is suitable for our development goals and aspirations and for the future of PNG.' Somare suggested that the outcome of the referendum should be implemented province by province. 'The results from each province would be given to parliament to consider,' he said. 'Those provinces where the majority decides for the change, their wishes will be respected'.

The reaction was predictable. The New Guinea island premiers issued a statement saying that their provinces would break away from PNG if Somare went ahead with the referendum. The referendum was dropped and a parliamentary committee established to do a comprehensive report on the provincial government system. The committee had just started its work when Somare was defeated in parliament in late 1985 and Paias Wingti became prime minister. Wingti disbanded the committee, claiming the answer was not to abolish provincial governments but to give them more support. But Mr Wingti was to suffer his own share of frustrations with provincial governments and, shortly before his government fell in mid-1988, it had drawn up plans to make provincial government subject to an ordinary Act of parliament. Enshrined as it is in the Constitution, provincial government is covered by an organic law that is just as difficult to change as the Constitution.

The theory behind this massive decentralisation experiment of provincial government was to improve delivery of services at the local level. But, while the number of schools and aid posts has increased, there are frequent complaints that the quality of service has declined since Independence. Tony Regan says not all the faults lie on the side of the provincial politicians and provincial administrators. 'The original idea was that with the implementation of provincial government, the national component of the public service would shrink,' he says. 'And that better quality people and larger numbers would be transferred to the provinces. Now that simply has not happened. All that happened was that large numbers of personnel down the line — teachers, primary industry field officers, health workers, forest workers, works and supply people — were transferred to the provinces and then there was a steady build-up again at the headquarters. They've continued to expand but not in the areas where they would be assisting provincial governments. Unless there's a massive effort across the board in the public service the problems are going to repeat themselves in the provinces that don't have the capacity to operate properly now.'

When the Wingti Government fell in July 1988, Father John Momis returned to the Provincial Affairs portfolio. In a major statement to parliament in September 1988, he outlined measures he intended to take to try to fix the system. First, he promised a complete review of the financial arrangements that were squeezing the provincial governments, especially the more backward ones. Second, he proposed a 'major reorganisation' of his department so that it would cease to have direct responsibilities at the provincial level and instead 'take on the much more vital role of monitoring and evaluation of the performance of the provinces and liaising between the provinces and national departments.' Father Momis said he was 'shocked' to find that his department had virtually no capacity to monitor when provincial governments were getting into difficulties. 'The chances are,' he said, 'the national Government will only know about it if the newspapers happen to hear about it.' Finally, he promised that increased allowances would be provided to public servants to encourage them to work in the provinces.

The eight suspensions of provincial governments have acted as a salutary warning to the others. But the errant provinces are not alone when it comes to financial lack of accountability. The Auditor-General was quoted during 1987 as saying that if some national government departments were provincial governments they, too, would have been prime candidates for suspension. There are encouraging indications that financial record-keeping in the provinces, or in some at least, is on the improve. The catastrophe that was revealed by the Auditor-General in the Sandaun province in the early 1980s may now be less likely thanks to computers. A simplified computer accounting system has been introduced and it has so impressed aid officials that both the United Nations Development Program and Australia have committed another $A3 million to the project. It began in August 1986, with the UNDP providing technical assistance to the national Department of Finance and Planning to help develop a computerised provincial accounting system.

One of the designers of the software, Darryl Higgins, says that Papua New Guineans at the provincial level have shown an aptitude for the technology that astounded the aid officials. He says one of the secrets was to create an extremely simple, user-friendly system. 'In the same way that a pencil or a pen and paper used to be the tool,' he says, 'now the keyboard is the tool. The idea is to keep it simple. Even the terminology. When we tested the system, we were fortunate to have on the team a former Kiap who had been in PNG for thirty years. He was instrumental in removing from the screen and from the terminology that we used any technical jargon that could not be understood in basic, simple English. We have put all the integral operations needed to keep the system running in simple step-by-step, on-screen prompts.

'The thing that has given me the biggest kick,' Darryl says, 'is that in the systems that have been effectively installed, no expatriates are needed. What has been surprising is the uplift in morale. They find they get the job done so much quicker. So that you find in a typical provincial headquarters most of the routine form-filling accounts work has been completed early in the morning. The people have been able to be redeployed into more exciting areas and do other jobs.' The Australian Government commitment to the computerised accounting project came in the form of a $2 million grant as technical assistance to the UNDP and a separate grant of

$600,000 to the PNG Government for the purchase of computers for the provinces.

Despite the problems, it appears that provincial government is going to be a reality in PNG for some time. The failures have been glaring and the temptation at the centre has been to try to sweep away the whole system. But the experiment of devolving decision making to the provincial level has gone so far and brought so many people into positions in which they can experience power that it may be irreversible. If the system continues to stabilise, that may not be a bad thing. A spreading of the sources of power has the advantage of limiting the excesses that could flow from having a powerful and autocratic central government. Father Momis argued before the parliament in September 1988 that successful decentralisation was 'essential to the unity, stability and peace' of PNG. He warned of the dangers of people becoming alienated and said the nation was beginning to suffer the consequences of a breakdown in law and order. 'Perhaps the most important factor' behind this, Momis contended, was 'rapid social change causing a breakdown of our traditional village based systems of social control'. The gap, according to Momis, could not 'possibly be filled by a monolithic centralised government'. In a country that speaks 700 languages, perhaps 700 politicians is not such a bad answer.

CHAPTER SEVEN

COULD A COUP SUCCEED?

'AT Military Staff College I made it my business to understand coups,' the ex-Brigadier General, Ted Diro, told the PNG parliament on 13 November 1987. 'I made it my business to understand military coups throughout Africa, Asia and the Latin American countries. The ingredients are here, whether you like it or not.' Diro, the commander of the Papua New Guinea Defence Force (PNGDF) from 1975 to 1981, and leader of the Papuan block in parliament, was heated. He had risen in the grievance debate to reject allegations of high treason that the Opposition Leader, Mr Somare, had levelled against him for accepting money from Indonesia's Armed Forces Chief, General Benny Murdani. 'I think it is time,' Diro warned the members around him, 'that somebody tells you, the leaders, the hard facts about Papua New Guinea's position. The situation is now tense . . . . I think the situation is now headed for crisis and I do not want to be blamed when that arises.' Diro's argument went that Papua New Guineans were not in control of their own economy and that the exodus of school leavers who could not be employed was placing intolerable strains on the political system. He claimed that his expertise as a long-time student of coups placed him in a position to know.

On 8 February 1989 four hundred unruly soldiers took to the streets of Port Moresby as a mob and marched eight kilometres from the Defence Force headquarters at Murray Barracks to the national parliament, threatening anybody in their way and smashing windows in the parliament building and car windscreens in the public carpark. They were angry over pay. In protesting they totally disregarded their officers, whom they bombarded with sticks, stones and bottles.

COULD A COUP SUCCEED?

The collapse in discipline shocked the Government and led to the establishment of a Defence General Board of Inquiry into the 'administration and management of the Defence Force and the Defence Department'. The Board found that 'some senior officers "lost rank" in not exercising decisive leadership'. Three lower rank soldiers, including a sergeant, were found guilty of mutiny by PNG's national court and jailed.

At dawn on 1 June 1988 military aircraft flew sixty combat soldiers from Port Moresby to Lae to defend the Lae airport against destruction. Operation 'Albatros' was under way. The soldiers secured the airport perimeter and refused to allow workers from the Government's own Department of Civil Aviation (DCA) on to the strip. The deployment of troops was authorised by the Defence Force commander, Brigadier General Rochus Lokinap, to stop the Civil Aviation authorities from sending bulldozers to tear up the runway. DCA and the Lands Department had won Cabinet approval to close down the Lae airport months earlier and DCA had ordered all operators, both civil and military, to shift to Nadzab, an international-standard airport, forty kilometres inland up the Markham valley. The PNG Defence Force maintained it did not have funds to keep its air element operating from an airstrip so far out of town when it had no hangars or facilities there and no money to build any. Prime Minister Wingti reprimanded the Brigadier General but the troops stayed at the Lae airport and the Defence Force was allowed to keep using Lae until new facilities to accommodate the PNGDF air element could be built in Port Moresby from Australian Defence Co-operation aid.

Over the Christmas–New Year period, as 1987 turned into 1988, Papua New Guinea's Defence Force went through the most dramatic shake-up in its senior officer corps since Independence. Four of the nation's top eight soldiers were removed from their posts. They were all Papuans: the commander, Brigadier General Tony Huai, and three colonels, including the officer previously thought most likely to succeed him, Colonel Robert Dademo. The sudden replacement of half of the top men in the PNGDF caused consternation, especially amongst Papuans, who make up one fifth of Papua New Guinea's population. Prior to what was called 'the Papuan purge', Papuans filled six of the top eight posts. Afterwards, they filled three. One Papuan was promoted to Colonel but the new commander, Brigadier General Lokinap, was the first head of the armed forces from a region other than Papua. He was from New Ireland in the New Guinea islands, the smallest of PNG's four regions. The Minister, James Pokasui, himself a former soldier, and the Secretary for Defence, Stephen Mokis, who had been promoted a short time before, were from Manus, also in the New Guinea Isands region. There were allegations of 'regionalism'.

All four of the above incidents — Ted Diro's predictions to parliament, the army pay riot, the takeover of Lae airport, and the sackings of the commander and three colonels — led to erroneous reports in one or another section of the Australian media that PNG was on the verge of, or had narrowly averted, a military coup. The two military coups in Fiji in 1987 demolished the myth that the Pacific was somehow different, that its recently independent countries had proven themselves able to sort out their post-colonial problems without the failure of this 'democracy' that they had been given. Fiji had been a symbol. When gloomy forecasts were being made as PNG's Independence approached, optimists pointed to Fiji, not to Africa, as the model to follow. The 'Pacific way' would see PNG through. The traditions of the Royal Pacific Islands Regiment, like those of the Royal Fiji Army, would ensure that civilian rule endured. But following Colonel Rabuka's dismissal of the Bavadra Government and his second usurpation of power four months later, the Fiji example took on an entirely different meaning.

What are the possibilities of a military uprising in Papua New Guinea and how seriously should the regular rumours and reports of an impending coup be taken? Firstly, the Fiji example is, and was, no reliable guide either way. The Fiji coups were racially driven. The Fijian Melanesians were outnumbered by the formerly indentured and more latterly immigrant Indians and they were fearful that they had lost control of government to an Indian dominated coalition. The Royal Fiji Army was almost totally Melanesian and Colonel Rabuka saw its role as being the guardian of the supremacy of the Melanesians in their own land. In PNG the non-indigenous residents comprise 1.3 per cent of the population. Amongst native Papua New Guineans there is a myriad of ethnic races. As well, the Fijian soldiers had been blooded in the Middle East in UN 'peace-keeping' missions — an experience that not only unified them but made them more internationally aware and politically conscious. The PNGDF's only outside venture was the short but highly successful excursion to Vanuatu in 1980 to help a newly independent

Melanesian country put down a 'French-inspired' uprising on Espiritu Santo. There are few similarities between Fiji and PNG or between their armed forces.

The strength of the PNG Defence Force is about 3400, although in early 1990 the PNG Cabinet approved a program of expansion to 5200 by 1994. It has a relatively large headquarters structure designed for an army infantry brigade. Operationally, there are three elements to the force — land, sea and air. The land element is the largest. It has two infantry battalions based on opposite sides of the mainland, an engineering battalion, a signals squadron, an explosives ordinance and disposal unit, and a preventative medical platoon. It has no tanks or artillery.

The naval element operates a patrol boat squadron of six ASI surveillance vessels, and a landing craft squadron of two heavy landing craft. The patrol boats were supplied by Australia under the Pacific patrol boat program to help South Pacific island nations with surveillance. However, at the request of the PNGDF, the six vessels supplied to PNG have been fitted with more powerful cannons than those to the smaller countries. The main patrol boat base is at Lombrum in the Manus province just below the equator, while there is a small forward base at Alotau in the Milne Bay province. The heavy landing craft operate out of the heavy landing craft base in Port Moresby.

The air element consists of four Iroquois helicopters and an air transport squadron with a fleet of four ageing DC3s, three Israeli short-take-off-and-landing Arava transport planes and four Nomads. The base for the air transport squadron is being moved from Lae to Port Moresby. The helicopters were donated by Australia in 1989 and quickly put into service on Bougainville. The PNGDF had no trained helicopter pilots to fly the Iroquois and let a contract to a commercial helicopter company, Heli New Guinea, to provide pilots and maintenance until pilots could be trained. Australia is providing the training in Australia.

The national Government in 1983 reduced the human resource ceiling for the Defence Force to 3050. But, although the full reductions were never achieved, that 1983 Cabinet decision and shortages of funds are held to be the main reasons for a gradual deterioration in the efficiency of PNG's armed forces. At the beginning of 1989 all the operational units of the PNGDF were well under establishment strength. One of the infantry battalions was 29 per cent below strength, with only 419 men out of an authorised establishment of 592, while the other was 26 per cent down, with 404 troops instead of 548. The engineer battalion was almost one third under-manned, with only 225 men out of 331. The most seriously deficient operational unit was the air transport squadron. It was 40 per cent under strength — 97 posted personnel out of an authorised establishment of 162.

The two infantry battalions are the 1st and 2nd battalions of the Royal Pacific Islands Regiment (1PIR and 2PIR), a regiment with a proud and tough record stretching back to World War II. While 1PIR is based at Tauarama Barracks on Port Moresby's south-eastern outskirts and has a border garrison at Kiunga on the Fly River near the Irian Jayan border, 2PIR has its home at Moem Barracks on Cape Moem overlooking the sea at Wewak, provincial capital of the East Sepik province on the north coast of the PNG mainland and its border garrison at Vanimo in the Sandaun province. Regimental headquarters are at Murray Barracks in the heart of Port Moresby. The Defence Department, the engineering battalion and the Defence intelligence branch are also located at Murray Barracks. Recruits are trained at Goldie River north-west of Port Moresby — the third military barracks in or around the capital. The Goldie River training depot is the largest single establishment in the PNGDF. Officer training is done at the Defence Academy at Igam Barracks in Lae.

Papua New Guineans proved themselves formidable soldiers during World War II. The Pacific Islands Regiment killed 2200 Japanese troops for the loss of only sixty-three men. The first unit of Papua New Guinean soldiers ever raised for a modern war was the Papuan Infantry Battalion, in Port Moresby in June 1940. It was an Australian Army Battalion and its officers were Australians. The Papuan Infantry Battalion fought with distinction in the Owen Stanley Ranges. Later, as the Japanese were slowly driven back, three more battalions were raised on the northern side of the mainland and in the islands. These were called the New Guinea Infantry Battalions and all four were grouped together as the Pacific Islands Regiment in 1944. However, they rarely fought as a complete unit, even at battalion level. The Australian and American troops quickly came to value the abilities of the Papua New Guineans on reconnaissance and other missions that could best be done by small detachments and so fragments of the regiment were in action in almost all the theatres of war in New Guinea. By the time the four battalions were disbanded in 1946, the regiment had won eleven battle honours and twenty-three soldiers had been decorated.

The Pacific Islands Regiment was formed again in 1951, its 1st Battalion once more raised in Port Moresby. A decision to raise the 2nd Battalion at Wewak was made in the early 1960s when Indonesia was confronting Malaysia in President Sukano's 'Konfrontasi' campaign. Australians dominated the officer ranks of the regiment right up until the post-Independence late 1970s. As Independence approached, officer training for Papua New Guineans accelerated. But it was May 1971 before the first Papua New Guinean — a man called Ted Diro — reached the rank of Major. Four years later Diro was a brigadier general and first commander of the PNG Defence Force.

Ted Diro was born on 14 December 1943 at Boku Village, in the Rigo sub-district of what is now the Central province. Boku village is about forty kilometres north-east of Port Moresby. Diro walked to Port Moresby to get himself enrolled for secondary education at the Kila Kila High School. Later he attended Sogeri High in the mountains behind Port Moresby and completed his secondary education at the Slade School at Warwick in Queensland where he successfully sat for his Senior Public Exams. In January 1963 he was admitted to officer cadet school in Australia and the following December graduated as a second lieutenant in the Australian Army. He was promoted to captain in 1967. When, on 3 May 1971, he became the first Papua New Guinean major in the Pacific Islands Regiment, there were still some six hundred Australians in the then 3200-strong PIR.

The Kumul Force

The radio in the Hotel Santo is tuned to the illegal Vemerana Republic Radio, which is broadcasting a call to arms. It is August 1980, three nights before PNG troops are to land on Vanuatu's northern island of Espiritu Santo to put down the Jimmy Stevens rebellion. Only two guests are in the hotel, which is 'behind rebel lines'. A British radio technician is attempting to jam the broadcast but a voice can be heard above the din.

After dedicating the song 'Daddy Cool' to 'Moli (Chief) Jimmy

Stevens', the rebel announcer, an Australian, Bob Schnell, launches into a tirade against the PNG soldiers. Schnell wears a pistol on his hip and each night sits behind the microphone of the Vemerana Radio's crude, transportable broadcast unit. Journalists covering the Santo uprising have dubbed Schnell 'Lord Paw Paw'.

'In a few days, probably starting this Sunday,' Schnell says, his voice low but gradually rising to reach a demonic pitch, 'three hundred troops from Papua New Guinea will be coming here to kill Man Santo. Man Santo will rise up with his bows and arrows and the few guns he has and he will kill these troops coming from Papua New Guinea. "In no way," and Man Santo is saying this. "In no way will he tolerate these troops from Papua New Guinea coming to his island." They have no right to come here to prop up the regime of Father Walter Lini.'

The broadcast continues: 'We all know of the violence and the bloodshed that has occurred in the Highlands of Papua New Guinea. The troops from Papua New Guinea are entirely ruthless. They are used to blood. And because they are used to blood they will be used to what will happen when they arrive on the island of Santo. If they do not come to respect Man Santo then they will have to be killed.'

Schnell is rumoured to be an intelligence agent. Even if he is not, his message that the PNG soldiers are to be feared fits well with the PNGDF's own propaganda efforts. A few days earlier, in Vila, Colonel Ian Glanville, a naturalised PNG citizen, stressed to me the World War II kill ratio that PNG soldiers set against the Japanese — 30:1. My reports over Radio Australia, I learnt that afternoon, were closely monitored by the rebels and their supporters on Santo. One threatened to 'cut [my] balls off' for an earlier dispatch he disagreed with.

(Recalling the successful Vanuatu operation on its fifth anniversary in 1985, former Brigadier General Ted Diro told the *Times of PNG*: 'There was a lot of propaganda in Santo and we published our significant military feat during World War II, where for every Papua New Guinean killed, thirty enemy soldiers died.')

In the Australian colonial days, the regiment's commander, an Australian brigadier, did not answer to the administration. He took his orders from army headquarters in Canberra. The role of the

PIR was predominately a regular army one. The soldiers went on patrols, occasionally doing minor civil aid works, but mostly they stuck to their role as army infantrymen. The Australian Army prided itself on the claim that 'to a notable extent tribal loyalties have been subordinated to esprit de corps'. There was much debate over what shape the force should take after Independence. Some argued that the PIR should be turned into a paramilitary force and given a police back-up role. In 1970, when the troubles on the Gazelle Peninsula were at their height and the Australian Government feared the Mataungan Association might whip up large-scale civil disorder, the Australian administrator in Port Moresby was authorised to call upon the military for support. He never did and the arrangement was revoked in May 1971, ten months after it came into force.

As Independence loomed, the PIR had no air transport. The Australian Navy operated its own Papua and New Guinea division with a small fleet of patrol boats based at Lombrum in Manus, which had been a huge American base in World War II. The cost of running a two-battalion-strong force in PNG was being met entirely by the Australian Government and it was obvious that an independent PNG would not have the resources to maintain the Pacific Islands Regiment by itself. In March 1973, the first Somare Government, formed barely six months earlier, considered what role it wanted the army to have in a self-governing and later independent PNG. There were some fears of what future role a powerful Defence Force might see for itself in the post-colonial period. According to the Deputy Chief Minister of the time, Sir John Guise, some people around Somare were advocating that the PIR be disbanded. Cabinet eventually directed the soldiers to devote their resources 'to economic development and the promotion of national administration and unity'.

PNG established its own Defence Department in October, 1974. Australia agreed that PNG could keep the patrol boats at Lombrum in Manus and the sailors became members of the naval element of a unified PNGDF. Full responsibility for Defence — one of the last functions handed over by Australia — was transferred to the Somare Government on 6 May 1975, and the Defence Force formed its embryonic Air Transport Squadron on 12 August, one month and four days before Independence.

In its October 1975 policy document, 'Programs and Performance', the Government of newly independent PNG set out its approach to the Defence Force. A certain ambivalence was evident. 'The primary roles of the force are to defend PNG from external attack and, if required, to assist the civil authorities in restoring public order and security in the event of a major civil disturbance. The force also performs other services of a civil nature which contribute towards building the nation . . . . The logistic self-sufficiency of the force, although costly in budget terms, means that it has a unique capability to carry out activities in support of the Government in remote areas.'

An optimistic plan to Papua New Guineanise the officer corps was outlined, 'aimed at reducing the numbers of Australian servicemen . . . from 550 in July 1975 to 17 by December 1980'. The reality fell a long way short. In 1990 there were still 29 Australians filling establishment positions in the PNGDF. 'The Defence Force has been reduced in strength since mid-1973 from 4200 to 3500 under Cabinet direction,' the policy document said. 'The reduction has been accompanied by a drastic reorganisation'. The cost factor was uppermost in the newly independent Government's mind: 'By the nature of its activities, the Defence Force is very reliant on a number of expensive, technology-intensive units such as the air and sea units and the engineer units within the land force. Wherever possible, more sophisticated equipment is being replaced by equipment more appropriate to PNG's needs and future maintenance capabilities.' That was a fond sentiment but it was not one the PNGDF agreed with. By the late 1980s, PNG complained that the new, free patrol boats were not sophisticated enough!

The funding problem facing that first Somare Government was eased when Australia agreed to continue providing substantial injections of cash under Defence aid. Despite this a number of the Government's early advisers still regarded the PNGDF as an expensive 'luxury' that PNG could ill afford. In PNG's first post-Independence financial year, 1975–76, the total Defence running costs amounted to $33.55 million. Of this, Australia put up $24.1 million, or seventy-two per cent. The Australian aid came in two ways. First, there was a direct grant from the Australian Defence Department of $8.1 million, which went into the PNG Budget, and allowed PNG to appropriate $17.55 million (4.7 per cent of total spending) to Defence in its 1975–76 budget ($8.1m from the Australian Defence Department and $9.45m from PNG sources). Second, there was a separate Defence grant in aid worth $16 million, which helped pay the salaries of the Australian servicemen seconded from the Australian Army and Navy to the PNGDF. Hefty Australian funding support for the PNGDF continues to this day, although the share of the total is closer to fifty per cent, recent grants having boosted it from thirty per cent.

The PNGDF's most successful post-Independence venture was the quelling of the Santo rebellion in Vanuatu in 1980. Seventy years of British and French condominium rule in the New Hebrides had created an explosive pre-Independence mixture. Father Walter Lini's fiercely pro-Independence, English-speaking Vanua'Aku Party had easily won the elections of late 1979, defeating the French-speaking moderate parties that were in favour of much more gradual political evolution. The Vanua'Aku Party had surprised the French by winning not only in areas where English influence had been strongest but also, albeit narrowly, on the main island in the north of the country, Espiritu Santo, and the main island in the south, Tanna, where the moderate parties had been expected to triumph. With the approach of Independence on 30 July 1980, trouble erupted on both islands. Skirmishes on Tanna between the rival political groups led to the fatal shooting of a Moderate Party Member of Parliament, Alexi Yulo. But the situation on Santo boiled over into an uprising.

Jimmy Stevens, a mixed-race, self-proclaimed chief, or Moli, with seemingly countless wives, became president of the 'Republic of Vemerana', and many of the English-speaking public servants and sympathisers of the Vanua'Aku Party were thrown off Santo. Stevens was supported by hundreds of bow-and-arrow-wielding tribesmen from the bush areas of Santo but there were other aspects to the Vemarana Republic. There was the right-wing, American, libertarian Phoenix Foundation, which provided money and even produced passports. There were French settlers, other long-term expatriate residents and disaffected, French-educated youths who saw little future for themselves in an English-speaking-led Vanuatu. And there were those who became its saddest victims when it collapsed — the mixed-race families who ended up as refugees living in the slums of Noumea. But during the excitement of the rebellion guns were ferried in from New Caledonia on a private launch and explosives stolen from government and private stores. The rebel republic began taxing companies and individuals who remained, not wanting to abandon their investments.

The British and French authorities refused to act. Father Lini appealed to the South Pacific forum for help. The forum was held in Kiribati in early July 1980. Father Lini was unable to attend formal sessions because Vanuatu was not yet independent. However, he did speak privately to PNG's Prime Minister, Sir Julius Chan. Sir Julius sent for the PNGDF commander, Brigadier General Diro, who flew into the coral atoll nation on the PNG Government's executive aircraft. While the forum meeting came out with a resolution of support for Vanuatu's coming Independence, the scoop of that year's forum meeting was that Papua New Guinea would send troops to put down the Santo rebellion.

Diro claims he was so enthusiastic that he told Chan that if the Government did not approve the deployment of the PNGDF, he would resign and personally go to Vanuatu to help. 'We spent many nights on top of the Pineapple building,' Diro recalls, referring to the distinctive building then housing the PNG prime minister's office, 'going over the scenarios, with Sir Julius again and again seeking assurances from the military that all would be well. I was not in a position to guarantee him no casualties but I assured him we would put up nothing but the best,' Diro says. 'I set the standards myself. Each unit was put through rigid battle indoctrination and the emphasis was on night manoeuvres, night shooting, physical fitness and generally bringing the Force into battle efficiency which we had never experienced during peace time. Company commanders were sacked if they did not perform to expectation and every officer and NCO had to justify his position in the Kumul force. That was the basis of our success. The training was such that they could hit rats and bandicoots at night if they moved. I have never seen our soldiers so efficient and highly motivated,' the former PNGDF commander says.

Australia provided logistical back-up. But no Australian soldiers seconded to the PNGDF were allowed to go into action on Santo. The PNG troops in Vanuatu were under the command of Colonel Tony Huai. At dawn on Sunday, 17 August 1980, two PNGDF DC3s and a Nomad dropped down onto the Santo airfield, disgorging ninety-five combat troops. Led by Huai clutching an Israeli sub-machine gun, the men leapt out prepared for trouble. They were in full battle dress, armed with automatic rifles and heavier weapons. They had the dark visors of their battle helmets pulled down over their faces and fearsome-looking, long-bladed bush knives strapped

COULD A COUP SUCCEED?

to their waists. They secured the airport. British commandoes and French paratroopers had been sent to Santo a week before Vanuatu's Independence by the condominium authorities on strict orders not to engage the rebels. All they were to do was guard the airport, and two or three other installations such as the fuel depot, against sabotage. The rebels had the run of the island. With the arrival of the Papua New Guineans, the British and French soldiers packed up and left, having picked up no honours but excellent suntans.

Within forty minutes the Kumul force secured the installations that the British and French left. Two PNGDF patrol boats moved into the Segond Canal, which flows past the main town, Luganville. They confiscated the rebels' motor launch. The previous evening more than fifty French citizens, most of them women and children, had been flown out to New Caledonia on aircraft chartered by the French Government. More left on a French warship standing by. The PNG soldiers set up roadblocks at either end of Luganville town and began confiscating vehicles. They had a list of vehicles commandeered by the rebels. Cars on the list were impounded, their drivers and passengers locked up. The troops shot out the tyres of cars that attempted to break through. Hundreds of shotguns and rifles, most of them hunting guns, were taken and piled up under guard outside the old British prison. After two weeks, the move on Jimmy Stevens's headquarters at Vanifo began. It was an efficient military operation. After it was over, the casualties stood at two rebels dead — one of them a son of Jimmy Stevens who was killed by grenade blast when he tried to break out of the Vanifo seige.

By September, two months earlier than expected, the Kumul force handed administration of Santo back to Father Lini's government. On 27 September the PNG troops returned home as heroes. Thousands gathered at Port Moresby's Jackson's Airport to cheer. The Vemerana rebellion had collapsed quickly and not a single PNG soldier had been lost. But the dangers for PNG had been high. At home the Opposition Leader, Mr Somare, had opposed the intervention from the start and had even gone to court to seek a ruling that Sir Julius had acted unconstitutionally. Fiji, too, had been critical. The Australians, who had to provide considerable back-up transport and logistics, had been anxious about the outcome but were delighted with the result. Huai was to write later that it took the Australians 'three flaming weeks to make up their minds'. But if the Kumul force had been a gamble, it was one that paid off. Over the following year, the PNGDF helped train the paramilitary Vanuatu mobile force — a display of Melanesian solidarity funded out of Australia's Defence Co-operation program.

The significance of this first deployment of soldiers from a Pacific island country to help another was that, for the first time in the Pacific, the use of force was no longer the sole preserve of the white administering powers. It marked a change in regional relations. For the French in particular, it set new parameters on what could happen. The deployment of the Kumul force raised the possibility in the minds of both the French and the Kanaks of New Caledonia that the intervention of Melanesian soldiers might, in extreme circumstances, be a possibility. It also led to a greater sense of cohesiveness amongst the new Melanesian countries, which eventually found its expression in the sub-regional Melanesian Spearhead Group of PNG, Vanuatu and Solomon Islands.

Australia had taken a keen interest in Vanuatu. Its Consulate in Port Vila was very active in the year leading up to Independence. Australia believed regional stability would be enhanced by an independent, stable and unified Vanuatu. And when the French Government dallied and the French Resident in the New Hebrides — as it was called pre-Independence — raised the expectations of the settlers on Santo by saying France would not abandon them, there was potential for mischief. Groups such as the American Phoenix Foundation and the extreme right in New Caledonia became involved. Australia did not want to intervene, so Father Lini's appeal to Sir Julius in Kiribati was secretly welcomed at senior levels in Australia. The Kumul force could intervene directly, with Australian back-up. Australia needed to take none of the risks.

While the Vanuatu operation boosted morale in 1980, it is symptomatic of the problems now facing the PNGDF that the Defence Department did not have the funds to strike a Vanuatu campaign medal for many years. The 1986 Annual Defence Report commented that concern had been raised 'by about 400 officers and servicemen regarding the proposed Vanuatu Operation Medal'. Indeed, the Defence Force's funding problems had become so severe by 1983 that the Defence Secretary, Gus Maketu, reported to parliament that the PNGDF would be incapable of staging another Santo operation. The 1983 Defence Report commented wistfully that both the PNGDF and the Defence Department had struggled through the year 'with high hopes and diminishing optimism'.

COULD A COUP SUCCEED?

An analysis of the funding provided to the PNGDF since Independence shows the force did not fare well for the first decade and a half at the hands of Finance Department bureaucrats and that, until 1990, it had few battling for it in Cabinet's deliberations on the Budget. The Defence Force's budget did not even keep pace with inflation. It went from K17.6 million in PNG's first year (1975-76) to K34.4 million in 1988. A better indication of the priority given the Defence Force is its relative share of total government expenditure. In the first year of Independence, 4.7 per cent of the Budget was allocated to Defence. By 1983, the Defence share had slumped to 3.4 per cent and by 1988 it was down to 3.3 per cent. The department constantly complained it was desperately short of cash and in 1988 could not achieve the cuts forced upon it. The Defence budget was overspent by 15 per cent or K5.2 million ($7.8m). In 1990 Defence was given a more realistic budget allocation of K43.2 million ($65m), which represented 4.2 per cent of total spending. But that surge of realism followed the 1989 army pay riot and the deployment of soldiers to Bougainville.

Troops' Pay Riot

Major Kavanamur stood, arms raised, in the twin beams of his vehicle's headlights and called on the approaching mob of angry soldiers to stop. Except for the headlights it was pitch dark on Taurama Road. The soldiers were swearing and cursing. More than 150 soldiers from the 1st Battalion, Pacific Islands Regiment, were on their way from Taurama Barracks to Defence headquarters at Murray Barracks ten kilometres away 'to get the support of our comrades' for a protest over pay. Major Kavanamur, Acting Commanding Officer of Taurama Barracks, was ignored. The soldiers brushed past.

Later that night, 7 February 1989, about four hundred soldiers from both barracks gathered at the Kingsbury Club inside Murray Barracks. When officers told them to disperse, there was a hail of sticks, stones and bottles. Next morning, the anger over pay had grown and even more soldiers assembled near the soccer field. They parked army trucks to block the main road passing through Murray Barracks, chased off paper boys at the nearby traffic lights and overturned a police vehicle.

The soldiers abused officers who tried to explain the new pay rates and ignored appeals to go back to barracks. One officer told them to 'go to Waigani' if they wanted more explanation and that is what they did. They marched as a mob to parliament, tearing off tree branches as clubs, threatening those who got in their way and chasing journalists, cameramen and photographers.

Along Sir John Guise Drive at Waigani one charged at me shouting and tried to snatch my cassette recorder. I held it. We struggled and the microphone went flying. Swearing, he let the recorder go, shaped to hit me, decided not to and gave me a shove before rejoining the others. I picked up the microphone, checked that I had the incident taped and headed off to file a news item on the Army pay demonstration for the ABC lunchtime news. As I passed soldiers straggling at the rear they recognised me and shouted, 'Shon Donny!' I looked up apprehensively. They smiled and waved.

The pay riot of early February 1989 was the result of a long build-up of dissatisfaction in the ranks over pay and conditions. When the Australian Army relinquished control over the PIR in 1975, soldiers were better off than most other Papua New Guineans on the public payroll. They also had first-class accommodation in some of the finest tropical barracks in the world. But soldier pay levels were not reviewed for the following thirteen years. Various submissions were put to a succession of governments but all were either ignored or referred back to the Defence Department for further information. In 1988, the Sydney company, Hay Consultants, was hired by the PNGDF to do a complete job evaluation of the force. The study was funded under Australia's Defence Co-operation program. Hay found serious anomalies. For instance, senior warrant officers with twenty or more years of service were being paid only about one and a half times what a raw recruit received. The Hay recommendations formed the basis of a new submission on pay rates that was presented to the national Government's Salaries and Conditions Monitoring committee, which revised the figures downwards.

There was strong speculation within the force as to what pay rises they would get. A figure of seventy-two per cent came to be believed. That had been the recommended rise for one position — force sergeant major, the rank Hay found most disadvantaged of all. But in the minds of many in the lower ranks, the figure rapidly assumed a legitimacy that was totally unwarranted. In October 1988 Cabinet approved pay increases. Media reports of the decision heightened expectations amongst servicemen of big pay rises. What had been approved was a complex range of reclassifications with a wide variety of different increases. For the sake of simplicity, the Defence Minister announced that the increases would average twenty-six per cent. Not everybody was to get twenty-six per cent. About six hundred privates were to get a pay rise of less than five per cent. Because some officers were to get substantially more, Cabinet decided to implement the new rates over three years with no one rank getting an increase in the first year of more than twenty-five per cent. But the details were never explained and the matter was appallingly handled.

There were long delays. Months elapsed. In early 1989 rumours spread amongst the troops that the 'big rise' would take effect in the first pay fortnight in February. A few days before payday, some lower ranking Defence Force members from the Naval Element who were to be away at sea received their pay early. In the mess at Taurama Barracks on the evening of 7 February they compared their back-pay with what they heard the officers were getting. Others gathered around and anger turned to fury. About 150 set out for Defence Force headquarters. The following morning, four hundred troops from both Murray and Taurama Barracks marched on the parliament, where they smashed half the plate-glass windows on the ground floor. Police restored control with tear gas and the Deputy Prime Minister, Akoka Doi, told the demonstrating troops they would get an adjusted pay increase before the end of February. Mr Doi blamed the Defence Department, saying Cabinet had approved significant increases for all. In a quick reassessment, the pay rise to the six hundred privates on pay level sixteen who were to move up just one step, to level seventeen, were promised a larger jump.

Three of the ringleaders of the pay demonstration were charged with mutiny. Convicting them on 31 March 1989, Mr Justice Bredmeyer of the PNG National Court found them guilty of the least serious of the three kinds of mutiny under the Defence Act. He found they had not tried to 'overthrow lawful authority' nor had they 'disobeyed orders'. However, the judge did find that they had 'impeded the performance of duty' of several hundred soldiers in encouraging them to march to parliament and therefore 'not to be on duty' when they should have been. Mr Justice Bredmeyer

sentenced Sergeant Albert Ugunnie and Private Matthew Davai —
'the leading spokesmen' — each to nine months' imprisonment with
hard labour and recommended their dismissal from the force. He
jailed the third man, Private Martin Taumu, for four months. In
handing down judgment, he said he had taken into account that
the men had 'a real grievance' over pay. 'There was a delay in paying
them,' Mr Justice Bredmeyer said. 'They saw that as a failed promise.
The pay rise was much less than they were led to expect and there
seems to have been a lack of communication between the officers
and the men as to the details of the pay rise.' The communications
problem was even worse than that. Branch heads and directors in
PNGDF headquarters were ignorant of the new pay rates even up
to a month after the riot.

Within days of the riot, the Government suspended the Defence
Force Commander, Brigadier General Lokinap, and the Defence
Department Secretary, Mr Mokis. The Defence General Board of
Inquiry absolved both men of blame. It said the commander had
been failed by his subordinates and that Mr Mokis, who had been
in the job for not much more than a year, had 'inherited a department
devoid of decisive leadership at the top'. Brigadier General Lokinap
had been out of Port Moresby when the riot occurred and the Board
was critical of some of the colonels, particularly the Chief of Staff,
Colonel Kerry Frank. However, others showed 'commendable
initiative' in rallying the officer corps and senior NCOs. 'Such timely
action helped save some degree of authority, albeit very much eroded.
The most notable and worthy of mention is Colonel Leo Nuia.'
Colonel Nuia, the chief of operations, was sent to Bougainville to
take charge of military operations in October 1989, after Brigadier
General Lokinap was reinstated.

The Defence Board of Inquiry was critical of the standard of
discipline in the PNGDF. A 'significant decline' in discipline had
occurred, it said, since the PNGDF started to implement the 1983
Cabinet submission reducing its manpower ceiling to 3050. It claimed
this had resulted in servicemen being overworked, recreation leave
accumulating and low morale. There was 'an apparent inability
and/or reluctance by commands at all levels to impose discipline';
officers and soldiers were 'becoming too familiar with each other';
there were 'inconsistencies' in the awarding of punishments; and
'undue delays' in the administration of discipline. The Board also
found that a 'significant deterioration' of all aspects of service

conditions had adversely affected discipline and there was 'an apparent failure by Defence Force training institutions to instil leadership qualities in the younger generation officers'.

Investigating whether the military discipline code was adequate, the General Board found that 'Junior disciplinary officers, senior disciplinary officers and officers generally are not conversant with the disciplinary procedures'. It recommended that all officers be forced to sit for examinations on the application and procedures of the code 'as a prerequisite for promotions'. It also found there were no provisions in the code for court martial! Actually, that was not so much a finding of the Board as a ruling of the courts. The PNGDF had court martialled more than thirty troops following the riotous march on parliament, but the men appealed and had to be reinstated. The Board said the Defence Minister should recommend to Cabinet amendments to the Defence Act to give the force the ability to court martial soldiers.

Concern about discipline was not new. One year before the pay riot, an extraordinarily public argument was conducted in the pages of the PNG newspapers between the Defence Minister, Mr Pokasui, and the Defence Force commander he had just sacked, Brigadier General Huai. Huai, who had led the men on Santo, became commander in late 1985 but Mr Pokasui, a former captain, removed him in late 1987. (Pokasui himself lost the Defence Ministry when the Wingti government fell in mid-1988.) In early 1988 he attacked Huai, claiming morale had slipped during his tenure as head of the PNGDF. Huai countered by saying the problems went back well before his time as commander. 'We were continuously under-budgeted,' he said. 'Our capital equipment, training and operational programs were always severely affected.' He claimed morale had been in decline since the mid-1970s. 'Gone are the pre-Independence days when we had stacks of personal equipment, stacks of air hours, stacks of land transport,' the ex-commander said, 'and we could travel anywhere in the country and spend weeks on patrol. Now we have to live with the reality of the economic situation. This one factor is the cause of morale and discipline problems.'

One practical consequence of the funding cutbacks has been the force's reduced capacity to patrol the Irian Jayan border. At Independence and for several years after, Defence Force units made a patrol a month along sections of the 750-kilometre border with Indonesia. In 1982 these were cut back to four a year. Tension on the border waxes and wanes. Since 1984, when more than 10,000 Irianese fled from Indonesia into PNG, one of the chief tasks of the force has been to ensure that elements from the rebel Organisasi Papua Mederka (OPM) are not trying to recruit new members from the refugee camps inside PNG or use PNG land for training. In 1986 one border patrol conducted by 1PIR, code-named 'Biku Namo', was sent to the Kiunga/Ningerum area in the central border region to investigate reports that the OPM was conducting guerilla training in the border refugee camps. The patrol found no basis for the reports.

Border Patrol

His jungle greens are grimy, the sweat glistens on his forehead. The unproductive, dry savanna bushland earth burns through the soles of his army boots. He leaves the stunted trees ringing the Morehead airstrip and heaves the cumbersome back-pack field radio from his shoulders. An ageing Defence Force DC3 with further rations should come lumbering down out of the sky any time now. His platoon has been patrolling the southern section of the Irian Jayan border on foot for several weeks.

Morehead is the district centre fifty kilometres north of the Torres Strait. It is the middle of 'the dry' and this low-lying country south of the Fly River is at its most unattractive. But it is easier to patrol now than during 'the wet', when the surrounding bush becomes swamp and the mosquitoes swarm instead of just harass. His PNG Defence Force patrol has not encountered any Indonesian troops. On the extremely rare occasions when this happens, standing orders for years have been to melt into the bush. However, when one group of Indonesian soldiers was found in 1988 to have set up camp inside the PNG border instructions came down that it was to be moved. As the Indonesians pulled out shots were exchanged. Nobody was hit.

In 1983 an Indonesian road being built along the Irian Jayan side of the border to the west of Morehead strayed across into Papua New Guinea in three places but it wasn't discovered for some time. The area is sparsely populated and the border, the 141st East parallel, is ill-defined in the extreme. The Indonesians have set up transmigration settlements on their side of the border — ten kilometres or more back inside Irian Jaya — settlements made up predominantly of formerly landless Javanese peasants. There are some Melanesian families interspersed in these settlements but thousands of the subsistence-farming, village-dwelling Melanesian Iranese fled across the border into PNG in 1984.

Part of the patrol's job is to ensure that these people, now living in refugee camps on the PNG side, are not providing succour and support to the scattered, poorly armed, virtually unorganised rebels of the Irian Jayan freedom movement, the OPM. The fear is that, should the rebels raid one of the transmigration settlements, the local Indonesian military commander might order a retaliatory attack against those suspected of harbouring them. The 1986 Treaty of Mutual Respect, Friendship and Co-operation is meant to ensure that this does not happen. But treaties need some physical back up. The soldier may have taken note of the relative better standard of health of the 'refugees' compared with his own fellow citizens in the village of Weam, between Morehead and the border. The 'refugees' are receiving internationally funded food and medical aid, the village people of Weam are not. And the children at Weam are suffering a variety of skin complaints, not immediately obvious in the camps. Such things can breed resentment. Melanesian brotherhood can come off second best when it collides with reality.

On the northern section of the border, also in 1986, a 2PIR patrol, code-named 'Bushman', went to the Wutung/Bewani area for fifteen days with the special task of investigating reports on the burning down of the government patrol officer's house, the stealing of food from local gardens and alleged intimidation of the Wutung villages. The patrol reported that the OPM was responsible. The 'Tully Gully' patrol to the Green River area in August and September of that year carried out surveillance on both Indonesian troops and OPM elements. One patrol in 1983 found that an Indonesian road under construction in the southern border plains swerved across into PNG territory in three places. The various dilemmas faced by the PNGDF and by Melanesian troops patrolling the Irian Jayan border were perhaps unconsciously summed up by the 'Sigirap Tumas' patrol report in 1983. It read: 'This patrol was deployed to the Bewani area of the West Sepik province and lasted seven weeks. Seventy-five rebels were caught during the course of the patrol, but all escaped whilst under guard.'

Frustrations with the Defence Force's capacity to manage to its own liking events on the border, and frustrations with what the force considered to be government mishandling of PNG's relations with Indonesia, led to what became known as the 1977 'Coup that Never Was'. Although it never got past dress-rehearsal stage, it was the closest PNG went in the 1970s or 1980s to a military takeover. Geoff Heriot, a former ABC correspondent in PNG, compiled a forty-five-minute radio program on this affair in 1983, six years after the event. A former colonel told Heriot: 'The plan was to blow the Waigani building and take a few of the political leaders, Somare and his advisers, hostage. And then commence some dialogue in order to get the Government to start thinking seriously about their policies and what to do with Indonesia.'

It was called Operation 'Electric Shock' and allegedly would have involved soldiers from 1PIR. Heriot reported that 'the catalyst for mutiny was an attempt to discipline or sack the Defence Force commander, Brigadier General Ted Diro'. Diro had met with Seth Rumkorem, a bush commander with the OPM operating at the northern end of the Irian Jayan border region, without telling the Government first. The Government was annoyed, fearing trouble with Indonesia, and Cabinet met on 6 October 1977 and reprimanded Diro. 'Had Cabinet sacked Diro,' Heriot reported, 'a soldier was waiting outside to signal the commencement of Operation "Electric Shock". Diro apparently did not know of the signal.' According to the ex-colonel, they rehearsed it twice in the days before the Cabinet meeting. 'We rehearsed it in full dress, full equipment.' Diro was not dismissed and the affair went no further. Government security personnel learnt of the alleged plot when one of those apparently involved got drunk at the Kone Tigers Rugby League Club and blurted out the story.

Papua New Guinea's first governor-general, Sir John Guise, who was approached by two military officers at this time, says he was aware of moves for a coup but he refused to have anything to do with them. Guise had stood down as governor-general to run for the 1977 elections and had been the Opposition's nominee to contest the vote for prime minister against Somare at the parliament's first gathering just a few months before. 'People say, you know, that we are unique from the States of Africa and Asia. We are not unique,' says Guise. 'During that period I did believe there was some move for a coup d'état. Now if anyone says that a coup d'état cannot happen in PNG, I say that that man is a mad fool.'

Geoff Heriot commented: 'Resentment within the Defence Force had been building up for some time. Soldiers complained they were either not given the material resources or the intelligence information to effectively monitor activity along the Irian Jayan border. They complained about the continuing influence of Australian military commanders attached to the PNGDF. And they complained the Somare Government failed to give a clear policy direction on how to handle the Irian Jaya border issue.' The ex-army officer who spoke to Heriot revealed that the Defence Force had initiated a relationship with the Indonesians. He said two military officers spoke with the Indonesian embassy to explain Diro's meeting with the OPM. 'It wasn't the PNG Government that defused the trouble with Indonesia,' he said. 'It was the Defence Force . . . . And I can tell you that during the Diro incident, the Indonesian military machinery was going to be mobilised to come over and clean up the border.'

The former colonel claimed the Indonesians were wary of Diro's meeting with the OPM. He held the PNG Government at fault because, he claimed, the Government was not talking enough with the Indonesians while prohibiting the PNGDF from speaking to either the OPM or the Indonesians. 'We are not battle hungry,' he said. 'We were thinking and we knew certain things were not right. We knew the Indonesians were planning an exercise and that was one of the reasons for the plot. We talked to the Indonesian Government, quietly, without the [PNG] Government knowing. We had to get both the Ambassador [Brigadier General Rogito] and General Diro together to talk. The Ambassador was planning the next day to fly to Sydney and then to Jakarta should the talks be as they suspected. So we talked to the Ambassador and that defused it.'

Diro left the Defence Force in 1982 to stand for parliament but he maintained connections with the Indonesians. Diro first met the former Indonesian armed forces chief, General Benny Murdani, in 1973, when Murdani was chief of intelligence with the Indonesian military. Murdani had his own memories of Irian Jaya. In 1962 during the Indonesian campaign to try to oust the Dutch, Murdani had led a commando parachute drop into Irian Jaya. Both men rose to command their countries' armed forces and Diro put great store by the friendship Murdani offered him. By early 1987 Diro was Foreign Minister in Prime Minister Wingti's government and he travelled to Indonesia in March for the ratification of the Treaty of Mutual Respect, Friendship and Co-operation which PNG and Indonesia had concluded late in 1986. Following the ratification ceremony in Jakarta on Thursday, 12 March 1987, ex-Brigadier General Diro and General Murdani, then commander of Indonesia's armed forces, met privately. Diro told Murdani of his difficulty in raising campaign funds for his People's Action Party for the national elections due in PNG in June/July. Murdani offered to assist, suggesting his own construction company could donate funds.

Foreign Minister Diro returned home via Australia. In Canberra he held a lengthy meeting with the Australian Prime Minister, Bob Hawke, whose mind at the time was on Libyan, not Indonesian, influence in the South Pacific. Hawke became so animated about the Libyan question, Diro informed an airport news conference on his return home, that their meeting went well over time 'and I almost missed my plane'. On 20 March, two days after Diro arrived back in Port Moresby, he called into the ANZ Bank in the Port Moresby suburb of Boroko and deposited $US69,700 into one of his accounts. Over the next three months another four deposits of American currency were credited to Mr Diro's ANZ Boroko bank accounts. $US5000 on 27 March, $US50,000 on 31 March, $US4500 on 9 April and $US10,000 on 23 June. At least one of these parcels of cash was ferried into Port Moresby by the Defence Attaché at the Indonesian embassy in Port Moresby.

News of the gifts spilled out in evidence before Mr Justice Barnett's Forestry Inquiry a few months later in October 1987. Diro had resigned from the ministry a day or two earlier, pending the hearing of perjury charges that the judge heading the inquiry had directed be laid against him. When Diro's People's Action Party Deputy Leader, Aruru Matiabe — who was Acting Foreign Minister in Diro's stead — claimed at a joint news conference with the visiting Indonesian Home Affairs Minister, Soepardjo Roestam, that it was 'the normal thing' for PNG's political leaders to accept money from influential people overseas, it cost Matiabe his job. Matiabe made the surprising comparison that Diro's taking money from Murdani was like 'Bob Hawke giving money to Paias Wingti'! Mr Matiabe admitted this had not happened but, he said, he was just trying to make a point. The point did not impress Mr Wingti, who sacked Matiabe as Acting Foreign Minister.

The Opposition in PNG accused Diro of treason. He defended

COULD A COUP SUCCEED?

himself and Murdani in parliament. 'Let me state from the outset that General Murdani is a great friend and a very great ally to PNG,' Diro claimed. He described Murdani as an upright and principled soldier 'not a politician'. Diro told the parliament there had been no border incursions by Indonesian troops since the Wingti Government took office, in November 1985, and he should be given the credit. 'As you know well when the Wingti Government took the decision to refer the problem of the refugees on our border to the United Nations High Commissioner for refugees, there was not one anti-PNG slogan in the papers in Jakarta. The problem . . . was so sensitive that previous Somare governments were powerless and gutless to do anything . . . . Mr Speaker, there is absolutely no hard evidence to substantiate claims of treason. On the contrary, there is hard and visible evidence of my successes in steering PNG out of grave security risk,' Diro argued.

General Murdani's campaign donations to Ted Diro totalled $US139,400 ($200,000). Diro claimed that these cash gifts were 'personal' and that he spent none of the money on himself, putting it all towards his party's election campaign. However, he could not deny that the gifts came from a man who, at the time, was the head of the armed forces of PNG's giant next-door neighbour and that he, Diro, at the same time, was Foreign Minister of PNG. Also, the request to Murdani for help in the election was not made during a 'personal' visit to Jakarta. It was made while Diro was in the Indonesian capital on official business for the ratification of the most important treaty PNG had signed with Indonesia. His contention that the gifts carried no reciprocal obligation was greeted with scepticism in PNG, where Melanesian custom has a very firmly structured tradition linking gifts and obligations. Diro claimed PNG could do little if Indonesia applied military pressure on the border and PNG's 'best option' for maintaining security was through friendship amongst leaders in the region.

Diro told parliament that he had received campaign donations from Australia but, he claimed, the reason General Murdani's gift had attracted so much attention was because some Papua New Guineans had inherited from Australia an anti-Indonesian 'phobia'. This 'phobia', he went on, had been passed on by others who paint Indonesia as an enemy country. 'In order to justify the defence expenditure that these countries go through they had to paint an enemy. And they have painted Indonesia as a potential aggressor and, quite wrongly, as an enemy to PNG.' Diro said PNG lived next-door to Indonesia and he accused other parliamentarians of being 'stooges' for third countries. 'Even though we are independent, the economy of this country is controlled by outsiders. Sixty-seven per cent of investment in this country is controlled by Australians. Twenty-three per cent is controlled by other foreigners. Papua New Guineans own ten per cent. We are guests in our own country,' Mr Diro said.

Attacking Australia was a tactic also employed by the dismissed Defence Force commander, Brigadier General Huai, when he defended himself two months later from allegations that he had 'leaked' confidential material to General Murdani during an unauthorised trip to Jakarta. Huai was sacked in December 1987, a year before his term was due to expire. Huai and the Defence Minister, Mr Pokasui, had fallen out over the Jakarta trip Huai had made in August 1987, when he spoke to General Murdani about the defence clause that was later to be proclaimed in the new joint declaration of principles (JDP) between PNG and Australia. Pokasui accused Huai of leaking the wording to Murdani while the joint declaration was still being negotiated. Huai defended himself by writing lengthy, exclusive articles for the *Niugini Nius*, which ran them as a frontpage series over three days.

'It was reported widely', Huai wrote, 'that I leaked the JDP document to General Murdani. I deny this categorically. I did, however, raise verbally in our discussions the final paragraph of the proposed arrangement'. This paragraph provides PNG with a stronger defence commitment from Australia than it ever had before. It makes provisions for immediate consultations in the event of PNG coming under attack, consultations aimed at determining what action the two countries will take, either collectively or separately. Huai claimed that this paragraph concerned him as a defence strategist because he felt it was 'inconsistent' with the Treaty of Mutual Respect, Friendship and Co-operation that PNG had concluded with Indonesia. 'It could easily be misread by Jakarta,' Huai contended, 'and therefore it could create unnecessary tension and suspicion between the two countries.' The clause has similar wording to that in the defence arrangements that Australia has with Malaysia and Singapore, and PNG had been trying to convince Australia for some time that it needed a stronger defence commitment, in writing.

COULD A COUP SUCCEED?

Various PNG governments since Independence have held the view that the country's security would be enhanced if Australia could be persuaded to enter into a defence treaty. The suggestion was resisted by Australia because there was a fear that a commitment to defend PNG in any circumstances might embolden some future PNG administration into blundering into a serious military confrontation with Indonesia. But, following the unilateral decision by the Hawke Government in late 1986 to slash PNG's aid budget by K20 million ($30m) and to abrogate the five-year aid agreement signed twelve months earlier when PNG celebrated its tenth anniversary of Independence, PNG demanded that the whole Australia/PNG relationship be put on a new basis. PNG proposed both a joint declaration of principles governing the relationship and an associated integrated package of agreements nailing down the various aspects of relations. One of these associated agreements was to be a defence treaty. After protracted negotiations, the integrated package was dropped but only when Australia had agreed to a strengthened defence commitment in the joint declaration. However, General Huai, who had not played a major part in any of the JDP negotiations, attacked this clause as a sinister Australian plot!

'The final paragraph is to Australia's advantage,' he wrote. 'They were shoving an arrangement down our throats that would continue their domination over PNG despite the usual political rhetoric to the contrary. There is so much at stake for the Australians in PNG and they do not want to see others take a leading role, be they Japanese, Americans, Chinese or whoever. . . . My view, therefore, of the final paragraph was to delete it altogether, that it was illogical, that it could be a thorn in our relationship with Indonesia,' Huai said. The Defence Minister, Mr Pokasui, replied that General Huai's claim that the Australians had forced PNG into accepting the Defence Clause was 'an utter lie'. He rejected as 'nonsense' the contention that the JDP was inconsistent with the Indonesian Friendship Treaty. But what worried the Defence Minister most was the relationship Huai had built up with Murdani that prompted him to fly to Jakarta to talk to Indonesia's armed forces chief about the Australian defence clause.

In a similar vein to Diro's claim that his acceptance of money from Murdani mattered little because the relationship was good, not bad, for the larger relationship, Huai wrote: 'I considered that my friendship with General Murdani . . . had put our countries' relationship at a height never experienced before... In my relationship with General Murdani, I considered it essential ... to constantly maintain dialogue that is long lasting as we share a common land border.' The Defence Minister said another reason for Huai's removal was that he had compromised himself by accepting a suite of furniture from Murdani. Huai had admired the Indonesian furniture during a meeting in the Irian Jayan capital, Jayapura, in May 1986. Murdani offered it to him and Huai had the suite flown back to Port Moresby on a PNGDF aircraft. Huai described it as part of 'a normal gift exchange between commanders' and said Murdani would 'have been offended' if he had refused.

The first four commanders of the PNGDF — Diro (1975-82), Gago Mamae (1982-83), Ken Noga (1983-85) and Huai (1985-87) — were all Papuans. The reason for the dominance of Papuans in the leadership is historic. They tended to be recruited by the Australians first and to remain in the force longest. Although there is no regulation governing the composition of the PNGDF, the recruitment policy has been to send teams around all nineteen provinces. Amongst the lower ranks at least, the Defence Force is made up of a cross-section of PNG's society. At the upper levels the two smallest regions, Papua and the New Guinea islands, predominate. Under the Namaliu Government in late 1989 there was a rehabilitation of some of the Papuan colonels removed by Pokasui. Colonel Robert Dademo was reappointed chief of staff.

At the beginning of 1990 there were ten colonels in the force — six were from Papua, three from the New Guinea islands region and one from the New Guinea mainland coast. The Highlands, PNG's most populous region, with thirty-five per cent of the people, was not represented at all at this level of the force. The New Guinea coastal and Highlands regions, which provide sixty-four per cent of the population, had only one man between them out of eleven at the top of the force. The removal of Huai and the other changes that followed resulted in no fewer than twenty-nine promotions within the ranks. Amongst those promoted to lieutenant colonel were two Highlanders — the first Highlanders to reach that rank since the late 1970s.

One former commander of the force, Brigadier General Ken Noga, heads Papua New Guinea's chief intelligence body, the National Intelligence Organisation (NIO). Announcing Noga's appointment in April 1989, Prime Minister Namaliu said his priority tasks included 'streamlining and reviewing the operations and the capacity of the NIO'. In the 1980s, the NIO was regularly held up to public ridicule. Its office was destroyed in a 'mystery' fire in 1987 and confidential NIO reports were leaked to the media with surprising frequency. One such report in November 1988, prompted Mr Namaliu to release a statement saying the allegations contained in the NIO report were a 'combination of guesswork and pure speculation'. The Prime Minister went on: 'As I have said before, we need to significantly upgrade our intelligence-gathering capacity. Documents such as this demonstrate how urgent this task is'! On his trip to Australia in May 1989 Mr Namaliu sought help from Bob Hawke. Later the PNG Prime Minister told journalists travelling with him that Hawke offered the services of ASIO to 'get the NIO back on its feet again'.

PNG's Intelligence Organisation

The front page of the PNG *Post Courier* newspaper screamed 'SUHARTO APPROVES GIFT TO DIRO — NIO'. Quoting from a leaked 'confidential' intelligence report by PNG's National Intelligence Organisation, the story claimed Diro had been 'picked as the man' by Indonesia and that General Benny Murdani's gifts of cash totalling $US139,400 to Diro for his party's 1987 election campaign involved so much money that it was 'considered highly unlikely' to have come from Murdani's own accounts.

After describing the details of the transaction as 'still murky', the NIO report speculated: 'In any case, President Suharto would have been informed and in all probability would have had to approve the transaction.' The *Post Courier* quoted the report as saying that, having won his seat, Diro would have had many people to thank, including Murdani. 'Murdani had placed a substantial bet on a horse that had won in convincing style. For Diro there was the law of reciprocity — you scratch my back, I'll scratch yours.'

But later in his report the NIO intelligence analyst seemed to lose confidence in his earlier assessment and qualified it with the comment that it would be 'very improper to pass judgment on Diro'.

The newspaper report appeared in November 1988, more than twelve months after Diro revealed the Murdani gift before a judicial inquiry into PNG's forestry industry. Prime Minister Namaliu claimed the allegations 'were a combination of guesswork and pure speculation' and 'such a combination lacked the credibility to be included in official intelligence reports'.

Mr Namaliu said the report had 'no value' as intelligence. He said intelligence assessments on such matters required the most detailed investigation and the co-operative efforts of the whole intelligence service. 'The document reported in the media today hardly fulfils that criterion at all.' The Prime Minister suggested that the report demonstrated PNG's urgent need to overhaul its intelligence service.

Concern within the Defence Force as to the quality of the NIO's work helped lead to the formation of a separate Defence Intelligence Branch (DIB) within the PNGDF in 1988. The NIO attempted to take over the new branch by arguing a case for rationalisation of intelligence services with the expected opening of a Russian embassy in Port Moresby in 1990. However, in a confidential letter to the chairman of the Government's National Security Advisory Committee in September 1988, the Defence Secretary argued vigorously against amalgamation. He rejected an NIO submission that the DIB was duplicating the NIO's functions and roles. 'We see the contrary,' the Defence Secretary wrote. 'DIB has been created to complement and support NIO. We will become a customer to NIO's products. But DIB's role is specific. It is there to provide professional advice to the Defence Council on military threats and how the nation must respond to those threats in terms of its military capabilities and defensive postures.'

The Defence Intelligence Branch is administratively part of the Defence Department. However, it is directly responsible to the Defence Council (the Defence Minister, the PNGDF Commander and the Secretary for Defence), with the Commander and the Secretary responsible for giving it tasks and directions. The DIB comprises an office of chief of intelligence and two directorates — the Directorate of Strategic Defence Intelligence and the Directorate of Military Intelligence. The chief of intelligence is a civilian with the status of assistant secretary in the Defence Department. The Strategic Defence Directorate is a civilian component of the branch and is responsible for providing strategic assessments; while the Military Intelligence Directorate is the military arm with the function of

COULD A COUP SUCCEED?

providing dedicated intelligence to support PNGDF operations. The DIB has an approved establishment strength of thirty-three — twelve civilians and twenty-one military. The appointment of Brigadier General Noga to the NIO in 1989 enhanced co-operation between the NIO and the DIB.

PNG is seeking to diversify its sources of foreign defence assistance. It has upgraded its links with the United States. In February 1989 the Namaliu Government endorsed a status of forces agreement with the US covering the presence of American and PNG military personnel in each other's country. A similar agreement exists with Australia and both provide legal coverage. The arrangements also include joint exercises, personnel exchanges, surveillance, military training, seminars, acquisition of equipment, consultations and visits by planes and ships. The United States sent an engineering unit to PNG in 1989 for a number of specific tasks. A unit of American Green Berets visited in 1988 to hold joint exercises with a contingent of PNG troops near Wewak. An erroneous report across the front page of the *Australian* interpreted the visit as a 'secret deal' in which PNG had agreed to station US Special Forces units on the Irian Jayan border. Wewak is 300 kilometres east of the border.

The PNGDF is in severe financial straits. The 1986 defence report claimed that this could result in 'longer term deterioration in military competence'. There were problems with supplies: 'With current allocations,' the report said, 'the supply system is unable to provide the force with an operational reserve and without such stock, the capacity of the system to support operations for extended periods is very limited.' A lot of equipment broke down and could not be repaired: 'The allocation of K190,000 ($285,000) for the repair and maintenance of well over two thousand units of land technical equipment was completely used up and found to be extremely insufficient.' The result? Operational effectiveness was down to sixty-five per cent. Although the Defence Force had assets that would cost some K170 million ($255m) to replace, the maintenance vote of K2.2 million represented just 1.3 per cent of replacement value — well below the 4–6 per cent required. The 1988 Defence report said things had not improved. 'The supply situation within the force is deteriorating rapidly with legitimate demands based on entitlements exceeding funds availabe by a larger margin each year,' it said.

Australian financial support for the PNGDF is still highly significant. Australia's Defence Co-operation program allocations to PNG totalled about $41 million (K30m) in 1989-90. Salary support for Australian loan staff stationed in PNG is a significant but decreasing component of this. Since 1986, the value of other projects under the program has been more than fifty per cent. The two largest equipment projects have been the supply of six patrol boats and four Iroquois helicopters. The helicopters were thrown immediately into action on Bougainville after their arrival in 1989, although Australia insisted that they not be turned into 'gunships' to strafe villages. More than 300 Papua New Guinean Defence Force officers and men visit Australia each year for study or training and their travel and living costs are met from the Defence Co-operation Program. There are still twenty-nine Australian defence personnel filling establishment positions in the PNGDF. Another nineteen are with the Australian Training and Technical Support Unit based at the PNGDF headquarters, Murray Barracks — a unit 'designed to provide advice, guidance and assistance in areas where the PNGDF has minimal expertise'.

Not all Australian defence personnel in PNG are attached to helping the PNGDF. Six airmen from the 8th Field Survey Squadron have been attached to the National Mapping Bureau and there is a communications expert working with the police force. But the highest profile Defence Co-operation project Australia runs in PNG is the long-term presence in the Southern Highlands of an Australian Army engineers unit. This 23-man unit, the 12th Chief Engineer Works, has been based in Mendi, the Southern Highlands capital, since 1971. These Australian Army engineers run the provincial Government's entire Works Department. The officer commanding the unit is the provincial works manager. In 1985 alone, the Australian engineers completed capital works costing K1.8 million ($2.7m). They supervised the construction of fifty new buildings in the Southern Highlands, including the Margarima High School.

This project has been so successful that, when it was suggested that the Australian Army engineers should shift to another province, the competition between provincial governments to secure their services was so intense the idea was dropped for fear of upsetting not only the Southern Highlanders but also those other provinces who had been overlooked in the switch. In 1989 a second Australian Army engineering unit was established in the Sandaun province. It is based at Vanimo and, as well as assisting the Sandaun provincial government with its works program, the unit will help improve civil works along the northern section of the Irian Jayan border.

The Defence Minister in the Wingti Government, Mr Pokasui, proposed that the PNG Defence Force should be expanded from three battalions to six over fifteen years, with the extra three all being engineering battalions, not infantry. He envisaged basing one in each of PNG's four regions. Mr Namaliu's government also favoured an increased civil engineering role for the force. But events on Bougainville propelled the Namaliu Government the other way — to deploying troops to put down insurrection. The Bougainville operation was a disaster for the PNGDF. The use of the troops in combating civil disorder is not a role many of the senior officers have much relish for. In the years since Independence, senior PNGDF officers have regularly stated that the force should not be used against Papua New Guinea's own people. Some Papua New Guineans fear that the Bougainville experience will have the effect of politicising the force.

The Defence Board of Inquiry criticised the current structure of the force, saying it led to unnecessary rivalry. 'The present headquarters PNGDF structure creates a plateau at colonel level,' it said, 'where the present colonels' vying for the commander's position inadvertently results in the formulation of inconsistent policies'. The Board said this adversely affected the efficient management of units. On Bougainville, this problem became quite obvious in September 1989, when there was uncertainty over whether Brigadier General Lokinap would be reinstated and Colonel Dotaona, the Deputy Controller of the state of emergency, was being considered for the job. A communications link was set up between Bougainville and Murray Barracks which bypassed Dotaona. The Board of Inquiry also said there was an absence of clear line management within the PNGDF. It proposed a new structure with a higher rank than brigadier general for the commander's position.

The PNG Defence Council also put forward a restructuring proposal. It wanted what it called a 'functional command' structure. This would consist of two major field units to be known as the Operational Command and the Support Command, while the existing headquarters would become Strategic Headquarters. The council argued that this line-command system would relieve the commander and headquarters staff of daily routine administration of units and allow them to concentrate on policy planning. The Board's recommendations on structure and those of the Defence

Council were being studied by the Government in early 1990. Nobody in the Defence Force favours its transformation into a paramilitary law-and-order force.

Mr Namaliu's defence minister, Benias Sabumei, advocated a program of civil action on Bougainville when the crisis was over. He wanted the army to return to the province to rebuild houses destroyed in the state of emergency operation and to build roads and bridges. Mr Sabumei said he did not want this work to go to private contractors. 'I want the Bougainville people to realise that it is their Defence Force as well as the rest of the country's. So we shall need a confidence-winning exercise.' Mr Sabumei said the PNGDF was already looking for land for a barracks. He said the Defence Force cost about K17,000 ($25,500) per soldier per year and he wanted to get more value out of the service through instituting a nationwide civic action program.

It is an ambition with which Australia's then defence minister, Kim Beazley, had no quarrel. On a trip to PNG in late 1987 Mr Beazley promised PNG the loan of as many army engineers as it wanted. He said one of the problems facing the army's engineering units in Australia was that they were not allowed to take work that might be done by private companies or with union labour. They were confined to 'digging holes and filling them up again'. Answering questions at a Port Moresby press club luncheon, Beazley said one of Australia's biggest benefits out of the Defence Cooperation program was the experience gained by its engineers. 'Our engineers who are up at Mendi and who are attached to the PNGDF down here get an experience for their capacities in both war and peace not to be gained at home. So basically you can have any number of Australian engineers you want because it is very useful to us.'

At that press club luncheon, Mr Beazley was asked the Australian government's assessment of the likelihood of a Fiji-style coup in PNG. After jesting with the PNG military men present, Beazley replied: 'I don't think there is really any comparison between the political and social situation in Fiji and the political and social situation in PNG. There are also very different military forces with different experiences and drawn from different social bases. In Fiji the armed forces definitely reflect a particular community that has some very substantial political coherence in the expression of its interest against other communities. That situation doesn't exist here and the PNG Defence forces are totally reflective of the diversity of this nation. Our assessment would be that there is not the remotest possibility of the events in Fiji repeating themselves here.' Mr Beazley said he could see the 'superficial' attraction to foreign commentators of drawing an analogy with Fiji. 'But in the same way as Chekhov once said, "All happy families look the same, it's the ones that are breaking up that break up in individual and very different ways".'

Coup talk is going to be a continuing and increasing part of political life and political news coverage in PNG in the 1990s. As the decade began, the likelihood of the 'talk' turning into anything more was slim. But Papua New Guinea's political process is inevitably one of compromise and frustration. Should a series of governments come and go every six months through votes of no confidence, as allowed under the Constitution, the instability created could provide a scenario in which the chances of a coup increase. The PNGDF was squeezed for cash all through the 1980s, its morale declined, and its level of discipline, even according to those in charge of it, left much to be desired. Its leadership was shared, or rather was the subject of competition, between men from the two least populous regions. The force's capacity to act with the singleness of purpose that a coup would require was questionable. And it was still dependent to a large degree on Australian assistance. This dependence rankles. The need to prove the force's philosophical independence may partly explain some of the anti-Australian sentiments often expressed by some current and former senior PNGDF officers.

The logistics of staging a successful coup in PNG are daunting. The geography is one barrier. While the infantry might be able to secure a few government buildings in Port Moresby or Wewak, it is an entirely different matter to control Bougainville, New Britain or the Highlands. The problems the PNGDF had in Bougainville in 1989 bear testimony to that. The police and the army at the lower ranks have a history of conflict rather than co-operation. The army pay riot of February 1989 and the widely reported instances of human rights abuses on Bougainville have lowered the previously high regard in which the PNG public held the Defence Force.

Perhaps the largest threat to continued parliamentary democracy in PNG is the one warned of in 1987 by Prime Minister Wingti when he was asked in parliament about the possibility of a coup. Wingti turned the question back on the members of parliament, including his own Cabinet, saying that if they wanted to avoid a coup then they must shun personal enrichment. A coup would only happen in PNG, he said, if people lost faith in their elected leaders.

CHAPTER EIGHT

CONFLICTING INTERESTS

'So much more is known about private lives here and so much more rumoured or suspected that the extent of corruption is difficult to hide. And, if the official cases are no more than the crumbs from a table laden with corruption, the knowledge circulating amongst the public of the true size of this repast is exaggerated to lavish banquet proportions by their imagination.' So says the most comprehensive study into Papua New Guinea's law and order problems since Independence, the Clifford report, published in late 1984. Politicians of all persuasions in PNG constantly talk about the need to stamp out corruption and, at election time, 'honest government' is a promise in almost every party platform. The PNG media, daily, carry stories of alleged corruption in government or court reports of the convictions of those who have been found out. The constant exposure of corruption is a tribute to the country's vigorously forthright media and its strong, independent judiciary. It also reflects the moral tone set by the major Christian churches which continue to be influential. But a major contributing factor is that those who framed the PNG Constitution were acutely aware of what a problem corruption would become in PNG's rapidly changing society.

PNG's Constitution is an impressive ethical document. It begins with a lengthy statement defining national goals and directive principles. These goals and principles commit the country to the pursuit of integral human development; equality; political and economic independence; the use and replenishment of natural resources for the benefit of all; and the application of primarily Papua New Guinean forms of social, political and economic organisation to achieve development. The rights of the country's citizens to freedom of speech, movement, religion and assembly are all spelt out. These noble ideals are backed by a strict leadership code and the creation, as a constitutional office, of what must be, potentially, the most powerful ombudsman's office in the world. The PNG chief ombudsman has the job of overseeing and enforcing the leadership code.

The code itself is quite broad: 'A leader has a duty,' the Constitution says, 'to conduct himself in such a way, both in his public or official life and his private life, and in his associations with other persons as not (a) to place himself in a position to which he has or could have a conflict of interest or might be compromised when discharging his public duties; or (b) to demean his office or position; or (c) to allow his public or official integrity or his personal integrity to be called into question; or (d) to endanger or diminish respect for and confidence in the integrity of government in PNG. In particular,' the code goes on, 'a leader shall not use his office for personal gain or enter into any transaction or engage in any enterprise or activity that might be expected to give rise to doubt in the public mind as to whether he is carrying out or has carried out the duty imposed by the above'. If the ombudsman believes a case of breaching the code has been established against a leader then he refers the matter to the public prosecutor for prosecution before a leadership tribunal consisting of a judge and two senior magistrates.

Several hundred people come under the category of 'leader'. Included are all members of parliament, heads of government departments, board members of statutory authorities, the police commissioner, the commander of the defence force, judges, ministerial staff and constitutional office holders. It is a wide net. The all-embracing nature of the leadership code was amply illustrated when an investigating authority set up by the ombudsman in 1987 to examine the Placer Pacific gold share float found that about fifty leaders were guilty of misconduct in office. Their offence? None of them had sought the necessary prior written permission from the ombudsman before buying shares in a foreign company. It was all highly embarrassing because amongst those who breached the code in this way were the chief ombudsman himself, the former chief ombudsman, the chief justice and three other judges of the national court. The public prosecutor decided that since all these breaches were technical, a simple warning was sufficient and he pressed no charges against those named. Only one case was to be pursued and that was against the Deputy Prime Minister, Sir Julius Chan, who had to answer the more serious charge of alleged conflict of interest. Nevertheless, the wide publicity and public shame involved undoubtedly ensured that the ombudsman's permission would be sought by leaders buying into any future share floats of foreign companies. Sir Julius was eventually cleared by a leadership tribunal.

The man who can take most credit for the worthiness of the ideals outlined in the Constitution is Father John Momis, who was deputy chairman of the Constitutional Planning committee. Father Momis, the member for Bougainville, has been at or near the centre of PNG politics since 1972. He has served as a minister under Michael Somare, Julius Chan and Rabbie Namaliu and he has been both deputy prime minister and Opposition leader. He is severely critical of almost every other senior figure in PNG politics for, in his eyes, they have all 'sold out' the lofty principles of the Constitution. Officially opening the seventeenth Waigani seminar at the University of Papua New Guinea in 1986, which had the theme 'Ethics and Development', Father Momis claimed PNG's political leaders had been too busy with crisis control and consolidating their own wealth to worry about keeping faith with the national goals.

'The corruption that has been endemic since Independence only confirms this,' Father Momis told the conference. 'Since 1975, over forty national parliamentarians have faced more than a hundred criminal and civil proceedings ranging from minor traffic offences to rape. Many of these members were ministers before, during or after these offences were committed. Far more members have faced serious allegations about their behaviour which have not been pursued,' he maintained. 'A considerable number of members have been involved in corrupt activities which directly concern their roles as leaders. Sometimes this involves out-and-out corruption, like misappropriation of funds; more often it concerns the abuse of power. Many leaders seem to consider it their right to use their position to further their own ends.'

It is one of the achievements of an Independent PNG that so many 'leaders' have been brought to book. There is no other country in the South Pacific or Asia where such a proportion of those occupying positions of power and privilege have had to face the criminal courts. The fearlessness of the various agencies in charging ministers and others with offences, be they only traffic infringements or something more serious, has to be admired. The first chief ombudsman and late governor-general, Sir Ignatius Kilage, launched regular attacks on the behaviour of leaders, parliamentarians in particular. In his annual report to parliament as Chief Ombudsman in 1979, he lambasted members of parliament for their bad debts. He said that at the end of June that year, twenty-four parliamentarians, including some ministers, had outstanding bad debts amounting to about K90,000 ($135,000). He urged people who were having problems recovering money owed by parliamentarians to contact his office and he revealed that some 'leaders' had made veiled threats to cancel liquor licences, stop land transactions and revoke visas of people threatening legal action against them for bad debts. Prime Minister Somare asked Mr Kilage for a breakdown of the figures and said he would speak to the ministers concerned. In his report the following year, the Chief Ombudsman said the number of members with bad debts had risen to twenty-six and the amount involved to K115,000 ($175,000).

Bad debts and other misdemeanours led to the first sacking of a parliamentarian in 1981. Following recommendations from the ombudsman, the public prosecutor instituted proceedings against the member for Central, James Mopio, for misconduct in office under the leadership code. A leadership tribunal headed by Mr Justice Greville-Smith found Mopio unfit to hold public office. The Tribunal convicted him on fifteen charges including accepting K4000 ($6000) from an executive of a foreign-owned construction company while he was a member of the parliamentary Public Works Committee, collecting rent on a house he did not own, taking an unauthorised trip overseas at government expense, and failing to pay his debts.

PNG's leadership code limits gifts that 'leaders' can accept to K10 ($15). Any gift worth more than that must be declared to the ombudsman for evaluation before acceptance. But, even before Independence, foreign businessmen were offering expensive gifts to people in authority in Port Moresby. In 1974 the Australian Department of Foreign Affairs approached the Japanese Government on behalf of the first Somare Government to ask that Japanese businessmen be informed that the giving of gifts of friendship could be misunderstood. In July 1974 Chief Minister Somare told the House of Assembly of how two ministers had been approached with gifts but had refused them. Ten years later, in 1984, the chief ombudsman in his annual report to parliament revealed how the vice-president of Japan's Sohbu Trading Corporation had given two senior government ministers each a package containing K1000 ($1500) in cash.

'These two gentlemen were amazed one day,' Ignatius Kilage said in an interview the day his report was tabled, 'to find a brown envelope given to each of them consisting of K20 notes. When they opened it they got excited. They rang me up and said, "Look, we have this money in our hands!" And I said, "Bring it to us." We asked the Sohbu company executives [about it] and they said this is their practice. And we told them it is not the practice in this country, not to cultivate such practices in PNG.' Sir Ignatius also revealed that the ministers told him Sohbu's vice-president had offered Prime Minister Somare K5000 ($7500) but that Mr Somare had refused to accept it. The ombudsman noted that the Sohbu Trading Corporation had considerable interests in PNG in timber, fishing, real estate and wholesale and retail trading. At the time of the gifts, several of Sohbu's companies had disputes with the Taxation Office.

Gifts also figured prominently in the 1982 executive diaries scandal. The ombudsman titled his special report into this irregular purchase of 15,000 'executive' diaries from a Singaporian company 'Corruption in Government — A Case Study'. The Government paid K82,500 ($124,000) for the diaries even though the Supply and Tenders Board had rejected the purchase three times 'on the grounds that procedures specifically designed to prevent corrupt practices and unbudgeted-for expenditure had not been complied with.' The Singaporian businessman involved, Anthony Shaw Kong Loh, testified to the ombudsman that he visited PNG six times in 1981 and spent at least K5000 ($7500) each time entertaining potential customers and giving them gifts. The gifts included safari suits. Several public servants received safari suits, as did one government minister. The Manus Premier, Barnabas Kombil, received one but, according to the ombudsman's report, it was 'too small and he gave it away'.

In a sworn statement to the ombudsman the State solicitor recounted his meeting with Loh: 'Mr Loh then offered me a free video set and free airline tickets for myself and my family to come to Singapore, stating that he would take care of us for a couple of weeks, if I would tell the Secretary for Works and Supply to authorise payment for the executive diaries. I then ordered him out of my office.' Another public servant told the ombudsman he was offered a video set, a camera and a case of whisky 'as a reward' for assistance. The Government's supply office found these 'executive' diaries an unwanted embarrassment. There were not 15,000 executives in the public service. At the end of 1982, about 14,000 of the diaries, which had cost the PNG Government K5.50 ($8.25) each, were still in storage. In 1983, the remaining 1982 diaries were given away to school children. The man who designed the diaries, Sition Gion, was charged with corruptly receiving money from an Asian businessman. Gion had been public services secretary in 1981. But he was acquitted in February 1988 by the Chief Justice, Sir Buri Kidu, who said the State had not proven its case against Gion 'beyond reasonable doubt'. He did find, however, that correct procedures had been breached and he commented that it was 'curious that nobody tried to stop this whole affair before it got out of hand'.

The Four Stages of Corruption

The PNG Chief Ombudsman's report 'Corruption in Government — A Case Study' included a chapter analysing how corruption starts and spreads in developing nations. 'Studies of corruption in other countries,' it said, 'have shown that, much like a disease, it develops through four progressive stages'.

> In Stage One, corruption begins and is localised at the top — the political leadership. In Stage Two, it filters down to the senior public servants where it is condoned and tolerated, of necessity, by the political leadership.
>
> By Stage Three, corruption has become pandemic throughout all layers of the bureaucracy and it becomes the norm for the public to have to pay something on the side for even the most routine performance of a public servant's duty (e.g. the renewal of a passport, granting of a licence, etc). In such societies, justice is bought and sold and public office becomes the gateway to personal fortune.
>
> History shows that Stage Four begins when the military, seizing upon the opportunity created by public disenchantment with widespread political corruption, takes power amid a rhetoric of righteousness and morality. Far from curing the evil, however, corruption becomes even worse. For, having become firmly embedded in the fabric of society, it is now enforced at the point of a gun, as the army simply takes the

place of corrupt politicians. Elections become a farce and personal freedom disappears.

In that essay on corruption written in 1982, PNG's Chief Ombudsman claimed that Papua New Guinea, at that point, had reached Stage Two.

The most devastating anti-corruption inquiry in PNG — the judicial inquiry into the forestry industry — uncovered many instances of money changing hands between Asian businessmen and people in positions of authority. The judge heading the inquiry, Mr Justice Barnett, said in his first report (there were seven of them over two years, covering twenty volumes) that documents seized by police in a raid on a company office in New Ireland revealed evidence that a Malaysian timber company called Santa Investments 'made payments to some twenty-five politicians and officials totalling approximately K165,000 ($250,000). The recipients of these payments,' the Judge said, 'appear to include a provincial premier, provincial politicians, national politicians, Forestry and Customs officers and other people able to favour Santa in its timber operations.' The Barnett inquiry was established by Prime Minister Wingti in April 1987, following a succession of newspaper articles in the *Times of PNG* detailing allegations of malpractice in the Forests industry.

In another section of his first report, Mr Justice Barnett said the former Forests Minister, Ted Diro, was using a timber company, Angus (PNG) Pty Ltd, to raise funds offshore for the use of his political party. The judge said his investigations had shown 'that the Angus timber operation raised questions of ministerial impropriety, corruption, transfer pricing and the abuse of government policy of a very serious nature.' He went on to say that his 'inquiry disclosed that the timber permit over the Gadaisu area of Central province was improperly issued to Angus (PNG) in complete contravention of forestry policy. The company, though posing as a national company, was in fact foreign controlled and funded. Neither it nor its Singapore parent company [was] pre-registered with the Forestry Department or with NIDA.' (By law all foreign businesses operating in PNG have to be registered with NIDA, the National Investment and Development Authority.) 'Angus (PNG) Pty Ltd was hopelessly under-capitalised and inexperienced in timber operations. Its operation was consequently financially disastrous for the company and severely damaged the timber resource, with no benefit flowing to the people.'

The judge found that from the very beginning of its operations, Angus engaged in transfer pricing, that is, exporting logs from PNG at a cheaper price than they were worth and cashing in on the extra profits overseas. 'It was able to declare a reasonable profit from its first shipments despite the fact that very substantial amounts were "dropped off" in a Hong Kong bank account,' Mr Justice Barnett said. 'When the company was placed under official management a scheme was discovered to be in place based on a six-monthly revolving Letter of Credit which was calculated to net illegal offshore profits of approximately K9 million [$13.5m].' In later reports, the judge said his investigations into other timber companies had revealed that transfer pricing schemes were rife with foreign timber companies taking illegal profits out of the country amounting to well over K10 million ($15m).

In his fourth report — which dealt with the 'rape' of the timber resources of New Ireland — Mr Justice Barnett said transfer pricing was 'universal' in the New Ireland timber industry. Under the sub-heading 'Obscene Greed', the judge wrote:

> The difference between the foreign timber companies in New Ireland is not that some did not transfer profits because they all did. The difference is that in addition to cheating the landowner companies of about $US10 per cubic metre by standard transfer pricing devices, operators like Francis Sia and Bruce Tsang could not restrain themselves from also plundering the landowners of their share of the falsely low FOB price which the contractor company had chosen to disclose in PNG. A combination of natural greed and dire domestic financial necessity drove them to cut into the landowner company's profits by unlawful deductions involving fraud and forgery in such an unrestrained way as to be actually obscene.

It would not be fair to imply it is only Asians who have taught Papua New Guineans how to flout the rules. Occasionally, the ombudsman has focused his attention on Australians. In 1980, the ombudsman's special report on Air Niugini opened with the memorable lines: 'The foundation of the house of Air Niugini is solid and healthy, it is the roof which is rotten. Up on the penthouse level where management lives we have discovered a den of iniquity.' The ombudsman conducted a seventeen-week investigation into Air Niugini at the behest of the Transport Minister at the time, Iambakey

Okuk. The ombudsman found that in the nineteen months to April 1980, free tickets worth about $2 million were issued by Air Niugini executives. Describing this as 'spectacular waste', the ombudsman said that virtually every category of free travel had been abused. One executive, the report said, appeared to have been 'the patron saint of the game of golf'. The report detailed commission on aircraft sales going to a company called 'Impossible Associates' registered in the Bahamas.

The ombudsman's investigations into members of parliament have often concerned abuses of the various 'slush funds' set up by successive governments to promote local development projects. The first of these special budgetary appropriations was called the Village Economic Development Fund (VEDF). The purpose of the VEDF was to give individual members access to money they could allocate to projects in their seats to spur local economic development. The argument was that members could often identify projects of potential worth that would never have a chance of regular government funding because of bureaucratic red tape. The name 'slush funds' originated with another of these early funds that in the 1970s went by the title of the 'Prime Minister's Discretionary Fund'. Amongst Finance Department bureaucrats this was referred to as the 'Prime Minister's Slush Fund'. The name stuck and eventually all these funds came to be referred to as 'slush funds'. Stories of alleged 'slush fund' abuses have provided unlimited copy for the vigilant PNG media. In the 1990 Budget, the 'slush fund' allocations jumped to K100,000 ($150,000) per member. The total amount appropriated — K11 million ($16m) — was almost double that allocated to the PNG equivalent of the ABC, the National Broadcasting Commission (NBC).

Back in March 1980, just a few days before Mr Somare was ousted for the first time in a parliamentary vote of no confidence, the then Opposition Leader, Iambakey Okuk, accused the Government of attempting to buy support with cheques drawn on the VEDF. In reply, the Commerce Minister, Karl Stack, told parliament that cheques totalling K735,000 ($1.1m) had been handed out to about fifteen members over the previous two weeks. Stack said the cheques were made out to village business groups in the members' electorates and the members would have to hand them over to the local business development officer. He defended the allocations, saying they had been approved months before and had gone both to government members and to its strong opponents. The Chan/Okuk Government that followed Somare's expanded the scope of these special allocations, setting up what were called 'sectoral program funds'. The sectoral funds covered not only economic ventures but also small-scale agricultural, transport and health projects. One of the professed aims was to restore the image of national parliamentarians as the 'bringers of goods and services'.

The first government minister to be referred to a leadership tribunal was the Commerce Minister in the Chan government, Opai Kunangel Amin. In January 1982, just six months before the national elections, Kunangel, a traditional bigman from the South Waghi valley in the Western Highlands, faced a series of alleged leadership code violations. Amongst the charges was misappropriation of K20,000 ($30,000) from the VEDF. The ombudsman alleged that Kunangel had allocated the money to a fictitious business group but that it wound up in a bank account in Mount Hagen operated by his three wives. Other charges related to further alleged abuses of the VEDF and some sectoral program funds. Kunangel managed to elude immediate conviction by exploiting a loophole in the law and resigning from parliament. The Supreme Court ruled that since he was no longer a 'leader', as defined by the leadership code, the tribunal could not proceed with hearing the charges against him. That Kunangel's resignation was simply a matter of using the law to beat the law and not an indication of his admission of guilt was clear when he nominated to recontest his seat at the elections only months later. He was beaten.

But the ombudsman was not to be thwarted. He persuaded the police to pick up the case and, following a lengthy investigation, they brought criminal charges against Kunangel. In April 1984, more than two years after he resigned from parliament, the former commerce minister was convicted and sentenced to two years' hard labour for 'obtaining by false pretences the amount of K20,000 — the property of the State — the people of PNG'. Handing down judgment, Mr Justice Amet told Kunangel he had breached the trust of the people who had elected him. 'At the time of the commission of the offence,' the judge said, 'you were the Minister for Commerce in the national Government, responsible for the administration of the Village Economic Development Fund. You were the final approving authority over applications for grants from the VEDF up to a certain maximum amount. You used that very high position of trust to benefit your nearest relatives and indirectly yourself.'

The judge then went on to broaden his comments in a sharp reprimand to national politicians and public servants. 'Most unfortunately this is becoming far too prevalent an occurrence in the highest ranks of Government and administration and it filters through to the rank and file,' he said. 'Every day one reads or hears about allegations of misappropriation or of theft by a senior official or allegations and concerns about persons in high positions of trust, such as you were, using their positions to better their own interests. These have to be deterred in the strongest possible way,' Mr Justice Amet said.

The parliamentary Public Accounts committee heard in 1983 how a minister's driver had obtained money from one of the 'slush funds' after claiming he was the president of a village youth group. Before handing over the money, the committee was told, the administrators of the fund had questioned the driver as to whether he was too old to head a 'youth' group. But he was given the money when he said there was no one else!

Several members of the 1982-87 parliament lost their seats after being charged before the courts. One, the member for Chuave, Robert Yabara, was sentenced to four years' jail for attempting to bribe a magistrate. The court heard that Yabara had presented a senior magistrate who was hearing fraud charges against him with an envelope containing K140 ($210). The fraud charges related to false declarations he had allegedly made in claiming reimbursement for hotel and car hire bills already paid for by the parliament. He was convicted on both counts. On the fraud charges he was jailed for six months, which was three months less than the term that would have automatically disqualified him from parliament. But on the bribery charge he was given four years and lost his seat. Mr Justice Amet said the courts would not tolerate any forms of corruption from the leaders who were elected to serve their people.

Shortly before the introduction of the 1988 Budget, Prime Minister Wingti announced that he intended to abolish the main 'slush fund', the National Development Fund, saying that the money could be better used. In a widely reported statement, Mr Wingti said he did not want members of parliament 'to be encouraged to behave irresponsibly and become dependent on hand-outs'. He said his decision 'to get rid of the NDF — commonly known as the 'slush fund' — is consistent with the Government's approach to careful economic management. This decision,' Wingti proudly proclaimed, 'sets the tone for the next five years. We will ensure that our scarce budgetary funds are carefully spent.' But it did not take long for the tone to be readjusted. The Prime Minister's announcement that he was scrapping the NDF set off howls of complaint, not least from Opposition members who claimed it was the only way of ensuring that small-scale village projects got any government support. Wingti was outvoted on the issue by his Cabinet. 'Clearly, most members of the NEC [National Executive Council — Cabinet] strongly see the Fund as playing a crucial role in bringing immediate benefits to the people,' the Prime Minister said, philosophically, announcing that he had lost the battle and the National Development Fund would be retained.

In June 1988 the purposes to which some members may have been attempting to put the 'slush fund' was back in the news. The PNG *Post Courier* claimed that it had been told that the Administrative Services Department which administers the fund had been asked by one member to take back a cheque for K10,000 ($15,000) which had been made out in favour of a coffee factory and reissue the amount in three separate cheques, two to be paid to individuals and the third to a local rugby league club in the member's electorate. The newspaper reported the next day that its 'reporters were threatened and senior public servants harassed' following the publication of the story.

Over the years the ombudsman, too, has come under an occasional barrage from PNG's elected representatives. Considering the commission's powers and its role of supervising the strict leadership code, it is not surprising that the ombudsman has not been popular with MPs. When the ombudsman's report into the executive diaries scandal was tabled in parliament by the Speaker in November 1982, much of the ensuing debate was taken up with attacks on the ombudsman. The ombudsman's report was stylishly presented and hard-cover copies were freely available from the ombudsman's office. That and the fact that action was recommended against several politicians sparked off bitter attacks. Many MPs claimed that those named had already been found guilty by the ombudsman and that they would be crucified by the media before their cases ever reached a court or a leadership tribunal.

In the late 1980s the police fraud squad was reinforced and it secured a number of significant corruption convictions. In mid-1987 the national court sent the general manager of the government-owned

Motor Vehicles Insurance Trust and one of his staff to jail for misappropriating K138,000 ($207,000) in compulsory third-party insurance premiums. The money had gone missing between April 1983 and February 1985. In 1983 the Motor Vehicle Insurance Trust, which handles all PNG's third-party insurance, began demanding that all payments be made in cash. The trust refused to accept personal cheques, and in many cases would not accept company cheques either. Convicting the former general manager, Rei Hamoka, and his accounts office manager of misappropriation, Mr Justice Barnett said that in one fourteen-month period the whole of the trust's daily takings were removed from the system on seventy-five separate days. All the cash receipt statements and the pink copy of registration certificates disappeared. The judge said: 'Somebody simply pocketed the money!'

The former chairman of the PNG Harbours Board was also jailed in 1987 for conspiring with others to defraud the Harbours Board of K80,000 ($120,000). Two other men were jailed with him, including the managing director of a real estate company who was sentenced to four years' hard labour. The judge, Mr Justice Hinchliffe, said the real estate managing director, Samson Yehere, was the ring leader in the fraud, which involved the Harbours Board buying two houses well above their market values. One of the houses was valued at K25,000 ($37,500) whereas the Harbours Board paid more than K75,000 ($112,000) for it. The Harbours Board Chairman, Leo Debessa, was given a three-year jail term. Debessa was a prominent PNG businessman having established a Port Moresby Security firm, Debessa Security, after leaving the police force ten years before.

Facing the Music

The country/rock band headed by the adopted son of the member for Manus, Michael Pondros, was a failure despite getting the best equipment that 'the people's' money could buy. The band played twice at the Lorengau Hotel in Manus 'but it was not appreciated and moved to Lae, Goroka and other centres' before breaking up. The group's vehicle was eventually abandoned in the Highlands.

The leadership tribunal set up to investigate charges of misconduct in office against Michael Pondros found he had spent about K12,000 ($18,000) of government money buying the band's instruments and a further sum on the vehicle. Convicting Pondros, the Tribunal Chairman, Mr Justice Gajewicz, began by saying it was time for Pondros 'to face the music'!

Michael Pondros was Public Utilities Minister in 1982 when suspended pending investigation. The leadership tribunal found Pondros guilty of misusing K60,000 ($90,000) that he had obtained when a backbencher from two separate funds — the Village Economic Development Fund and the Prime Minister's Discretionary Fund. The K60,000 was supposed to have bought a barge to 'assist the people in the isolated areas of Manus to bring their crops' to town. Instead, the tribunal found, Pondros spent the money buying buses in Port Moresby, purchasing musical instruments and on his own re-election campaign.

'The tribunal has no hesitation in saying,' Mr Justice Gajewicz told a crowded court, 'that Mr Pondros tricked the government by false representation into giving him the grant of K60,000. The tribunal is satisfied that Mr Pondros is a shameless liar, a thoroughly dishonest man who used government funds of K60,000 for his own personal enrichment and for the benefit of his associates.' He was dismissed from parliament.

In his mammoth corruption study into the PNG forestry industry, Mr Justice Barnett said his detailed investigations into the allocation of timber resources and company operations on New Ireland indicated that bribery, corruption and the buying of support were so widespread they had become a 'major social sickness'. He said speedy decisions on forestry matters by ministers in both national and provincial governments and by public servants 'without bothering to consult other authorities or to check the facts, and without regard to due legal process' raised suspicions that benefits had been given. These suspicions, he said, were confirmed by oral and documentary evidence that in some cases was 'overwhelmingly strong'. The judge then went on to detail a list of fifteen people to be referred — for follow-up action — to the police commissioner, the foreign investment control body, NIDA, the registrar of companies, the ombudsman commission and the president of the Law Society.

One of the fifteen, the national Government's Housing Minister, Gerard Sigulogo, was later found guilty of misconduct in office by a leadership tribunal that recommended his dismissal from parliament. The leadership tribunal found that Sigulogo had corruptly asked a Malaysian logging contractor, Francis Sia, for K30,000 ($45,000). The request was contained in a letter Sigulogo wrote to Sia in October 1987, a few months after he was elected to parliament. It was discovered in a police raid on the office of Sia's company, Malaysian Overseas Investment (PNG) Pty Ltd, in the New Ireland provincial capital of Kavieng. In the letter, Sigulogo told Sia that he needed an 'incentive' to put his support behind Sia and promised that as long as he remained a member of parliament, Sia's logging company would continue to operate on his island of New Hanover. Sigulogo also thanked the Malaysian businessman for a trip that he and Mrs Sigulogo had just made to Singapore at Sia's expense and for the gold watch that Sia had given as a gift to the member's wife.

The tribunal's judgment reinforced Mr Justice Barnett's findings about the extent of corruption in the forestry industry. And it made particular reference to both the role of the former Forests Minister, Ted Diro, and a leading New Ireland lawyer and former Chairman of the government-appointed Forest Industries Council (FIC), Miskus Maraleu. Before entering parliament in 1987, Sigulogo had been secretary of what was supposed to be a landowners' company called Mamirum Timbers on New Hanover. Mamirum Timbers had, in mid-1986, been granted a timber permit over more than twelve thousand hectares of forest on New Hanover and it engaged Sia's company, Malaysian Overseas Investment (PNG) Pty Ltd (MOI), as its logging contractor on the advice of Maraleu. The leadership tribunal — which quoted extensively from Mr Justice Barnett's reports — said Maraleu was 'well qualified' for the task of adviser. He was a lawyer, Chairman of the FIC, and principal of a timber consultancy company. But Sia also engaged Maraleu at K1500 ($2350) a month and he became lawyer for both parties.

Quoting from one of Mr Justice Barnett's reports the tribunal said that Maraleu was 'clearly in an untenable and unethical position and could not possibly advise both parties fairly'. There was 'no doubt [Maraleu] betrayed [the landowners'] trust in a most disgraceful way in favour of his "paymaster", MOI.' The extent to which the landowners on New Hanover were cheated is revealed in the breakdown of payments from the first two log shipments. Mamirum Timbers was supposed to get twenty-five per cent of the proceeds but Sia designed the contracts so that the landowners' company not only paid all the royalties, the export tax and the industry levy from its share but also paid Sia's company, MOI, K40 ($60) per cubic metre in logging, administrative and other charges. The first log shipment grossed K284,236 ($425,000) but Mamirum's share of the profits was only K1844 ($2750). According to the Tribunal and Judge Barnett this was 'absurdly small'. But it was almost forty times as much as Mamirum made from the second log shipment. Sia's company received K413,330 ($620,000) of which Mamirum's eventual share was K48.66. That is less than $75! 'The smallness of the financial return to the landowners from an unusual and unfair agreement was a disgrace,' the judge said, 'and it was only made possible because Maraleu betrayed his own people for financial reward'.

The story of how MOI was granted approval to log in PNG was also detailed in the tribunal judgment. MOI received pre-registration by the PNG Forests Department on 17 October 1986. 'All the normal checks and procedures had been bypassed, including referral to the pre-registration committee,' the tribunal said, quoting from Mr Justice Barnett's findings. 'Sia had previously been involved with his brother, Michael, in another timber company, Santa Investments, but, had even a basic check been run on MOI by the Department of Forests, it would have shown that, although it was a foreign company, it lacked the necessary NIDA approval to be involved in the timber industry and that it had, almost literally, no working capital at all,' the judge said. 'This irregular pre-registration granted in October followed after a direction which Minister Diro gave to the Secretary of Forests in May 1986. On 15 May, Diro had received a letter on Santa Investments' letterhead, signed by Francis Sia as managing director of MOI, in which he sought pre-registration for MOI. Mr Diro penned a note at the foot of the letter to Department of Forests Secretary Mamalai, directing that pre-registration be granted.

'On the same day as he directed MOI's pre-registration, Mr Diro wrote a letter to Francis Sia seeking donations for his political party for its coming elections campaign. He sought donations totalling K117,500 ($175,000) to be paid between May 1986 and 1 June 1987.' Mr Justice Barnett's twenty-volume report was tabled in parliament over a twelve-month period, with his final report being presented in July 1989. Mr Sigulogo was the first to be charged following his recommendations. Prime Minister Namaliu said the reports and recommendations had all been referred to 'the appropriate authorities'. Mr Diro did face a number of perjury charges following his appearance before the inquiry. But the charges were dismissed because perjury was found not to be an offence under the Commissions of Inquiry Act. The anomaly was amended in 1989, but not made retrospective.

The forest inquiry commissioner recommended that Miskus Maraleu and another New Ireland lawyer, Sebulon Watt, be referred to the president of the PNG Law Society for professional misconduct. He said both men operated what he called 'hybrid lawyer/consultant firms' that acted for both the exploiters and the exploited. 'Both these men are New Irelanders and have taken advantage of this fact to induce less sophisticated landowners to trust them to advise on their affairs. By simultaneously working for the foreign contractor these lawyers betrayed this trust.' Towards the end of his two-year inquiry, Mr Justice Barnett became concerned that there was little action being taken to correct the abuses and corruption he had uncovered earlier. In his report dealing with New Ireland, he said he had drawn public and government attention to various irregularities in 1987 and 1988 but that they were still happening in 1989. 'People publicly exposed by the commission for fraudulent (and in some cases criminal) malpractices . . . continue those same malpractices,' he said. The judge named both Watt and Maraleu, amongst others, saying that Maraleu, who had 'admitted serious professional malpractice for personal gain and abuse of public office', had again 'found favour with the provincial Government' and been appointed chairman of its Development Corporation.

In one of his earliest reports, Mr Justice Barnett said that he had found the PNG Forests Department in a state of 'thorough demoralisation'. One of his terms of reference was to report on what the Government's forestry policy had been since Independence and how it had been implemented. The judge reported that, in the absence of any coherent policy, what had evolved was a de-facto policy that was resulting in some of the country's best forests being mercilessly ripped apart and the owners cynically ripped off. 'Such formulated policy that does exist is frequently and openly contravened by ministers, senior officers, inspectors and timber operators. The result,' Judge Barnett reported, 'is that the national department has lost its sense of purpose and provincial forestry officers are wandering leaderless with no sense of belonging to a profession of foresters. Most are thoroughly demoralised and are coming under more and more pressure from provincial governments wishing to stimulate "development" and revenue, and of timber operators who are exploiting the lack of clear policy and enforcement of policy to maximise their profits at the expense of present and future generations of landowners.'

The judge then listed thirteen separate 'worrying aspects' of the de-facto policy 'based upon an assessment of the Government's action and inaction over the past ten years'. Amongst these worrying aspects were:

- 'The government no longer puts effective emphasis upon the concept of sustainable, renewable resource management.'
- 'There is no policy to ensure in practice proper logging techniques.'
- 'The main thrust of forestry policy is to maximise revenue by a startling over-emphasis on exporting logs.'
- 'The encouragement of local processing seems to have been abandoned and there has been a drastic reduction in the production of sawn timber over the last ten years.'
- 'The effective policy is to allow foreign capital, foreign control and foreign profits to dominate the timber scene to the severe detriment of local landowners who are losing their resources for very little benefit; sometimes for no benefit at all.'
- 'The policy is to tolerate blatant schemes for transfer pricing and related schemes which are systematically defrauding the government and the local landowners of millions of Kina per annum.'
- 'The policy is to tolerate the continued existence of forestry legislation which is dangerously out of date.'

The forestry laws pre-dated Independence and, although a study in 1974 — the year before Independence — found them to be seriously defective, nothing was done to correct the problems. Indeed, Mr Justice Barnett found that the flaws noted a decade and a half before were being outrageously exploited in the late 1980s. The inherent dangers warned of then, the judge said, had 'exploded into reality'. One item of legislation, the Forestry (Private Dealings) Act, allowed foreign timber companies to deal directly with the local landowners without any reference at all to the national Government. These deals bypassed any official regulation or supervision and it was up to the village people to fend for themselves. Mr Justice Barnett said the villagers, lured by the promise of 'quick cash' and urged on by politicians wanting to see 'development', were signing away their resources. 'The situation is now chaotic,' the judge said. 'Foreign timber enterprises are exploiting the situation to the full as, to some of them at least, it promises quick "in and out" "mining" operations, without the burdens of fulfilling the onerous conditions' that might be imposed by dealing with the national Forestry Department. 'Recent applications for local forest area declarations (under the Private Dealings Act) involve 300-400,000 hectares,' he reported.

A second regulation that the inquiry found being shamelessly abused related to what were known as timber authorities — licences that could be bought for a nominal amount from forestry inspectors. These timber authorities were intended to facilitate sales by landowners of small amounts of timber for essentially domestic use. Mr Justice Barnett said this timber authority system was 'being deliberately and systematically abused with the knowledge and encouragement of previous ministers and officials. Forestry records disclose that official guidelines have been issued which quite deliberately break the law. Although timber authorities are by law to be limited to purchases not exceeding forty cubic metres, the guidelines permit up to 5000 cubic metres. There are several log-exporting operations,' the judge said, 'which are now based entirely on timber authorities and they are being issued by provincial forests officers, with the connivance of the department, in such a way as to allow the purchase and export of up to 20,000 cubic metres or more at a time.'

Because of the chaos in the industry and the transfer pricing, the PNG Government missed out on massive amounts of revenue. A report prepared for the United Nations centre on transnational corporations estimated that the PNG Government received approximately half of the average revenue that the Philippines did for its logs and one third of what was received by the Government of Sabah in Malaysia. As a result of Mr Justice Barnett's inquiry, the PNG Taxation Office recovered several million Kina from a number of the major timber operators who were prepared to settle backdated tax claims out of court. The PNG national Government was considering new forestry legislation as the 1980s ended but the story of the first fifteen years of Independence was of an industry lacking any real national supervision. Decisions were being made at the local level with no regard to national interest and often by people ill-equipped to ensure their rights were safeguarded. 'The national minister and the Department of Forests are in real danger of becoming redundant,' Mr Justice Barnett said. There were virtually no controls and, the judge warned, 'the future timber industry and the forests themselves could well be destroyed.'

The Forestry Department may be an extreme case. The PNG Department of Minerals and Energy, by contrast, has a solid reputation for straight dealing. But in the PNG public sector as a whole there is a shocking lack of accountability. The Auditor-General's office in the early 1980s reported that it had fallen more than a hundred work years behind in its government audits. It had problems recruiting experienced auditors. The Auditor-General regularly complained of the huge increase in workload that had resulted from the introduction of nineteen provincial governments. The situation improved towards the end of the 1980s when the Auditor-General was allowed to contract out some of its work. As the 1990s began, the Auditor-General's office had significantly caught up on the backlog. However, in many government departments files get lost regularly and records of transactions sometimes are just not kept.

How Not to Sell a Jet

The Pelair inquiry — which cleared Michael Somare of allegations that he had business associations with men named in the Stewart Royal Commission into drug trafficking in Australia — uncovered a case of gross administrative incompetence that cost the PNG Government up to $US2 million. Mr Somare returned to power in the 1982 elections promising to sell the executive jet that Sir Julius Chan had bought for PNG during his term. Responsibility for selling the jet was delegated to 'a young man with an economics degree' in the Prime Minister's Department whom the inquiry described as 'incompetent to handle a matter of this importance'.

Mr Justice Bredmeyer and his fellow commissioners found that the aircraft, a Grumman Gulfstream II, was given to an agent, World Jet Trading of Denmark, who flew it to Europe claiming it could be sold for $US8.5 million. 'That was mere salesman's puff,' the inquiry said. The only sale World Jet Trading arranged was with a Nigerian company, Dantata, for $US6 million. But because of the collapse of the Nigerian economy, Dantata could not pay in any convertible currency — only in Nigerian Naira. However, the PNG Cabinet approved the deal unaware of this complication. 'It is crystal clear Cabinet was misled,' the Pelair inquiry found.

In the meantime a PNG-based company, PNG Aviation Services (PNGAS), made an offer of $US6 million on behalf of the computer company, Atari, but the offer 'was treated casually' and Atari lost interest. After Mr Somare found out about the currency fiasco, he raised it with Nigeria's president at the Commonwealth Heads of Government Meeting in New Delhi in late 1983. President Shagari was unsympathetic, saying he suspected that the Dantata Group wanted to buy the jet only to resell it illegally.

Finally, in August 1984, twenty-four months after Cabinet's initial decision to sell, PNG made a direct sale to an American buyer, Robey Smith, for $US4.35 million. Robey Smith complained about the state of the aircraft and PNG had to pay for flying it from Denmark to the US. But in agreeing to the Robey Smith sale, Cabinet was 'misled' again and approved payment of a commission of $US180,000 to the company in Denmark. The PNG official handling the affair had received legal advice that the Dantata deal might be still legally valid and the Danish company was entitled to its three-per cent commission! The commission of inquiry said 'anyone reading this Cabinet submission would be led to believe that it was the commission payable on the Robey Smith purchase' of which there was none, being a direct sale.

The Clifford report into law and order felt that some of the prevailing lack of accountability may have been 'attributable to a cultural lack of familiarity with written records. Pre-literate societies used public ceremonies for the exchanges of gifts or the marking of events so that these would be recorded in everyone's memory,' the study said. 'The transition to an appreciation of written records takes time. However, this lack of skill in keeping — or conscience about losing — records is intensified at the provincial and local government levels by the fact that the national Government, simply because it realises the lacunae of competence and systematic recording, keeps as much as possible under its own control. So, at the local level, the need for precision and accountability just seems to be so much less important.' Both Clifford in 1984 and Mr Justice Barnett in

1989 commended the work of the PNG media in attempting to keep the public informed and the government of the day accountable.

Papua New Guinea has had a remarkably free and vibrant media through its first decade and a half of Independence. Visitors with experience elsewhere in the developing world are astounded at the standard. In very few countries that have won their Independence since 1950 has the media grown, as it has in PNG, to be more robust and free from government control than it was in the dying days of the colonial administration. This freedom to expose and criticise has often annoyed those in power. Mr Somare, when Prime Minister, constantly lectured the media about how 'freedom' imposed obligations of 'responsibility' but that, far too often, he had found the media's sense of responsibility wanting. But while he got upset, Michael Somare, who as a young man worked as a broadcast journalist for the Australian colonial administration's district radio service, never moved to legislatively curb the media.

The communications minister in Mr Wingti's Government (1985-88), Gabriel Ramoi, did. And to draw up his plans for 'licensed' media, Mr Ramoi called on the services of the Australian media critic and lawyer consultant, Stuart Littlemore. In late 1987 Mr Ramoi announced plans to introduce legislation to license the media and establish a powerful mass media tribunal. In double-page advertisements in all the written media in PNG, Mr Ramoi explained his aim. He said the country 'must be assured of complete control of the media free from foreign interference or influence. Without such control,' he wrote, 'radio and television broadcasting and the print media can never become a great agency for communication of matters of national concern and for the diffusion of national thought and ideals.' He went on to say that 'without such control it can never be the agency by which national consciousness may be fostered and sustained and national unity still further strengthened'.

The foreign 'interference and influence' that Mr Ramoi saw and wanted to curb was mostly Australian. But only part of that was a hangover from pre-Independence days. When the colonial era ended in 1975, there was only one foreign media proprietor. That was the Melbourne-based Herald and Weekly Times, which was the majority owner of the then sole national daily newspaper, the *Post Courier*. The only other significant media organisation in PNG at that stage was the National Broadcasting Commission, the NBC, a government-funded statutory authority that was formed in late 1973 through an amalgamation of what had been the ABC's Papua New Guinea radio network and the administration's district radio stations. By early 1988, when debate on Mr Ramoi's proposed Mass Media Bill reached its pitch, the media had grown in depth and diversity. There were two fiercely competitive national dailies, the *Post Courier* and the *Niugini Nius*; a quality weekly in English, the *Times of PNG*; a weekly national Pidgin newspaper, *Wantok*; a monthly magazine, *New Nation*; and two commercial television stations, the Niugini Television Network (NTN) and EM TV; while on radio the NBC had set up a national FM service to complement its national medium-wave network and had increased the number of provincial radio stations to nineteen.

NTN, which had been the first to broadcast television in Papua New Guinea, closed in March 1988. It had been ninety per cent owned by the West Australian businessman, Kevin Parry, and was a victim of Mr Parry's financial collapse after the October 1987 stock-market crash rather than of any move by Mr Ramoi. The Communications Minister had tried to stop NTN opening but he had not succeeded. Parry Corp's Newcastle television station which went by similar initials to his PNG venture — NBN — had signed an agreement with the Somare Government in 1985 allowing it to start a commercial PNG television station. Following the change of government at the end of that year, Parry spent much of 1986 fighting Mr Ramoi and the new Wingti administration through the courts to establish the validity of the 1985 agreement. The introduction of broadcast television was hotly debated in PNG for more than a decade. Those opposing it argued that it would swamp the culture with dated, foreign 'rubbish' and raise expectations to levels impossible to satisfy. Supporters argued that well-managed television would be a powerful educational tool in a country with only 33 per cent literacy. The argument was never resolved. Television just arrived. Having won its court battle, but in the absence of any specific legislation governing television, NTN began broadcasting in January 1987.

Bond Media's EM TV followed six months later. Bond had inherited the plans for EM TV when he bought out the Nine Network from Kerry Packer. When EM TV was launched in late July, 1987, the ownership was announced as 50 per cent Bond Media, 25 per cent Peter Sam — a Papua New Guinean lawyer, and 25 per cent

Alun Beck — a New Zealander who ran a video production company in PNG. But Bond provided most of the money. The PNG market, limited at first to Port Moresby, was not large enough for one profitable television station, let alone two. The prospect of a long-drawn-out ratings battle between the two Perth businessmen who had fought for the right to defend the America's Cup ended abruptly with Parry's financial troubles forcing NTN to shut, having lost an estimated $7 million. Despite its short time on air (fourteen months) NTN had set a high standard, with its aggressive nightly news service regularly breaking major political, business and crime stories.

Of the five main media organisations operating in PNG at the start of the 1990s, only two were fully Papua New Guinean owned. They were the government-owned NBC and Word Publishing, the company producing the *Times of PNG*, *Wantok* and *New Nation*. Word Publishing was set up by the Catholic, Anglican, Lutheran and United Churches of PNG and has made a distinguished contribution to the liveliness of the country's media industry. One of the two daily newspapers, *Niugini Nius*, was owned by Dennis Buchanan, an Australian living in the Highlands of PNG who also owned and operated PNG's largest commercial light aircraft company, Talair. The other national daily, the *Post Courier*, fell into Rupert Murdoch's News Limited empire when Murdoch took over the Herald and Weekly Times. News Limited held a controlling 62.5 per cent interest in the paper. Bond Media, which had increased its share of EM TV to 90 per cent by the end of 1989, was the fifth of PNG's media proprietors.

Mr Ramoi's proposals to license the media lapsed when Prime Minister Wingti's government fell in mid-1988. However, the debate that his plans generated raised a number of pertinent questions about the role of the media in a developing and rapidly changing country such as PNG. The idea for his mass media tribunal evolved during 1987 when, having lost his battle in the courts to prevent the introduction of television, the Communications Minister drew up several items of legislation aimed at controlling television broadcasting. For a variety of reasons, including lack of numbers on the floor of parliament for crucial votes, none of this legislation was ever passed. Then, in November, 1987, Mr Ramoi scrapped all the previous work and announced his plans for the media tribunal that would license not just television, but all media — television, radio, the newspapers, magazines, video and even outdoor advertising.

Licences would be subject to review every six months, and the licensees would have to follow a 'fairness code' that Mr Ramoi had drawn up as one of the schedules to be presented with the Mass Media Tribunal Bill. The Bill would empower the tribunal chairman to order that certain matters be published or that others be suppressed — one of the matters being 'issues of national importance' as determined by the Communications minister. In a concession, Mr Ramoi later changed this to be 'as determined by the governor-general'. Strict foreign ownership regulations would force foreign shareholders to divest, over a period, all but 17 per cent of the ownership of any media organisation to Papua New Guinean citizens.

Gabriel Ramoi is a committed ideologue. He told EM TV News in June 1988 that he regarded himself as a Marxist. Ramoi was a co-founder of Prime Minister Paias Wingti's People's Democratic Movement, the PDM. From the West Sepik or Sandaun province, Ramoi is a graduate from the University of Papua New Guinea where he was president of the Students' Representative Council. He once led a students' march on the parliament where he burnt a copy of the Constitution in front of Prime Minister Somare. On another occasion, Ramoi, the student leader, was charged with harbouring an illegal immigrant, an Irianese dissident who had crossed the border from Indonesia's Irian Jayan province but who had disappeared into student hands when the Government was attempting to deport him to a neutral third country. Like Mr Wingti, Ramoi went directly into politics from his university studies — although for him it was one election and five years later. Wingti entered parliament in 1977 and Ramoi in 1982.

Ramoi's proposed Mass Media Tribunal Bill created controversy. The Catholic Church called on its one million followers throughout PNG to sign a petition to let the parliament know that they did not want their right to freedom of expression cramped by legislation. At a seminar organised by the PNG Institute of National Affairs in February 1988, Mr David Gela, chairman of the Melanesian Council of Churches' Media Council, summed up the apprehension about the Bill when he said: 'Today, within thirteen years of gaining Independence, Papua New Guinea is standing on the threshold of legislation which might provide opportunities for a healthier and more integrated national development, or may well pave the way for the curtailment of democracy and a slide towards tyranny.'

In his address to the seminar, Mr Ramoi claimed that his efforts to bring change to the media in PNG should be seen, understood and supported in the light of the Wingti Government's determination to find a 'development strategy' for PNG. He argued that the inherited institutions had let the country down since Independence. 'This understanding and support is needed more urgently now than ever before,' the Communications Minister said, 'in the face of a growing resurgence of nationalism in Papua New Guinea as people become frustrated over developmental trends over the past ten years when the institutions we have inherited, or built, have not been able to respond fast enough to the expectations of our people. The developmental trend in PNG today can be described as chaotic and wasteful, with eighty per cent of the economy in the hands of foreigners while in rural Papua New Guinea state services are barely reaching our people. This situation is compounded with an education system that is turning out 40,000 school leavers while the economy can only create 10,000 jobs annually,' Ramoi said. He went on:

> The nation today is at the brink of a major, national disaster. It is within this political context that the Mass Communications Tribunal Bill must be read. The concept of a mass-media regulatory body must be seen as a manifestation of our political will in the face of failed expectation to determine the destiny of our nation by moulding a national character that can be described as Papua New Guinean; so as not to allow the media to foster false hope and expectation among our people as a result of their pursuits of profit. And, secondly, it must be seen as a continuation of a process of distributing modern wealth in a more equitable manner from the control of foreigners and foreign managers to a new class of Papua New Guinea managers and entrepreneurs.

Papua New Guinea's journalists presented a submission to Mr Ramoi supporting the moves to localise the ownership of the media but rejecting clauses that would allow the Government to dictate what could or could not be published or broadcast. The chairman of the PNG Press Club and then editor of the *Times of PNG*, Neville Togawera, said the journalists were keen to see Papua New Guineans take greater control over the foreign-owned media. However, he said, they were extremely wary of the possible 'censorship implications' of Mr Ramoi's proposals. 'Many journalists,' he said, 'see the Bill as the beginning of a conscious attempt by government to restrict, by legislation, freedom of the media in PNG.'

The churches, which play a big role in public life in Papua New Guinea, made a separate submission on the proposed mass media tribunal. They asked the London-based representative of the World Association of Christian Communication, Neville Jayaweera, to help prepare their case. Mr Jayaweera said that what Mr Ramoi was trying to do should come as no surprise. It had numerous precedents in the third world. He said it was a natural consequence of what he called 'the third stage of decolonisation'. First, he said, came political decolonisation; then attempts at economic decolonisation; and thirdly, efforts to try to achieve what he called 'information and cultural decolonisation'. He went on:

> Generally, they have made a mess of it. In country after country in the third world, in their attempt to evolve a model which would give them some degree of cultural and information autonomy, they have fallen into the trap of going to the other extreme and foisting upon themselves a controlled information system. This controlled information system has ultimately defeated not only the political goals which those governments had sought to secure, but it has even destroyed the very governments who imagined that by choosing this particular model, they could consolidate themselves in power for all time. This has been the invariable lesson.

Mr Jayaweera concluded that PNG was on the verge of a very critical decision. 'In which way this particular country, this government, chooses to go will depend crucially, not only on the understanding the government and the Minister has of the problem, but equally on the understanding and the sensitivities of those who control the press and the media'.

Black Superman

The seven student teachers from the Goroka Teachers' College had a complaint against the PNG *Post Courier* newspaper. 'Your top three comic strips on 10 August had one message,' their letter to the editor read.

'Rip Kirby, the Phantom and Flash Gordon were all male, all resolving conflict violently, all white, uninvited in countries not their own, all sure that they know what is right for the nationals, all overcoming nationals who are criminals, incompetents or cowards.

'This message may have been good enough in the time of the Kiaps [Australian colonial patrol officers]: it is not good enough after fourteen years of Independence to have this kind of racist propaganda disguised as entertainment.

'We would like Melanesian comics reflecting Melanesian culture.'

Mr Ramoi had hoped to get his mass media tribunal legislation through the PNG parliament in April 1988. In the fortnight leading up to that session, Mr Ramoi and the Labour Minister, Masket Iangalio, attacked the media, alleging a plot to topple the Wingti Government. Mr Ramoi claimed that the 'foreign-owned and foreign-dominated media' was involved in a 'major conspiracy to destabilise and remove an elected government from office'. Two days later, the Labour Minister claimed the government had in its possession 'tangible evidence' of a conspiracy between the foreign-owned media and the Opposition. Mr Iangalio, whose department controls work permits, said the Government would 'not hesitate to terminate the work permits of foreigners found to abuse their residency privileges by conspiring with the Opposition' to bring down the Government. The number of non-Papua New Guinean journalists working in the PNG media was small. There was none at the NBC; none in the newsroom at EM TV; one, a Catholic priest, at Word Publishing; one, the brother of the owner, at *Niugini Nius*; and there were four at the *Post Courier*. Not a single one was on the reporting staff; all were sub-editors or editorial support staff.

This threat of deportations prompted Australia's High Commissioner, Lance Joseph, to issue a statement saying that 'in the absence of having sighted any evidence of a conspiracy or conspiracies, the High Commission must naturally express skepticism'. Mr Joseph said that the High Commission would be particularly concerned if Australian journalists, normally resident in PNG, were singled out for discriminatory treatment. The conspiracy accusations were rejected outright by both the *Post Courier* and the *Niugini Nius*. 'I can say categorically there is no conspiracy to bring down the Government,' said Don Kennedy, managing editor of the *Post Courier*. 'There is no collusion between any of the media.' The April parliamentary session was aborted by the Government after less than three hours to avoid a vote on a motion of no confidence.

When the parliament next met, three months later, the Wingti

CONFLICTING INTERESTS

Government was replaced by the Namaliu Government in a parliamentary vote. A few days before that vote, the owner of the *Niugini Nius*, Dennis Buchanan, grounded his airline, Talair, saying he could not work with Mr Wingti's Aviation Minister, a naturalised PNG citizen, Hugo Berghuser. Mr Berghuser had moved to limit Talair's ability to compete on main routes with the government airline, Air Niugini. Buchanan said he would not put Talair's fifty-two aircraft back into the air unless the Wingti Government was replaced. Talair services 138 airstrips around PNG and the cessation of flights caused considerable inconvenience in rural areas. The *Niugini Nius* gave extensive coverage to the Talair grounding, but its editorial on the morning of the no-confidence vote took a neutral line. A week before, the paper had predicted Wingti would survive. After the fall of the Government, Ramoi vowed that when he got back into a position of power again the first thing he would do would be to demand Buchanan's deportation.

The National Broadcasting Commission is the most vulnerable to government pressure of all media outlets in PNG. It depends upon the Government for its budget, which has been progressively cut in real terms for fifteen years. By the end of the 1980s, the NBC was receiving about one-third of the proportion of government expenditure it received when it was established. In its first year, the NBC was given K5 million — 1.6 per cent of the total national Budget. By 1989 its budget was K7.5 million — 0.6 per cent of the Budget. As a result of funding cutbacks and mediocre management, the national broadcaster was, by the end of the 1980s, in danger of going off the air in many parts of the country. The three short-wave transmitters for the national service of the NBC were not functioning and the service had to rely on a much weaker stand-by transmitter normally used by Radio Central, the NBC's provincial service for the rural areas around Port Moresby.

Despite the funding problems, the NBC's News and Current Affairs Division had not become a government information bureau. It had its shortcomings but any member of the public had access to expressing a point of view on NBC news broadcasts. Government pressure on the NBC has, at times, been crude. In the early days of the NBC in the mid-1970s, the NBC's chief political reporter broke a story on details of a proposed mini-budget on the morning the mini-budget was going to be introduced. Senior NBC executives were called before Cabinet and told that the mini-budget would be put off and the loss of revenue deducted from the NBC. The commission's director of news and current affairs was demoted in the early 1980s after the Prime Minister disapproved of the way an address of his was edited. Perhaps the most newsworthy case of interference was when the former Deputy Prime Minister, the late Sir Iambakey Okuk, charged into an NBC studio and physically put a current affairs program off air. NBC journalists protested but the then NBC Chairman, Leo Morgan, apologised publicly to Mr Okuk for the 'misunderstanding' that led to his intervention.

These isolated incidents indicate that the independence of the NBC can be fragile but, according to one former NBC chairman, Mr Austin Sapias, himself a former journalist, the media in PNG needs to become more professional if it is to protect itself. Mr Sapias fears the media in PNG is too free for its own good. He spent a term in Australia as Papua New Guinea's High Commissioner in Canberra. 'The media is more free here than it is in Australia,' Mr Sapias says. 'Some of the reports we read in the newspapers here could never appear in Australia. Our papers defame people all the time. The biggest problem facing the PNG media,' he says, 'is that our journalists need to be better trained. They are too young, they haven't had the exposure. The country needs good investigative reporters. Journalists to look behind the news.' Mr Sapias claimed that when he was NBC Chairman the most constant source of complaints from government ministers was about reporters' inaccuracies, not their alleged political bias.

The long-time Papua New Guinean editor of the *Post Courier* newspaper, Luke Sela, said that at one stage in the early 1980s, Iambakey Okuk attempted to put pressure on the paper by contacting the paper's ultimate bosses in Melbourne at the Herald and Weekly Times. But, he said, the matter was left to the paper in Port Moresby to handle. He welcomed the increased competition of the 1980s, saying that the greater number of media outlets had forced all the media to be more alert. He claimed that the diaries scandal of 1982 would not have been uncovered if there had been only one newspaper. 'We started that story off, the *Post Courier* did. But because of competition we all kept after it and eventually an inquiry was set up. Before, we might have just dismissed it as just another government bungle and left it to the Government to sort out.'

There is ample evidence to back up Mr Ramoi's claim that the development goals set at Independence have been frustrated because, to repeat his words, 'the institutions we have inherited, or built, have not been able to respond fast enough to the expectations of our people'. But the media has been one of the few institutions in PNG that has responded to the expectations of the growing proportion of the population that is literate. The gravest danger facing the PNG media is inaccuracy. The more times journalists do not get the facts correct, the more ammunition they give those in parliament who want to be given the power to silence them. But, as one government backbencher said during the Ramoi media tribunal debate, 'we can't afford to silence the media because it is the media who will let us be heard when we're back in Opposition again'.

Papua New Guinea has produced a large number of fine journalists since Independence. One of the better ones has been Sinclair Solomon. Sinclair's investigative exposés on the forest industry in 1986 and 1987 when he was working for the *Times of PNG* ultimately led to the Barnett commission of inquiry. A few years earlier, when editor of the *Niugini Nius*, Mr Solomon told an ABC radio program examining media freedom that journalists in PNG would refuse to bow to government pressure. 'We have plenty of freedom to express what we want,' he said. 'And I'd like that to be maintained. We will continue to be outspoken on issues like the border problem between Papua New Guinea and Indonesia. And where we feel we are being cornered by the Government we'll start to yell and we will not hesitate to yell!'

CHAPTER NINE

IRIAN JAYA — BORDER TRAUMA

A few nights before Christmas, 1983, the people of Papua New Guinea, sitting around in the kerosene-lamp semi-gloom of their village huts or shanty shacks or in the sharper electric light of town, heard their Prime Minister tell them he knew that in their hearts they feared Indonesia. But, in a broadcast aimed at calming fears of an Indonesian invasion, Mr Somare went on to tell his people that this fear was just a hangover from the expansionist days of President Sukarno. 'Since General Suharto gained power,' Somare said in the broadcast, which he recorded in all three official languages (English, Pidgin and Motu), 'Indonesia has consistently strived for regional peace and stability. Its policies have been consistent and non-expansionary. From their point of view their annexation of East Timor was consistent with their desire for peace and stability. They saw East Timor as being a possible base for political extremists. Without endorsing that view in any way, I can see from their point of view they have been consistent . . . Papua New Guinea need not fear any invasion from Indonesia,' Mr Somare assured his nationwide audience.

Indonesia and Papua New Guinea share a 750-kilometre land border. That is roughly equivalent to the New South Wales–Victoria border, or twice as long as the border between France and Germany. This chopping of the New Guinea mainland in two is a nineteenth-century European map dividers' legacy that dominates both military and foreign policy thinking in PNG. PNG's vulnerability was stated starkly to the parliament in Port Moresby in November 1987, by Ted Diro. 'I want to tell you a few hard military facts,' Diro told his fellow parliamentarians. 'If Indonesia with its size of population, its armed forces, its level of defence technology and its geographic location was to take on PNG, there is absolutely nothing that anyone in this region can do about it. Our best defence is probably a prayer and the Bible.'

The border cuts across some of the worst terrain on earth — thick jungle in the north, nigh-impenetrable mountains in the centre and swampy, savanna country in the south. It is impossible to police effectively, and small bands of Irianese dissidents have little trouble slipping across to gain sanctuary in PNG. The indigenous Melanesians of the Indonesian province of Irian Jaya are ethnically and socially the same as Papua New Guineans and equally diverse in their local identities. But increasingly the population of the Indonesian province west of the border is made up of formerly landless Javanese and other Indonesian racial groups who have shifted there on their own or under the Indonesian government's transmigration program.

Indonesia's population is 180 million, Papua New Guinea's 3.8 million. Irian Jaya, which comprises more than one-fifth of Indonesia's total landmass, is home to only 1.5 million. In Indonesian eyes this vast Irian Jaya area with a population density of just three people per square kilometre is practically uninhabited compared with Java's 760 people per square kilometre. The name 'Irian' comes from the language of the Biak people. Biak, an island off the north Irian Jayan coast, was the setting of an early pro-Indonesian, anti-Dutch Independence movement just after World War II. Frans Kaisieppo, a member of that pro-Indonesian movement who became governor of Indonesian Irian Jaya in the late 1960s, popularised the use of the word *Irian* to describe the whole province. It means 'a hot place'. Hot as an issue Irian Jaya has certainly been for Papua New Guinea ever since the latter's Independence in 1975.

In a major defence statement to the PNG parliament in September 1987, the Defence Minister, Mr Pokasui, described three levels of possible threat to PNG, the highest being a full-scale invasion, the second being external pressure and the lowest level being internal instability such as secession movements, tribal fighting and insurgencies. Although Mr Pokasui said PNG must maintain a defence force of sufficient capability to 'meet as far as possible any external pressure that may be applied,' it was only the third — low-level conflict — he said, 'that was expected to confront PNG in the next ten years'. An earlier Defence Minister, Epel Tito, lost his job when he gave a different assessment of what he thought was going to happen. In 1983 Mr Tito, on a trip to Australia, told Radio Australia's Canberra reporter that he thought Indonesia was going to invade 'within ten or twenty years'. Tito was sacked by Prime Minister Somare for this gaffe. Mr Pokasui, in referring to Indonesia, stated: 'Although the relationship is mature and stable, the new Defence Policy also recognises that mismanagement of problems related to the border has the potential to cause tension between the two countries.'

PNG's deep concern about Indonesia is reflected in the constant questioning of Indonesia's intentions. The official 1986 defence report describes the results of a courtesy call PNG's Defence Force Commander, Brigadier General Huai, made on President Suharto. 'The President gave a verbal assurance,' the annual Defence Report said, 'that Indonesia has no intention of launching military operations against Papua New Guinea.' This seeking of reassurance has been repeated year after year and in 1987 culminated in a formal, written, non-aggression pact called the Treaty of Mutual Respect, Friendship and Co-operation. Article Seven states that Indonesia and PNG 'shall not threaten or use force against each other.' Much of the impetus for that treaty came from the border-crossing refugee crisis of 1984 when well over ten thousand Melanesians fled into PNG. Six years later, at the close of the 1980s, more than eight thousand were still in refugee camps on the PNG side. The handling of this matter tested PNG's diplomatic skills to the full and the pragmatic result has been disappointing for supporters of the Irian Jayan Independence cause.

The Dutch claimed possession of the western half of the main island of New Guinea in 1848 and it became part of the Dutch East Indies. It remained largely neglected for a century. Apart from setting up the infamous Boven Digoel prison camp for political dissenters in the desolate, swampy Tanah Merah region a few hundred kilometres north of the Torres Strait in 1927, the Dutch did little in Irian Jaya before World War II. At the end of the war, when the Dutch attempted to return to their former East Indies possessions, Irian Jaya was made a separate district with its administrative centre at Hollandia — now Jayapura — where General MacArthur had established his military headquarters after advancing from Port Moresby. By 1949 the Dutch could not keep hold of most of their old colony. Indonesia, supported vigorously at the diplomatic level by Australia, won Independence. However the 1949 Independence Agreement left control of Irian Jaya for further talks. These talks were never held and Holland began a concerted political development program in Irian Jaya.

Several factors were involved. The Dutch were annoyed and shamed at the loss of their rich islands in the Far East. They were under pressure from the far right in Holland. They were seeking a home for the Dutch who were reluctantly leaving Indonesia as well as for members of the mixed-blood Indo-European population who felt they had no home in an independent Indonesia. (In the three years to 1953, the number of Dutch citizens in Irian Jaya jumped fourteen-fold, from 900 to 13,500.) And there was the concern of the Christian churches in Holland for their Melanesian converts whom they feared would be swamped by the predominantly Moslem Indonesians. Indonesia claimed that Irian Jaya rightfully belonged to it under the successor State principle, a principle strongly supported in the United Nations as the post-war world decolonised.

As the dispute between the Dutch and the Indonesians intensified, Holland suggested a case before the International Court of Justice but the Indonesians disagreed, claiming that the issue required a political, not a legal, resolution. President Sukarno made 'unification' a national crusade. Peter Hastings, who reported on Irian Jaya for more than forty years and who visited the province more than any other Australian journalist, wrote in 1969 that in Sukarno's Indonesia 'the emphasis on symbols of national unity and national identity became all pervading and in inverse proportion to the decline in administrative capacity and of pragmatic values'. Hastings related that, in 1950, Australia's Deputy Opposition Leader, Herbert Evatt, suggested that Australia buy Irian Jaya from the Dutch. This was the year after Dr Evatt had been president of the UN General Assembly. Speaking in parliament in reply to a Menzies government statement on the growing Dutch–Indonesian hostilities, Evatt said that, if Holland were agreeable, Australia should buy the territory in its own security interests and for the good of the people of the entire New Guinea mainland.

Through the 1950s the Dutch poured money and effort into creating an elite to take over an independent Irian Jaya. The pace at which they pursued this objective came to concern the Australians next door in PNG who were promoting more evenly spread development. The Dutch grants to Irian Jaya began to match the

Australian grants to PNG, which had three times the population. Crash political and education programs produced high school graduates and a class of indigenous public servants not matched in the Australian Territory. By 1961 the Dutch had held elections (in which 100,000 voted — of a population of 800,000) for a national council, the Volksraad. The Volksraad adopted a national anthem, a coat of arms, a flag, and the name 'Papua Barat' — West Papua. The 28-member Volksraad had 80 per cent indigenous membership — of the 16 elected members, 13 were Irianese, and of the 12 appointed members, 10 were Irianese. Across in Australian-administered PNG, the 1961 Legislative Council had less than thirty per cent Papua New Guinean membership — 11 out of 37. And only 6 of those 11 were elected, chosen not by the ballot box but by electoral conferences.

In that same year there was the first-ever meeting between indigenous politicians from both sides of the border. It was held in Hollandia in April after the official opening of the Volksraad. According to Hastings, who was present, the Dutch-educated Irian Jayan leaders, Nicholas Jouwe and Herman Womsiwor, argued persuasively, in English, for a political union. John Guise translated their words into Pidgin for the other PNG politicians present. Jouwe and Womsiwor were to flee to Holland with the Dutch less than two years later to set up the Organisasi Papua Merdeka (OPM) government-in-exile in The Hague. John Guise became Sir John Guise, PNG's first governor-general.

The Dutch efforts were doomed by international power politics. What they left behind was acute, burning frustration. Indonesia's General Nasution described as a 'Dutch time bomb' the increasing social and economic expectations of the Irianese in the late 1950s and early 60s. President Sukarno applied increasing pressure on the Dutch and by early 1961 he had broken off diplomatic relations with The Hague and ordered $450 million worth of military equipment from the Soviet Union. This included a squadron of Badger fighters and a Sverdlovsk-type battle cruiser, called 'Irian'. Although invited, neither Britain nor the United States sent representatives to that opening of the Volksraad in April 1961. In September, as its options narrowed, Holland proposed to the General Assembly that an international authority take over Irian Jaya to prepare the people for self-determination. Indonesia fought the suggestion and defeated, by 53 to 41, a separate proposal sponsored by central African states for an interim international administration.

In December 1961 Sukarno issued commands for the 'liberation' of Irian Jaya. Paratroop units moved to east Indonesian airfields. On 4 January 1962 Australia revealed its impotence. Menzies declared Australia's neutrality. The following week Sukarno appointed newly promoted Major General Suharto commander of the West Papua operation. But while President Sukarno made progress with bluster on the world stage, the Indonesians did not do well in the early military engagements. One of Indonesia's most senior military men, Commodore Jos Sudarso, was killed in a naval engagement in January. A furious President Sukarno ordered paratroop drops. By the time the 'war' for Irian Jaya was over, 1500 Indonesian troops had been dropped into the province. More than two hundred men were killed or never found and hundreds were captured. The Dutch claim they lost fewer than a dozen men.

Liberation Hero

The statue honouring Irian Jaya's 'hero of liberation' stands in the main square of central Jayapura. His arm points over the Provincial Assembly building across the harbour to the horizon. This liberation hero is not Melanesian. He was the Indonesian hero of the war against the Dutch for Irian Jaya, Commodore Jos Sudarso.

Commodore Sudarso, second in command of the Indonesian Navy, was killed on 14 January 1962, when leading a patrol boat raid against Dutch New Guinea. The heavily armed patrol boat he was aboard, the *Matjan Tutul*, had set out from the island of Gebe with two others that day and they were met by two Dutch frigates. One of the frigates, *Evertsen*, sank the *Matjan Tutul*.

Twenty-eight years after his death, the taxi cabs circling Sudarso's statue soliciting fares are driven by Indonesians from other provinces, not Irianese. The commercial life of Jayapura is dominated by Javanese, Bugis, and Makassarese. It is a distinctly Asian city — food trolleys are being wheeled down side streets, a large mosque dominates the tin-roofed buildings surrounding it, wooden scaffolding hugs building sites, the recorded voice of an Asian female vocalist singing a popular Bahasa song wafts from a loudspeaker outside the picture theatre and garish billboard posters advertise coming Indonesian movie attractions. Not many Melanesians are on the streets.

On the other side of the mainland, Australians in Port Moresby were nervous about the developing conflict. By early 1962 Russia had delivered to Indonesia four new destroyers, four submarines and seventy-five fighters and bombers. The Dutch backed up their forces with an aircraft carrier and, by mid-1962, had twelve thousand troops in Irian Jaya. On 25 June 1962 the Port Moresby Town Advisory Council called on Australia to strengthen Port Moresby's defences. Australia's Territories Minister, Paul Hasluck, on a visit to Port Moresby, reassured the population that Australia would not abandon them. The Americans, concerned not to lose any initiative to the Soviets, established links with the Indonesian military and helped Sukarno arm more divisions.

While the Dutch may have been ahead on the battlefield, the future was decided at a different level. In February 1962 the late Robert Kennedy, then US Attorney-General, went to The Hague and made it clear that the US would not support Holland in the event of a full Indonesian attack. The next month the Dutch sat down to talk with the Indonesians under the chairmanship of a UN special representative, American diplomat, Ellsworth Bunker. Bunker drew up a set of proposals that were presented to both parties in July. These called for the Dutch to hand over Irian Jaya to an interim UN administration which in turn would hand full administrative responsibility to Indonesia by May 1963. Bunker further proposed an exercise of free choice by the end of 1969. The Dutch gave in and agreed to the Bunker plan on 15 August 1962. 'We are ashamed before the world,' the Dutch Prime Minister, Professor de Quay said. In Sydney, Herman Womsiwor, hearing about the Dutch acceptance while visiting Peter Hastings, told him bitterly, 'I spit upon the Dutch!'

Other Irianese reacted in different ways. Elizier Bonay, a prominent Volksraad member, co-operated and became the first governor, although he was later to flee across the border into PNG. In 1981 Bonay became an embarrassment to the PNG Government when he appeared as the star witness before an unofficial South Pacific Human Rights Tribunal at the University of Papua New Guinea.

The tribunal was headed by Bernard Narokobi, later to be PNG's justice minister, but who then had just completed a year's appointment as an acting judge on the PNG Supreme Court. Hundreds of students packed the main lecture theatre at the Waigani campus on the Tuesday night of the four-day mock trial to hear Bonay claim that the Indonesians had killed thirty thousand Irianese in the six years from 1963 until the Act of Free Choice in 1969. By speaking, Bonay broke the conditions of his permissive residency in PNG and was deported the next month to Sweden.

The interim United Nations administration did little as they oversaw the departure of the Dutch at the end of 1962 and the entry of the Indonesians in early 1963. In the northern border region the people of the Sentani area tried to leave, too, and 7500 asked to be resettled in PNG. Australia refused to accept them. Between 1963 and 1969 about four thousand Irianese crossed the border, the majority being sent back home. Some families with genuine concern for their safety were granted permissive residence in PNG but by the time of the Act of Free Choice in 1969, they numbered fewer than three hundred.

Those six years were not happy ones for Irian Jaya. Sukarno turned his attention to his next venture, 'Konfrontasi' with Malaysia. Irian Jaya was not an attractive posting for Indonesian public servants or military officers and the previous enthusiasm shown for unification was not reflected in the quality of the administrators sent there. The relatively well-stocked and equipped administrative structure left behind by the Dutch was stripped. Much that was moveable was shipped out to the black markets of Jakarta or Indonesian provincial capitals in between. A $30-million grant that the Dutch had set aside for the United Nations to use for development in Irian Jaya was frozen when Sukarno pulled Indonesia out of the United Nations in March 1965. Irianese who had received rapid promotion and good pay under the Dutch had great difficulty adjusting to their new, much more poorly paid positions in the Indonesian system. A number had to surrender their government houses to their incoming bosses. Soon, repressive measures were the norm, such as the compulsory carrying of travel documents for Irianese wanting to move from one centre to another. By 1966, 369 Irianese were in jail as political prisoners.

The province's administrative apparatus all but seized up. This was well documented by a visiting UN team in 1967 after the demise of Sukarno. In late 1966 General Suharto had taken Indonesia back into the United Nations following Sukarno's rapid decline after the failure of the Communist coup of 1965 and the military's successful counter-coup. This UN team, which had the job of deciding how the $30-million Dutch grant should be spent, found that 43 of the 76 government vessels were out of action because no maintenance had been done. The other 33 were declared unfit to take to sea and should have had their seaworthiness certificates cancelled. The anti-malaria campaign had collapsed. The team reported that assets had been shipped out, and stated bluntly: 'The explanation was really quite simple: it was plunder.'

President Suharto promised to honour the Bunker plan and hold the exercise of free choice by the end of 1969, although everybody involved recognised that this would be nothing more than the final legitimising of Indonesian sovereignty. The August 1962 agreement had carefully avoided mentioning a plebiscite and indeed the final report on the 1969 charade by the United Nations special representative, a former Bolivian diplomat and journalist, Fernando Ortiz-Sans, states that 'an act of free choice has taken place in West Irian *in accordance with Indonesian practice* [author's emphasis].' Only 1025 people actually had a say. Mr Ortiz-Sans did suggest that the Indonesians adopt a one-man, one-vote procedure in the more developed urban centres. But Indonesia rejected this, something the special representative did criticise in his report to the UN. He also recorded that 'certain elements of the population of West Irian held firm convictions in favour of Independence.' But the former Bolivian diplomat's most positive, if limited, achievement was to secure the release from detention of 195 political prisoners held in Jayapura, Biak and other centres and to get more humane treatment for others.

The Act of Free Choice was held between July and August 1969. Consultative assemblies, called 'Pepera', were held in various district centres with the assembly members being drawn from the surrounding populations by the Indonesian authorities. The Pepera at Manokwari had seventy-five members who made the decision on behalf of the fifty thousand people in that district. The Jaya Wijaya Pepera in the central Highlands consisted of 175 delegates representing 168,000 people. Hastings, who went to them all, reported that 'the Pepera were conducted with all the familiar instruments of Indonesian political persuasion and intimidation. There were free cigarettes, cheap plastic brief cases, and food and goods specially flown into all centres for the occasion combined with heavy-handed police and security activities, gaily decorated towns [and] endlessly exhortative posters declaring solidarity.'

Across in Port Moresby the House of Assembly supported a motion by the member for Moresby Open, the Reverend Percy Chatterton, deploring Indonesian repression in West Irian and condemning the UN for not actively intervening on behalf of the West Irianese to ensure that the act of self-determination truthfully reflected the wishes of the people. The House moved that the motion be passed to Canberra for transmission to the UN. Australia was not about to curdle the improved relations that had followed Suharto's rise to power and no action was taken.

The Irian Jayan rebel movement (OPM) has never been a military force of any significance. In early 1990 it had no more than four hundred men in the bush, in small, widely scattered groups, most armed with spears, bows and arrows rather than with automatic weapons. Further, the movement has been riven by bitter factionalism. It has been said that the OPM is more a state of mind of the Irianese people than an army. It has caused headaches of varying intensity to Indonesia but even more acute ones to successive governments in PNG. For Papua New Guinea has had to contend with the competing passions of Melanesian brotherhood and pragmatic self-preservation. An OPM government in exile was formed in Holland in the early 1960s, but it was not until after the Act of Free Choice that the OPM proclaimed independence. At a gathering in the bush at Markas Victoria in the northern part of the Irian Jaya/PNG border region, self-styled Brigadier General Seth Rumkorem declared West Papua's unilateral Independence on 1 July 1971.

In a way Rumkorem's history sums up the sad plight of the Irianese nationalist movement. Rumkorem, from Biak, opposed the Dutch and was incarcerated in the Boven Digoel prison in 1958. He was freed by the Indonesians and, in 1964, made officer rank in the Indonesian military. He deserted and set up camp near the Irian Jayan/PNG border from where he operated for more than ten years, fighting almost as much with other factions of the OPM as with the Indonesians. In 1976 he and the other major OPM bush leader, Jacob Prai, had a dispute over the supply of arms to their ragged supporters. Rumkorem wanted to make contact with arms dealers. Prai disagreed. They split up. A few months later one of Prai's men led an attack on Rumkorem's group, taking thirteen captives. Although OPM spokesmen claimed that the rift between the two was resolved in 1978, Prai's successor, Elky Bemay, led a surprise raid in 1981 on Rumkorem's sanctuary camp in the Bewani mountains on the PNG side of the border. Bemay's guerillas killed several men and took eleven hostages. Rumkorem held out in the bush for another year but in September 1982, tired and dejected, he and nine others set out on what they planned to be an epic trip by motorised outrigger canoe to Vanuatu.

They made it to Rabaul — a quarter of the distance — where they were detained by PNG authorities. Rumkorem and his companions were all charged with illegal entry. However, in a decision that stunned the Government but was welcomed by many Papua New Guineans, the Rabaul Magistrate, Dangs Mila, dismissed the charges. He ruled that Rumkorem and his men on the motorised canoe had not entered PNG until 'invited to do so by the police and customs officials at Rabaul who had intercepted them at sea'! In fact, Rumkorem's group had made many landfalls along the northern coast of the mainland and then along the coasts of West and East New Britain. The following year, Rumkorem was deported to Greece after the Greek Government agreed to accept him.

Papua New Guinea has had a general policy of seeking out 'third countries' to take Irianese dissidents whom it is reluctant to send back to Indonesia but whom it does not want in PNG as a continuing embarrassment to relations with Jakarta. The United Nations High Commissioner for Refugees (UNHCR) has acted on PNG's behalf in approaching various countries over the years. Most go to Europe. Even if Rumkorem had made it to Vanuatu, he would not have been given asylum there, according to Vanuatu's Prime Minister, Walter Lini. Father Lini was visiting PNG on a private church visit the day Rumkorem was freed in Rabaul. He said Vanuatu would have charged Rumkorem with illegal entry as PNG had done and then it, too, would have sought a third country to accept him.

There is a long list of OPM rebel leaders who have been broken by the difficult, frustrating, dangerous and health sapping life of being an ill-equipped guerilla soldier in the malarious, unforgiving border region. A few years before Rumkorem left, his chief rival, Jacob Prai, had struggled across the border into PNG dispirited and ill. He and his lieutenant, Otto Ondawame, were charged with being illegal immigrants and were deported to Sweden. Prai's successor, Martine Tabu, was captured by the Indonesians and the next leader, self-styled General Elky Bemay, disappeared in 1981. The bush generalship of this faction then passed to James Nyaro, the man interviewed on the ABC 'Four Corners' program in 1984 which led to my temporary expulsion from PNG.

Nyaro, an agriculturalist, lived in the jungle from 1982 until November 1985 when, together with his deputy, Alex Donald Derey, he straggled out of the jungle and into a PNG prison. Ten months later these two were deported to Ghana along with the most effective southern border region commander the OPM ever had, Gerardus Thommy. While Rumkorem, Prai, Tabu, Bemay and Nyaro were active in the northern border region, it was not until Thommy trekked across the mountains and into the central and southern border regions that the OPM came to cause serious problems there. Raids he led against Indonesian posts in April 1984 precipitated Indonesian retaliatory action that resulted in eight thousand Irianese fleeing across the border into PNG. He is also credited with encouraging these people (who are mostly from the one language group) not to return home. Thommy surrendered to PNG authorities in the south only days after Nyaro did in the north in the closing weeks of 1985.

The most prominent OPM guerilla leader of the late 1980s, Melchior Salossa, ended the decade in a PNG prison. Salossa was sentenced to four months' jail by the district court in Vanimo in December 1989 for illegally possessing a firearm and ammunition. He had been arrested in a PNG village near the border a few days earlier. Salossa had served an earlier prison term. In 1984 he had been with Nyaro's guerilla group when they killed two Indonesian Government officials while kidnapping a Swiss mission pilot at Yuruf on the Indonesian side of the northern border region. Grisly photos of the Indonesians' bodies, bristling with protruding arrows and spears, appeared in PNG and Australian newspapers. But Salossa's earlier jailing for two years was for his part in another kidnapping near the border in 1984 — that of a PNG schoolteacher. After his release he stayed in PNG and was arrested in a Port Moresby market in March 1987. PNG's Foreign Affairs Department tried to deport Salossa to Jayapura but the PNG Chief Justice, Sir Buri Kidu, granted an injunction until his case was heard by the National Security Council. Sir Buri ordered Salossa be set free pending the Security Council's decision being conveyed to him as chief justice.

The factionalism of the OPM has been just as acute in Port Moresby as in the bush. One of the most vigorous OPM spokesmen is Henk Joku, a naturalised citizen who was secretary to the Volksraad in West Papua prior to the Indonesian takeover in 1963. Henk Joku supports the Prai faction and like other OPM 'spokesmen' throughout PNG is almost endlessly available for comment. Shortly after the 1981 inter-factional warfare on the border, Joku issued a statement saying that PNG should arrest Rumkorem's men. On the morning of 16 July twenty-three Irianese men stormed into Bible House near Port Moresby's Koki market, grabbed Joku from behind his desk, and, as other Bible House staff watched, manhandled Joku into the back of a truck and sped off. A passing police vehicle was waved down and it spun around and gave chase. The police forced the truck off the road bringing to an end, after less than half an hour, Henk Joku's dramatic mid-morning kidnapping by the Rumkorem faction. The twenty-three Irianese, who had come down from a rubber plantation on the Sogeri plateau inland from Port Moresby, were charged with offensive behaviour.

Henk Joku was chief negotiator for the James Nyaro group when Salossa and his men kidnapped the Swiss Catholic mission pilot in April 1984 and demanded $2 million in ransom from the Swiss Government. Later they changed the claim to Swiss recognition of the West Papuan Independence struggle. Joku flew to Vanimo with the Swiss Ambassador to Australia, Dr Rossi. And together with the Swiss Consul, Rolf Meyer, and the Catholic Bishop of Vanimo, Bishop Etheridge, Joku flew into a bush airstrip near the border to arrange the noon handover of the pilot, Werner Wyder. Dr Rossi stayed in Vanimo on advice from PNG Foreign Affairs that he could be a far more tempting hostage than the poor pilot. Wyder said of his ordeal that he had been well treated, but that they had been constantly on the move. A few days later, he was ill with malaria.

PNG's then Foreign Minister, Rabbie Namaliu, described the kidnapping of Wyder and the killing of his two Indonesian passengers as 'an irresponsible criminal act of terrorism'. A few days later PNG moved armed riot police to the border posts of Amanab, Green River and Imonda to force rebel groups back into Irian Jaya. And Prime Minister Somare broadcast on radio that, while he understood that people in PNG had sympathy for the Irianese, 'what we cannot tolerate is when this sympathy extends to violent threats, blackmail and kidnapping. We are not going to allow PNG to become a base for those who would use violence to achieve their aims,' Somare said. Despite his close involvement, Henk Joku never appeared in court. The PNG Government has often warned Irianese who have become naturalised PNG citizens about the duties they owe their new country, but PNG's Constitution confers on its citizens strong rights to freedom of expression and despite some official annoyance little action is ever taken against the OPM 'spokesmen'.

About 250 Irianese have been granted PNG citizenship and hundreds more have permissive residency. The urban Irianese community in PNG totals several thousand. They live in a number of provinces with concentrations in Port Moresby, Madang, Wewak and Manus. A prerequisite of PNG citizenship is eight years' continuous residence. The majority of Irianese granted citizenship won it in the first few years of Independence and were some of those who crossed the border in the early 1960s. A ten-year freeze on granting citizenship to Irianese applicants was imposed in 1978 but since its lifting a number of long-term Irianese residents have joined Joku and the others as PNG citizens.

The freeze came after the 1978 naming by the OPM of a West Papua Cabinet that included ten naturalised PNG citizens and permissive residents. The then Foreign Minister, Ebia Olewale, said this confirmed his 'growing disquiet at the activities of certain persons . . . who appear to be attempting to use PNG as a base for promoting an independent West Papua movement.' Olewale warned that any person, 'in particular a citizen', who conspired with others in PNG to commit criminal offences, either inside or outside the country, or who assisted 'any organisation in the contravention of the laws of PNG' would be prosecuted. He threatened to seek to revoke the citizenship of those who had 'abused the trust' placed in them. By 1990 not one naturalised citizen had been stripped of citizenship. However, a number of permissive residents had been deported for breaking the conditions of their residency — that they do not engage in political activities to the detriment of PNG.

The OPM made an attempt in 1985 to heal its factionalism. The West Papuan Peoples Front (formed a year before) arranged for Jacob Prai and Seth Rumkorem to travel to Vanuatu where they signed a pact called the Prai Rumkorem Port Vila Declaration. Rumkorem had some difficulty getting to the meeting. He had to re-route through the United States when told in Athens that the Australian

Government would not allow him to transit through Australia. Nevertheless he got there and the two most famous of the OPM bush leaders met again. The Port Vila Declaration read: 'We earnestly admit our mistakes in the past nine years [1976-85] of disunity that has caused serious setbacks in our Independence Struggle . . .we have agreed Mr Jacob H Prai will lead the Political Arm of the Free Papua Movement [and] Mr Seth J Rumkorem will take charge of the Military Arm . . . . We appeal to the West Papuan people, freedom fighters and leaders . . . to liberate our rich country from the neo-colonialist, imperialist, expansionist, fascist and militarist Indonesian regime under Suharto.'

The pact also called for a national convention that would adopt a new constitution and a new structure for the independence movement. But by 1990 that convention had not been held. Speaking in Port Vila in March 1988, three years after the declaration, one of the principle figures in the West Papuan People's Front admitted that factionalism continued. Within a year, that man was not even welcome in Port Vila! The falling out between Father Lini and his former right-hand man, Barak Sope, in Vanuatu had repercussions for the OPM. Sope had been a strong supporter of Irian Jayan independence and had arranged for an exiled Irian Jayan rock group, Black Brothers, to settle in Port Vila. The group was jailed after Sope's supporters confronted the Vanuatu mobile force during the political troubles in Vanuatu towards the end of 1988. Australia later agreed to accept the band members and a number of other Irianese as temporary residents.

PNG and Indonesia have regularly revised their border agreements and each new signing has been heralded as marking a new era of friendly co-operation and, more lately, 'maturity'. Even prior to self-government, there was a recognition that a peaceful relationship with the giant neighbour on the western border would have to be a cornerstone of any stable, independent PNG. In House of Assembly debates in 1969 — the year of the Act of Free Choice — the politician who later became PNG's first foreign minister, Albert Maori Kiki, stressed the need for stability in the Indonesian relationship. One of the earliest acts of the first Somare coalition Cabinet was to deport eight border crossers to Indonesia. That was in July 1972, sixteen months before formal self-government, and it seemed that the first PNG Government was determined to prove it was going to be even tougher on border matters than the outgoing Australian administration. Australia's External Territories Minister, Andrew Peacock, said: 'It is their country and they are entitled to decide who resides there.'

The border agreement allows for 'traditional movement' across the border. About ten language groups straddle the border and some village people own land in both countries. The ruler used to draw colonial borders in nineteenth-century Europe was not sensitised to the concept of Melanesian land boundaries. Traditional movement is approved for 'traditional activities within the border area such as social contacts and ceremonies including marriage, gardening, hunting, collecting and other land usage and customary border trade . . . Normal immigration, customs, quarantine and health requirements shall not apply.' The most frequent complaint of the Indonesians has been that certain groups regularly cross the border not for any of these 'traditional' purposes but for one that is perhaps almost as old — the need for dissidents to seek refuge in an area out of reach of the authorities against whom they are dissenting. An early change to the border agreement was the inclusion of the obligation on both countries to prevent their respective territories being used for hostile activities against the other. That came in 1974.

There are five-yearly reviews. The 1979 agreement added provisions for improved border liaison and for the use of the Fly River bulge — where the border follows the meandering river across the 141st parallel for some fifty kilometres — by barges servicing PNG's Ok Tedi mine. The border in this area is 'the waterway'. Shifts in the main channel of the Fly River have seen the border move by up to 3.5 kilometres as the course has cut through some of the more snake-like bends. The changes to the 1984 agreement reflected PNG's concern with transmigration settlements near the border and destructive incursions by Indonesian military patrols. New clauses provided for exchanges of information on major construction within five kilometres of either side of the border and compensation for damage caused in either country by people performing 'acts' while being responsible to the other government. The agreements have been useful in managing an extremely complicated border but they have not been able to prevent several periods of crisis — most notably in 1977-78, again in 1982 and most seriously of all in 1984.

Ill-treatment

Yulianus Sapioper fled across the border from Indonesian Irian Jaya into PNG's Sandaun province along with thousands of others in 1984. He claims to be a genuine refugee. Many of the others who fled, although wary of going back, are village people, border crossers, whose lives are unlikely to be in danger should they return. But Yulianus will be allowed to settle permanently in PNG at East Awin, a large stretch of scrub land to the east of the Fly River, upstream from Ok Tedi's river port of Kiunga.

Yulianus tells a harrowing tale of what he claims were his times of detention by the Indonesian military in Irian Jaya. While it is difficult to verify his statements, this account records what a number of the politically motivated, pro-Independence Irianese claim has been their lot in Irian Jaya under Indonesian rule:

> Since 1960 I worked as an employee at the nutritional section of Jayapura hospital. I have eight children. I am from Bosnik village, Biak, and was born on 6.7.42. I was arrested first in 1967. I was severely beaten until the blood came. I was also given electric shocks. But they did not keep me that time. I was detained on May 9th, 1968. The OPM had convened a meeting, but it was discovered. I chewed the letter we had received from Holland and swallowed it. During detention I was severely beaten with a wooden bar and a gun as well as kicked hard many times. I was transferred to a jail at Ifar Gunung. I recollect being knocked down here with a wooden chair till it broke to pieces. The next thing was to stand for four hours in a water tank. Then lying in the sunshine. I was released in August.
>
> I was detained again in April, 1969, after joining a demonstration led by Arnold Ap. [Ap was an internationally respected Irianese museum curator who was shot dead by the Indonesian Military in 1984.] I spent six months in a police cell. Lieutenant Joko once burned my left arm with a lighted cigarette. They released me in November. My third detention came ten years later in 1979. I was held for three months from June to September. My fourth detention was in 1982, July until October. At one time I was prohibited from using the toilet for five days. I was detained for a fifth time in March 1983. On the fifth night I got violent beatings that made me cry vehemently. Blood dripped from my bruised face and left brow, while my back was afflicted with severe pain. Because

of my heavy cry the commander attended to me and requested his men to leave. He sanctioned my release.

I fled on February 10th, 1984. I swear to God that this is not invented.

The OPM maintains a stream of propaganda via numerous sources, much of it wildly unbelievable. The South Pacific News Service of the Provisional Revolutionary Government of West Papua New Guinea, which operated a news drop in the late 1970s, regularly claimed large-scale military clashes. Its release Number 73 stated: 'More than 55 Indonesian troops have been killed at Skofra . . . trapped between advancing OPM/Papenal forces and the border . . . Between 500 and 1000 Indonesian soldiers are lost and cut off in the jungle.' While there have been large-scale Indonesian sweeps against the OPM, the rebel movement has never had the capacity to mount open resistance, certainly not as described here. Release Number 74 claimed 'villagers aided by OPM militants captured a platoon of 43 Indonesian soldiers. Enraged by the destruction of their homes, food gardens, by the senseless slaughter of women and children, the villagers fell on the 43 and hacked them to pieces, throwing the dismembered corpses into the river.' The Campaign for an Independent East Timor, which printed the releases, attached the disclaimer: 'We accept no responsibility for material included in this Press Release.'

Whereas those boasts about pitched battlefield victories by the OPM were fantasy, the Indonesian offensives referred to were quite real. In 1977 and 1978, Indonesia conducted military actions which involved some 'bombing' of villages. There were two main trouble spots — in the Highlands of central Irian Jaya and along the northern border. There was widespread disruption in the Baliem Valley in the Highlands in mid-1977. Closer to the border sweeping actions led to hundreds of Irianese crossing into PNG. Some military operations coincided with the Indonesian presidential election. Relations between Port Moresby and Jakarta became strained and PNG's Foreign Minister, Sir Albert Maori Kiki, expressed concern to his counterpart, Dr Adam Malik. But he was told it was 'tribal fighting' and an internal matter. 'Indonesia would not tolerate those who attempted to exploit the tribal clashes for political purposes,' Malik said. In June 1978 the Jakarta nationalist newspaper, *Merdeka*, detailed this 'tribal fighting'. Of the 13,500 people living in the Jaya Wijaya region in the central Highlands, a thousand had been killed in the previous year. It spoke of bitter fighting, with schools and houses burned. The newspaper said peace was restored when six thousand people attended a ceremony, ate pigs and burnt their weapons.

A month later, in July 1978, Indonesia's ambassador to PNG told reporters on his return from a visit to Jakarta that the bombs being dropped on suspected OPM positions along the Indonesian side of the border were 'non-lethal'. The Ambassador, Major General Busiri Surjowinoto, said the bombs had a plastic casing and contained no shrapnel. 'They make a loud noise but cause little harm,' he said. The bombing was to flush out rebels who had taken seven Indonesian officials hostage and destroyed their helicopter. Later that year, Indonesia announced a change in policy towards the rebels which came to be called the 'smiling policy'. This was a welcome relief to the PNG Government and in June 1979 Indonesia's President Suharto made his one and only visit to Port Moresby. The new 1979 border agreement was signed a few months later with provisions for improved border liaison. But that proved an elusive goal.

The OPM's most effective campaigns, apart from propaganda, appear to have been sabotage and kidnappings. In 1977 rebels disrupted production at the Freeport copper mine at Tembagapura, wrecking some mine infrastructure. In 1978 a group led by Martine Tabu captured seven Indonesian officials, including a senior soldier, Colonel Ismael. This led to intense military activity. Colonel Ismael was eventually released unharmed. In another attack on a timber yard near Jayapura in 1982 eighteen Indonesian hostages and one Malaysian Chinese were led off into the bush. The rebel faction responsible demanded a ransom of $2m and a hundred machine guns but, after some months, PNG officials sought out the rebel group responsible and secured the hostages' release. In 1984 came the kidnappings of the Swiss mission pilot and, later, the PNG schoolteacher.

The first Somare Government attempted talks with the OPM. Foreign Minister Kiki tried secret diplomacy and offered to act as a mediator between the OPM and the Indonesians as early as 1973. But he found the OPM too factionalised. In early 1977 he had Seth Rumkorem flown to Port Moresby for talks. Indonesia was not happy. News of the talks leaked. In confirming them, Kiki said

Prime Minister Somare had also held a brief meeting with the OPM rebel leader in Wewak. Sir Maori said Rumkorem had crossed the border in December but that it 'was not pre-arranged'. Nor did it have 'any connection with the previous secret initiatives' he had taken. The Foreign Minister said he had wanted to find out from Rumkorem why he had crossed into PNG. Sir Maori said he had told Rumkorem PNG had approved more than 150 applications for citizenship from Irianese permissive residents and he had 'emphasised to Mr Rumkorem that once these permissive residents had been granted PNG citizenship they had a certain duty and obligation to the independent state of PNG' — an obligation not to cause trouble. He said Rumkorem had then 'returned to the Indonesian side of the border'.

In April 1978 Rumkorem was again flown to Port Moresby for talks. This time the other major faction leader, Prai, went too, both travelling by PNG military aircraft. Over three days they held talks with the new foreign minister (Kiki had lost his seat in the 1977 elections), Mr Olewale, the Defence Minister, Louis Mona, the Foreign Affairs Secretary, Tony Siaguru and the Commander of the Defence Force, Ted Diro. Olewale said he 'told the two rebel leaders quite categorically and firmly that they were not to use PNG territory as a sanctuary'. He said he told them that PNG recognised 'Irian Jaya as an integral part of Indonesia' and it would 'continue to take all reasonable steps' to prevent its territory being used for anti-Indonesian activities.

The Indonesians were not convinced, especially since the two major rebel leaders had been flown across the country and back in PNG Defence Force aircraft. They had then been allowed to return to their men in the bush. On the day Mr Olewale spoke to the media, the Indonesian embassy put out its own news release saying: 'If we really want to crush the rebels . . . we would do it . . . But since we always respect our neighbour, its sovereignty and integrity, we didn't want to cross the border.' The embassy said, 'Papua New Guinea's citizens must not be allowed to have "double loyalties".' Indonesia wanted PNG to grow strong and be a good neighbour, it said. But, in a comment that caused considerable uproar, the Indonesian embassy statement went on: 'Therefore, if there is a dream that we want to invade Papua New Guinea, we would do it now when Papua New Guinea is still weak, rather than to wait [for] Papua New Guinea to become strong.'

The Indonesian embassy has issued other warnings. Its most extraordinary contribution to PNG's public debate came during the 1982 election campaign when it warned about the dangers of Iambakey Okuk becoming prime minister. Okuk, then deputy prime minister, had seized on the Irian Jayan cause as a possible vote winner. In a series of statements he attacked Indonesia's record in the province. He claimed Indonesia's transmigration policy meant that the Melanesians of Irian Jaya would 'within a few years' be outnumbered by Javanese and PNG could face 'disastrous consequences' if it failed to develop its side of the border. Okuk pledged that if he were elected Prime Minister he would 'alert the conscience of the world' to what was going on in Irian Jaya. The Indonesian embassy released a newsletter in April 1982, saying 'if one would become a leader of a certain nation, one has to understand the nature of international politics. Otherwise such a person will create disaster instead of developing peace and harmony between neighbouring countries.' And the Embassy said pointedly, 'A nation's leader must understand the difference between a nation and an ethnic group.'

It is inconceivable that the Indonesian embassy in Canberra would issue a statement during an Australian election campaign rooting for either side. But the Indonesian embassy in Port Moresby had no hesitation in letting the people of PNG know the possible dire consequences of having a prime minister who was openly hostile to Jakarta or Jakarta's policies. Okuk hit back furiously at the Indonesians, accusing the embassy of 'grossly unjustified interference' in PNG's national elections and he asked what would happen to PNG diplomats in Jakarta if they issued a newsletter taking sides in the elections then under way in Indonesia. He also claimed that the Indonesian embassy was 'grossly overstaffed' and he wondered what they all did. Okuk lost his seat in the subsequent elections but the issues and factors that determined that result had more to do with rivalries in the Simbu province and the vote-splitting tactics of Okuk's Simbu opponents than anything said by Indonesian diplomats. Nevertheless, since then no political party in PNG has put any store in the vote-pulling power of cross-border Melanesian Brotherhood as an election issue.

In that year, 1982, relations with Indonesia were poor even before Okuk's outbursts. Early in the year PNG's Foreign Affairs Department refused to renew the visas of two Indonesian embassy officials. The reason given was that the Indonesian embassy, second largest after the Australian High Commission, had not complied with staff limits set eight months earlier for all foreign missions. The Indonesians retaliated by closing down their visa section. As the 1982 PNG election campaign intensified, there were a number of border incidents, including three crossings by Indonesian army patrols searching for an OPM rebel group that had taken nineteen hostages from a timber camp near Jayapura. Indonesia's Irian Jayan military commander also arrived unannounced at the Wasengla Catholic Mission seven kilometres inside PNG. Brigadier General Sentosa's Puma helicopter dropped into the mission in the Bewani mountains. The Indonesian general apologised, saying bad weather had forced him off course. But the same day, PNG's chargé d'affaires in Jakarta, Wilson Ephraim, was summoned to the Indonesian Foreign Office and told that PNG had failed to abide by the 1979 border agreement by allowing 'wild gangs' to seek sanctuary in PNG territory.

A few weeks later, on the Saturday that voting started in the PNG elections, another Indonesian patrol crossed the border, raided two settlements and escorted back to Irian Jaya nineteen Irianese who had been living in PNG for five years. In a diplomatic protest note delivered to the Indonesian embassy, the Foreign Minister, Noel Levi, said PNG was extremely annoyed at what he called 'the continued violation of its territory by the Indonesian military'. Back in Opposition after the 1982 elections, Levi revealed he had threatened the Indonesians with changing PNG's United Nations vote on East Timor in an effort to bring the incidents to a halt.

However, the border incidents of 1982 were minor compared with the developments in 1984. On 11 February 1984 the OPM planned to stage a co-ordinated revolt in a series of centres throughout Irian Jaya. Papua New Guinea's intelligence officers found out on 8 February and the PNG authorities asked their Indonesian counterparts what was going on. The Indonesians replied that they were unaware of any potential trouble. That was not true and the OPM uprising which would have been doomed anyway turned into a military fiasco. On the allotted day, 11 February, there were desertions from the Indonesian Army but it was not until the thirteenth that an abortive attempt was made to raise the OPM flag outside the Provincial Assembly in Jayapura. That night more than fifty Irianese families fled Jayapura to seek refuge in Vanimo, the capital of PNG's Sandaun province fifty kilometres away along the coast. The 1984 uprising was precipitated by the then burgeoning transmigration program. During 1983 it had become increasingly clear that the influx of Javanese was having a profound impact on the traditional village people whose land was being taken over for transmigration settlements.

Transmigration in Indonesia began in a small way under Dutch rule and was directed mostly at Sumatra. But in the 1960s it was adopted wholeheartedly by the Indonesian Government, with substantial financial support from the World Bank. The idea is to relocate the landless poor from overcrowded Java to Indonesia's more sparsely populated outer provinces, Sumatra, Kalimantan, Sulawesi and Irian Jaya. Australia's Ambassador to Indonesia, Bill Morrison, visited Irian Jaya's transmigration sites in September 1985 and said that, as a former politician, he could appreciate the motives: 'There is a compelling attraction to politicians in the notion that there are 1.2 million people in an area as large as Spain. On the island of Java, one-third that size, there are a hundred million people. And many of the people of Java have no land. They are landless peasants.' In the early 1980s the American aircraft manufacturer, Lockheed, ran glossy advertisements which, under a large photo of a Lockheed Hercules, read: 'The largest transmigration on Earth needs a big lift. Indonesia chose Hercules for the job.'

Falling oil revenue, poor soils and the reluctance of many Javanese to move led the Indonesian Government into a major scaling down of the program in the late 1980s. But earlier in the decade the political and bureaucratic enthusiasm for shifting hundreds of thousands of people a year threatened full-scale disaster for Irian Jaya. Maps of the Irian Jayan transmigration plan presented a startling picture. Almost all the flat, fertile land was to be handed over to the scheme. In the Merauke district alone three million hectares were to be divided up into some 130 separate settlement projects which, it was estimated, would support a transmigrated population of four million. The indigenous population of that area is about seventy thousand. The transmigration program operates on five-year plans. In the first five-year plan, Repelita I, from 1969-70 to 1973-74, only three hundred families (representing some 1700 people) were moved into Irian Jaya. That was less than one percent of the total number of transmigrants. The second five-year plan, Repelita II, from 1973-74 to 1978-79, shifted another thousand families (or 4300 people) on to blocks in Irian Jaya — still about one per cent of the total.

But as land in Sumatra ran out the plans for Irian Jaya grew.

Repelita III, 1979-80 to 1983-84, saw the percentage of the total transmigrants sent to Irian Jaya jump to about five per cent or about twenty thousand families (80,000 people). The numbers never kept pace with the plans but, by late 1983, well over fifty thousand people had been settled in Irian Jaya's transmigration camps. The number of non-Irianese who had moved to Irian Jaya of their own volition or as workers for government or business numbered about one hundred thousand. The original plans for Repelita IV, 1983-84 to 1988-89, called for Irian Jaya to take fifteen per cent of the transmigrated landless from Java, a total of 137,000 families (or almost 600,000 people). This would have meant that, by 1990, the Irianese would have been under threat of being outnumbered in Irian Jaya by other Indonesian ethnic groups. But in the transmigration camp areas they would have been totally swamped. In 1983 Utula Samana, then premier of the Morobe province, visited Irian Jaya. 'Definitely it's going to mean a lot of Melanesian people not owning land,' he said. 'And I believe they will lose their traditional rights.'

PNG's attention was further drawn to the possible impact of the Transmigration Program when it discovered in March 1983 that Indonesia's Trans-Irian Highway crossed over into PNG territory. Satellite fixes commissioned by both countries confirmed that in the flat southern lowlands the road strayed into PNG's Fly River province three times. This road was no bush track. From the air it was a thick red scar through the green savanna landscape. The road corridor was about fifty metres wide and the forty units of heavy equipment engaged in the project were pushing the road north very fast. The Japanese contractors had erred in surveying the ill-defined border region. Indonesia ordered work to stop, closed the sections that strayed on to PNG territory and apologised for infringing PNG's sovereignty. Commodore Soedarsonu, one of the most senior Indonesian Foreign Affairs officials, said in Port Moresby some months later that the cross-border road was an expensive mistake for Indonesia, 'psychologically, politically and economically'. And the Foreign Minister, Dr Mochtar, told a banquet in Port Moresby in August 1983 that he hoped history would recognise that 'such an admission was rare internationally' and he saw it as testimony to a strong and enduring relationship.

Many in PNG were perturbed not so much by the road but by the transmigration development blocks it was to service. Mr Samana felt that it raised a lot of questions: 'Alongside the road they are creating nuclear estate projects together with the transmigration policy. Now one could easily say that perhaps that is to minimise the problem of border crossing by sealing the border line with populations that are more ethnically related to a Java-orientated government. A buffer zone for the interests of the stability of the Indonesian State. That raises a lot of implications for future problems purely from the PNG perspective.'

President Suharto had decreed that Irianese families were to make up twenty-five per cent of the families on each settlement block. The idea was to teach Indonesia's Melanesian citizens more modern farming methods and to encourage their economic development. But Melanesian subsistence farming and hunting do not blend easily with Javanese agricultural practices. The member for the border electorate of North Fly at that time, Warren Dutton, said one of the concerns of the people in the Fly River bulge was that dispossessed Irianese who might refuse to be assimilated on the transmigration blocks might move across into PNG and try to hit back at the settlers through guerilla action, which in turn would precipitate Indonesian retaliation.

PNG did not have to wait long for the effects of transmigration to be felt across the border. But the first wave of border crossers in 1984 was not from the inland areas where large tracts of traditional land were being appropriated, without proper compensation. The first people to flee were a cross-section of the Melanesian middle class of the Irian Jayan capital, Jayapura — public servants, academics, students and deserters from the Indonesian Army. They, their families and the families of those who had been detained by the Indonesian military were slipping out of Jayapura at night to make clandestine crossings of the border by sea. The PNG Government arrested and charged all the men with being illegal immigrants.

Escape By Night

The long-hulled, finely decorated outrigger canoes of the Serui fishermen put to sea from Jayapura's magnificent harbour every night to bring back their catches for the morning market. But for a few months in early 1984 they carried out a cargo that they did not bring back. The cargo was human and hidden as best it could be. Melanesian Irianese — men, women and their children — were fleeing to Papua New Guinea following the abortive uprising of 11 February.

The Serui fishermen, who charged for the side trip, dropped off their unauthorised human cargo at Vanimo before dawn. Vanimo, provincial capital of PNG's Sandaun province, is fifty kilometres from Jayapura. Amongst those to cross this way was the pregnant Mrs Cory Ap whose husband, Arnold, curator of the Ethnology Museum at the Cendrawasih University, had been detained. Arnold Ap had an international reputation. When he was shot dead by Indonesian security forces two months later, in April 1984, allegedly while trying to escape, there was uproar in regional academic circles.

Other early crossers included some involved in organising the proposed 11 February uprising. One, from the Cendrawasih University, spoke about it: 'We planned to take over West Irian from the Indonesian Government to play out our Independence. We coordinated the plan over several towns in West Papua. The Melanesian military personnel stood by to take up arms and fight back against the Indonesian military. But the secret was revealed and Indonesian intelligence began to chase people, so we had to escape from Jayapura.' They had tried to raise West Papua's Morning Star flag.

> It was on 13 February at 7 a.m. on Monday. Five people, four from the army and one student, went to the provincial parliament House. One army member hoisted the flag but before it reached the top he was shot by one Indonesian intelligence officer and killed on the spot. Our men then shot back but they were quickly outnumbered and had to withdraw. A cleaner at the parliament who they suspected of opening the gate for our men was also shot.
>
> Soon the Indonesians started going from house to house searching for OPM people. Some houses they found empty, they burnt. They are calling it Operation 'Sate'. Sate — something killed, chopped into pieces and cooked. Operation 'Sate'!

Amongst those charged was a group of Indonesian Army deserters from Indonesian Battalion 751, one of the four battalions permanently based in Irian Jaya. Standing around in the sun outside the Vanimo court house, they were still wearing the Indonesian

Army battle fatigues. Their leader, a corporal, said they deserted on 11 February. 'It was at 11 p.m.,' he said, speaking through an interpreter, 'there were sixty altogether but we did not run away together, but separately, in small groups. We were acting on the orders of Seth Rumkorem. He had issued instructions that we had to rise up and fight against the Indonesian occupation. The date was set a long time ago.' The corporal said there were about 150 Irianese in Battalion 751 and 400 from other Indonesian provinces.

The prosecution of the Irianese men was extremely unpopular in PNG. Critics included government backbenchers. One, Mark Ipuia, said he was worried that if the men were convicted, they would be turned back over the border. 'I strongly believe that if these guys are sent back, well, that's the end of them!' The Catholic Bishop of Vanimo, Bishop John Etheridge, was so annoyed by the arrests that he issued a pastoral letter strongly criticising the Government. PNG's public solicitor provided free legal counsel to fight their cases. Harassed, Prime Minister Somare lashed out at those he described as 'humanitarians who were happy to put PNG's freedom in jeopardy'. Mr Somare repeated the official policy that PNG recognised Irian Jaya as an integral part of Indonesia and what went on there was an internal affair for the Indonesians. He did offer to act as what he called 'an honest broker' to help bring the OPM and the Indonesian Government to the conference table.

Under attack in parliament, Somare said that, if it had been 1963 and if PNG had been independent then, he would have been the first to demand Independence for the Melanesians of Irian Jaya. But, he said, the United Nations approved the 1969 incorporation of Irian Jaya into Indonesia six years before PNG's Independence and nobody could change history. When asked at a news conference whether his government's border policy was, like the people of Irian Jaya, a prisoner of history, Somare gave a sharp lecture on PNG's Independence struggle in the 1960s when, he said, there were Australians who wanted Papua New Guineans to become second-class citizens in a seventh Australian State.

One of the refugees, an academic from Jayapura's Cendrawasih University, claimed the Irianese were angry about transmigration. 'It brings a lot of social problems because the transmigrants take a lot of land from the local population. Many think they are pushed away from their land and they're not given much attention to develop. We think that in a couple of years they will dominate the whole of West Papua and outstrip us in population,' he said. 'The Indonesian Government sees transmigration as part of the economic development of West Papua. The people see it from a different angle. They lose their land and suffer social problems. They are not paid for their land and the emphasis is on development. In the process the Papuan feelings and traditions are being wiped out and they are pushing the Indonesian, the Asian way, so that the feelings towards Papua will be eradicated.'

Intelligence sources in Vanimo in early 1984 predicted that over the following few months many more people would cross the border in inland areas as Indonesia pursued known OPM groups and sympathetic villages. That came true. By August more than ten thousand Irianese had fled into PNG — many moving from the fear of military action rather than actual conflict. For the PNG Government this created a problem that could not satisfactorily be resolved. The 'improved liaison' provisions of the 1979 border agreement failed abysmally. The so-called 'hotline' between Vanimo and Jayapura was out of action for months. PNG officials found it impossible to get information from the Indonesians and PNG's official anger grew. At the end of March, after two Indonesian jets buzzed the border post of Green River, PNG was so fed up that it threatened to expel the Indonesian military attaché at the Port Moresby embassy, Colonel Ismaeil. Fear on the border led teachers and students to abandon schools. In a diplomatic protest note, PNG claimed that the jets incident was 'a serious breach of international law and a flagrant violation of PNG's territorial sovereignty'.

Several days later Prime Minister Somare said on national radio that if Indonesia did not give PNG an adequate reply to its protest note by the following afternoon, his government would have no option but to expel the military attaché. The Indonesian ambassador delivered a diplomatic note to PNG's Foreign Minister the next morning but the minister, Mr Namaliu, said it did not deal 'directly or in full' with all the matters raised by PNG. The note announced that Colonel Ismaeil would be leaving PNG within three days. But within minutes that statement was withdrawn. When reissued, it said the military attaché was being replaced. This was a face-saving measure on both sides, with PNG deciding it should not complicate a mission Mr Namaliu was about to make to Jakarta at which he would raise the border problems with his counterpart, Doctor Mochtar.

On the night before those talks began in Jakarta, PNG made its first official comment that transmigration might be the crux of the problem. Acting Foreign Minister, Tony Siaguru, who had been PNG's first secretary for Foreign Affairs, said Mr Namaliu would be asking Indonesia to halt its military exercises in the border region and to reassess its transmigration policy. 'The time has come,' he said, 'to make it clear to the Indonesian Government that many of its policies and actions in Irian Jaya affect PNG directly.' Siaguru said Namaliu would be seeking assurances that Irianese were not being forced from their land to make way for transmigrants. The Jakarta meeting was tough. But Foreign Minister Namaliu announced on his return that he and Dr Mochtar had agreed 'to co-operate in ensuring that our crossers are returned to their homes in an orderly manner'. But the border crossers kept coming. Soon they were flooding across in the central border region.

PNG officials on the border privately predicted in early May that the repatriation plan would fail. Under the plan PNG officials were to escort the crossers to the border where they would be met by the Indonesians. A single PNG diplomat from the Jakarta Embassy was to be allowed to check that they came to no harm. But the sceptical border officials said the Irianese who fled out of fear would refuse to go back. They would either disappear into the bush and remain in PNG or, if rounded up and escorted back, would slip over into PNG again afterwards. The officials were right.

The military exercises on the Indonesian side of the border did not stop either. On 21 May Mr Namaliu told the members of parliament that he 'regretted' to have to inform them 'that, despite the assurances given to me in Jakarta, the Indonesian Government has not given us adequate, advance notice of a military exercise which we understand is currently taking place near the border.' By then, 6800 Irianese had fled into PNG. Mr Namaliu promised parliament that their repatriation would begin before the end of the month. However, the Indonesians stalled. The border crossers were a much bigger headache to Port Moresby than they were to Jakarta. In a move that infuriated PNG, the Indonesians asked for the names of all the people who were going to be returned — an impossible task for the undermanned PNG border administration.

In the midst of this the PNG national court freed 164 Irianese from amongst the first group jailed in Vanimo in March. The Deputy Chief Justice, Mr Justice Mari Kapi, discharged them, saying he was convinced that the magistrate who jailed them had overlooked a possible defence under the criminal code. In the Bewani mountains near the northern part of the border PNG forces captured and disarmed six Irianese men and charged them with belonging to an outlawed group, the OPM. This was the first time the name 'OPM' had been on a criminal charge sheet in PNG.

Then there was another incident involving the Indonesian military on the border and the PNG Government lost patience. An Indonesian patrol crossed the border near the northern coast in late June and burnt down village huts in Sowampa village. Mr Namaliu protested officially to Jakarta, threatening to raise border violations at the coming ASEAN meeting. (Although not a full member of ASEAN, PNG has 'special observer' status at the annual ASEAN foreign ministers gathering, enabling it to attend closed-door sessions and raise matters impinging on PNG.) He carried out his threat and eventually also raised PNG's concerns at the General Assembly of the United Nations in October.

In Jakarta, Dr Mochtar said Indonesia itself had 'run out of patience' with PNG. He repeated the long-held Indonesian complaint that PNG did little to stop the OPM using PNG territory for sanctuary. PNG could hardly reject this charge but the events through 1984 disclosed how the border agreements provisions on consultation were violated as much on the Indonesian side as the sanctuary provisions were on the PNG side. The reality of the terrain and the vastness of the areas involved meant that PNG would have to spend a fortune on border patrols if it was rigidly to keep its side of the bargain. As if to underline the dilemma facing its own officials in the border region, the Government charged one of its own senior border station officers, Sumata Ebuk, with harbouring an illegal immigrant, namely the nine-year-old daughter of rebel leader, James Nyaro.

In August 1984 news broke that border crossers at the Komokpin refugee camp in the Fly River bulge area were dying of starvation. Early reports said fifty-four had died since crossing the border, thirty-three in the previous three weeks. The local member, Warren Dutton, said two thousand people were attempting to live off food gardens that normally supported 150. He accused the Government of following a policy aimed at starving the people into returning to Irian Jaya. Investigations found the starvation stories to be substantially true and while the number of deaths at Komokpin was revised downwards to forty-two, the total deaths for the six border camps in that region was put at ninety-three. Aid was forthcoming. Australia contributed funds to the United Nations High Commissioner for Refugees but the UNHCR's work was hampered by the PNG Government's reluctance to agree to the international refugee body playing any more than a minor role. These people were not 'refugees', PNG's secretary for Foreign Affairs argued. They were 'border crossers' who would return home forthwith.

PNG persisted with its repatriation plan, even though it was increasingly obvious that it was not going to work. Statements emanating from the Foreign Secretary's office were peppered with official starting dates for the repatriation, none of which was ever met. The Secretary, Paulius Matane, was a former school headmaster, who took over as head of Foreign Affairs in 1981 after serving as PNG's ambassador to the United Nations. A gospel-singing novelist, columnist and nationalist, Mr Matane laid down the department's policy with a certainty born out of a firm belief in his own righteousness. Soon after taking over the job, he had tightened the PNG policy on the border to shut it completely to non-traditional crossers. He announced in 1981 that in future people crossing from Indonesia seeking permissive residency would be sent back immediately and he made the bold but ultimately flawed prediction: 'We can reasonably expect this problem to disappear.' By late 1984 the problem was the worst it had ever been. And the confusion went on for more than a year. In October 1985, when PNG deported a dozen Irianese to Jayapura, other residents of the Blackwater refugee camp rioted in Vanimo, attacking government buildings and wrecking cars. Police had to use tear gas to quell the trouble.

The way the Government's border policy had fallen apart became blindingly obvious in late 1985 in the dying days of the Somare Government when Australia's Foreign Minister, Bill Hayden, made an official visit. The week before Hayden's arrival, Prime Minister Somare, at a news conference on his return from CHOGM in the Bahamas, was woefully underbriefed when confronted with a series of questions. At first, he professed not to be aware that Mr Hayden was coming. Then he expressed surprise at a Cabinet decision, taken in his absence, to ask other countries, such as Australia, to share the burden of the border crossers by taking some as immigrant refugees. If Cabinet had taken such a decision, Mr Somare said, he was unaware of it. Asked if he agreed with his Acting Foreign

Minister, Tony Bais, that Australia's $2 million assistance to the UNHCR to help feed and provide for the people in the border camps was 'mere token assistance', Mr Somare said he didn't know Australian money was involved. When told it was he seemed surprised, saying he thought all the money had come from the UN. But he finally seized one issue. Mr Somare said he was very annoyed with Australia's refusal to accept as refugees five Irianese who had turned up on Thursday Island seeking asylum.

At the end of his visit, Mr Hayden was blunt: 'The government of PNG does not seem to have a policy concerning those ten thousand people, and certainly if it does, it's not putting it into effect,' he told the ABC's Trevor Watson. 'Now, there's been no objective assessment of the people to establish whether in fact there are any genuine refugees among them. The fundamental fact,' Mr Hayden continued, 'is that the Government of PNG must make decisions. It must make hard decisions, and it must act resolutely. If it expects Australia to jump in every time it has a problem which it is not prepared to address and resolve — and if Australia does it, it will never handle its own difficult domestic or bilateral affairs. And that is an overwhelming concern I have.' Mr Hayden said another matter worried him. 'We were told when we arrived there were three hundred genuine refugees. The second night it rose to six hundred! What is the figure? We established that, in fact, there's been no objective assessment! Now it's all very messy and the Government of Papua New Guinea must tidy it up.'

PNG's new Foreign Minister, John Giheno, reacted angrily. 'I find such a statement to be patronising and it obviously casts doubts on the humanitarian basis for Australian refugee policy!' Mr Giheno said the decision to 'internationalise' the border issue was in no way an attempt to blame Australia or any other country for PNG's border problems. 'It was intended to request countries which normally receive refugees to consider taking a few from Irian Jaya,' he said. Earlier that year, in February 1985, Mr Hayden was denied a trip to a border refugee camp by the Foreign Secretary, Mr Matane, who felt it might be misinterpreted by Indonesia. PNG's Deputy Prime Minister, Father Momis, added to the confusion, saying the Irianese should be allowed to stay in PNG if they wanted to. Mr Somare said resettlement in PNG was totally out of the question.

In November 1985 the PNG parliament replaced Somare as Prime Minister with his one time deputy, Paias Wingti. Wingti moved fast to implement an entirely new policy. Within two months he announced that PNG would accede to the United Nations Refugee Convention and the 1967 protocol relating to the status of refugees. He said the UNHCR would be involved in dealing with the future of the border crossers and refugees. Wingti said that 'after a comprehensive review' of the issues, he had decided to reduce the number of camps and relocate them away from the border. All border crossers were to be interviewed. 'Those granted refugee status and their immediate dependents will be allowed to remain as permissive residents until arrangements can be made for them to be permanently resettled in third countries,' Wingti said. He claimed that the Somare Government had become entangled by indecisiveness, poor coordination and misunderstanding of refugee arrangements and definitions as well as protracted public discussion. 'What was required,' he said, 'was firm and resolute action' to address the 'serious problems affecting PNG's security as well as the plight of border crossers and refugees.'

The UNHCR welcomed PNG's new refugee policy, describing it as humane and, for the first time, 'resolution oriented'. The UNHCR's legal adviser for Asia, Shun Chetty, praised the Wingti Government's decision to move the existing border camps away from the influence of the OPM. He said there was no doubt that some of the camps were being used as rest and recuperation centres by the rebels. Moving the camps, he believed, would depoliticise the issue and lead to a dramatic improvement in relations between PNG and Indonesia. That dramatic improvement in relations came rapidly but the new 'away from the border' camps were a longer term proposition. Almost a year later Mr Wingti announced that the Government was buying some hundred thousand hectares of land in the East Awin area of the Fly River province. Cabinet agreed to the proposed purchase from the PNG traditional landowners at a cost of about K1.5 million ($2.2m) to be paid in 1987, 1988 and 1989 at K500,000 a year. Mr Wingti said the area would be suitable for growing oil palm and rubber with potential, too, for raising livestock. He said border crossers granted refugee status would be engaged in smallholder rubber development while awaiting placement overseas.

Within weeks of the new Wingti Government announcing the policy change, Mr Wingti's first Foreign Minister, Legu Vagi, was despatched to Jakarta to explain it all to the Indonesian Government.

Although the Somare Government had rejected an increased UNHCR role because of a possible adverse reaction from Indonesia, Vagi met with a good reception. The joint statement issued by Dr Mochtar and Mr Vagi at the conclusion of his visit recorded that 'the Indonesian Government respects PNG's decision to assign a greater role to the UNHCR on PNG Territory'. It went on to say that both ministers 'reaffirmed their commitment not to allow their territory to be used as sanctuary or staging areas for hostile or illegal activities against the other's'. PNG appeared to have accepted Indonesia's suggestion for an extradition treaty and officials were to discuss this further. There has been no extradition treaty signed yet and PNG is reluctant to have one in place because of the adverse publicity each case would attract. But there was, in the space of a year, the negotiation, signing and ratification of the Treaty of Mutual Respect, Friendship and Co-operation.

This twin approach — the treaty and the UNHCR involvement — appears to have served PNG well. One effect is that the guarantees on PNG's part not to allow OPM sanctuaries on its territory have been elevated to a much higher status — that of an international treaty. Article Eight of the treaty provides for each country to 'respect the other nation's right to be free from coercion, external interference in internal affairs and subversion'. Article Nine has two clauses. One states that each country 'shall not co-operate with others in hostile or unlawful acts against the other nation, or allow their territory to be used for such acts'. While these sentences seem specifically aimed at the OPM, PNG won a considerable concession in return from the Indonesians in the second clause of Article Nine, which says both PNG and Indonesia 'shall endeavour to conduct their respective nation's affairs in the border region bearing in mind the other nation's interests'. PNG believed that the transmigration program was just such an 'affair' and, while it has been scaled back for other reasons, too, the slower pace of resettlement in the border region has been welcomed by Port Moresby.

When this treaty was signed in October 1986 the Opposition in PNG claimed that the Wingti Government had become party to 'a conspiracy to legalise the passive genocide of thousands of Melanesians in Irian Jaya'. The Opposition Foreign Affairs spokesman, Mr Giheno, claimed that the treaty was 'a duplicate of the existing border agreement but with new and sinister additions'. He called it a foreign policy blunder that would turn PNG into a 'puppet for Indonesian manipulation'. Mr Giheno is one of the most able of PNG's politicians and such an outburst did not sit too comfortably with statements he had made a year earlier as Foreign Minister about 'Irian Jaya being an integral part of Indonesia' and 'non-interference in Indonesian internal affairs'. But when it comes to 'the border' there is often a sharp contrast between what PNG politicians say when they are in government and what they say when they are in opposition.

This is best illustrated by selecting quotes from the political career of Noel Levi. Levi, the first secretary for Defence, held the seat of New Ireland for ten years and in the late 1980s he was posted to Beijing as PNG's ambassador to China. Mr Levi was Foreign Minister in Sir Julius Chan's government from March 1980 until August 1982. His statements in government and opposition reflect the real dilemma many senior Papua New Guineans have over the Irian Jayan issue. When the late Sir Iambakey Okuk attempted to campaign on 'Melanesian brotherhood' in the 1982 elections, Foreign Minister Levi dismissed Okuk's attacks on Indonesia as 'election bumpf'. He said PNG had nothing to fear from Indonesia. This assurance was at odds with Mr Levi's own campaign in the 1977 elections. He was extremely critical then of the Somare Government's handling of the Irian Jayan issue and in 1979 told parliament that PNG had given away too much to the Indonesians in the 1979 border agreement negotiations. And, he claimed, Indonesia had many spies in PNG.

Two years later, in July 1981, Foreign Minister Levi authorised the deportation to Indonesia of three Irianese permissive residents. He came under heavy attack from the Somare-led Opposition for allegedly sending the three to their deaths. Stung by this allegation, Levi claimed that the deportations followed approaches being made to 'the Cuban and Russian consulates in Sydney for money and guns for the Irian Jayan rebels'. Mr Levi released what he said was previously 'top secret' intelligence on the activities of an underground political movement, the Melanesian Socialist Party, which, he claimed, was offering Russia a 'communist foothold' in PNG in exchange for money and guns. A year after that, back in Opposition, Levi attacked the Foreign Minister in the new Somare Government, Rabbie Namaliu, for 'appeasing' Indonesia by cracking down on border crossers. He claimed that Namaliu's September 1982 visit to Jakarta and East Timor was like 'visiting the home of a burglar to discuss his crimes'.

Indonesian Diplomat Murdered

An alleged Indonesian 'murder list' naming nine prominent Papua New Guineans was produced as evidence in the PNG national court in August 1983. Simon Allom, an Irianese, had pleaded 'not guilty' to murdering an Indonesian embassy official, Meinard Poluan, in Poluan's flat at the Indonesian embassy flats at Gordons, Port Moresby.

The alleged 'murder list' was part of his defence case. Allom's counsel, Bernard Narokobi, was on the list, as was the Justice Minister, Tony Bais. Narokobi claimed that Poluan had given Allom a list of nine prominent people in PNG he wanted killed. The Court heard allegations that Poluan had given Allom money, a camera and keys to a car but when Poluan returned without photos of the nine, a dispute broke out and in a scuffle Allom had stabbed Poluan with a bread knife.

The Indonesian embassy pays close attention to the activities of Port Moresby's Irianese community, which is deeply factionalised. Some Irianese are paid informants. Many believe those in rival factions have been bought off by the Indonesians and are spying on them. If there was a list it was more likely to have been an observation list than a murder list.

The Chief Justice, Sir Buri Kidu, convicted and jailed Allom for fifteen years. Sir Buri said he could not believe that the official Allom killed was a spy. However, in passing sentence he did accept and take into account that Allom's father had been hanged by the Indonesians and his mother disembowelled.

The Russian connection mentioned by Mr Levi appears to have been all one way — approaches without result. The OPM spokesman, Henk Joku, has said often that the OPM has approached the Eastern Block for guns because their cause has been rejected by the West. At one stage, a letter bearing a Bible House stamp and addressed to a Mr George in Turkey was returned to Port Moresby undelivered and was intercepted by PNG intelligence. This letter invited Mr George to act on the OPM's behalf in making contact with Moscow. There was a raid on Joku's house. He protested, saying the approach was nothing new, and pulled out five-year-old newspaper headlines to prove it. Another Irianese PNG citizen, Moses Werror, who is the Madang-based 'chairman of the OPM revolutionary council', claimed in May 1987 that the organisation had established links with Libya.

A report out of the Netherlands had quoted the ageing Nicholas Jouwe as saying a number of young exiled Irianese living in Holland had been lured to Libya by Colonel Gadaffi 'with false promises and fairy tales' to undergo training as terrorists. Moses Werror claimed that the men the OPM had in Tripoli were being trained as 'freedom fighters', not terrorists. He said the OPM had turned to Libya because it had failed to get regional support. He claimed these 'freedom fighters' were receiving training as guerillas who would attack Indonesian military targets, not civilians. Werror described Jouwe as a respected elder of the movement who was not in touch with 'current OPM diplomacy'. The Libyan connection has naturally been of some concern to the Indonesians. In July 1987 Indonesia's Foreign Minister, Dr Mochtar, accused the Libyans of helping the OPM. And he made pointed reference to moves then under way to set up a Libyan People's Bureau in Vanuatu. That bureau was never established. There was no evidence by the end of the 1980s of any Libyan-trained guerillas active in Irian Jaya.

Transmigration goes on, although the ambitious, original target in Repelita IV of transferring six hundred thousand Javanese peasants to Irian Jaya in the five years to 1988–89 was abandoned. There were about two hundred thousand transmigrants in Irian Jaya at the beginning of 1990. Several transmigration sites failed to impress the settlers, with some abandoning their free plots of land to head into Jayapura, Merauke and other towns. Another limiting factor was cost — an estimated $900 per transmigrated settler. In November 1986 the minister in charge of the transmigration program announced that the number of Javanese to be settled in Irian Jaya in 1986-87 would be only eleven thousand. The official reason given for the cut in the transmigration program was budgetary cutbacks forced by the drop in revenue from Indonesian oil exports. However, the President of the World Bank, Mr Barber Conable, on a visit to Indonesia in March 1987 said Indonesia had been responsive to outside critics of its transmigration policies.

Prime Minister Wingti made an official visit to Indonesia in January 1988. He was impressed by the welcome given by President

Suharto. Three-metre-high portraits of Paias Wingti lined the streets and school children packed footpaths, waving miniature PNG flags as he zoomed past. During the trip both President Suharto and General Murdani confirmed to Wingti that Murdani had given $US139,400 to Ted Diro during the 1987 elections. 'General Murdani did not disclose to me why he gave Mr Diro this money,' Mr Wingti said on his return to PNG. 'And thus the reasons remain private between General Murdani and Ted Diro. President Suharto had earlier told me of his knowledge of the affair when we sat together for the State Banquet'. He said the President claimed that his first knowledge of the matter was when Diro revealed the gift before the Barnett inquiry into the PNG forests industry three months earlier, in October 1987. Diro had said some of the money was carried into PNG by Indonesia's military attaché.

Mr Wingti said he appreciated President Suharto's assurance that the campaign contribution to Diro's party was not officially condoned by the Indonesian government. He said President Suharto told him that General Murdani had admitted making the gift but that it was 'purely a private affair between the two of them and did not involve the Government or armed forces of the Republic of Indonesia. President Suharto told me that he accepted General Murdani's explanation, and that he, Suharto, was satisfied that it did not compromise Indonesia's relationships with PNG.' Mr Wingti said the reason General Murdani had at first publicly denied the story was because of extreme embarrassment but 'in the interests of PNG's and Indonesia's overall relationships and to demonstrate Indonesia's genuine desire to place our relationship on a very honest footing, he decided, after discussions with President Suharto, to clear up the mystery once and for all,' Mr Wingti said.

This claim that it was a 'private' gift, even if true, does not lay the issue to rest. From Indonesia's point of view, Diro was the perfect PNG Foreign Minister — a former brigadier general who understood the military mind and who was fully aware of how vulnerable PNG was to military pressure on the border. Had Mr Diro's People's Action Party won enough seats at the 1987 elections for him to become prime minister, PNG would have had a leader owing a large debt of gratitude, if nothing else, to the head of the Indonesian armed forces. General Murdani and Mr Diro both suffered career setbacks after the $US139,400 gift became public knowledge. But, in PNG at least, the ease with which the affair seems to have become accepted sets an amazing precedent for the 1992 elections.

The problems of the border have not been solved although tension eased considerably following the Treaty of Mutual Respect, Friendship and Co-operation. The Namaliu Government opened a consulate in Jayapura in 1989 to facilitate increased 'travel, trade and business' and to help 'practical border arrangements'. The first test for the consulate came within three months with dissident Irianese seeking asylum in December 1989. Asylum was not granted. Speaking at the September official opening, PNG's Foreign Minister Somare predicted that the border would 'no longer be a mystery to either country. It will not be a closed area,' Somare said. 'And it will not be a matter which third countries will seek to manipulate for their own interests.' This reference to 'third' countries was interpreted by some Australian officials as being a message to Australia to mind its own business when difficulties arise on the Irian Jayan border.

The head of the PNG Foreign Affairs Department in the late 1980s, Bill Dihm, must be given much credit for PNG's surer stance in its relations with its neighbours since the difficulties of 1984. Mr Dihm, who was deputy secretary under Mr Matane, took over as departmental head at the time the Wingti Government took power in late 1985. A younger man than Matane, Dihm is one of PNG's most impressive bureaucrats. He led negotiations on the Treaty of Mutual Respect, Friendship and Co-operation and was the architect of the change in relationships that PNG forged with Australia and the Melanesian island States of Solomon Islands and Vanuatu. A joint declaration of principles between PNG and Australia aimed at putting their relationship on a more even, 'mature' basis was signed by Mr Wingti and Mr Hawke in late 1987. The Melanesian Spearhead Group was formed in 1986. Although all three — the treaty with Indonesia, the declaration with Australia and the spearhead — were initiatives taken during Mr Wingti's 1985-88 term, all three have been endorsed by the Namaliu Government.

Indonesia's former Foreign Minister, Dr Mochtar, called on PNG to try to forget the fears of the past when he spoke at the banquet in Port Moresby the night the two countries signed the historic Treaty of Mutual Respect, Friendship and Co-operation in October 1986. He said that he understood how memories of what happened under Sukarno still lingered in PNG. But times had changed, he claimed, and the people who had fled Irian Jaya during the 1960s should return to see the difference. He made a comparison with Indonesia's own experience with Chinese support for the failed Communist coup of 1965. 'We have the same problem with China,' Dr Mochtar told the banquet guests, who included a number of Irianese naturalised PNG citizens. 'We still have those fears against them — and if it takes us twenty-one years to get over our trauma, it will take time for suspicions to wear off in PNG.' What PNG has to accept is that it has an 'Indonesian' province next-door. A province that is being converted away from Melanesian ways. It is being Indonesianised. The heartaches and the problems of this process are never going to be easy for PNG to live with but pragmatism demands that it find ways to do so.

CHAPTER TEN
CRIME, PUNISHMENT, JUSTICE AND THE FUTURE

WITHIN Papua New Guinea village society the most serious crime of all is not murder. It is adultery. Killing within traditional society was more likely to have been a sentence than a crime. Killing was often the product of other actions that disrupted society in the small, unitary village community. In my wife's village on Manus Island the most traumatic event of the past one hundred years followed an order by her great grandfather, the village bigman, that his younger brother be assassinated for allegedly coveting an elder brother's wife. The killing went horribly wrong. The hired assassins from another part of Manus took advantage of the dispute to slaughter not only the brother but most of the rest of the village as well. Rural Papua New Guineans still rate adultery as worse than murder. A University of Papua New Guinea Psychology Department survey has discovered big discrepancies between village assessments of the gravity of crimes and the severity of punishment allotted to them in the PNG criminal code which was drawn from the Queensland code.

A former Justice Minister, Paul Torato, suggested that PNG revert to traditional penalties for traditional offences. In his province of Enga in the Highlands, he claimed, a woman committing adultery would be punished by having her nose cut off 'so she cannot be beautiful any more' while a man guilty of the crime would be 'hung from the ceiling' and smoked over a low fire to 'suffocate him to death'. The university survey showed that crimes against property such as breaking and entering and car stealing are considered far less serious by villagers than the relative loading given to them on the criminal code. Of the nineteen crimes listed, the people rated breaking and entering eleventh most serious and car theft fourteenth, whereas the criminal code ranked them fifth and seventh.

The crucial point about the 'law' in traditional society was that it was aimed at restoring balance to the community. It was rough, it was ready, it was swift. It was not always fair. And some powerful men avoided it altogether. It also often involved compensation to the victim or victims. The accused had few rights. In Mr Torato's words: 'Things have changed since we have moved towards civilisation. In the Western kind of law which we adopted, the offender is protected. They usually get away with it and the innocent are being victimised. But in our law, in our customs, we knew exactly who did it. Or we presumed who did it!'

PNG's justice minister in the late 1980s, Bernard Narokobi, ordered work to begin on an extensive overhaul of the PNG criminal code so that a new, 'more appropriate' code could be introduced in the 1990s. Narokobi was the first justice minister to take the title 'Attorney-General' because he was the first qualified lawyer to hold the ministry. Narokobi, a former acting judge and civil rights lawyer, has written extensively about 'the Melanesian way' and may be the best man to try to resolve the huge dilemma of drafting appropriate legislation for a country as culturally diverse as PNG. There is no single, agreed body of customary law. What held traditional society together were mechanisms and understandings that often varied significantly from place to place. What might quell feuding in one locality might be a recipe for conflagration in another.

Disregard for the rule of the current laws makes governing PNG extraordinarily difficult. Lawlessness is the aspect of the country most featured overseas, and that annoys the authorities. The image of PNG being a land almost beyond the rule of law where the white woman lives in fear of rape and her life, is a recurring one in the Australian media. Incidents such as the rape and murder in mid-1987 of a young female Australian helicopter pilot, Heather Mitchell, reinforce that perception. 'Sixty Minutes' followed up Mitchell's murder with a segment titled 'White Prey', which infuriated Papua New Guineans who saw it on video in Port Moresby. The 'not a white woman safe' cliche is vastly overdone. Either that, or the ten thousand or so expatriate females in PNG are the most violated people on earth. Flippancy aside, crime is a very serious problem.

While it might scare away tourists, the real worry is the way it is shaping the internal economy of PNG and shaking the confidence of the population in the ability of the system to deliver peace and order.

The difficulty with maintaining law has much to do with the astonishing rate at which more than seven hundred separate and tiny independent society States, each with its own language, customs and traditional practices, have been compressed into a modern nation State. For almost the whole of PNG it is less than a hundred years since first permanent contact with forces outside the village group, and for many areas it is a period of half or a quarter of that. Perhaps the surprising thing about PNG is not that law and order is a perplexing problem but that things are not a great deal worse.

The Australian patrol officers, the Kiaps, who first brought 'government' to the bulk of the people of PNG, subdued the fighting and introduced a veneer of harmony. But of all the colonial tasks performed by Australia (and considering the time frames involved and the enormity of the job, Australia scored fairly highly in most), the one in which achievements were most ephemeral was in establishing a system of peaceful dispute resolution. The aims were high but the execution was confused. The Kiap courts (courts of native affairs) were a logical first step. The Kiap, usually a young Australian in his twenties, aided by older PNG policemen under his command, acted as prosecutor, defence counsel, magistrate and, if need be, jailer.

Dame Rachael Cleland, whose husband, Sir Donald Cleland, was Australian administrator from 1952 to 1967 and who was from a legal family herself, claimed that the system suited the people's own notions of justice, with the simple face-to-face hearing of the dispute 'when either an acceptable compromise was reached between the parties or, when necessary, justice was meted out and the wrongdoer taken away'. She claimed that the justice dispensed had to be sound because good order depended on it. 'If (people) were not satisfied, resentment smouldered and the trouble broke out again. So an officer learned in a hard school to ferret out what had actually happened.' While that was the ideal, the Kiaps did not visit some remote villages more than once every two years. Also, the young patrol officers mostly did not know the languages of either those they tried or any of the witnesses. Interpreters held great power and there were many misunderstandings.

Towards the end of the 1950s, a fundamental philosophical difference on the conduct of justice in PNG arose between the Australian administration in Port Moresby and the Territories Minister, Paul Hasluck, in Canberra. Some preliminary work had begun in PNG on an attempt to codify a system of village courts that could draw on both village custom and the introduced law to establish a lasting mechanism for dealing out appropriate justice. Hasluck, however, believed that if the principle of justice was to be instilled in PNG then there had to be one set of laws covering the whole population — not a separate system for the Europeans and sophisticates and another for the 'natives'. And he believed the courts had to have absolute independence from the administration. The chief justice appointed by Hasluck in 1957, Justice Alan Mann, told him that a 'territory common law' could only be built up by recorded judicial decision and not by decisions applied by Kiaps ad hoc in local tribunals whose main objective was to fix up a local situation.

Hasluck argues that he wanted 'to familiarise the people with the idea of justice as a principle to be applied without discrimination in all situations, the idea of law as a code that applied evenly and justly to all citizens, and the idea of courts of justice as institutions that were independent, not subject to, the direction of those in authority, not to be used as one of the agencies of governmental administration, and equally accessible on the same terms to all persons.' In his book *A Time for Building*, Hasluck says he was worried that 'in too many newly emerged countries there were the signs of the colonial system of domination by white over black offering an easy transition to the substitution of a dominant black for the former dominant white group, leaving no greater liberty or freedom and possibly less just treatment for the subordinate indigenous populace than they had under colonial rule.'

The problem with Hasluck's proposed system — which came out of recommendations by Professor Donald Derham, of Melbourne University, in 1960 — was that it depended on an expensive system of visiting foreign magistrates. Hasluck was an impatient man well aware of the immense job facing Australia in preparing PNG to rule itself and he became convinced that the administration in Port Moresby was resisting Derham's recommendations. So in September 1962 he laid down the policy on justice as it was to apply from that day on. There was to be a single system of courts administering a single body of law; the Kiaps courts were to be abolished and 'nothing similar to them' was to be substituted; and all courts were to be 'equally independent of the legislature and the executive'. The work on village courts came to a stop. At that stage, also, the administration had only just established a separate Police Department. Prior to this the police were subject to the Kiaps. Australia's worst legacies to PNG were to be the lack of any established court system with relevance at the village level and a police force designed for colonial convenience.

Village courts now operate but the system did not win favour until after Papua New Guineans took control of the House of Assembly in 1972. The first village court was not set up until 1975, Independence year. That was a time of rapid change and disarray in rural administration and the effectiveness of village courts today would be far greater had they been introduced earlier and had a more tranquil settling in period. Back in the 1960s, the rapid implementation of Hasluck's single justice system meant that Kiap courts ended before there were enough magistrates to take over; the hopelessly undermanned Public Solicitors Office had to take total responsibility for defence cases; and untrained police suddenly had to accept complicated legal prosecution duties. The most comprehensive study yet done into PNG's post-independence law and order problems highlighted that failings in all three areas had reached dreadful proportions. The Clifford report, named after its chairman, William Clifford, ex-director of Australia's Institute of Criminology, ran to two volumes and 543 pages. It presented a devastating picture of the state of law administration in PNG in the mid-1980s.

The Clifford report put a 'conservative' estimate on the cost of crime in PNG each year at K76 million ($A115m) for the private sector and K56 million ($A85m) for the Government. It said this bill of K132 million ($A200m) put 'a sizeable hole in the economic bucket — more than half of the aid received annually from Australia'. Although some of Clifford's recommendations have been followed and there have been improvements in some areas, much of the analysis remains valid. The report revealed a system of justice overwhelmed by the job before it. It estimated that at least eight thousand crimes were committed in 1983 and said, 'the criminal justice system is in serious danger of losing the battle to manage and process, let alone constrain, the existing rates of crime.'

'This is not the same,' Clifford said, 'as saying that the criminal justice system verges on collapse. For the reality is that long after the rate of crime exceeds the processing capacity of the system, the system will continue to function. To any casual observer, an overburdened, totally inefficient criminal justice system still appears to operate normally . . . and, superficially, so it does. Police, courts and jails continue to process offenders through the system. Whether they are the ones who should be processed, whether the majority of serious offenders escape, whether the courts work expeditiously and with justice, whether the prison service aggravates rather than ameliorates the situation — all of these questions arise only for the person affected by this structure or for those who are interested enough to examine it in action.'

In attempting to answer the question 'Who is to blame for the startling demise in the ability of the justice system to respond to crime?', Clifford said the National Court was where most of the problems surfaced. By the mid-1980s, conviction rates had fallen from 80 per cent to just over 50 per cent, cases struck out had leapt from 3 per cent to more than 20 per cent and court delays had exploded so that the processing time for cases had climbed 300 per cent — to a mean time of 344 days from committal to ruling. 'But this court cannot be held primarily to blame,' the report said. 'It seems the deficiencies in every criminal justice agency are reflected in the problems manifested in the national court. The police and Public Prosecutor's Office appear to be responsible for most of the problems in the National Court: the police chiefly through their incompetent investigations, and the Public Prosecutor's Office through their ineptitude in prosecuting cases.' Clifford said both agencies were 'severely handicapped by the common ills of the system — no training, no supervision and consistent overwork'.

One lesson criminals in PNG learnt by the mid-1980s was that the surest way of tangling up the system and avoiding punishment was to plead 'not guilty'. If they could then get bail, the chances of conviction almost disappeared. Police prosecutors in the district courts and lawyers from the Public Prosecutor's Office in the national court won few contested cases. Conviction rates before the national court came almost wholly from those who admitted guilt. Clifford and his committee found that everybody they interviewed believed the most significant cause for the number of cases 'delayed, withdrawn, struck out, discharged or dismissed could be traced to deficient police investigations'. They said a lack of training, improper supervision and inadequate resources 'deny police a fighting chance against most crimes [and] cause many cases to be dropped out of the system'.

The judge's annual report to parliament in 1983 said that police had 'come to rely on confessions as the primary, if not the exclusive, means of proving their case. Because offenders are not properly warned of their constitutional rights, confessions obtained by the police are inadmissible in court, and cases are withdrawn or lost at trial due to the absence of other evidence. Frequently,' the judges said, 'the entire prosecution rests on the admissibility of a confession, as police do not know how, or lack the skills and forensic services, to acquire other incriminating evidence.'

The inability to cope with difficult investigations led to a reluctance to prosecute serious cases. Clifford said that this shifted police resources from chasing hardened criminals to first offenders. 'The full force of the law thereby increasingly falls upon shoplifters, highway traffic violations, and drunks; while rapists [and] streetwise and hardened criminals enjoy increasing immunity from justice.' The problems fed on themselves. As the public became more and more aware of police failings, public attitudes worsened. 'Deteriorating public respect fosters frustration, undermines confidence, adversely affects motivation and commitment and in turn intensifies the very causes of public disrespect,' the Clifford report said.

No Appearance

'Can you be at Port Moresby courthouse tomorrow? Ten?' the policeman asked over the telephone. He wanted me to testify in a case against a youth charged with stealing the ABC vehicle. The car had been stolen months before. It was recovered the next day with the windscreen smashed and the radio ripped out. A fingerprint check led to the case.

It was the second time the policeman had asked. Some weeks earlier, I had been unable to oblige because I was off to Vanuatu and he had said they would seek an adjournment. I presented myself to the Port Moresby District Court. The policeman thanked me for coming. We then waited two hours.

'That is us now,' he said. I followed him into the court as the defendant's name was called out. I sat astounded as the officer assisting the court walked out into the public corridor, yelled out the man's name twice, and then returned to pronounce, 'No appearance.' The magistrate issued an arrest warrant.

I grabbed the policeman by the shoulder and asked what had happened to the fellow they caught whose fingerprints matched those on the car. 'Oh, while you were away,' he said with disarming frankness, 'that guy was taken by mistake to the Boroko District Court and we have not seen him since.'

Annoyed and incredulous, I wanted to know why I had been kept waiting as a potential witness for more than two hours. The policeman shrugged. As I was leaving I met a lawyer I knew who was waiting to defend another case. He was not surprised. 'There was a bloke here the other day up on a fairly serious charge,' he said. 'He just walked out, down to the wharf there and hopped on a boat for Daru. They won't see him again!'

The Clifford report related how defence counsel consider securing bail as a most important step towards eluding conviction: 'Many offenders released on bail never appear for court and can never be found by the police. In time everybody gives up and the case is dropped. Many judges, magistrates and lawyers believe the clearance rate of outstanding bench warrants (for arrest) is less than 5 per cent.' In Port Moresby in the twenty months to March 1984, of 3500 warrants issued, only sixteen per cent were executed. Police put the total of unexecuted warrants at more than fifteen thousand. 'Warrants float loosely about police stations and can be found buried on or in desks, mixed inadvertently with other papers,' Clifford said. 'Many warrants simply disappear. One police station is reported to have reduced its backlog by burning two thousand outstanding arrest warrants.' Those who do not honour bail often win by having their cases struck out. In 1982 the national court struck out a long list of cases including wilful murder, rape, indecent assault, unlawful wounding, and breaking, entering and stealing because they had been unattended to for years.

In the late 1980s the Chief Justice, Sir Buri Kidu, said the national court had been able to fix some of the problems identified by Clifford but that long court lists and delays remained. 'Since that report,' he said, 'almost every case which was outstanding then before the national court here in Port Moresby was struck out because witnesses had disappeared or the accused who was on bail had disappeared. A very high number of cases were struck out, too, in Lae and Mount Hagen. To look at the clearance rate,' the Chief Justice said, 'you might get a false impression that we were getting rid of the list. But no! And now it has gone back to Square One. I was just going through the April and May lists for Port Moresby [1988] and they are still as long as when Clifford's report was published.'

Many prosecutions foul up on legal technicalities. In April 1988 three men accused of taking part in PNG's largest ever armed robbery were discharged by a national court judge in Lae because they had not been brought to trial fast enough. Two of the men had been in custody for more than a year. The armed robbery occurred at the Lae Airport in February 1987, when K165,000 ($270,000) was stolen while in transit from a bank's branch office to head office in Port Moresby. Mr Justice Amet granted an application from the defendants' lawyers that, under the criminal code, a person was entitled to be discharged if the court was satisfied that the prosecution had not made a genuine attempt to complete its case. The State prosecutor told the judge that the State case had been delayed by various logistical difficulties and the fact that a police officer investigating the case had been charged with official corruption for allegedly receiving K3000 ($5000) to destroy evidence against the three men. Judge Amet said he sympathised with the difficulties but he had to follow the law.

Amongst problems hindering the national court's work that Clifford highlighted, three — staff, money and access — have been addressed. After a bureaucratic battle, Sir Buri Kidu won the right to hire and fire staff. 'At one stage there were ten judges and only five secretaries,' he recalls. 'And the judges were fighting over whose work was going to be typed first. Eventually a sympathetic Justice Minister, Mr Warren Dutton, appreciated the impossible situation and he pushed through legislation which now enables us to recruit staff.' Also, the judges no longer have to write everything in longhand. Trials that should have taken two days took a week. Another breakthrough came when the Chief Justice won parliamentary approval for a constitutional amendment that allows him to submit his own budget proposals direct to Cabinet. Sir Buri said the judiciary previously had to argue its submissions right through the bureaucracy, and the Finance Department always slashed its estimates. The third improvement in the court's functional ability is the basing of judges in centres other than the capital. Since 1989 judges have been based in Mount Hagen and Rabaul.

While the police prosecutors are blamed for the disastrous standard of prosecutions in the district courts, the Public Prosecutor's Office attracts similar criticism in the national court. Clifford said it was not surprising that counsel were so widely condemned for incompetence, nor that so many quit young. 'Counsel are neither stupid nor particularly incapable of learning; they are simply inexperienced, unsupervised and grossly overworked. Prosecutors a few short years out of law school are thrust into criminal litigation with responsibility for prosecuting murder, rape and fraud,' Clifford said. 'Unquestionably they are a major contributing cause to the breakdown in the justice system, but not because they are not trying; they simply do not know how to litigate properly serious criminal cases. There is no one with the time, ability or experience to teach young national counsel how to become competent barristers.'

The lure of better paid private practice is strong. Few young lawyers stay with the Public Prosecutor's Office for more than three years and the system perpetuates its own failings. One defence lawyer told the study team he never had to do very much to win. The prosecutor would 'usually find a way to lose. They simply do not want to take on tougher cases and the others they do take on, the chances are good they will forget to do something important.' Sir Buri Kidu sees this as a continuing problem, although he is encouraged by some of the younger prosecutors. However, he fears they, too, will be lured away by the more substantial financial rewards that await solicitors in private practice 'where they can make more than I do'.

Of all the agencies examined by Clifford, the police force had the biggest problems. The report said that the intrusion of Western law, with its strict impartiality and high standards of proof, was one. 'Originally, serving the Kiaps the police had a friend in court, for the Kiaps were also the magistrates: it took an unusual set of circumstances for the magistrate to doubt the word of the policeman; and his position of authority in the villages assured him of support — and a flow of fairly accurate information from the Luluais and Tultuls.' Luluais and Tultuls were the village men appointed by the administration to be the Government's link with the people. They were replaced when local government was introduced and councillors were elected.

'The decline in the centralised authority of the Kiaps,' Clifford pointed out, 'the shift to more and more professional magistrates and the isolated role of the police in barracks in town changed all that. No longer were people compliant. They would dodge the police or defy them. Raided in their settlements by police in force, they began to regard the police as alien. Police were not as much a part of the community, so that neither information nor support were readily forthcoming. Then to make life impossible for the police, the magistrates were likely to treat them like any other witness, and a generation of young trained lawyers ran rings around them in court. Yet to cope with this the police were progressively receiving less training than before.'

The Clifford report maintained that the breakdown in police communication with the people was one of the gravest problems facing the force. The communication links shattered following the separation of the police from being subject to the patrol officers in the old Department Of Native Affairs. 'The community did not desert the police so much as the police deserted the community,' the Clifford report said. 'The barracked police in towns were not at all like the Kiap's rural police. They came under a centralised police authority and when they went to rural areas it was to deal with disorders or to become instruments of pacification. They operated in large groups and quickly developed a "them" and "us" mentality which they maintained back in town.'

This led to its own complications in carrying out investigations into crime. The people would not co-operate. The report found that 'there are large pockets of intense hostility against the police. In each instance examined, the hostility was based on police discourtesies, abuses of their power, violence or repugnant public behaviour. The fact is the police do not respect the communities. Their arrogance and indifference dries up any co-operation. Sometimes it even generates fear of the police. For wrongdoers to fear the police is appropriate. For communities to feel like this is to kill co-operation and to kill successful investigation, thus providing the criminal with support which in other circumstances would be denied.'

The police force that Australia handed to PNG at self-government was the most crippled of any government agency. In the year of Independence police responsibility covered only ten per cent of the land area and forty per cent of the population. A PNG policy document produced just one month after Independence stated that the force faced 'major problems' because of inexperienced and untrained staff. 'Of a total force strength of 4400,' it said, 'there are 239 commissioned officers, 96 below established strength. Sixty-two officers are expatriates and 177 are Papua New Guineans'. On average the 177 PNG officers were aged 28 and had been policemen for less than five years and commissioned officers for less than three years. Worse were the severe shortages of senior non-commissioned officers (NCOs). There were only 149 sergeants instead of 324; and only 306 senior constables when there should have been 575. Hardly the law enforcement agency one would wish upon a new nation with PNG's complexity of problems! The document noted that 485 recruits graduated from the Bomana Police College in 1974-75, while 448 NCOs left the force in the same period.

David Tasion, PNG's most respected post-Independence police commissioner, says that when the Australian officers started leaving, there were no PNG officers sufficiently trained to take over either the key operational positions being vacated or the senior executive positions in police headquarters. 'The PNG officers lacked the confidence to tackle the jobs involved,' he says. 'Hence we had a lot of very junior officers — at the inspector and sub-inspector level — who were rapidly promoted to higher ranks to fill positions they were not trained for. The police force started losing its effectiveness in both planning and management. It was not until the early to mid-1980s that we started picking up again,' Tasion says. 'That came about because we started to have officers who were trained and who had undergone enough experiences on the ground and they had moved up more slowly through the ranks.'

Tasion, from Pak Island in the Manus province, turned the police force around in his four years as police commissioner from 1985 to 1988. He accepted many of Clifford's criticisms and set about correcting the problems. A glaring deficiency identified by Clifford was the absence of any up-to-date police reference manual, something the report referred to as 'an indispensable tool of trade'. The absence of a manual compounded deficiencies in training. Without it there was no way for policy decisions to be communicated to the men; there was no uniformity of systems, so that local commanders generated their own methods of handling problems and men transferred to a new post had to learn an entirely new way of doing things; and there was no acknowledged way of handling difficult situations, which often led to inappropriate police responses. The lack of a good manual contributed to 'the shocking rate' of disciplinary charges levied against all ranks.

'Those were very true criticisms,' Tasion says. 'The first manual that was produced for us was around 1974-1975. That was when the Australian officers were still here. But that manual became out of date very quickly. There were a lot of changes with Independence, a lot of laws changed, police procedures and police administration changed and no one took the effort to either upgrade the manuals or rewrite the lot. It was not until Clifford did his study that it dawned on us the manuals were so out of date.' Tasion set up a task force and it took them almost two years to rewrite the manuals. They were completed and distributed in 1988.

Tasion agrees that police became divorced from the community. 'A policeman in the old days was simply an extension of the work being done by the administration — the Kiaps. At that time a policeman was not allowed to make his own decisions. He was saying "Yes, Sir, No, Sir" all the time. Every time a Kiap went on patrol, a policeman went with him to deal with the natives, to do everything the Kiap says. From that day onwards the policemen were seen as the heavy hand of the administration. No one dared to speak out against the policemen. Hence policemen were brought up in a situation whereby, almost like the military, they had to live in barracks. If there was trouble, a police bus went to the barracks and picked up the whole lot. They would go out, deal with it and come home together. They became isolated and there was very little understanding between the two,' Tasion says.

Tasion tried several measures to overcome the problem. He attempted to move police families out into the community, swapping houses with the Housing Commission so that other families could move into the police barracks, thus reducing the 'police only' atmosphere. 'We liaised with the Housing Commission and with the former Urban Management Department,' he says, 'but we received little response. One problem was that our houses, although not perfect, were often better maintained than some of the Housing Commission stock and we wanted those places at least brought up to the same level so that my men and their families would be moving into comparable housing to what they would have to leave. But we could not get any action — a real disappointment.' However, under a police community housing program, money raised from private firms built police homes in various settlements, especially around Port Moresby. Tasion feels this has been a success and where it has gone well the policemen have enhanced the power of the village courts in the settlements by co-operating with the village court magistrates and peace officers.

As police capacity deteriorated during the 1970s and early 1980s, the nature of the problems they faced became more complex. The population of Port Moresby doubled in the first ten years of Independence. Urban drift, unemployment, the spread of squatter settlements — all presented problems the police were not adequately equipped or trained to meet. Port Moresby's infamous rascal gangs grew and became more brazen. An American sociologist with PNG's Institute of Applied Social and Economic Research, Dr Bruce Harris, spent two years in the late 1980s mixing with the rascals of Port Moresby and his detailed report, 'The Rise of Rascalism', describes the gangs as 'efficient criminal organisations which operate with little fear of apprehension'.

Rascal

Joe, a Simbu, was first caught in PNG's Independence year, 1975, for stealing a bicycle. He was thirteen. He had done three years' school up in the Highlands before coming down to Port Moresby where his father got a job as a council worker. Joe began mixing with a rascal gang in Boroko. He was given two months' probation.

The next year, he ran away from home to live with his gang friends at the Four Mile settlement. He became adept at breaking, entering and stealing and rose to form his own gang, Joe's Mob. Joe organised his gang into specialist groups — some to steal cars, others to break into homes. Joe's Mob grew and its membership spread to several suburbs and settlements.

Joe was caught inside a house at Six Mile in 1976 and sent to the Catholic Boys' Town near Wewak for nine months. He returned to Moresby and made enough from crime to take a holiday, buying a ticket to Simbu where in his spare time he stole chickens. Back in Moresby leading his gang, he was arrested in 1978 for breaking into Carpenters store. He got two months, which he spent at the Salvation Army Boys' Town at Sogeri, inland from Port Moresby.

In 1979 police traced Joe by his fingerprints and charged him with breaking into Steamships store, two dentists' premises and other shops in Boroko. But he was not convicted. Later in 1979 he was caught again. This time police matched his prints with seventeen break and enters. This time he got a six-month sentence and a four-year bond.

Released from jail in 1981, Joe was arrested again in 1982 on two counts of breaking and entering. The national court jailed him for two and a half years. In Bomana jail near Port Moresby, Joe organised the escape of seven prisoners. He made no secret, when interviewed in prison by sociologist Louise Morauta in 1984, of his intention to return to run his gang upon release.

Joe's Mob took different names. At one stage it called itself 'Macarthurs'. In the late 1980s it was known as 'Apes'.

Dr Harris says gangs have consolidated in recent years and a dozen Rascal Gangs now control crime in the city. There were forty gangs in 1980 and maybe fifty ten years before that. Gangs are highly organised, with a structure of command and blood initiation ceremonies in which members cut their palms or fingers and swear allegiance to the 'King' of the gang and swear not to discuss gang actions outside. Gangs use 'strike forces', which are sent out nightly to break, enter and steal. They have strong links with other criminal groups in the country for the distribution and sale of stolen goods; they are heavily involved in the drug trade (mostly cannabis); and they have close links with some politicians and businessmen who use them for political purposes and to 'pay back' their enemies.

Dr Harris says policy makers have to get to understand the gangs if programs to combat them are to be effective. 'We will get nowhere by assuming rascal gangs are groups of sick, crazed young men who senselessly inflict damage and suffering on society,' he says. 'They are a part of society. The development and actions of rascal gangs make sense given the goals of the members, the means available to them for achieving those goals, the responses of the rest of society, and the reactions of the rascals to those responses.' Dr Harris stresses: 'Rascals are not dumb. They see corruption and self-interest in the political arena. They see the police and the courts as inefficient and powerless to stop them from doing exactly what many of the powerful members of society are doing. And they are good at it. Today, rascals feel they have the ability to perpetrate whatever crimes they like, virtually without fear of arrest or punishment. This is a dangerous situation, which, if left unchecked, can have very serious consequences.'

The word *rascals* was first used in the 1960s to describe Port Moresby's youth gangs but it gained currency after the gangs themselves adopted the name in the 1970s as a badge of notoriety. Dr Harris says frustration and anger were cogent forces in the emergence of the first rascal gangs a quarter of a century ago. Frustration and anger that the attractions of the city did not live up to their promise for rural migrants. He says young, often ill-educated, men unable to find work turned to each other, trying to re-establish self-esteem. Cultural factors also contributed. 'The idea that one could suffer in the midst of plenty,' Harris claims, 'contradicted the individual's most basic beliefs and values. In the village, no one went hungry as long as someone had food.' But the city turned society upside-down. 'Those who were successful had relatively immense amounts of wealth, of a quantity and quality beyond the dreams of any village bigman. Yet this success seemed to bring with it no obligation to share ... This was not merely a matter of selfishness. To the recent migrant it was morally wrong,' Dr Harris contends.

To combat the gangs in the early 1980s the then Police Commissioner, Phillip Bouraga, who had been one of the first Papua New Guineans to rise through the Kiap ranks, gave David Tasion the job of forming a specialist anti-rascal unit. 'I had just been promoted to Assistant Commissioner, Logistics,' Tasion recalls. 'Bouraga called me down from my room in Kundiawa one night — we were touring police stations in the Highlands — and he said, "What we can do in Port Moresby?" Logistics was the last thing in the force I could do so I said, "Why don't we start something like the New South Wales Squad 21? A hard-hitting unit to get out every night and crack down on these gangs? I'll volunteer to head it up." ' Tasion hand-picked thirty policemen and, while they waited for their specially commissioned vehicles to arrive, he put them through a month's intensive training at Port Moresby's Gordons police barracks.

'At the end of the month we went out on the streets in four cars,' Tasion says, savouring the memory of forming a unit that was to get dramatic results and equally adverse publicity. 'One of our major tactics was to go out every night. Any youth we found on the streets after ten, although he might not be doing anything wrong, was picked up. My attitude was: given the opportunity, he was capable of breaking the law. We were out to identify every gang operating in Port Moresby. We had cameras, we had spotlights in small interview rooms. We would get a photo, we would interrogate him, demand to know who his gang leader was, which gang he belonged to, where he lived, where his father was. We also ensured any gang member who was in jail was picked up the day he walked out of the prison and his movements were monitored from there on. If a crime was committed in any particular part of the city we would jump on those gang members we knew operated in that area.'

The so-called '21 Squad' became feared and controversial. 'After six months the crime situation in Port Moresby became so quiet!' Tasion says. 'We had a lot of problems, though. We had the Public Solicitor's Office, the Minister for Police, even senior police officers from headquarters coming investigating our activities. And I was pretty strong to keep them away. But we ended up having several of my policemen charged. They went right to the national court. But we managed to win, have them discharged. We managed to keep very high morale.' Tasion says they identified about forty gangs in the city and they had more than a thousand dossiers with photos and details. 'Before that,' he says, 'the police had very little idea of gang activity. They just had no idea! The 21 Squad was effective. Almost every night we would raid the squatter settlements and we picked up a lot of information.'

Dr Harris says that squatter settlers complained to him that any time the police found valuable items such as electrical goods for which the people had no written receipt, the goods were seized and the people taken away and charged. He argues that although some items were stolen, the actions bred resentment. The settlers felt they had all been labelled thieves. 'Had the police approached recognised leaders or local people who had prestige in the community and requested their aid,' Harris argues, 'they would have been much more successful in actually capturing criminals.' Instead of enjoying police protection, settlement residents found themselves 'victimised, stigmatised and, ultimately, isolated'. Tasion accepts the criticism but points out that when he set up the 21 Squad in the early 1980s, the police had lost so much ground to the criminals that appeals to settlement leaders would not have worked.

Jail the Girl

'You must go to jail for seven months,' the Morata Village Court Magistrate told the girl, aged seventeen, who had refused to marry a 45-year-old man already with one wife. Morata is one of the largest and longest established squatter settlements in Port Moresby. The girl had not been in Port Moresby long. Just months before, she had been an unemployed village girl at Kainantu in the Eastern Highlands with no formal education. The Chief Ombudsman took up her case after discovering the girl languishing in the Bomana prison outside Port Moresby.

'She was persuaded by a 45-year-old married man to come with him to Port Moresby,' the Chief Ombudsman reported, 'under the pretext that she was to marry his son. No bride price was paid to her parents. Shortly after arrival, the man revealed his true intentions that he wanted her for himself. She refused to marry him and ran away to relatives in Morata. The man went to Morata Village Court and obtained an order requiring the girl to pay him 280 Kina ($400) compensation.' This was to reimburse him for the 'wasted' airfare. The girl was given one week to pay. When she was unable to raise the money, she was sentenced to seven months' jail. The Chief Ombudsman arranged for law students from the university of PNG to lodge an appeal and the girl was released.

'At the Village Court proceedings,' the Chief Ombudsman said, 'the girl was told by the Village Court Magistrate to shut up when she tried to speak, because young women like her tend to "fool a lot of our men".'

'It is true, we engendered resentment,' Tasion says. 'We would hit the settlements any time, anywhere. One day, I got into trouble with the Minister. We had just raided a hamlet and I came home about six in the morning. At eight o'clock they came from the office to pick me up. The Minister said, "Tasion. Your job is on the line. You get out of here and go to the ombudsman." So I went. They made me take an oath and started interrogating me. I just said, "If you have enough evidence, charge me. If not, I'm going to walk out of here." I walked out.' Tasion says the complaint was that his men pointed guns at people, knocked their heads, and stole property from their shop. 'There was a sly grog operation and we picked up a lot of beer. They said it was not for sale. You couldn't believe that,' Tasion says. 'Although we were clearing a lot of crime, the village elders were not happy. We were not liaising through them. And that was because we didn't trust a lot of them. I believed then a lot of them lived off the activities of their sons and daughters. Having liaised with them prior to a raid would have been fruitless. They would have disclosed our intentions.'

Dr Harris also claims that police tactics forced the gangs to tighten up their organisation and encouraged them to become vertically integrated into other criminal networks because it became increasingly dangerous to hold on to stolen goods. By the early to mid-1980s a fully formalised distribution network had been set up. Gangs had established links with certain businessmen who bought stolen goods and resold them. 'Currently there is a thriving business which is run particularly through small shops throughout the Central province region,' Harris says. Certain shops depend on illegal goods for much of their stock. In some cases gangs have even opened their own shops which members control and operate. Harris says the older gang members graduate through the ranks to become storekeepers.

The shake-out of gangs in the mid-1980s involved inter-gang warfare. In some instances the clashes were violent. 'The Texas Gang in the town area was especially renowned as one which brutally suppressed competition,' says Harris. 'Members of other gangs found in the area claimed by the gang were often severely beaten, and groups of Texas Gang members would search out individuals known to be members of other gangs in their homes or in places they frequented. This often led to a continuing series of "pay-back" crimes. . . . This could involve direct attacks on the members of the transgressing gang, or it could involve attacks on people related to that gang.' One type of vengeance attack was to rape women associated with or related to members of the opposing gang. Dr Harris says the increased incidence of reported rape during this period can be directly related to this element of gang warfare. 'Rape as a means of pay-back fits comfortably into the traditional Melanesian complex of male-female relations,' he says. 'The establishment of control over the women of a rival has been a traditional means of establishing a dominant-subordinate relationship.'

Harris says the consolidation of the gangs and their increased sophistication meant that 'by the mid-1980s, the game, to put it directly, had been lost'. He quotes from Clifford that in 1983 only 5 per cent of stolen property was being recovered, while just 7 per cent of stolen vehicles and 3 per cent of break and enters resulted in arrests. 'Inter-gang violence was escalating and had come to include interpersonal aggression, which itself included violent sexual attacks. It was open season for gangs.' Port Moresby became a city under siege. Those who could afford it barricaded themselves in their houses protected by high, razor-wire-topped fences, security guards and growling dogs. Those who could not sometimes lost everything, and some over and over again. In 1985 the Somare Government was under huge media and public pressure to take action and the Government imposed a curfew and declared Port Moresby under a state of emergency.

The emergency ran from 17 June until 4 November 1985, and it was a dramatic success, if only in reducing the incidence of violent crime and in fostering good public relations. Soldiers joined police on the streets. At the start, nobody was allowed out after 10.30 p.m. or before 4.00 a.m. without a special pass. Discos, nightclubs and places of entertainment had to close at 9.00 p.m. Take-away liquor sales were banned after 5.00 p.m. from Monday to Thursday and completely on Friday, Saturday and Sunday. Prime Minister Somare claimed that in the first three months of the emergency, serious crime fell seventy-five per cent, with pack rapes being eliminated altogether. He told parliament that the clear-up rate for crime had improved from thirteen per cent in June to around eighty per cent at the end of September. The emergency cost the Government about K3 million.

The state of emergency gave huge powers to David Tasion, who by then was Police Commissioner. 'The state of emergency was an extreme measure,' he says now. 'At that time the image of the police in the eyes of the people was very bad. Although the state of emergency gave me a lot of powers — much more power here in Port Moresby than the Prime Minister — I decided I had to use the powers intelligently to the long-term advantage of the force.' Tasion consulted with businessmen, diplomats, the press, and settlement leaders and personally kept discipline tight amongst the security forces. 'We did a lot of things during the emergency that had lasting benefit. For instance, the curfew freed up police vehicles which were used to help transport people who needed urgent medical treatment to hospital and back. I knew it was a situation that, if we did not handle it properly, could attract a lot of criticism and generate a lot of bad feelings between the community and the force. We dealt heavy handedly with criminals we picked up but we restored our image with the community.'

Doctor Harris says gang members he spoke to claim they went underground during the emergency, that it forced them to rethink their tactics and even become more sophisticated. 'Doctor Harris probably has some points I would not disagree with,' David Tasion says. 'But it was not only rascal gangs we were dealing with. At the time of the 1985 state of emergency we had about four hundred hard-core criminals who had escaped from prison. We rounded up more than two hundred of them. I was determined to ensure that the goodwill we won from the community was built on after the emergency was over. I think I managed to do that successfully. In fact, during the emergency we completely changed the approach of the 21 Squad. It is now called Force 10. The emergency was the start of better relations between the police and settlement and community leaders. There are two hundred peace officers around the settlements and suburbs in Port Moresby and about fifty magistrates, and during the emergency they were the ones who were given the responsibility to police all the squatter settlements throughout the city.'

Crime against the home dweller in Port Moresby has risen again since the lifting of the state of emergency in late 1985 and at the end of the 1980s it was returning to the level it had been in the years leading up to the declaration of the emergency. Theories abound that in the mid-1980s the smarter criminals shifted out of the capital and into other cities such as Lae, Madang, Rabaul and the Highlands centres of Goroka, Kundiawa and Mount Hagen. Crime in Lae reached crisis point in early 1987 and a modified emergency was applied there for a few months but it was not the extensive clampdown that Port Moresby had in 1985. In 1989 a breakdown in authority in Lae led to a looting spree that shocked the Namaliu Government into imposing a curfew on the city and suspending the Morobe provincial Government.

Looting in Mt Hagen

The Engan, face daubed with mud, led the mob as it surged across the highway. He charged towards Bromley and Manton's Reinbo Store and, with a mighty swing, buried his axe into the aluminium security roller door. Others joined in, chopping their axes into the metal sheets protecting the entrance to Mount Hagen's largest supermarket and department store. In less than a minute, some were inside.

Those at the back turned our way and, perhaps seeing the television camera, ran in our direction. Frank Mills, my contract cameraman, could not see this for he was concentrating on the destruction. I tapped him on the shoulder and suggested strategic withdrawal. As we hopped into the car, the policeman who had driven with us to the John Paul II oval told us to move fast. Some in the crowd picked up rocks and threw them as I reversed up the highway out of trouble.

The Communications Minister and member for Enga, Malipu Balakau, had been shot dead outside his Mount Hagen home the night before. Mount Hagen is capital of the Western Highlands and when news of the murder reached Wabag, the capital of Enga, there was a riot. Buildings in Wabag owned by companies with alleged Western Highlands connections were attacked, looted and burnt. Truckloads of Engans had then driven, that morning, the ninety kilometres to Mount Hagen to demand compensation. Police corralled them on the John Paul II oval but, fed up with several hours of talking, the mob acted.

Riot squad police firing tear gas cleared the looters from the Reinbo store but goods worth K70,000 ($105,000) had been stolen. Employees cleaning up found piles of old boots, some falling apart, left behind in the cleaned out footwear section and, next to where racks of jeans used to be, discarded tanget leaves (the bunch of leaves, also called 'arse grass', which Highlands men wear as traditional garb, tucked into the belt at the back of the waist).

The suspension of the provincial Government had political overtones. The Government was dominated by the Morobe Independent

Group (MIG) whose leader, Utula Samana, headed the Melanesian United Front (MUF) in the national parliament. Samana was in the national Opposition, and the Morobe province for years had been the scene of a struggle between MIG and Prime Minister Namaliu's Pangu Pati. Samana had been premier of Morobe for seven years until standing for national office in 1987. During that time he had motivated youth groups into politically active units and was a constant critic of the police. He was arrested at one stage when he tried to prevent police detaining a youth during a demonstration and, as premier, he publicly demanded the removal of the head of the police force in the province. Relations between the police and the MIG-run provincial Government were bad. The Pangu-led Opposition in Lae had adopted Samana's tactic of involving youth groups in politics and so trouble between gangs in Lae came to have a political dimension.

The Lae looting of September 1989 followed the killing of an off-duty policeman, Charles Wala Ipne, from the Southern Highlands, by a gang who raided a house at Six Mile. Six men, some armed with guns, pushed their way into the house and attempted to take away a young woman. Constable Ipne, who was staying with the family, struggled with one of the men and he and the head of the household, Gewa Estumai, were shot dead. That night, police tracking down the killers raided the Three Mile settlement near where Samana lives. Hearing a commotion, Mr Samana attempted to intervene. He claimed at a news conference the next day that he was punched and kicked by policemen whom he accused of 'behaving like hooligans'. One of the suspected killers was caught and admitted to Lae's Angau hospital but police had to take him away to the police station for his own protection when relatives of the two dead went to the hospital seeking revenge. Two days of trouble followed. A proposed 'peace protest' march rapidly ran out of control.

On the worst day of looting, men, women and children broke into stores, taking whatever they could put their hands on — food, liquor, mattresses, clothes, video players and television sets. Stores owned by one Indonesian/Chinese businessman, who trades under the name of Papindo, were singled out for special attention. One youth group alleged that Papindo was a friend and supporter of Utula Samana. A television news cameraman from the PNG-based television network, EM TV, shot graphic footage of the looting at

Papindo's new department store at Eriku. Included in the coverage shown on the television news in Papua New Guinea were shots of policemen standing by while the looting went on.

The Australian Government has provided one specific aid package to the PNG police force aimed at what is called 'capacity building'. It involves a specialist team led by the former South Australian Police Commissioner, Lou Draper, concentrating on specific areas within the force, such as criminal investigation and police prosecution. But there is one problem facing the police for which imported expertise provides no solution. That distinctly Papua New Guinean problem is tribal fighting. In the late 1980s tribal fighting took a nasty turn for the worse with firearms replacing bows, arrows and spears. The reasons for tribal fighting are complex. It happens mostly in the Highlands, mostly in areas that were contacted relatively late in the colonial period and mostly in places where there is increasing population stress. Tribal fighting traditionally was a method of resolving disputes. Most of the investigations into why fighting remains endemic conclude that, for many Highlanders, the modern mechanisms for dispute resolution are just not working.

In coastal Papua New Guinea before the war, the two Australian administrations sometimes took extreme measures to stamp out intervillage warfare. While fighting on the coast appears to have been less common traditionally anyway because land pressures were not as high, the actions taken to end tribal warfare by the colonial power are not available to the authorities in an independent PNG. For instance, head hunting disappeared from the Sepik only after punitive expeditions in which alleged head hunters were rounded up and hanged. The legendary New Guinea District Officer, Kassa Townsend, in the 1920s used to trail the hanging rope out behind his boat so that everybody up and down the Sepik River knew when there was a hanging. Afterwards, the rope was cut up into little pieces and sent out to the tribes involved as a warning of what would happen in future.

David Tasion says present-day Highlands tribal fighting presents the police with a 'huge' problem. 'Whatever the police do,' he says, 'we can't seem to provide a lasting peace between two clans. More and more the police force is being regarded as a third tribe. Our men go into tribal fights with a hard-hitting approach. So now, almost every major tribal fight generates massive complaints and compensation claims against the police from the participating clans.

And more and more tribal fights involve guns,' the former police commissioner says. He frankly admits the police do not have a solution and do not know if there is any. 'Maybe, in time, the situation will improve. There is no instant solution, none. We can't crack down like the colonial power did. Unlike under the Australian administration, we are now living in a democracy.' PNG does not have the death penalty for any crime except treason, although many PNG parliamentarians have advocated its reinstatement.

Barry Shaw, an economist who did an extensive report on agriculture for PNG's Institute of National Affairs in 1985, commented that in the Highlands 'the official emphasis seems to have shifted to stopping fighting rather than solving disputes'. He said that, while warfare had to be discouraged, it had to be replaced by a suitable means of settling rural group disputes in a manner respected by all parties. 'A personal example of this,' Shaw said, 'was when all adult males of a group I had close contact with in 1981 were jailed after a man was killed. The women and children fled, all houses and food gardens were destroyed by the "losing" side and possessions of value, including pigs, food and bilas [traditional decorations], were distributed to neighbouring groups and provincial politicians to form alliances against the jailed group.'

Shaw claimed that, while the men were in jail, 'the unprotected women and children had to live in a near town with *wantoks* [people from the same language line], to whom they are now heavily obligated. On their return to the area from jail six months later, they were demoralised and starving as they rebuilt their village and replanted their gardens. The didiman [agricultural extension officer] and other officials visited them and recommended a grant of food: this was approved and then blocked by the same politicians who had been given the spoils. The village children cannot now go to school, since that means walking through enemy territory. The net result is that the dispute remains unresolved in an atmosphere of intense bitterness and economic and social deprivation.'

More than a hundred people are killed every year in tribal fights in Papua New Guinea. The authorities fear the death toll will climb because of the new reliance on twentieth-century weapons in combat fashioned in a different age. Although the first reported use of a gun in a tribal fight occurred in the 1970s, it is only since 1986 that the use of shotguns in tribal wars has become commonplace. Joe Mek Tierne, senior public prosecutor in Mount Hagen for much of the 1980s, says the use of guns has added a new dimension. Mek Tierne, a Highlander from the Simbu province, built up an enviable reputation as one of PNG's most fearless lawyers. Amongst his successful prosecutions have been three provincial premiers — all convicted and jailed for misappropriation. He says that the introduction of shotguns has fundamentally altered the nature of the conflict.

> In pre-colonial times tribal fighting was a ritual. The people would take a long time to prepare themselves. They would set up an area where they wanted to fight and they would pay great attention to dressing up properly. They would stay away from women. All sorts of ceremonies would take place before the fighting actually started. Then, when it did, they would use only traditional weapons like spears, bows and arrows and shields. However, since Independence tribal fighting has increased in frequency and the old rules are breaking down. They now fight over very little things. They fight over a bottle of beer. They fight over women, they fight over pigs trespassing on somebody else's land. They fight when political candidates lose an election.

John Burton of the Department of Anthropology and Sociology at the University of PNG, having witnessed a tribal fight at Minj in 1989, wrote that shotguns had 'swept bowmen off the battlefield as surely as the Panzers brushed aside the valiant Polish cavalrymen on the North European Plain in September, 1939'.

Shotguns for the Clan

The Constable in charge of firearms at the Mount Hagen police station — headquarters for the Western Highlands command — has an armoury full of confiscated home-made shotguns. Some have sickeningly bent barrels where they have blown up in the faces of those firing them. But most still look lethal.

Picking up one gun, he explains how the amateur village gun maker first carves out a wooden frame, then attaches a metal pipe for a barrel. 'They use water pipe or sometimes they hack up sections of a [Hills Hoist] clothes line to be used as a barrel too. They fit them into this grooved-out bed here,' he says, running his finger along the channel in the wooden frame.

'In this one they've used strips of rubber to tie down the barrel. You see how they've wrapped it around about twenty times to keep it tightly attached. Some are tied on with wire or nailed on with the nails bent or hammered across the top to keep the barrel in place. The firing pin here is a piece of iron that they have filed down. It, too, is tied up with rubber and they stretch the rubber back to cock it. So it is fired just like a spear fishing gun.'

Constable Leapi puts that one down and picks up another, which has a metal spring. 'Actually, this one is a bed spring. For ammunition,' he says, 'they use normal shotgun cartridges. You can see that we have plenty of these home-made guns here. Almost all of these were confiscated from tribal fights.'

The number of shotguns being used in tribal fights seems to be four or five per tribe. But the number is on the rise. Joe Mek Tierne claims that the Firearms Act is not properly administered. 'I know for a fact many people have applied for shotguns when they really do not need them. For instance, local businessmen claim their property will be stolen or that their lives are at stake. But this is not the case. When they apply, they usually get them. Their *wantoks* borrow the shotguns for use in tribal fights. I think the best solution is to stop issuing shotgun licences.' It is a subject that exasperates David Tasion. 'We have tightened up,' he says. 'In 1984 we banned the importation of all weapons. No gun dealer can import a gun from outside without the police commissioner's permission. The only two bodies that can import weapons are the police and the Defence Force.' But John Burton claims those two organisations have been the source — without official knowledge — of some of the guns and a deal of the ammunition now used on the tribal battlefields.

The former Police Commissioner, Mr Tasion, believes home-made shotguns are a direct result of the 1984 ban on gun imports. He also says there is a strong trade in smuggled guns. 'There are about ten thousand shotguns in this country which are unlicensed,' he says. 'Ten thousand shotguns that are out there in the hands of people who should not have them.' Guns fetch handsome prices on the PNG black market. In 1984 Tasion sacked one policeman who got involved, lured by the money to be made. 'In that year we had an amnesty during which we appealed for guns to be surrendered,' he says. Quite a lot were. But we found one policeman who was working in Mount Hagen selling some of these guns back to villagers in the Western Highlands. He had to be dealt with very seriously. In fact he went to court and got sacked.'

The link between beer consumption and tribal fighting is well established. Several Highlands provinces have attempted to ban beer sales. One such attempt led to one of the more bizarre compensation claims. A truckload of young men from one province went into the next-door province to buy beer and had a fatal crash on the way back home. The relatives of the dead lodged a compensation claim against the provincial Government claiming that their young men would not have died if they had not been 'forced' by the beer ban to make the journey.

Paias Wingti, who is a Jiga clansman from the Western Highlands, maintains that economic development is the solution, not only to tribal fighting but also to PNG's other law and order problems. Throwing more money into police activities, he says, is not the way to resolve problems that are being aggravated by rapid population growth. Wingti is optimistic that tribal fighting will die a natural death in the 1990s. In tribal fighting one of the major aims of the combatants is to destroy the property of the opposing clan. Coffee trees are a prime target. 'Right now the leadership in the villages is torn between the Western system and the traditional system,' Wingti says. 'Many of the old leaders aren't financially affected too much by the fighting. But what I forecast is a modern leadership emerging in the rural areas. They are going to take care of their investments. They are the leaders who will control the tribes and clans. So in the long run it is by doing more in the rural areas, by our encouraging agricultural development that we will minimise the problem.'

Some attempts to curb tribal fighting have been thwarted by the PNG Constitution. The Constitution emphasises individual rights and this led to one Supreme Court ruling that the Group Fighting Act was unconstitutional because it enabled police to arrest groups of people at the scene of a tribal fight and the onus was on the accused to prove that they had not been fighting. The Clifford report highlighted the dilemma that the Constitution poses. 'This Constitution was adopted from Western laws and based on a distinct tradition of individualism which derived from Greek and Roman patterns of thought incorporated in a Judaeo-Christian ethos,' Clifford argued. 'It had little to do with the "obligations orientation" of the Asian and Pacific region or with the "underlying law" of

PNG.' Clifford said there was frequently a serious clash between the two concepts of personal rights and group obligations, and this confronted the Government with a dilemma of both principle and practice:

> Group obligations and individual human rights are dramatically opposed in, for example, a woman's freedom of choice to marry, the group control of an individual's right to drink, in the imprisonment of people not obeying the village courts, in the legal denial of a customary right to commit a "pay-back" murder if compensation is not satisfactory, in the way group obligations and status are ignored in definitions of crime and corruption. If such principles of the underlying customary law are to inform future legal development then the Constitution has to be suitably amended to accommodate tradition. Alternatively, tradition can be subordinated to the written law of the land; and the rights of individuals, which are enshrined in the Constitution can be the ultimate standard. But the present schizophrenic condition of shifting between the old and the new with no recognition of their fundamental conflict contains the seeds of disaster.

Self-reliance

The three thousand people living in the Burum community government area in the remote hinterland of the Finchhafen district are surrounded by mountains. For years they were told by colonial administration officers and Lutheran Church pastors that if they wanted development they should send their children to school in Finchhafen or Lae. To get their coffee out they had to walk for several days down to Finchhafen on the coast.

Eventually, they decided that instead of looking to outsiders for development they should take affairs into their own hands. Led by a community schoolteacher, they built an airstrip. The Kiaps told them that their airstrip was not planned but they built it anyway and started to fly their coffee to Lae.

With income flowing back into the Burum valley they built a school — again against the advice of the authorities. But they could see advantages in educating their children at home. With the confidence gained from building their own airstrip and building their own school, they built a sub health centre. That was not in line with the Morobe provincial health plan but they did it anyway.

The Burum community Government has done almost everything outside the official plans of both the national and provincial governments. Their latest self-help venture is to buy a D4 bulldozer costing about K50,000 — money they collected from various villages in the valley. And they are building a road from the community government centre near their airstrip all the way across the mountain ranges to Lae.

Changing the Constitution is not easy. Members of the national parliament are the only ones who can do it legally. And it must win their overwhelming support twice. Constitutional amendments require majorities of two-thirds or three-quarters (depending on the provision) on two votes taken at least two months apart. The politicians have shown a marked reluctance to change provisions that strike in any significant way at the existing system. In the middle of 1988, the parliament did vote through one constitutional change by a huge majority. This won such bipartisan support that the first vote occurred while Paias Wingti was prime minister in May 1988, and the second after Rabbie Namaliu had replaced him. On its second reading, only two members voted against it — the Justice Minister, Bernard Narokobi, and the Opposition Justice Spokesman, Albert Kipalan. That amendment abolished the independent parliamentary Salaries Tribunal headed by a judge and replaced it with a commission dominated by parliamentarians.

This move by the members to take control of setting their own pay was greeted cynically by many in PNG. One of the country's most articulate public figures, Tony Siaguru, claims that this decision may have helped create the climate for the Bougainville crisis, industrial trouble at the Ok Tedi mine and the army pay riot of February 1989. He says people who were already suspicious of self-seeking politicians lost all confidence in the fairness of the system. The politicians could change the system when it did not suit them while telling everybody else who had grievances that they had to go through the correct channels. 'No longer did we have one set of laws applying to everybody across the board,' he wrote in his weekly newspaper column. 'From then on, we would have two different sets, one for those within the system and one for those outside the system.'

Siaguru elaborated on his theory by listing a series of reports of alleged corrupt activities. 'When we see what is going on around us and hear the stories about the actions of our leaders, we react in the only way we know. We rebel. Not in an open confrontationist way, but in small incremental steps. First,' he wrote, 'like a neglected child we create a lot of noise to attract attention. We make excessive our demands for compensation for land, minerals and environmental damage. Then we issue threats. And if our threats are not acted upon immediately, we take the law into our hands — because we realise that we cannot get satisfaction from the existing system, as there seem to be two systems — one for us and one for them. We cannot help ourselves, but they can help themselves. Ultimately, this road will lead to tragedy, a national catastrophe.'

It is not hard to be pessimistic about Papua New Guinea's prospects. The most worrying statistic about PNG is the ratio of young people leaving school each year to new jobs created — about eight to one. Many of those leaving school have dropped out of the system and not graduated. Only one in three children completing the final year of primary school is able to find a place in a secondary school. That one-in-three chance is about the same as it was at Independence in 1975, but the statistic obscures the progress in access to education that has been made since the colonial days. In 1962, thirteen years prior to Independence, 128,000 PNG children were enrolled in primary schools in the Australian Territory of Papua and New Guinea. Of those, only 30 per cent were educated by the Australian administration. The other 70 per cent went to schools run by the Christian missions. When Independence arrived, total primary enrolments had grown to 237,000, with government schools educating about 40 per cent and the Churches 60 per cent. Thirteen years after Independence, in 1988, primary students numbered 374,000 — almost three times the 1962 figure — with half of them attending government schools.

The story of secondary education is even more dramatic. Back in 1962, the Australian administration had not managed to set up any secondary schools at all for Papua New Guineans. The only secondary teaching was in classes added to the top of some primary schools or at the rudimentary teacher training colleges. By 1975 there were twenty-eight thousand PNG students attending high schools. This figure had jumped to more than fifty thousand by 1988. The narrow workforce base in PNG means that the prospects for paid employment for high school graduates have been declining. Whereas about seventy per cent of the students who completed their final year of provincial high school in 1978 were placed in employment or tertiary education, the percentage had dropped by forty-six per cent for those who did their final year in 1984. It is even lower now.

High school selection involves a public examination. In 1988, 49,119 students sat for the grade six examination. Contrary to what many in PNG fear, the standards at community school appear to have been improving since the early 1980s. Standards fell after Independence, with the rapid departure of Australian teachers at the same time as student intakes were expanding. However, a detailed study of grade six exam results by the Education Department's Measurement Services Unit reveals a turnaround since 1982. The study has shown that on the Rasch analysis scale the mean score throughout PNG in English went up from 1.36 in 1982 to 1.84 in 1986. In Mathematics the jump was from 0.48 in 1982 to 0.96 in 1986.

These are encouraging results for the future. But at the other end of the education scale the 1980s ended on a sorry note at both universities. Student lawlessness at the University of Papua New Guinea in Port Moresby and the Lae University of Technology resulted in police being called on to both campuses. At Lae, police shot one student dead. In Port Moresby the vice chancellor, Professor John Lynch, suspended the student disciplinary statute, stood down the discipline committee and ruled on seven cases himself, banning two students for life. He found them guilty of assault, theft, threatening behaviour, consorting with known criminals, refusing to vacate student accommodation and continued violent and criminal behaviour. Female students, outnumbered seven to one, complained of rape and harassment. The university's chief of security claimed that student indiscipline was 'alarmingly high' and said two of his men had been hospitalised after drunken students beat them up while three others had been stood down because of threats to themselves and their families. The wife of one took her own life.

Papua New Guinea will never be what outsiders want it to be. It will continue to perplex. It will find its own Melanesian way, sometimes to its own surprise, and oil and gold might keep it economically afloat. The changes taking place are so rapid and the interest groups so many and so diverse that it is difficult to make any predictions about the future. The best I can offer is what I have written — in the hope that when the extraordinary does happen, as it regularly seems to, at least the observer may better understand why.

EPILOGUE

Paias Wingti, back in power less than a month, stood just inside the entrance to the cavernous basketball arena at Port Moresby's Sir John Guise Stadium, and declared to his 1,200 guests that he had wasted his time when he was previously Prime Minister. The stadium had been built by the Chinese so PNG could host the 1991 South Pacific Games but, on this night, 7 August 1992, it more resembled Beijing's Great Hall of the People than any sporting venue. Among the many attending the State Reception honouring the start of the new, five year (1992-97) parliamentary term were foreign diplomats and businessmen none too comforted by what Paias Wingti was telling them.

'I wasted my time,' Mr Wingti's voice boomed. 'This time my Government is dedicated to building up and supporting Papua New Guinean entrepreneurs. It is only through our own businessmen, our own entrepreneurs, that we will succeed in bringing development to our people.' He said the Government would reserve all public works contracts worth less than K5 million exclusively for PNG-owned businesses, and those between K5 million and K10 million for 50/50 joint venture operations. Prime Minister Wingti singled out the mining sector saying he expected foreign mining companies to co-operate. 'I will not hesitate to legislate to help Papua New Guinean entrepreneurs,' he said. Mr Wingti's address was punctuated by agitated shouts from the Member for Moresby North-East, David Unagi, who was stalking back and forth just metres from his leader. 'White men to the back of the stage,' Unagi yelled again and again, 'black men to the front!'

Ironically, one of Mr Wingti's most decisive early actions had quite the opposite effect. An Australian mining industry figure, Bob

Needham, was given an immediate star role while the Papua New Guinean he replaced exited stage left. Mr Needham was appointed to the crucially important position of managing director of the government-owned Mineral Resources Development Corporation, the MRDC, bustling aside one of Papua New Guinea's most gifted and well-qualified indigenous technocrats, Melchoir Togolo. Togolo was sacked. The MRDC holds the State's shareholdings in the Bougainville copper mine (19 per cent), the Ok Tedi copper mine (20 per cent), the Misima gold mine (20 per cent) and the Porgera gold mine (10 per cent) while MRDC's subsidiary, Petroleum Resources Kutubu Pty Ltd, PRK, holds the State's 22.5 per cent stake in the Kutubu oil development. Mr Wingti's Minister for Mining and Petroleum, Masket Iangalio, defended Needham's appointment, saying PNG was not getting as good a deal as it should from its resource agreements and that the government needed an experienced miner to advise it. One who, he said, would not be hoodwinked by the foreign multinationals.

Three other expatriate advisors to Mr Wingti quickly came to prominence. Dennis Reinhardt, who had known Wingti from when they were university students in the 1970s, became his foreign media advisor. Another journalist, Trevor Kennedy, formerly an executive for Australia's richest man, Kerry Packer, was appointed to the Board of the newly created Papua New Guinea Holdings Corporation, Mr Wingti's privatisation vehicle. The third was long-time PNG-resident lawyer, Peter Steele. Steele drew up the legislation for the Holdings Corporation and he became its first managing director. The Holdings Corporation Bill was passed without debate in the very first session of the new parliament. The powers of this company—whose job it is to privatise PNG government assets—are extraordinarily broad. It can do almost whatever it wishes and a separate item of legislation has removed it from the normal government auditing obligations.

Mr Wingti's haste in establishing the PNG Holdings Corporation and his other frenetic activity in the opening period of his new term as Prime Minister had much to do with his belief that his time was limited. The previous parliament had passed the long demanded amendments to the Constitution to expand the period between successful votes of no confidence in a prime minister beyond six months. Although the original proposal was to extend this period of grace to thirty months, the Namaliu Government agreed to the then Wingti-led Opposition's proposal that it be eighteen months. With that constitutional change in place, Paias Wingti became the most powerful prime minister since Independence. He was the first one to be guaranteed at least a year-and-a-half in power free from challenge.

This gave Wingti almost presidential powers, despite the fact that his re-elevation to Prime Minister had been by the slimmest of margins. The vote for Prime Minister in the new parliament between Mr Wingti and the former Prime Minister, Rabbie Namaliu, was tied at 54 each. Mr Wingti won on the casting vote of the Speaker, Bill Skate, a first time member of parliament. Mr Skate had plenty of company. Of the 109 members who walked onto the floor of the parliament that day, 58 were first termers. At the 1992 elections, the voters rejected 62 sitting members including fifteen ministers in Mr Namaliu's outgoing government. In one province, Simbu, the failure rate of sitting members was total, 100 per cent, while in the largest province, Morobe, it was 90 per cent with only one of the ten sitting members getting back.

Nomination fees had been increased ten-fold to K1000 but this had not deterred a record 1645 candidates. The large numbers and the first past the post system resulted in the election of many Independents. Thirty-nine members were elected without the formal backing of any political party. Thirty-two of these were new to the parliament. The Pangu Pati had the most endorsed candidates returned but Pangu lost more seats than it held while its gains were limited. Wingti's People's Democratic Movement came in second while the Peoples Action Party, leaderless following the banning from parliament for three years of Ted Diro, came third. Sir Julius Chan's People's Progress Party rose from near oblivion to be fourth largest.

These official figures of how the members lined up after the return of the writs are taken from the lists of endorsed candidates held by the PNG Electoral Commissioner. However, they have only the vaguest similarity to how the members aligned themselves in parliament on the day of the vote for prime minister, 17 July 1992. Wingti and Chan moved quickly after the election, dispatching helicopters to collect new MPs and fly them to a protected camp on Doini Island in the electorate of the new Member for Milne Bay, Tim Neville. Namaliu's Pangu Pati gathered its coalition forces in the Madang Resort Hotel owned by another new, white member

PARTY	SEATS WON	BEFORE '92 POLL	GAINED	HELD	LOST
Pangu	19	32	4	15	17
PDM	15	17	2	13	4
PAP	12	13	6	6	7
PPP	8	2	7	1	1
MA	7	7	4	3	4
LNA	5	4	3	2	2
NP	2	3	2	0	3
LP	1	0	1	0	0
BAP	1	0	1	0	0
PSP	0	2	0	0	2
CP	0	1	0	0	1
Indep.	39	28	32	7	21
Total	109	109	62	47	62

(PDM—People's Democratics Movement; PAP—People's Action Party; PPP—People's Progress Party; MA—Melanesian Alliance; LNA—League For National Advancement; NP—National Party; LP—Liberal Party; BAP—Black Action Party; PSP—People's Solidarity Party; CP—Country Party)

of the PNG parliament, Peter Barter.

The game started to move Wingti's way when the League For National Advancement, now under the leadership of John Nilkare, withdrew from the old govenment. Nilkare, one of the LNA's founders who was back in parliament after a five year absence, won guarantees from Wingti that the LNA's major party platform—the introduction of a Village Services Scheme—would become a key Wingti Government policy. As the numbers narrowed, attention focused on the long term independent member for Rabaul, John Kaputin. Kaputin was in Brisbane visiting his cousin, Margaret Nakikus, Namaliu's wife who had been diagnosed as being terminally ill only a week earlier.

Back in 1988, shortly after his rise to Prime Minister, Namaliu had told a large crowd of fellow Tolais in Rabaul that Kaputin would be brought into his ministry as soon as the opportunity arose. It was a promise he had not been able to keep. And when John Kaputin flew into Port Moresby from Brisbane after seeing Margaret, he went off with Paias Wingti. He voted for Wingti on 17 July, helped him score his one vote victory, and became Foreign Minister.

While a majority of one may present difficulties in other democracies where it would leave the leader of government in a precarious position, this is not so in Papua New Guinea. The PNG Prime Minister cannot be brought down by failing to get legislation passed, but rules until defeated in a vote of no confidence. The strength of Mr Wingti's position became evident over the weeks following the 17 July vote as members who had supported Namaliu flocked to Wingti's side. He had a comfortable majority to pass the privatisation bill.

Rabbie Namaliu's fortunes went rapidly in the opposite direction. In December 1992 he was charged with seven counts of misappropriation of public funds, and seven counts of attempting to influence members of parliament in how they intended to vote. The charges dated back to Namaliu's successful attempt in mid-1990 to head off a vote of no confidence. Police alleged that he and his Finance Minister, Paul Pora, had illegally made payments from the Prime Minister's discretionary fund to four former cabinet ministers to keep them on his side of the parliament. Mr Namaliu protested his innocence of any criminal wrong doing and announced he would vigorously defend himself when the case went before the courts in 1993.

A Leadership Tribunal set up to hear charges of misconduct in office against two of the four former ministers found them guilty, and both were dismissed from parliament. Originally, all four were to face the Tribunal. That was prior to the 1992 elections and the four took the well-worn escape route of PNG politicians wanting to evade leadership charges. They all resigned from parliament, and since they were no longer leaders, the Tribunal had to be disbanded. It was a ruse, of course. All four nominated again to stand for the upcoming elections. Three of the four got back in but one, Galeng Lang, died shortly afterwards of a heart attack. The Ombudsman sought a Supreme Court ruling on whether a Leadership Tribunal could be reinstituted to hear charges arising from a member's previous, uncompleted, term as a leader. The Supreme Court said, 'Yes'.

The Tribunal, consisting of a judge and two senior magistrates, found the former Minister for Labour, Peter Garong, and the former Minister for Prisons, Melchoir Pep, guilty of thirteen misconduct charges each. The Tribunal said both had signed a letter to Prime

Minister Namaliu in mid-1990 demanded K100,000 in 'special packages' as compensation for 'voluntarily' stepping down from the ministry. The Tribunal's final report included copies of the letter and of Mr Namaliu's reply in which he said K100,000 was too much, but suggested packages of K50,000 instead. The use of discretionary funds to help Members out with projects in their electorates has been a feature of PNG politics since Independence and all four Prime Ministers have done it.

In Peter Garong's case, the Tribunal found he had requested an additional K40,000 to help him buy a house in Port Moresby—quite a distance from his electorate in the Morobe Province. Garong had written to Namaliu asking for the money as a deposit on a house at Section 388, Lot 19, Boroko. The Tribunal said Namaliu gave him K20,000. The other member sacked, Melchoir Pep, had a housing charge too. The Tribunal found that Mr Pep, while a minister, threw a public servant out of a government house in Gerehu, a Port Moresby suburb, and became an illegal tenant. While occupying the house without paying any rent, Pep collected K23,325 in Ministerial Housing Allowances.

The Ombudsman Commission forced at least ten members out of parliament in the early 1990s. In the most notable Leadership Tribunal case, the former Deputy Prime Minister, Mr Ted Diro, was found guilty of 81 charges of misconduct in office, 70 of which warranted his dismissal from parliament. Many of the charges arose from the Barnett corruption inquiry into the PNG forestry industry. The conviction of Mr Diro precipitated a short-lived constitutional crisis. The Governor-General, Sir Serei Eri, who had been President of Mr Diro's Peoples Action Party prior to becoming Head of State, refused to accept the Tribunal's recommendation that Diro be sacked. The Namaliu Government was about to have Sir Serei sacked by the Queen when both Mr Diro and the Governor-General resigned.

Shortly after his return to power, Prime Minister Wingti announced a series of anti-corruption moves. One was abolishing what was commonly called the members slush fund, the Electoral Development Fund. This Fund provided each of the 109 members with K100,000 a year to spend as they saw fit on development projects in their electorates. 'The problem it has created,' Mr Wingti said, 'is making the Member become like a banker to his people.' PNG's shadow Attorney-General, Bernard Narokobi, said the Fund had become a monster. He tabulated the thousands of demands put to him in 1991 and in that one year he was asked by people in his electorate of Wewak to hand out to them a total of K3 million ($4.5m). People wanted money for funeral expenses, bride prices, school fees, travel, seed funding for chicken farms, trade stores, boats, outboard motors, anything. Mr Narokobi said it was impossible to ensure grants were spent properly. 'I'd probably say that 70 per cent to 80 per cent of the funds I've given out have not been used for the purposes for which they were given. People say, 'That's not right!' And I agree, I agree. But if I had to control these funds strictly and look after them properly, I would need to employ a lot of people.'

Mr Wingti claimed demands on members so outweighed their K100,000 allocation that many were 'forced to look at other ways of looking after their people and that is the breeding ground for activities that are not proper'. However, he said, members would still be entitled to apply for projects to help their constituents. True to his word when the 1993 Budget was brought down there was no Electoral Development Fund. But there was plenty of money for members' projects! This was set aside in departmental allocations. For instance, in the Transport Budget there was K23.8 million ($35m) for 'the allocation of funds to Members of Parliament for construction of road projects in their electorates'. This discretionary fund was in the hands of the Transport Minister. Shadow Attorney-General Narokobi welcomed the abolition of the Electoral Development Fund, but he claimed Mr Wingti was creating a climate for even worse abuse.

'The ministers that possess those discretionary funds,' Narokobi argued, 'their powers have been increased. I controlled a discretionary fund through Law and Order, and, in my view, it's very, very difficult for a busy minister to do anything properly. So you're going to have to leave it to quite junior officers to make decisions about the funds. And, in the end, it's quite likely these funds are going to be abused just as much. Substantially greater sums will be abused. And because they are hidden in different activities—like Agriculture, Fisheries, Law and Order—the potential for abuse is going to be enormous.'

The 1993 Budget was radical. The Finance Minister, Sir Julius Chan, back in charge of PNG's finances for the third time in twenty years, was as determined as Mr Wingti to implement dramatic change. He aimed, he said, to 'jump-start' the economy. 'The 1993 Budget is revolutionary,' Sir Julius told Parliament. 'Revolutionary because it deliberately foregoes revenue for the short term but for a definite purpose. Revolutionary because it cuts infrastructure and utility costs but again for a definite purpose, and revolutionary because it puts more money back into the pockets of the people.' The top Personal Income Tax rate was chopped from 45 per cent to 28 per cent; fringe benefits taxes, which had been amongst the toughest in the world, were abolished; and the company tax rate was cut to 25 per cent, one of the lowest corporate tax rates in the Asian/Pacific region.

The definite purpose Sir Julius aimed for was the stimulation of the non-mining sectors of the economy, all of which were in decline. Amongst the economic measures was the introduction of a five year price support scheme for agricultural crops—guaranteeing prices that in the case of coffee was twice the world price. The government also endorsed a Minimum Wages Board decision slashing the urban minimum wage by two-thirds. The new urban minimum wage became K22.96 a week. It had been K61.60. In its determination, the Minimum Wages Board accepted arguments put by government economists and employers that PNG's urban wages were too high for the country to be competitive. The Board claimed its responsibility extended to the whole population not just those lucky enough to have paid jobs. Trade unions threatened industrial strife. The head of the Labour Department, Aphemeledy Joel, attacked the determination, saying K22.96 would not be enough to buy a family of four in Port Moresby breakfast each day. Mr Joel had been a previous Chairman of the Minimum Wages Board and he claimed the new wage would not keep anybody fit enough for work, either mentally or physically. He was ignored.

Sir Julius said the tax cuts, the new minimum wage and other concessions had created favourable conditions for foreign investors. He said the PNG economy had been very ill. The goal was an economy that would work for Papua New Guinea. 'An economy which will create employment and national wealth simply by making it attractive enough for everyone—workers and employers—to come out from the intensive care ward,' was how he put it in his Budget speech. Sir Julius was going for growth and he was prepared to gamble the income from PNG's resources boom in a bold attempt to restructure the economy so that when the boom was over there would be secondary industries in place to take up the slack.

The strategy was based on the resources boom continuing well into the 1990s. Gold, copper and oil were expected to make up 83 per cent of Papua New Guinea's export revenue in 1993. Government revenue from these extractive industries would climb to 30 per cent of total revenue. The Kutubu oil field began production in mid-1992 and its impact on exports was immediate. In the September quarter, oil exports jumped from zero to one fifth of total exports, some K100 million out of K500 million. The next major gold mine, Lihir Island, was expected to begin construction in 1994. Investor confidence in PNG underpinned Sir Julius's plans.

However, the Wingti Government's relations with the main players in the extractive resources sector began poorly and deteriorated rapidly. The selection of Environment Minister was an immediate concern for Australia's BHP, 30 per cent owner and operator of the Ok Tedi copper mine. Mr Wingti chose the Member for South Fly, Perry Zeipi, through whose electorate 30 million tonnes of waste from the Ok Tedi mine flowed down the Fly River each year. Mr Zeipi had campaigned long and hard for the closure of the Ok Tedi mine. He announced that as Minister he was determined to shut the mine unless it built a permanent tailings dam. BHP's Chairman, Brian Loton, flew to PNG in September 1992, visited the mine and proclaimed himself satisfied with the mine's operations. But the chairman of Australia's largest company could not get to see Mr Wingti.

Institutional investor confidence in Papua New Guinea was rattled in the concluding months of 1992. The share prices on the Australian Stock Exchange of PNG-related stocks collapsed. More than $1.5 billion was wiped off the market capitalisation of three mining companies alone. The immediate cause of this crisis in confidence in PNG was Prime Minister Wingti's decision to increase Papua New Guinea's ownership of the very profitable Porgera gold mine from 10 per cent to 30 per cent. Both Mr Wingti and his Mining and Petroleum Minister, Masket Iangalio, accused the Porgera Joint Venture partners (Placer Pacific, Rennison Goldfields Consolidated and the Mount Isa Mines subsidiary, Highlands Gold) of having misled the Government as to how profitable Porgera would be. Porgera produced 1.4 million ounces of gold in its first year of full production. Mr Wingti claimed that when the Government was making its final decision on its 10 per cent equity holding in Porgera in the 1980s it had been told the mine would be marginally profitable. The Porgera joint venture partners denied the allegations that they had tricked PNG authorities and then bluntly replied that they regarded the Government's moves as attempted appropriation.

It was not only the Porgera issue that was causing nervousness amongst the major miners. Some said that Dennis Reinhardt's involvement with the Prime Minister had helped create uncertainty in the minds of the mining companies because of Reinhardt's position as a shareholder and consultant to a small Western Australian company, Ramsgate Resources, which was trying to evict CRA as the developer of the Mount Kare gold resource. Mt Kare, the scene of the 1988 gold rush, became the site of a small alluvial gold mining operation which CRA had set up with a landowner company, Karepuga Development, which was supposed to represent 6,000 landowners in the Enga and Southern Highlands provinces. Supported by Ramsgate, some of the landowners mounted a series of court challenges to CRA. A violent raid in January 1992, closed the mine.

The influence of Mr Bob Needham, the new boss of the MRDC, also worried the multinationals. Needham was a former chief executive of Placer Pacific but he had left the company in 1986 to start up an ill-fated mining house, Giant Resources, which became a victim of the 1987 share market crash. Mr Needham claimed detailed knowledge of the Bougainville mining operation and he maintained CRA over-estimated the costs of reopening the mine. After a visit to Bougainville in which he'd flown in an Iroquois helicopter a thousand metres or so above the Panguna pit, Mr Needham declared it to be in great shape. Prime Minister Wingti announced the Bougainville Mine would reopen in 1993. CRA, the majority owner, described both statements as wildly optimistic.

Mr Needham drew fire from the Bougainville rebels as well as from CRA. A Bougainville Revolutionary Army sniper shot at the Iroquois when Needham put down at the Tunuru Catholic mission, the PNG military's front line camp. The military advanced to Tunuru in October 1992, taking them to within three kilometres of the rebel provinicial capital, Arawa. PNG had effectively regained control over three-quarters of Bougainville. They had done it with a limited number of troops and with the support of self-styled Bougainville Resistance Fighters. These were young Bougainvilleans, who with the support of their chiefs, had turned against the BRA.

At Wakunai, on the north east coast of Bougainville, the local resistance group numbered fifty-five. Their leader, Paul Akotai, said his people initially had favoured secession but that anarchy had followed the withdrawal of the PNG security forces in March 1990. 'We supported secession because we thought the BRA would control its men and look after the welfare of the people,' he said. 'Instead, they killed people, destroyed things, raped women and stole property.' Paul said his people had appealed to the interim Government to control the BRA gangs. They had been visited by the Chairman of the Interim Government, Joseph Kabui, and the BRA military commander, Sam Kauona, but they never saw President Ona. 'Kabui and Sam Kauona both came to receive a petition we wrote asking for Francis Ona to come out of the jungle and explain to us what was happening. We saw that Ona was just hiding in the jungle and he would send messages out saying who was to be executed. People were dying like frogs on the road!'

By year's end, the BRA was still a force to be reckoned with but it had been driven back into its heartland, Central Bougainville. Taking Central Bougainville remained a formidable task. The military expected a tough fight from the people who had begun the revolution. Mr Wingti's government, however, was predicting victory by April 1993. It appointed a new Defence Force Commander, Brigadier General Robert Dademo, the former Chief of Staff, and allowed him to carry out a purge of the senior ranks of the Force. Four colonels were banished from military headquarters, Murray Barracks. Three, including Colonel Leo Nuia, the officer who had directed much of the course of the Bougainville operation, were sent overseas to Defence Attache posts. The Namaliu Government had tried to sack Nuia in 1991 after he frankly admitted to ABC television's Debora Snow that, in late 1989, his men had dumped the bodies of rebel suspects at sea from an Australian donated Iroquois helicopter. Colonel Nuia was reinstated after the National Court found he had been dismissed incorrectly.

Papua New Guinea's relations with Solomon Islands plummeted in September 1992, when soldiers from the Small Boats Unit on Bougainville crossed the sea border in search of hard core BRA and shot dead two Solomon Islands citizens, one of them a pregnant woman. They abducted a third and shot his daughter through the knee. The incident happened at Komalaie village in the Shortland Islands at night. Prime Minister Wingti apologised to the Solomon Islands Prime Minister, Solomon Mamaloni, and said the soldiers involved would be withdrawn from Bougainville and dealt with under the Defence Force Act. Mr Mamaloni and his government were in no mood to forgive and they took the matter to the United Nations Security Council.

As 1993 dawned, the father of the nation, Sir Michael Somare, distressed at the general level of crime in Papua New Guinea, said he hoped the new year would bring with it PNG's first official execution. The death penalty was back in the statute books following its approval by parliament. Sir Michael demanded a hanging and he nominated his own province, East Sepik, as where the first one should happen. Sir Michael admitted he was furious about a vicious killing of a young relative of his from Murik Lakes. 'They hacked his head, ripped his stomach open and cut up his hands and legs,' Sir Michael said. 'This is barbaric and those found guilty must be punished by death. There is no time to waste debating hanging,' Sir Michael stated. 'Parliament has made its decision. Our forefathers administered the death penalty under our customary laws and we should not let Western attitudes dictate how we should administer justice.'

APPENDIX

PROVINCIAL POPULATIONS

These 1990 population figures are taken from the 1990 Census. No Census was possible in the North Solomons because of the Bougainville crisis. The North Solomons figure is an estimate based on projections from the 1980 Census.

REGION	PROVINCE	POPULATION	TOTALS
Papua	1 Western (Fly)	108,998	
	2 Gulf	68,122	
	3 Central	141 197	
	4 NCD*	195,382	
	5 Milne Bay	157,880	
	6 Northern (Oro)	96,638	
			768,217
Highlands	7 Southern Highlands	321,349	
	8 Enga	238,988	
	9 Western Highlands	337,200	
	10 Chimbu (Simbu)	183,857	
	11 Eastern Highlands	299,445	
			1,380,839
Momase	12 Morobe	364,563	
	13 Madang	269,600	
	14 East Sepik	252,855	
	15 West Sepik (Sandaun)	138,930	
			1,025,948

Islands	16 Manus	32,830
	17 New Ireland	86,867
	18 East New Britain	184,941
	19 West New Britain	128,348
	20 North Solomons	608,886
		3,783,890

*NCD—National Capital District

1990 populations of main cities and towns:

	CITY	PROVINCE	POPULATION
A	Port Moresby	NCD*	195,382
B	Lae	Morobe	80,400
C	Madang	Madang	27,175
D	Wewak	East Sepik	23,154
E	Goroka	Eastern Highlands	17,855
F	Mt Hagen	Western Highlands	17,392
G	Rabaul	East New Britain	17,035

Source: *PNG National Statistical Office, December 1991*

INDEX

Abaijah, Josephine, 155-6, 158, 159-60
Abal, Sir Tei, 62
administration
   Australian, 40-6, 152-3
   pre-European, 40
adultery, 286
agriculture, 87, 89, 93-8
   early, 24-7
Air Niugini, 103, 222-3
aircraft sale inquiry, 234-5
Alatas, Ali, 333
alcohol, 313
Angus (PNG) Pty Ltd, 221-2
anthropology, 35-6
'apartheid', 125-7
archaeology, 25, 29, 30
army *see* Defence Force
Asia Pacific Communications (firm), 327
Australia
   administration, 40-6, 152-3
   aid, 159
   colonisation, 39-40
   defence aid, 186-7, 204-5, 209-10
   during Bougainville war, 321
   during Dutch-Indonesian conflict, 252
   justice administration, 288-90
   market, 87
   police aid, 309
   refugee assistance, 277

Australian Defence Co-operation Program, 321
aviation industry, 329-30

bad debts, parliamentarians', 218
Bais, Tony, 55
Balakau, Malipu: murder, 77
ballot papers: portraits, 57, 72
Barnes, Charles Edward, 45-6
Barnett, Mr Justice Tos, 21, 221-2, 228-34, 328-9
beer, 313
Bemay, Elky, 256, 257
Berghuser, Sir Hugo, 74, 143, 243
betel nuts, 95
Bika, John: assassination, 138, 142, 324-5
Bismarck Archipelago, 29-30
Blackwood Hodge (firm), 173-4
bombing of Irian Jayan border, 264
Bonay, Elizier, 252
Bond Media, 237-8
border with Irian Jaya, 198-201, 246-85, 333
borrowing, 85, 96-7
Bougainville, 117-49, 158-60, 211, 212, 319-28
Bougainville Copper Limited, 10, 85, 88, 92, 106-7, 121-33, 155, 172, 319, 326
Bougainville Revolutionary Army, 119, 142, 145, 319-20

Bouraga, Phillip, 68, 301
bribery *see* corruption
British colonisation, 39
Buchanan, Dennis, 243, 329-30
Budget
  1989, 91
  1990, 319
Buka, 324-5
Buka Liberation Front, 325
bureaucracy *see* public service
business interests of politicians, 63
businesses, government, 102-3, 173-5

cabinet reshuffle
  1982, 64-5
  1984, 69
  1985, 70-71
capital works spending, 171-2
cash cropping, 93
Catholic Church
  Bougainville, 124, 134, 144, 149
  opposition to media licensing, 239
cattle, 95-6
Chan, Sir Julius
  Bougainville, 130
  corruption charges, 217
  economy, 83-4, 104
  parliament, 60-1, 63, 65-7, 69, 71-2
  Vanuatu rebellion, 190
Chatterton, Sir Percy, 155-6, 255
Christianity, 38
church
  ownership of plantations, 98
  see also Catholic Church
Clifford report, 235-6, 290-1, 293-6, 313-14
Clowes, Waliyato, 59
coastal areas
  languages, 31
  origin of peoples, 29

cocoa, 97-8
coffee, 49, 87, 96, 97
colonisation, 38-9
commercial statutory authorities, 102-3
Committee of Inquiry into the Work Permits Division of the Labour Department and the Immigration Division of the Foreign Affairs Department, 104-5
compensation, 10-11, 18, 118, 121, 122
  see also royalty payments
computer accounting system, 178
Constitution, 159, 215-17
  change, 78-82
  individual rights, 313-5
  parliamentary pay and conditions, 57
  parliamentary sittings 332-3
  provincial, 175-6
  role of Parliament, 61-2
Constitutional Planning Committee, 153-4, 157
copper mines
  Ok Tedi, 35, 107
  Bougainville, 117-49
copra, 97-8
corruption, 56, 202-3, 215-35, 316
  electoral, 21-23
  timber industry, 20-21
coup
  1977 preparation, 200
  1990 attempt, 322-3
  journalists' alleged conspiracy, 242
  possibility, 180, 212-14
courts, 289-91
CRA, 107, 117, 133
credit, 85, 96-7
crime, 286-313, 333
  see also corruption; murder

INDEX 335

crops, 26-7
currency launch, 83
customs, traditional, 15

death penalty, 310
Debessa, Leo, 227
debt, 87-8
decentralisation, 150-79
Declaration of Peace,
    Reconciliation and
    Rehabilitation, 323
Defence Force
    Bougainville, 144, 147-8
    coup preparation 1977, 200
    discipline, 196-7
    formation, 187-8
    funding, 188-9, 209-10
    intelligence service, 208-9
    international aid, 209-10
    Irian Jaya border, 198-200
    leaders' corruption, 201-6
    pay dispute, 180-1, 193-6
    staff shake-up, 181-2
    strength, 183-4
    structure, 211-12
    Vanuatu rebellion, 189-92
deportation of foreigners, 242-3
deserters, Indonesian, 271-2
devaluation, 319
development forum, 112-13
devolution, 150-79
Dihm, Bill, 185, 284
Dion, Leo, 322
Diro, Ted, 185
    Bougainville, 143
    corruption allegations, 201-4,
        207, 221, 229-31
    coup attempt, 180, 200
    Irian Jaya, 246-7, 283
    Parliament, 67, 69, 74-5, 76
    Vanuatu rebellion, 190
dissolution of parliament,
    unwillingness for, 61

doctors, 43
Doi, Akoka, 137, 139, 143, 195
Dotaona, Colonel Lima, 143, 147-8,
    211
Dutch in New Guinea, 39, 248-51,
    252

earthquakes, 33
Ebeial, Premier, 176
Ebi, Kuberi, 326
economy, 83-116
education, 19, 316-17
    Bougainville, 127
    provincial government, 162
    spending under Australian
        administration, 41
Education Department, 162
elections
    1964, 46-7
    1972, 49
    1982, 21-3, 66, 267
    1987, 57-8, 72
electoral system, 81
Electricity Commission, 103
employment, 89
Employment of Non Citizens Act,
    331
Endeavour Accord, 323, 325
Enga province
    spirits, 37
    suspension of government, 151,
        168-9
entrepreneurs, 12, 13-15, 86
Evara, Roy, 63-4, 67-8
executive diaries scandal, 219
expatriate workers, 99-100
    Bougainville, 128-9
exports, 87, 97, 115, 326

Fiji compared, 182, 212-13
financial management, 169-74, 178
financial scandal in Sandaun
    province, 150-1, 170-1, 173-4

Fly province: suspension of
  government, 151
Fly River, 34
Food Marketing Corporation, 95
food shortages, 94
Foreign Affairs Department, 105
forestry industry
  administration, 328
  corruption, 20-21, 221-2, 228-34
  royalty payments, 19
Forests Department, 231-4
fraud, 56, 202-3, 315-35, 316

Gaius, John, 164
gangs, 299-308
Garnaut/Baxter report, 99
Gazelle Peninsula, 153
Gebusi people, 36
Gemel, Cecilia, 10
Genia, Jack, 55
geology, 33-5
German colonisation, 39-40
ghosts, 37-8
gifts, political, 218-20
Giheno, John, 277
Gion, Sition, 220
gold, 107-9
  Bulolo, 41
  export, 87
  Misima, 88
  Mount Kare, 11-12, 152
  Porgera, 110-11, 326
  prospecting, 12
  rushes, 12
Goroka, 26
Gouna Development Corporation, 86
government businesses, 102-3, 173-5
Gross Domestic Product, 85, 88
group obligations, principle of, 313-14
Grynberg, Dr Roman, 109, 115

Guise, Sir John, 187, 200, 250
Gulf Papua Fisheries, 175
Gunther, Dr John, 42-3

Hamoka, Rei, 227
Hannett, Leo, 136, 143
Harbours Board, 103, 227
'hard Kina' policy, 84-5
Harris, Dr Bruce, 299-301, 304-6
Hasluck, Sir Paul, 43-5, 289
Hayden, Bill, 159, 276-7
head hunting, 309
health care, 42-3
Heriot, Geoff, 200-1
Highlands
  languages, 31
  origin of the peoples, 28
  provincial government, 152
  topography, 33-4
  tribal fighting, 309-11
  view of Independence, 49
Hiri Motu language, 32
Holland: colonisation, 39, 252, 284-5
Holloway, Sir Barry, 71, 72
Honiara Declaration, 323
Huai, Brigadier General, 197, 204-5, 248
human rights abuses, 144
Huon Peninsula, 29

Iangalio, Masket, 242
Ijape, Mathias, 144-5
immigration, 104-5
Independence, 45-6, 48-51, 155, 158-9
Independents (parliamentarians), 72-3
individual rights, 313-14
Indonesia
  administration of Irian Jaya, 253-75
  and the Dutch, 248-9

INDEX

Indonesia *continued*
  fear of, 246-8
  fight for Irian Jaya, 249-51
  PNG's relations with, 201-4, 266-75
  see also Irian Jaya border
industry *see* agriculture; manufacturing; minerals and mining
Institute of Medical Research, 27
intelligence, military, 206-9
investment, 104, 106, 327-30
Ipimeian Revolution, 27
Ipuia, Mark, 54
Irian Jaya border, 198-201, 246-85, 333

Japanese
  business ethics in PNG, 218-19
  invasion of PNG, 42
  market, 86
Joku, Henk, 258-9, 281-2
Joseph, Lance, 242
journalists, 242, 245
Jouwe, Nicholas, 250
judges, 294
justice system, 286-313
  Australian administration, 41

Kabui, Joseph, 123, 130, 136-8, 141, 324
Kainantu, 26
Kakabin, Gideon, 13-15
Kange, Pundia, 58-9
Kapal, Philip, 166
Kaputin, John
  Bougainville, 143
  customs, 15
  economy, 85
  parliament, 65, 66, 71
  provincial government, 154, 157-8
Karava, Sepoe, 165

Karkar, 31-32
Kauona, Samuel, 119, 141, 320-1
Kavali, Sir Thomas, 66
Kekedo, Jean and Rose, 329
Kemelfield, Grahame, 319
Kerepia, Pins: murder, 333
Kerowagi, 57-8
Kerr, Sir John, 153
Kiaps, 40, 288, 295
kidnapping, 258, 264
Kidu, Sir Buri, 293-5
Kiki, Sir Albert Maori, 135, 260, 263, 264-5
Kikori Landowners Development Corporation, 326
Kilage, Sir Ignatius, 64, 218, 219
Kina (unit of currency), 83-5, 319
Kina Gilbanks & Co., 16
Kipalan, Albert, 55
Koleala, Nat, 330
Kumbon, Daniel, 37-8
Kumul Force, 185-6, 190-2
Kunangel Amin, Opai, 224-5
Kutato, Jolson, 110-11
Kutubu Oil development, 326
Kwapena, Mark, 165
Kwarara, Galeva, 71, 74, 77

labour Department, 105
labour mobility, 331
Lae
  Defence takeover of airport, 181
  looting, 308-9
land
  disputes, 17-18, 19-20
  ownership, 17-18
'landowner participation', 326-7
Langro, Paul, 151
languages, 31-2
Lapun, Sir Paul, 136
law, criminal, 286-313
lawyers, 295
leadership code, 216, 218

League for National Advancement, 68, 72, 73, 80
League of Nations, 40-1
Leahy brothers, 12
Leiba Party, 60
Levi, Noel, 267, 280
Libya approached by OPM, 282
Lihir goldmine, 108-9
Lini, Father Walter, 189-90, 256
loans, 85, 96-7
local government, 153
'localisation', 330
Loh, Anthony Shaw Kong, 219-20
Lokinap, Brigadier General Rochus, 181, 196, 211, 322
looting, 307-9
Loudon, Geoff, 108-9
Lucas, Luke, 59, 81
Lus, Sir Pita, 47, 61

macro-economic management, 116
magic, 36-7
Maiah, Joel, 151, 169
Malaysian Overseas Investment (PNG) Pty Ltd, 229-30
Mamirum Timbers, 229-30
manufacturing, 103-4
Manus province: suspension of government, 151, 169
Mara, Nambuga, 151, 165-6
Maraleu, Miskus, 229, 231
market economy, 85-6
markets, 95
Marsipal, Arnold, 144
Masandanai people, 17
mass media tribunal proposal, 238-40
Matane, Sir Pauliias, 36, 276, 277
Matiabe, Aruru, 52, 67, 202
Meade, Margaret, 36
media, 236-45
Mel, Michael, 73

Melanesian Alliance, 64, 66, 70-71, 139
Melpa (government business), 175
Millett John, 330-1
Mineral Resources Stabilisation Fund, 92-3
minerals and mining, 87-9, 92-3, 106-16
  see also Bougainville Copper Limited; gold
Minimum Wages Board, 99, 100
ministerial reshuffle *see* cabinet reshuffle
ministers: number of, 80-1
Misima goldmine, 107
missionaries, 39
Mochtar, Dr, 275, 282, 284-5
Mokis, Mr, 196
Momis, Father John
  Bougainville, 123-4, 130, 132, 135-7, 139, 142, 149
  Constitution, 217
  government contract, 327
  Irian Jaya, 277
  parliament, 64-6, 70
  provincial government, 154, 157-8, 162-3, 177, 179
Mopio, James, 218
Morauta, Mekere, 175
Morobe province, 164
  suspension of government, 306-8
Motor Vehicle Insurance Trust, 227
Mount Hagen, 12, 307
Mount Kare gold rush, 11, 152
Mount Lamington eruption, 33
Mount Victor mine, 107
Mugugia, Francis, 323
Murdani, General Benny, 202-3, 283
murder, 286
  Bika, 138, 142, 324-5
  Bougainville, 138, 140, 142, 322
  Emmanual, 154

INDEX

murder *continued*
  Kerapia, 333
  Indonesian diplomat, 281
  Balakau, 77
Murray, Sir Hubert, 40-1

Nakikus, Margaret, 15-16
Namaliu, Rabbie, 15-16
  Bougainville, 120, 130, 138-40, 142-3, 145, 319, 321
  coup attempt, 322
  defence, 206-8
  economy, 90-1, 102, 108-9
  Irian Jaya, 258, 273-4
  on crime, 333
  parliament, 52, 68, 75-7, 332
  provincial government, 161-2
Narokobi, Bernard, 120, 253, 287
Nasioi people, 122
National Alliance, 67-8
National Broadcasting Commission, 243-4
National Development Fund, 225-6
National Housing Corporation, 103
National Intelligence Agency, 206-9
National Investment and Development Authority, 104
National Parliament building, 75
National Party, 62, 66-7, 70-71, 73
Negints, Thomas, 56
Nelson, Hank, 40
Nenega people, 13
New Ireland timber industry, 21
newspapers, 237-8
Nilkare, John, 22, 56, 68, 72, 172
Ningini Nius, 329
no-confidence motions, 52-3, 62, 69-71, 77-8, 176
Noga, Brigadier General Ken, 206-7, 209
North Solomons government, 166
Nuia, Colonel Leo, 147, 196, 320
numeration, 32-3

Nyaro, James, 257

oil, 113-16, 326
Ok Tedi mine, 35, 107
Okuk, Sir Iambakey, 21-3
  alleges corruption, 223
  Bougainville, 130
  economy, 85
  Irian Jaya, 266
  media pressure, 244
  parliament, 50-1, 56, 62-3, 65-6, 69-72
Olewale, Ebia, 259, 265
ombudsman, 216, 218, 220-1, 222-3, 226
Ona, Francis, 10-11, 117-20, 124-7, 137-8, 140-3, 320, 324
OPM *see* Organisasi Papua Merdeka
organic law, 161, 167-8
Organisi Papua Merdeka, 198, 199, 250, 255-9, 263-4, 267, 275, 281-2, 333
origin of PNG peoples, 27-9

Pacific Islands Regiment, 185, 187
palm oil, 98
Pangu Pati, 47, 49-50, 60, 62, 66, 68, 75, 76
Panguna Landowners' Association, 10, 118, 121-4
Papua
  naming of, 39
  secession movement, 155-6, 158
Papua Besena, 156
Papua Party, 71
Papuan Block, 74
Papuan National Alliance, 59
parliamentary sittings, 332-3
parliamentary terms, 61
Parry, Kevin, 237
party discipline, 62
patrol officers (Kiap), 40, 288, 295

Paua, Joel, 77
pay
    expatriates compared, 46
    mining, 115
    parliamentary, 53-7
    plantations, 98-100
Peacock, Andrew, 48
Pelair inquiry, 234-5
People's Action Party, 71
People's Democratic Movement, 68, 76
People's Progress Party, 62, 66, 71
Pidgin, 32
plantations, 98, 115
planters, 39-40
Planters Association of Papua New Guinea, 97
PNG Shipping Corporation, 102
Pokasui, Mr, 197, 211, 247-8
Pokawin, Stephen, 169
police, 291-2, 295-9, 301-6, 309
    Bougainville, 137-40, 144-5
    fraud squad, 226-7
pollution, 118-19
Pondros, Michael, 55, 227-8
population, 152, 247
Porgera
    goldmine, 102-7, 326
    people, 110
portraits on ballot papers, 57, 72
Portuguese, 38-9
Post Courier, 329
Posts and Telecommunications Corporation, 103
Prai, Jacob, 256, 259-60, 265
Premdas, Ralph, 63-4
premiers' conference of 1983, 164-6, 168
prime minister's powers, 61
privatisation, 102-3
provincial government, 150-79
Public Accounts Committee, 91-2
Public Prosecutor's Office, 295

public service
    employment, 100-1
    pay, 46, 54-5
    power, 153, 154
    provincial government, 161-4, 166, 177

Rabaul, 33
Ramoi, Gabriel, 80-1, 236-40, 242, 244-5
rape, 287
rascal gangs, 299-308
Reddaway, Brian, 330-1
referendum on provincial government, 176
refugees, Indonesian, 248, 262-3, 270-1, 273-8
Regan, Tony, 81, 160-1, 167-8, 177
repatriation plan, Irian Jaya, 274-80
resettlement scheme on Bougainville, 126
revenue of provincial governments, 166-7
rice, 95
Rio Tinto Zinc, 125
Rooney, Nahau, 63-4
'Rooney Affair', 63-4
royalty payments, 19, 111, 121, 122, 134, 138, 167
Rumkorem, Seth, 259-60, 264-5
rural economy *see* agriculture; minerals and mining
Russia approached by OPM, 280-1

sabotage, 119, 137, 264
Sabumei, Benias, 212, 321
Salossa, Melchior, 257
Samana, Utula, 19-20, 60, 73, 74, 77-8, 164, 308
Sandaun province: financial scandal, 150-1, 170-1, 173-4
'sanguma' men, 36
Sapioper, Yulianus, 262-3

INDEX

Sarei, Alexis, 134, 136
school-leavers, 316
schools in Bougainville, 127
Sea Park, 101-2
Searson, Bill, 327
secession movement
  Bougainville, 134-5, 155, 158-60
  Papua, 155-6, 158
sectional votes, 80
'sectoral program funds', 224
Seeto, Robert, 20
self-government, 45-6, 48-51, 155, 158-9
Sentosa, Brigadier General, 267
Serero, Pepetua, 10, 117-18, 126
Shaw, Barry, 94, 95, 96, 310
shotguns, 311-13
Sia, Francis, 229-30
Sia, Michael, 20
Siaguru, Tony, 68, 71, 72, 79-80, 274, 315-16
Sigulogo, Gerard, 228-9
Simbu province
  elections, 21-23
  suspension of government, 151
Singkai, Bishop Gregory, 140, 149
Siune, Matthew, 151, 165
'slush funds', 223-7
smallholder farming, 95-7
socialism, 60
Sohbu Trading Corporation, 219
soldier settlement scheme, 40
soldiers *see* Defence Force
Solomon, Sinclair, 245
Somare, Michael
  attitude to the media, 236
  Bougainville, 133, 134-6, 323
  corruption attempt, 219
  defence, 187
  Irian Jaya, 246, 258-9, 265, 272, 273, 276, 277, 284, 333
  parliament, 47, 62-5, 67-76, 79
  provincial government, 153, 155, 156-60, 165, 168, 176

Somare, Michael *continued*
  Vanuatu rebellion, 191
Southern Highlands constitution, 175-6
spirits, 35-8
squatter settlements, 302
Stack, Karl, 223
Stevens, Jimmy, 185, 189
strike in Bougainville, 134
subsistence agriculture, 89, 93-4
Suckling, Robert, 74
Sudarso, Commodore Jos, 251
Suharto, President (of Indonesia), 246, 248, 254, 265, 283
Sukarno, President (of Indonesia), 249-51
Surjowinoto, Major General Busiri, 264
suspension of provincial governments, 151, 168-70, 306-8

Tabu, Martine, 257
Tago, Stephen, 70
Talair (airline), 243, 329
Tasion, David, 297-8, 301-6, 309-10, 312
tax
  laws on mining and oil, 115
  paid by CRA, 133
  provincial governments, 167
television, 237-8
Thommy, Gerardus, 257
timber authority system, 233
timber industry *see* forestry industry
Tindiwi, Malip, 12, 151
Tito, Epel, 247-8
Togolo, Melchior, 131
Tohian, Paul, 139, 147, 320, 321-2

Tolai people, 15
Torato, Paul, 53-4, 68, 69
Torres Strait Islanders, 29
trade, lack of, 26
traditional customs, 15

Trans-Irian Highway, 269
transmigration policy, Indonesian, 266, 268-70, 272, 282
Treaty of Mutual Respect, Friendship and Co-operation, 284
tribal war, 12-13, 18, 27, 309-14
  Irian Jaya, 263-4
Tsiamalili, Peter, 146
Tul, David, 58
Tuya, Theodore, 53, 73
21 Squad, 301-2

United Nations
  administration of Irian Jaya, 252-4
  High Commissioner for Refugees, 276-9
  visiting mission 1962, 46
United Party, 49, 62, 64, 67, 71
United States defence agreement, 209
universities, 317

Vanuatu rebellion, 185-6, 189-92
village courts, 289, 303
Village Economic Development Fund, 223-5
violence, 37
  over elections, 58-9
  over land disputes, 11, 17-18
  troops' pay riot, 180-1, 193-6
  see also murder; rape; rascal gangs; war
visas, 104-5, 329
Vulpindi, John, 91-2

Wabo, Thomas Torame, 11
Wagambie, Tony, 145-6
wages *see* pay
Wagner, Merlyn, 37
Waipek, Gabriel, 166
Waka, Lukas, 56

Walter, Dr Michael, 81
Wama, Peter, 166
war
  Bougainville, 119-21, 131-2, 319-22
  tribal, 12-13, 18, 27, 263-4, 309-14
Water Board, 103
Watt, Sebulon, 231
wealth, 55
weather patterns, 34-5
West, Richard: *River of Tears*, 125
West German market, 86
West Papuan Peoples Front, 259-60
West Sepik Development Corporation, 173
Western Highlands province: government suspension, 166, 169-70
Whitlam, Gough, 47-8
Wingti, Paias, 16-17
  deals with corruption, 202, 225-6
  economy, 89-90, 102
  Irian Jaya, 277-8, 282-3
  on possibility of a coup, 213-14
  on tribal war, 313
  parliament, 54, 68-77, 332
  provincial government, 166, 176
Wiru people, 59
witchdoctors, 36
Womsiwor, Herman, 250, 252
Woolfers, Ted, 81
work permits, 104-5, 329
working class culture, lack of, 60
World War II, 41-2, 184
Wright, Dr Eric, 159

Yabara, Robert, 225
Yaki, Roy, 59
Yehere, Samson, 227
Yer Waim, Jim, 58
Yonki: agriculture, 25-6
Young, Dennis, 57, 73
Yule, Charles, 38